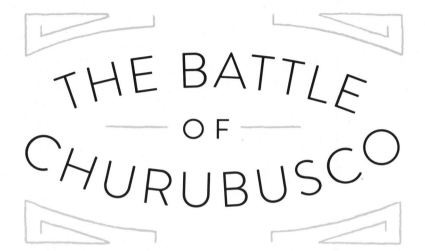

THE BATTLE
— OF —
CHURUBUSCO

AMERICAN REBELS
IN THE
MEXICAN-AMERICAN WAR

ANDREA FERRARIS

FANTAGRAPHICS

To Giorgio, Lilla, and Barbara

Translator: Jamie Richards
Editor: Kristy Valenti
Designer: Keeli McCarthy
Supervising Editor: Gary Groth
Production: Paul Baresh
Editorial Assistants: RJ Casey, Sabrina Futch,
Conrad Groth, Mackenzie Pitcock, Heidi Swenson
Associate Publisher: Eric Reynolds
Publisher: Gary Groth

Fantagraphics Books, Inc.
7563 Lake City Way NE, Seattle, WA 98115
(800) 657-1100 • www.fantagraphics.com
Follow us on Twitter @fantagraphics and on Facebook
at Facebook.com/Fantagraphics.

ISBN: 978-1-68396-057-7
Library of Congress Control Number: 2017938733

First Printing: November 2017
Printed in China

LIKE A PUNCH, LIKE A POEM

THE TOWN AND THE PEOPLE of Churubusco have always been close to my heart.

With his drawings, Andrea has transformed it into a mythical landscape, a symbol of unrelenting courage and resistance. Churubusco is but a faint memory, if that, for most Americans—at best, a tiny thorn in the side of history. But to Mexicans, it represents hope itself and a reason to stand forever firm. With few frills and a style as direct as death, Andrea unfolds a cruel and violent history. Like a punch to the stomach it leaves you breathless—just like a poem.

When we met in Dublin, Andrea told me he had learned the story of the San Patricios thanks to the album I produced with the Chieftains, in collaboration with Ry Cooder. Others will learn the same story when they read his book. I have thought about our meeting many times. Just as the Italian soldier Rizzo and John Riley, the Irish Captain of the San Patricios, met across the bloodstained fields of history, Andrea and I, another Italian and another Irishman from another time, met once again to discuss this age-old battle.

The courage of men who saluted their past and forsook their future shall never be forgotten.

Churubusco lives on!
Viva la San Patricios!

Paddy Moloney
Lead singer of Irish folk band the Chieftains

THE MARTYRS' COURAGE

CHURUBUSCO: THE SCENE of lost battles and heroes who found immortality and glory on its path.

Not for nothing did the ancient Nahuas call its people the Tzulupuchco, or Huitzilopochco, in honor of Huitzilopochtli, the Aztec God of War. The Spanish conquistadors transformed this name—that was, for them, unpronounceable—into "Churubusco," a place that, centuries later, would become the site of the Museo Nacional de las Intervenciones, justly commemorating all the people who have fallen defending Mexican land.

Ferraris draws Churubusco, now a neighborhood of Mexico City, as a phatasmagorical setting. There, in the mid-nineteenth century, some Mexicans, a handful of Irishmen, a couple Italians, and a few other Europeans, banded together, as if washed up from a shipwreck, to fight for a cause they knew was lost, yet just, illuminated by nothing but a beautiful, benevolent moon.

Today, in the twenty-first century, Ferraris's Churubusco brings together Mexicans, Irish, and Italians once again in tribute to the martyrs of the San Patricio [Saint Patrick's] Battalion.

Carlos Garcia de Alba Zepeda
Consul General of Mexico in Los Angeles
Former Mexican Ambassador to Ireland

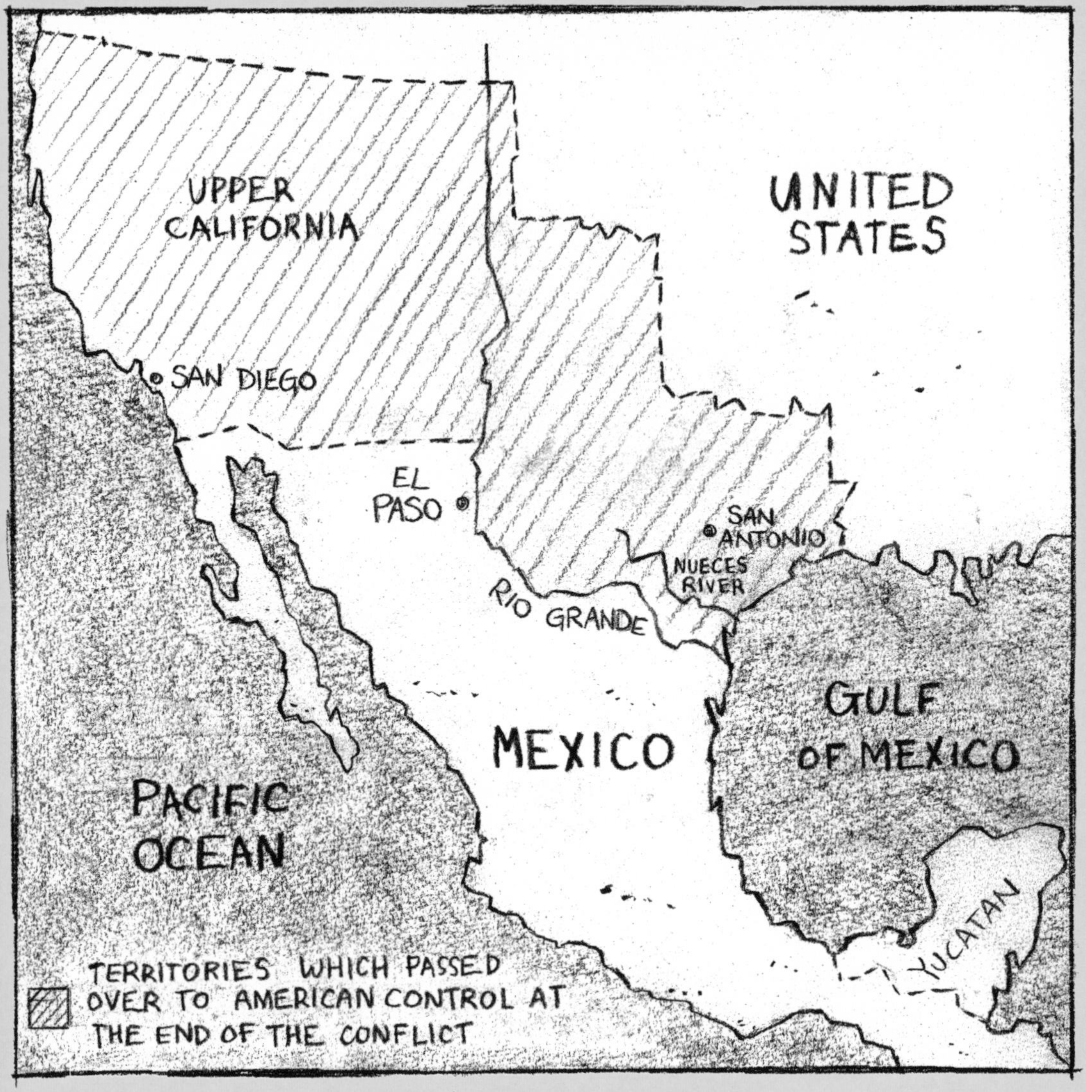
UPPER CALIFORNIA
UNITED STATES
SAN DIEGO
EL PASO
SAN ANTONIO
NUECES RIVER
RIO GRANDE
MEXICO
GULF OF MEXICO
PACIFIC OCEAN
YUCATAN
TERRITORIES WHICH PASSED OVER TO AMERICAN CONTROL AT THE END OF THE CONFLICT

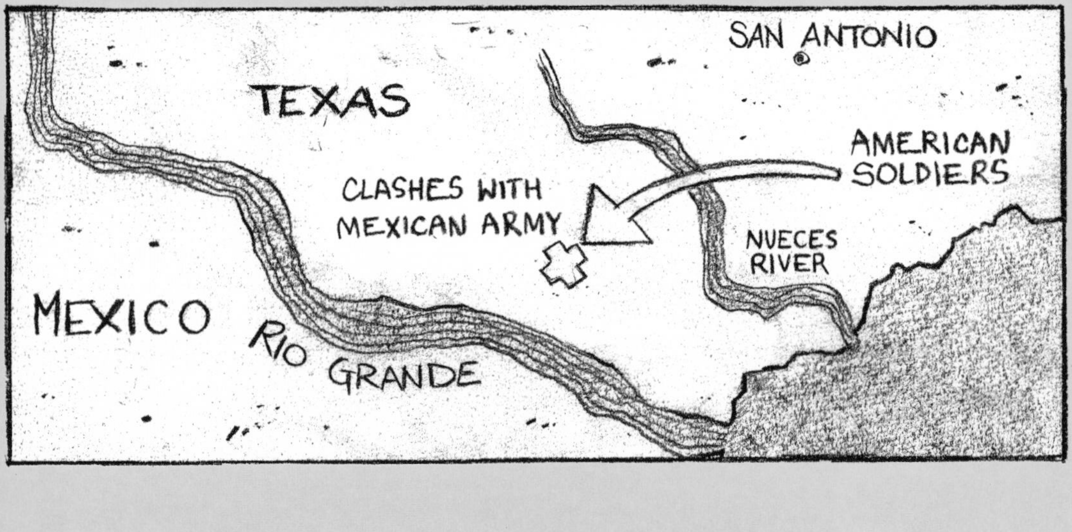
SAN ANTONIO
TEXAS
AMERICAN SOLDIERS
CLASHES WITH MEXICAN ARMY
NUECES RIVER
MEXICO
RIO GRANDE

IN 1840, THE UNITED STATES was looking for a Pacific Ocean outlet that would allow them to embark on lucrative trade with Asia. So, they set their sights on California, which was, at the time, under the authority of the Mexican government. They made many futile attempts to purchase it.

In January 1846, taking advantage of the disputes between Mexico and the then-Republic of Texas, the United States sent troops to the disputed territory between the Nueces River and the Rio Grande.

That invasion led to skirmishes and the deaths of several American soldiers. The US Congress seized the opportunity to declare war and invade Mexican territory.

Mexico wasn't equipped to deal with armed conflict. They didn't have weapons, ammunition, or a fighting spirit. The people were poor. Many Europeans signed up for the American army. Irish, Spanish, German, Polish, and Italian immigrants, seeking their fortunes, agreed to fight upon promises of citizenship and a parcel of land. A group of Irishmen, known as "St. Patrick's Battalion," deserted the American army, switching sides to fight alongside Mexicans. Other Europeans followed their lead and joined them in battle.

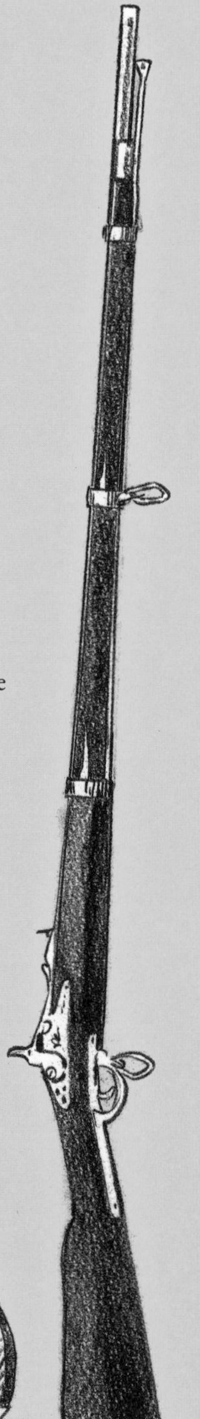

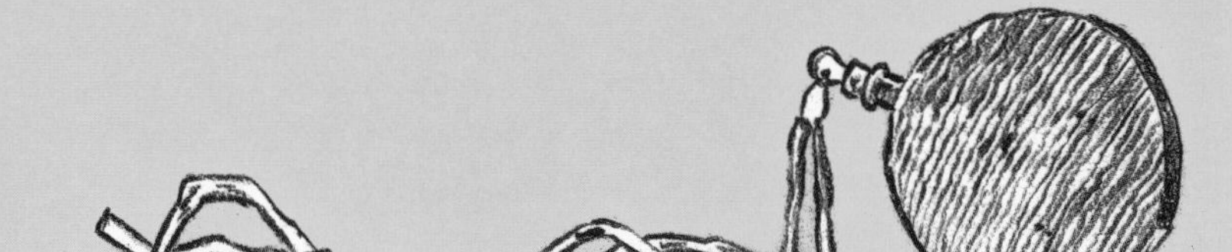

CHAPTER ONE

ADIOS SAN PATRICIOS

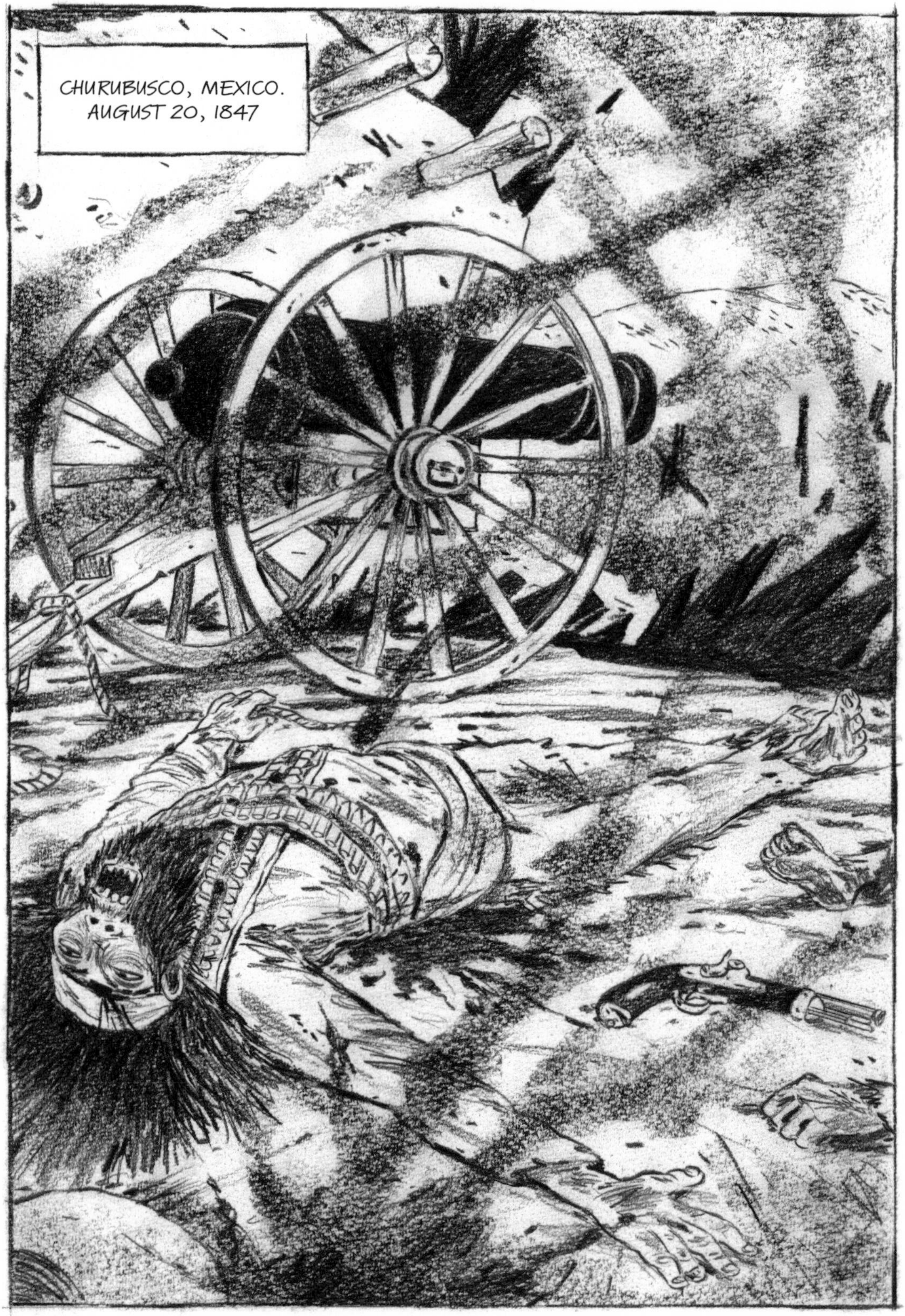
CHURUBUSCO, MEXICO.
AUGUST 20, 1847

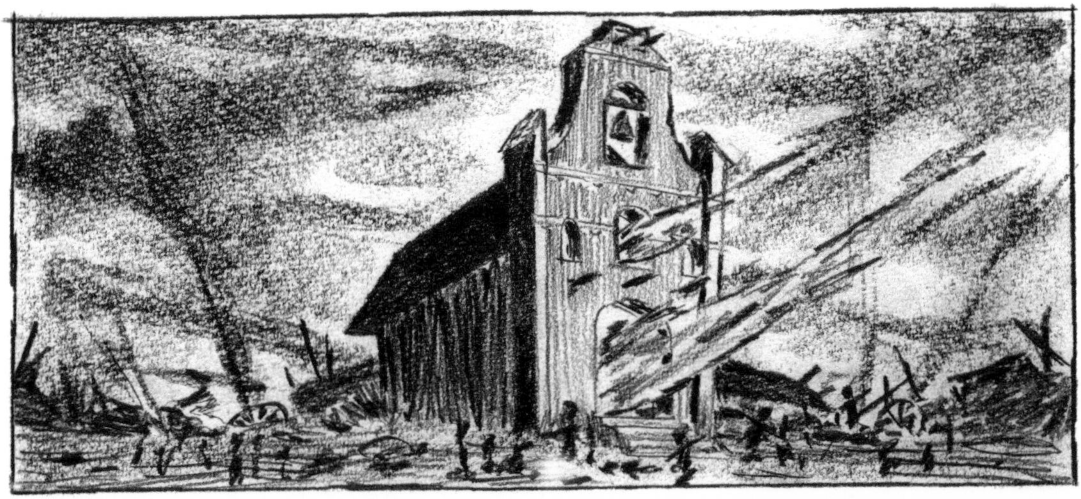

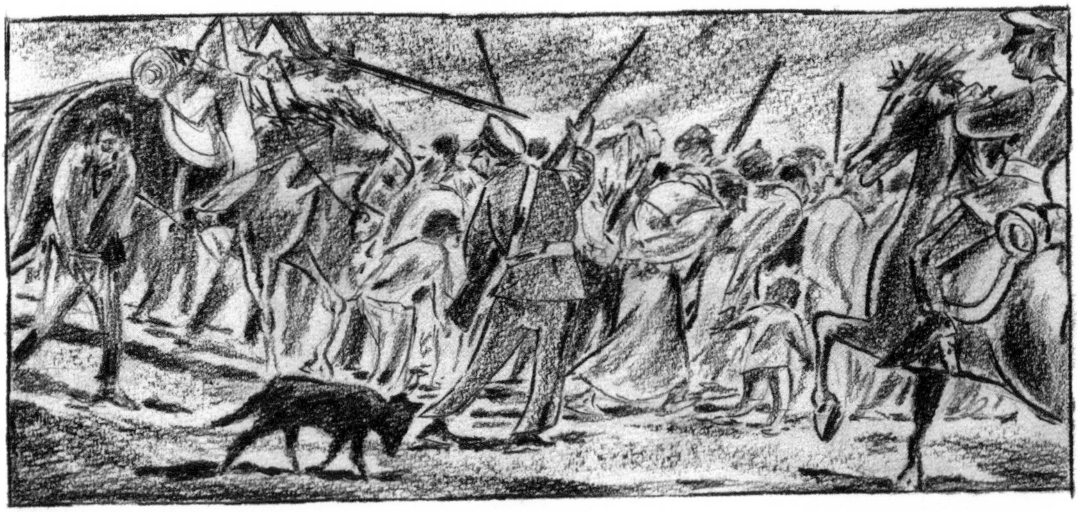

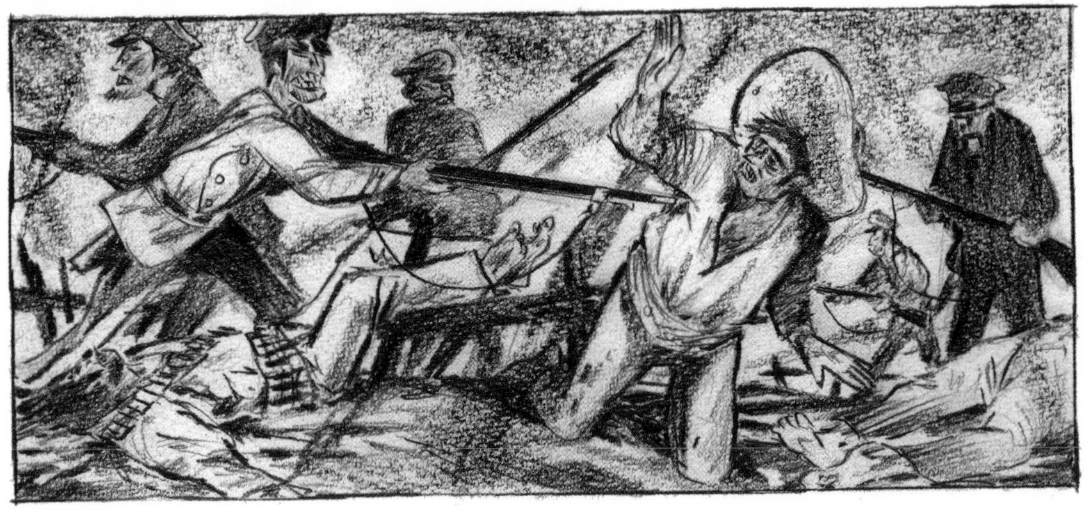

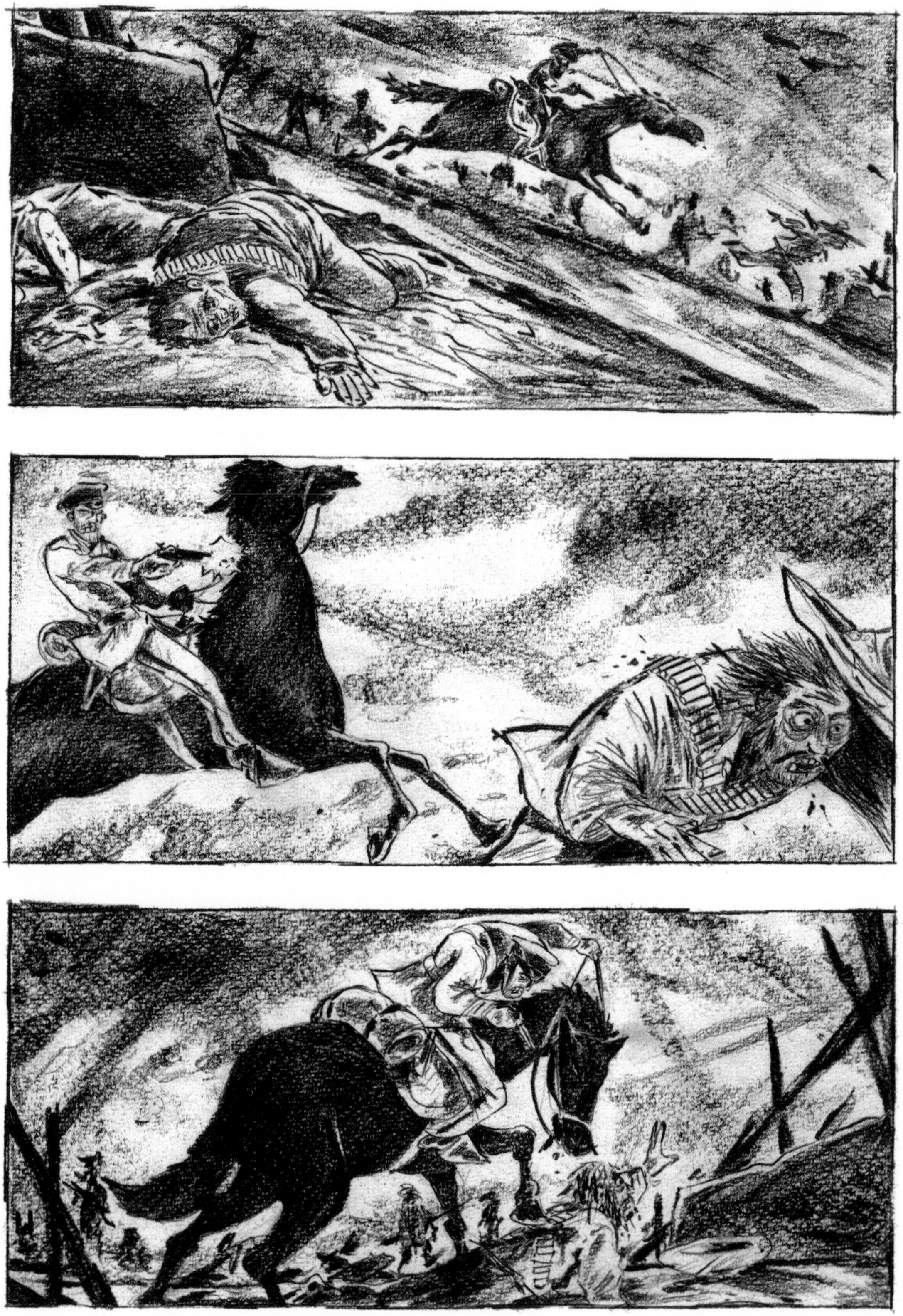

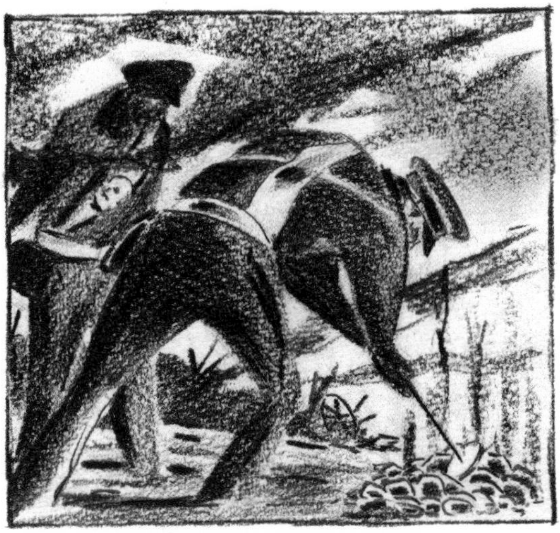

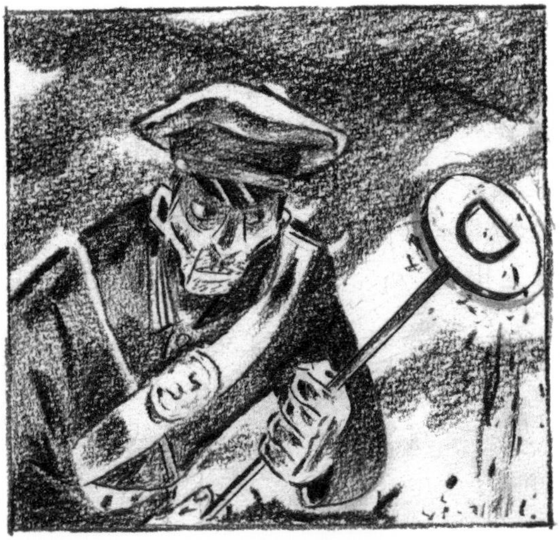

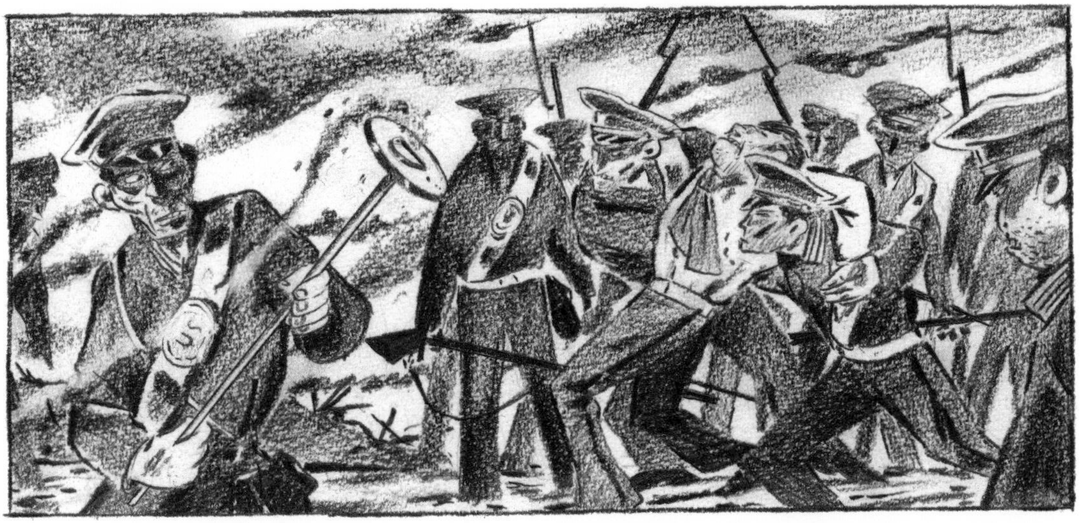

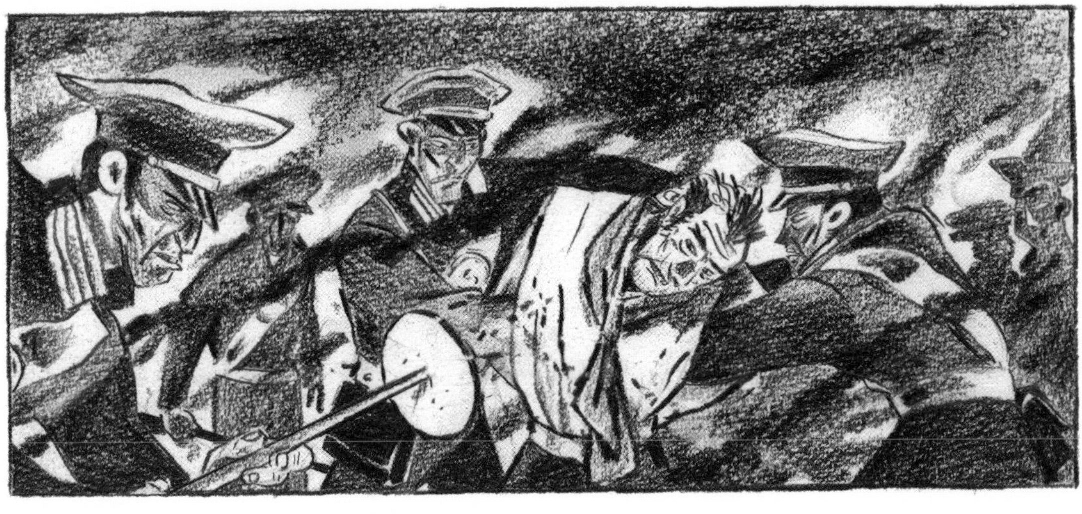

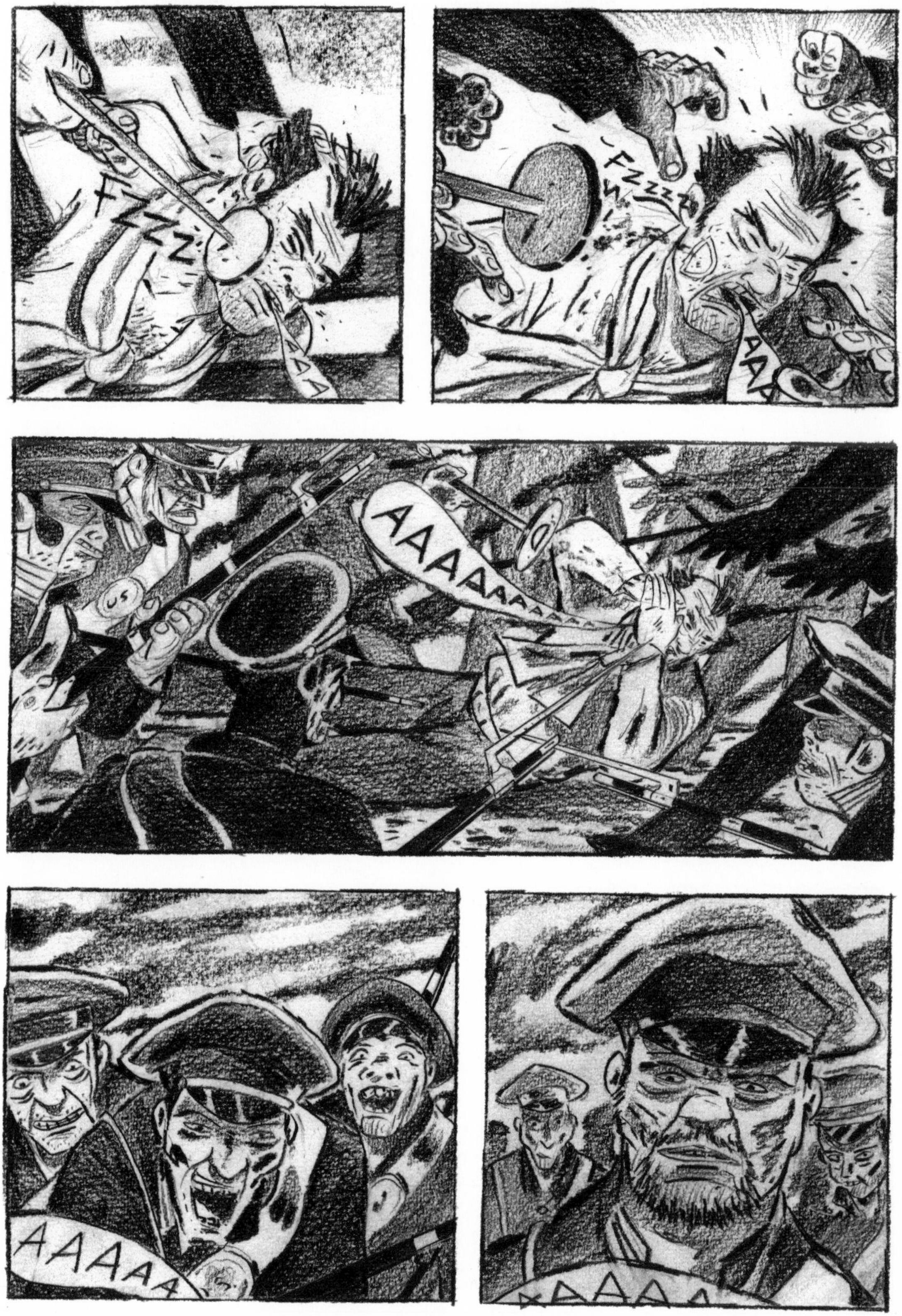
FZZZ
AAAA
FZZZZ
AAA
AAAAAAAAA
AAAAA
AAAA

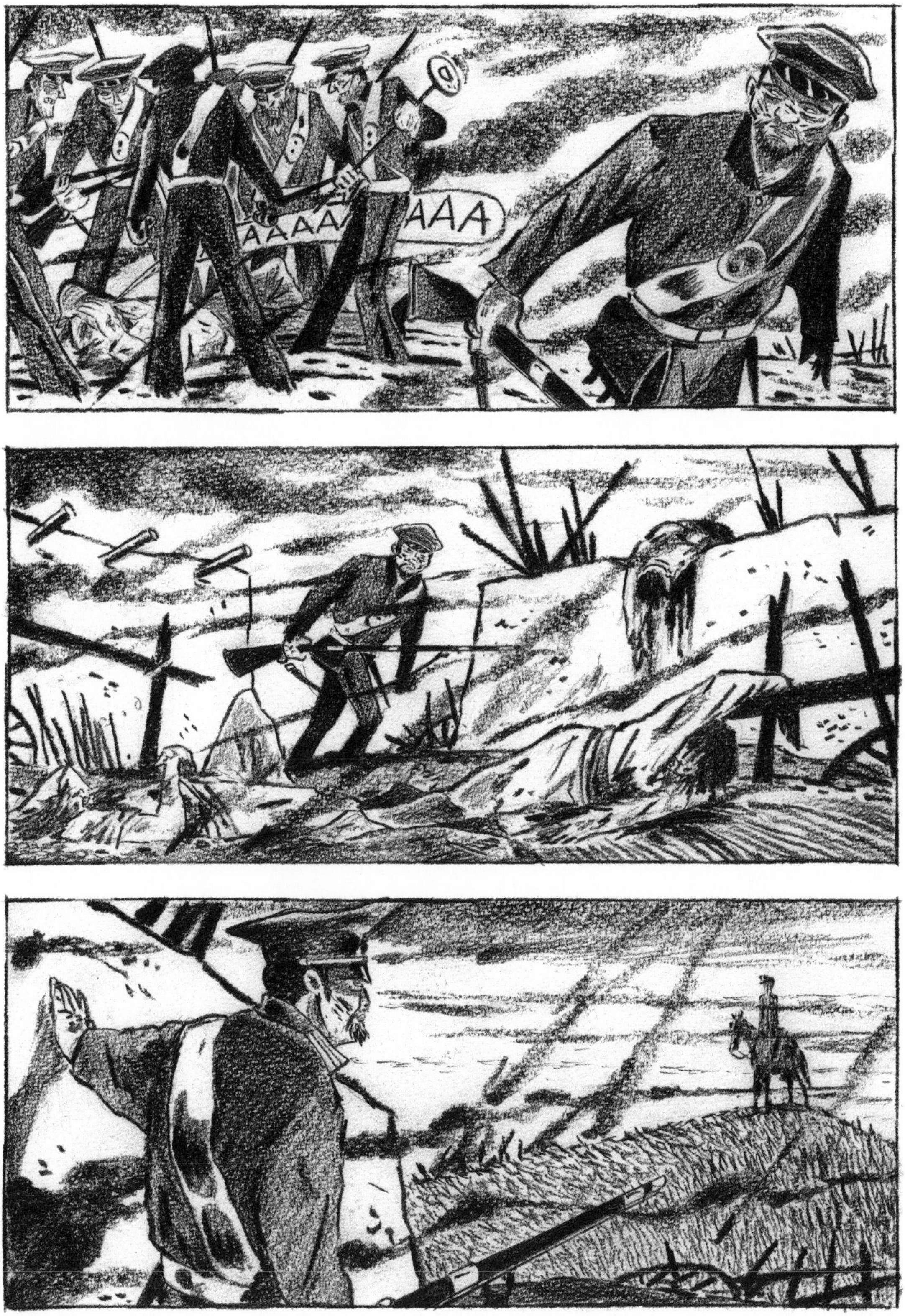
AAAAAAA

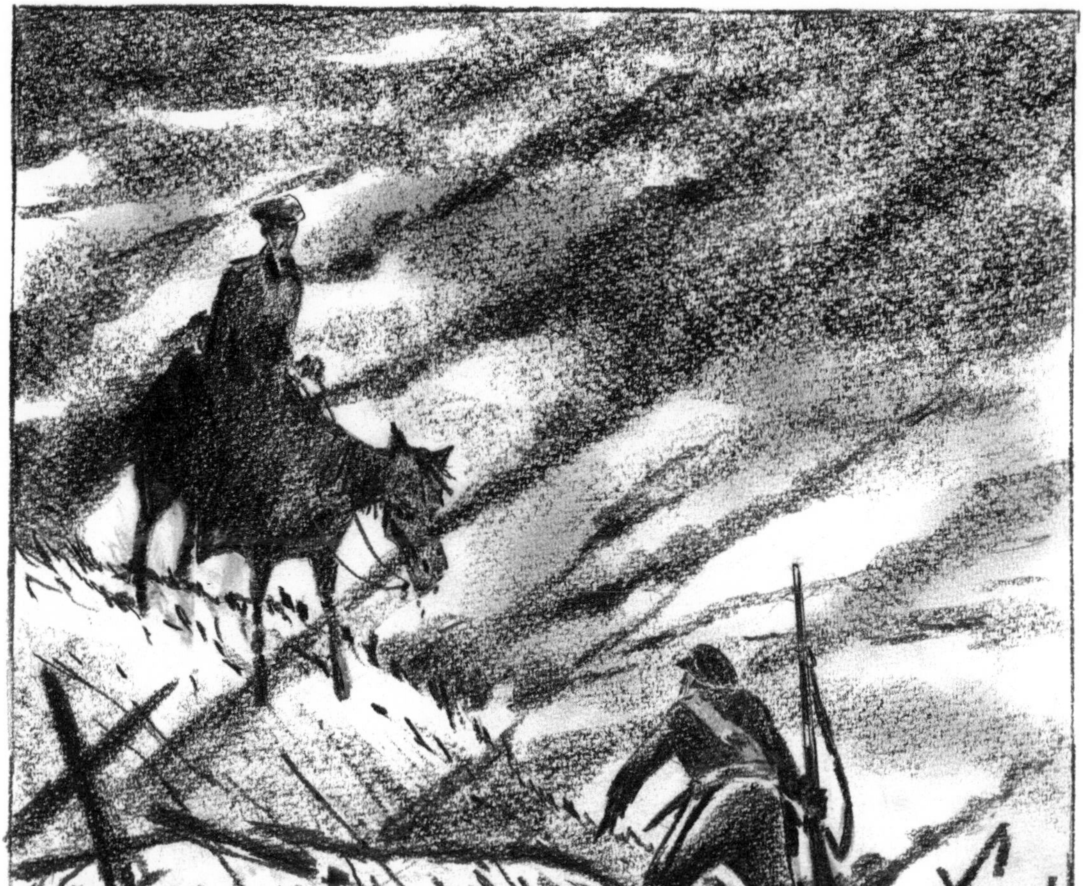

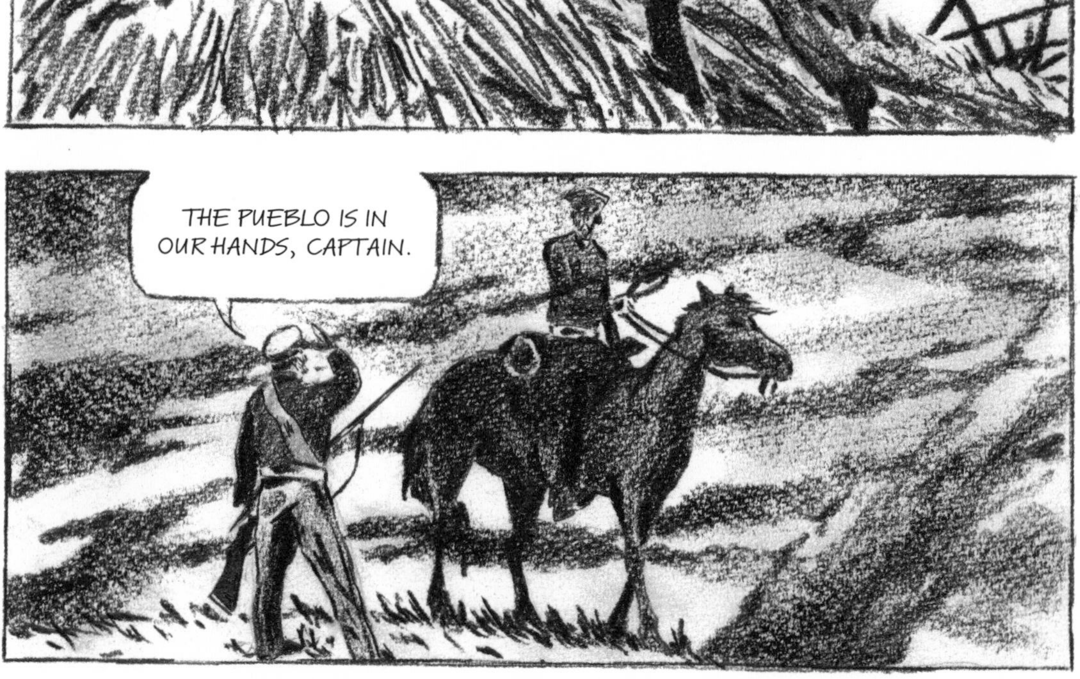
THE PUEBLO IS IN OUR HANDS, CAPTAIN.

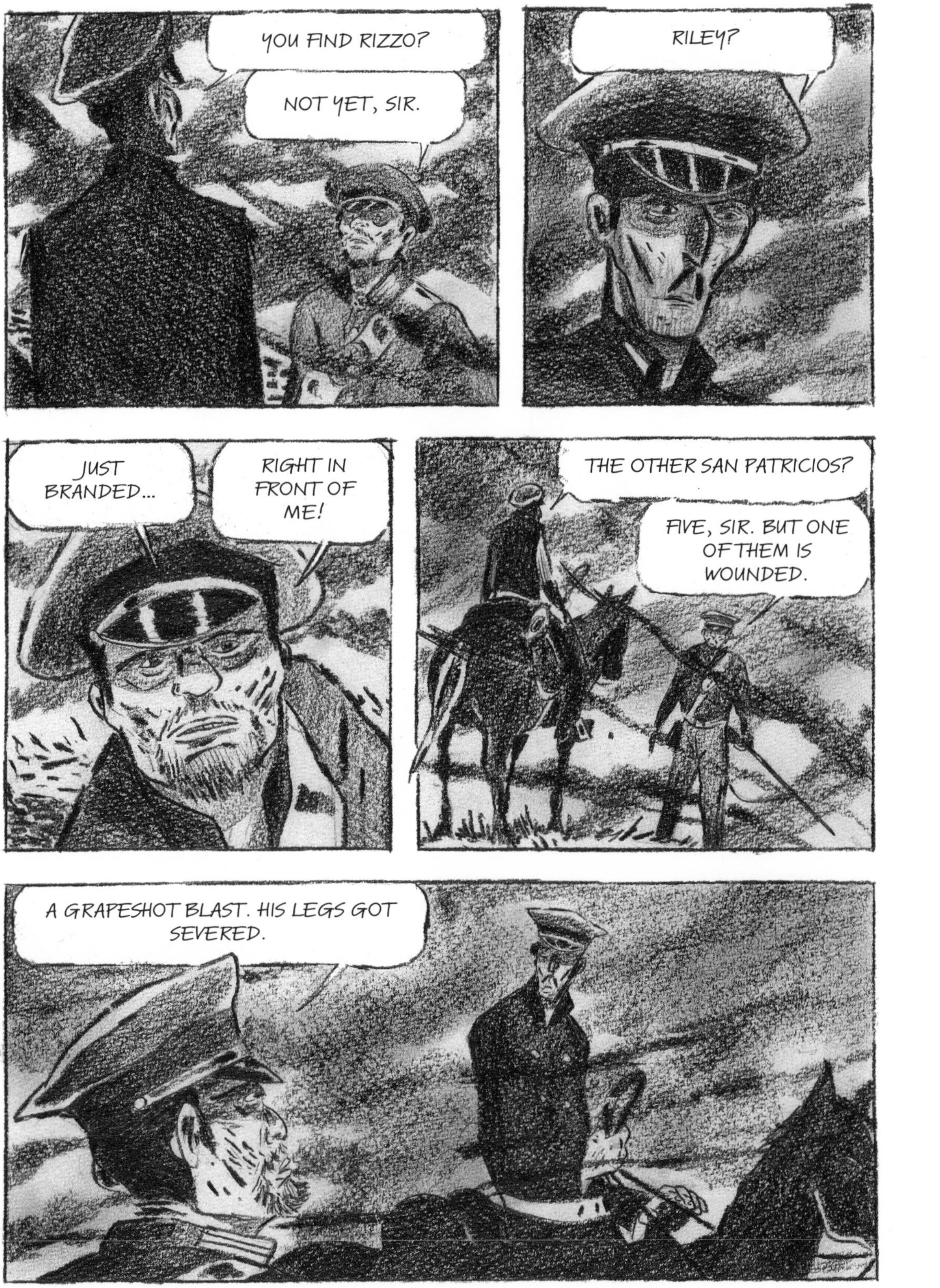
YOU FIND RIZZO?
NOT YET, SIR.
RILEY?
JUST BRANDED...
RIGHT IN FRONT OF ME!
THE OTHER SAN PATRICIOS?
FIVE, SIR. BUT ONE OF THEM IS WOUNDED.
A GRAPESHOT BLAST. HIS LEGS GOT SEVERED.

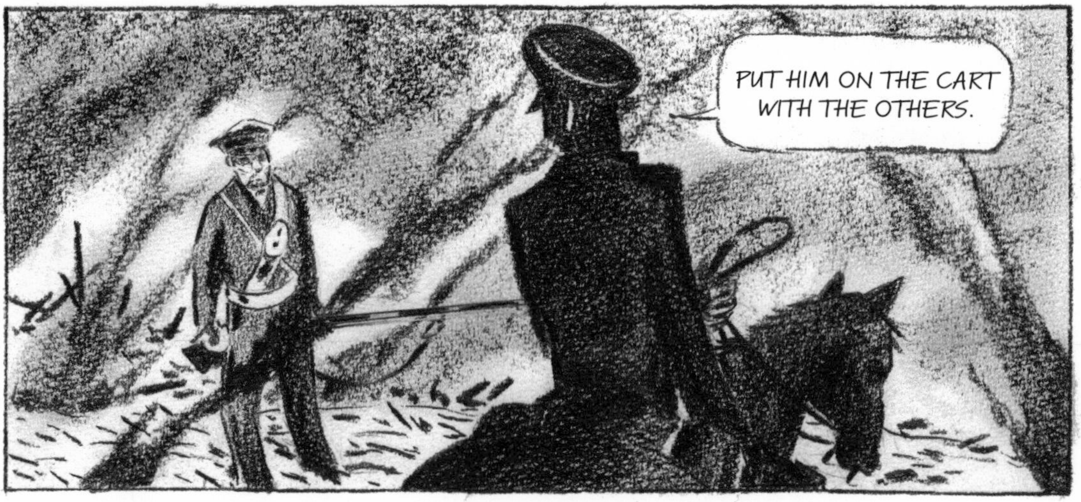
PUT HIM ON THE CART WITH THE OTHERS.

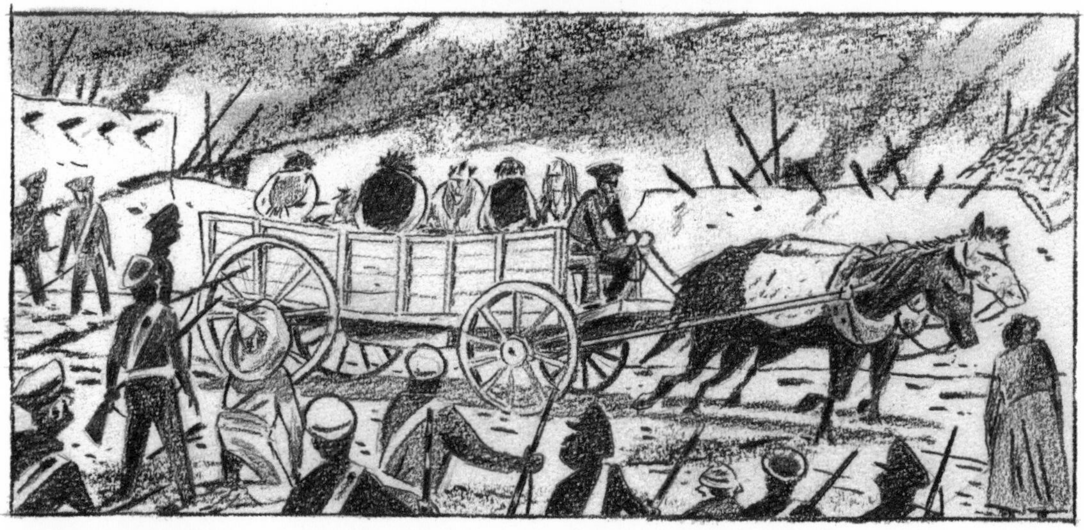

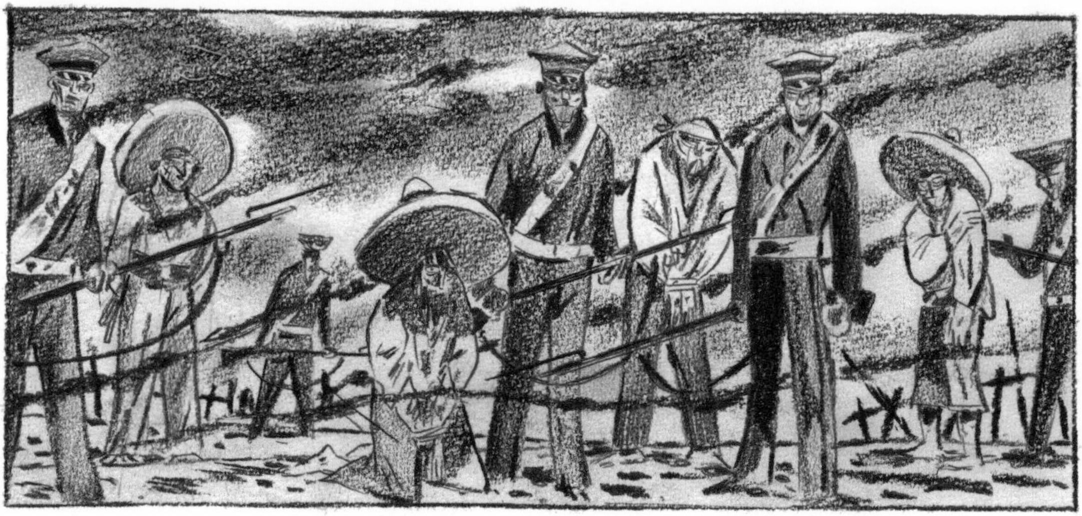

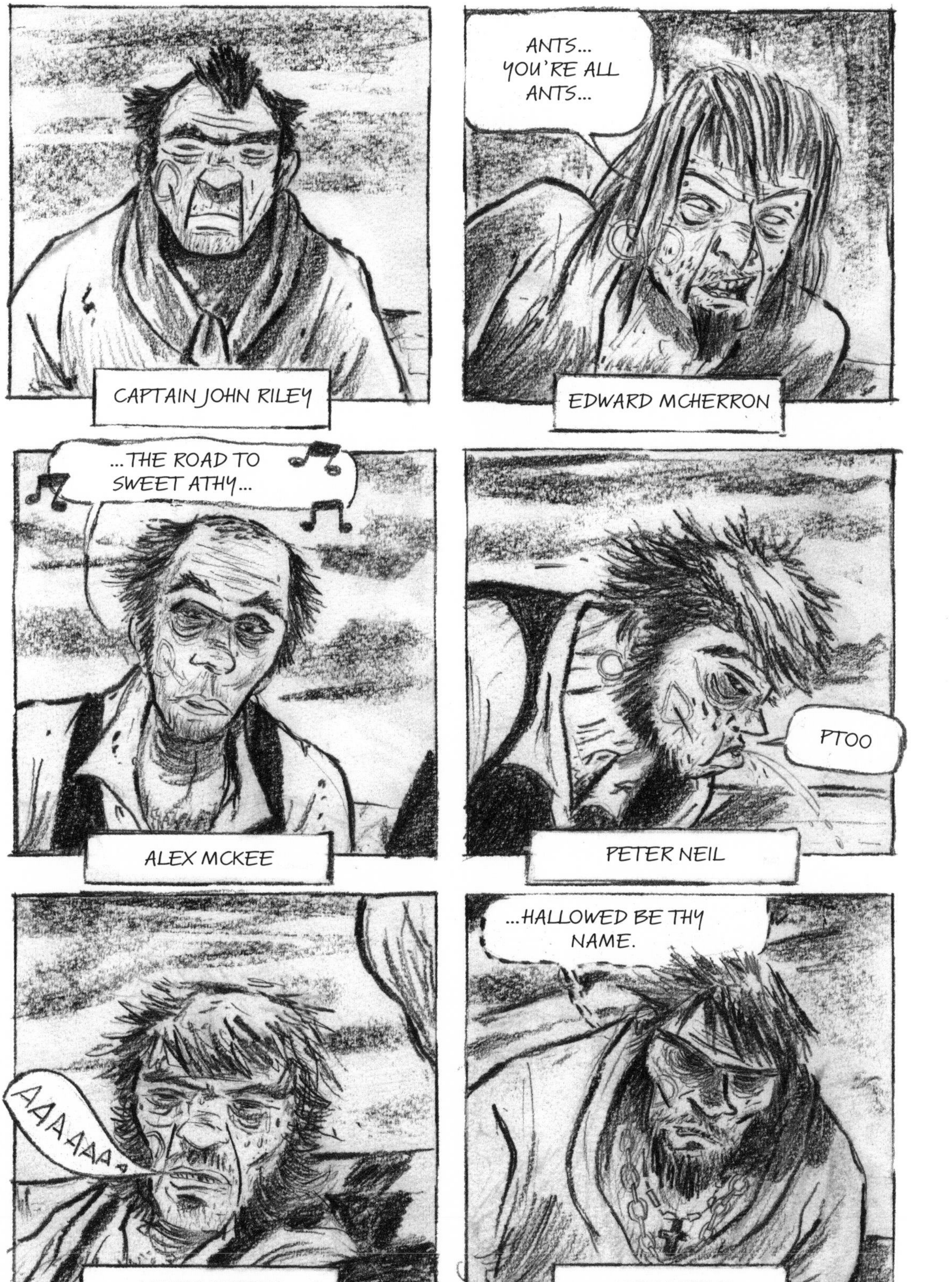
CAPTAIN JOHN RILEY
ANTS... YOU'RE ALL ANTS...
EDWARD MCHERRON
...THE ROAD TO SWEET ATHY...
ALEX MCKEE
PTOO
PETER NEIL
AAAAAA
JAMES SPEERS
...HALLOWED BE THY NAME.
JOHN LITTLE

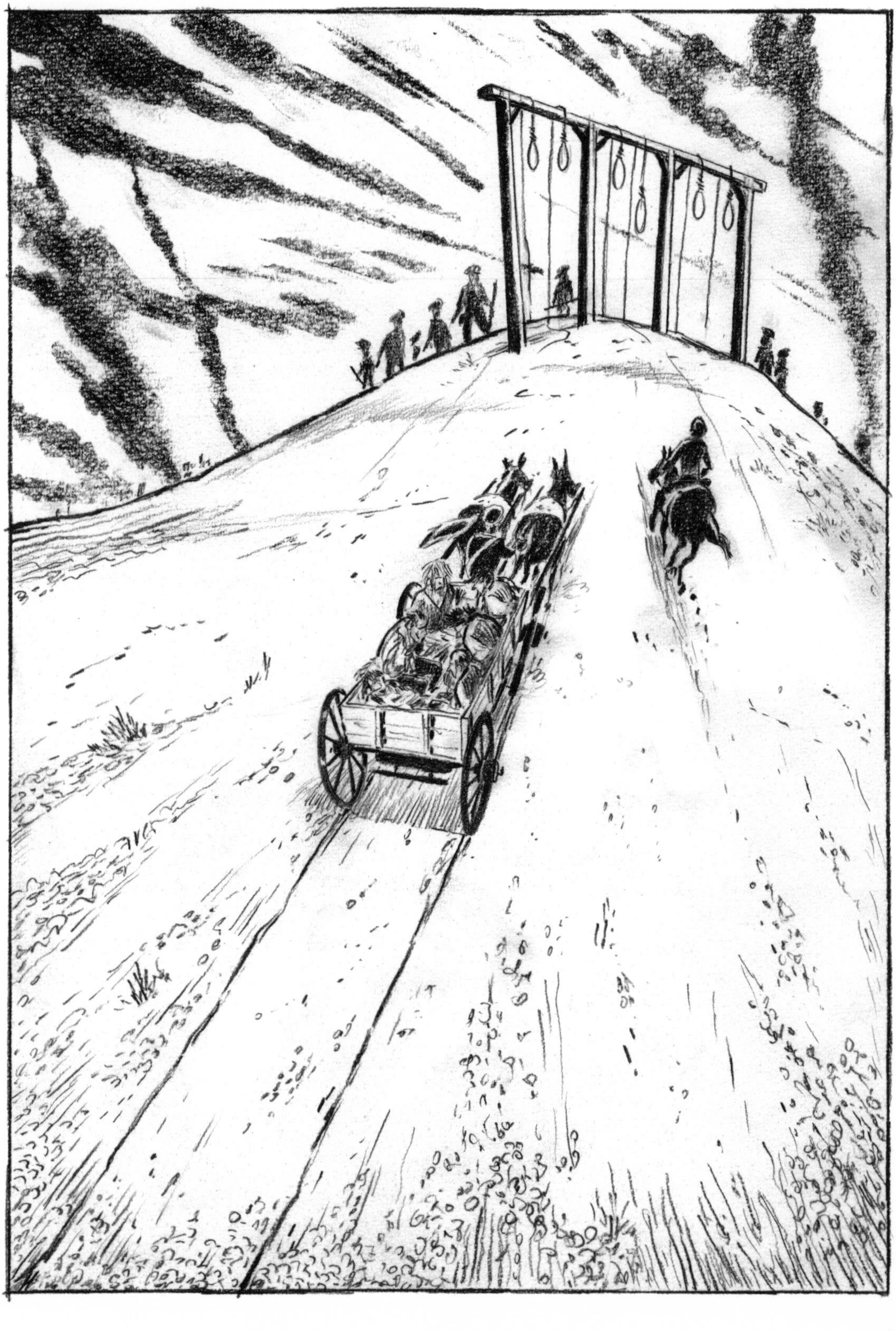

AAAAR
ADIOS, SAN PATRICOS.

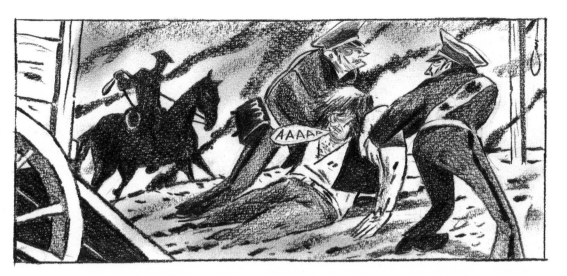

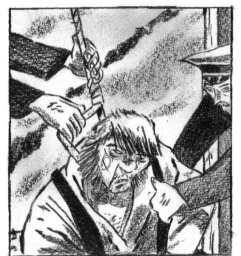

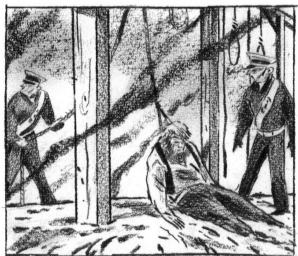

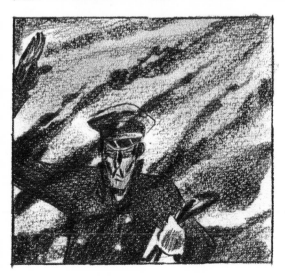

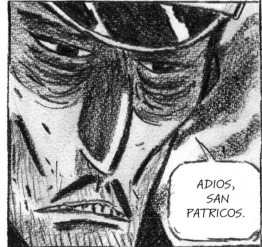

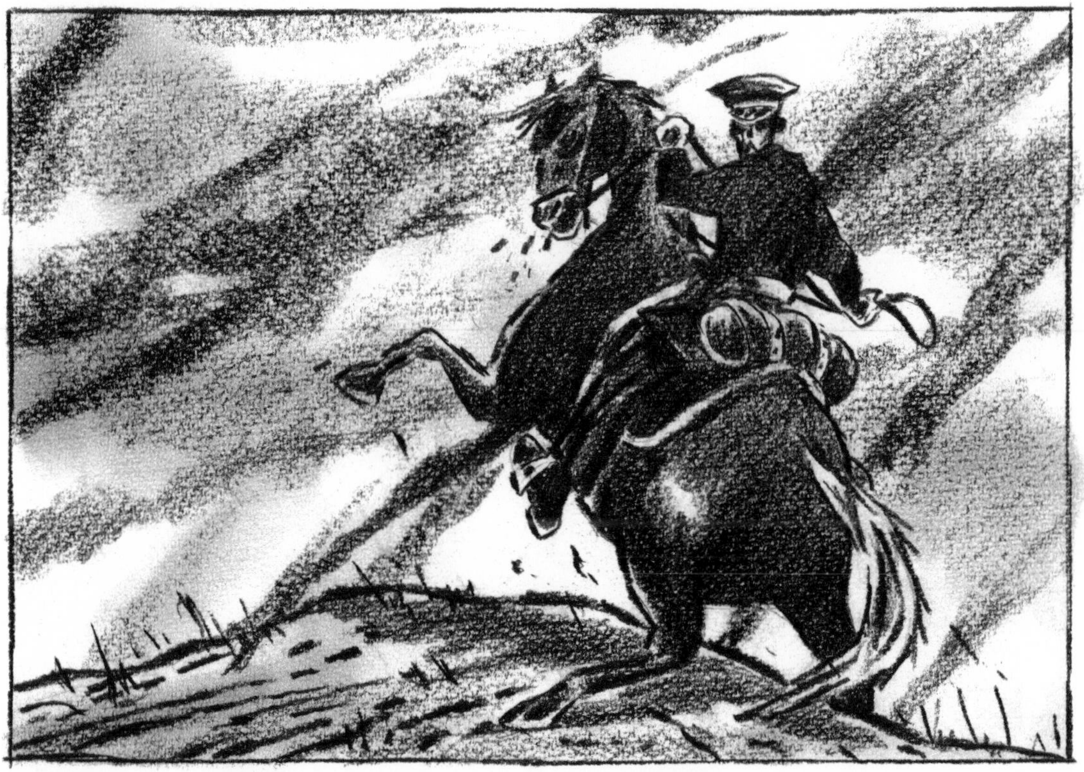

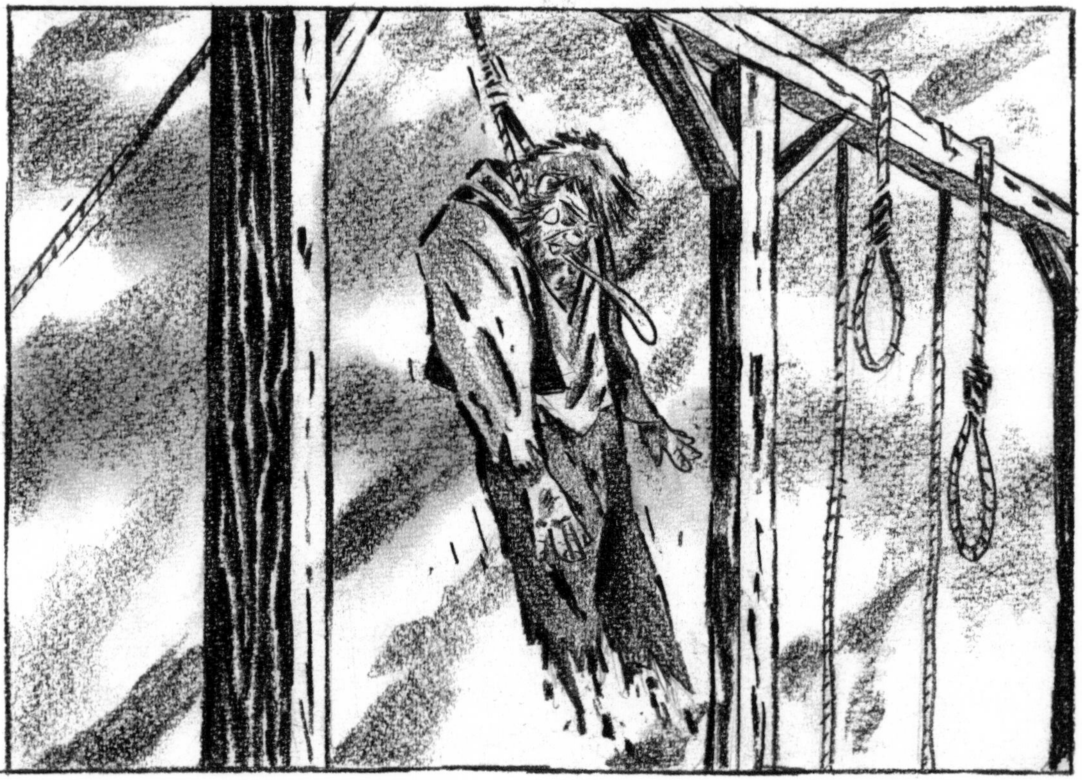

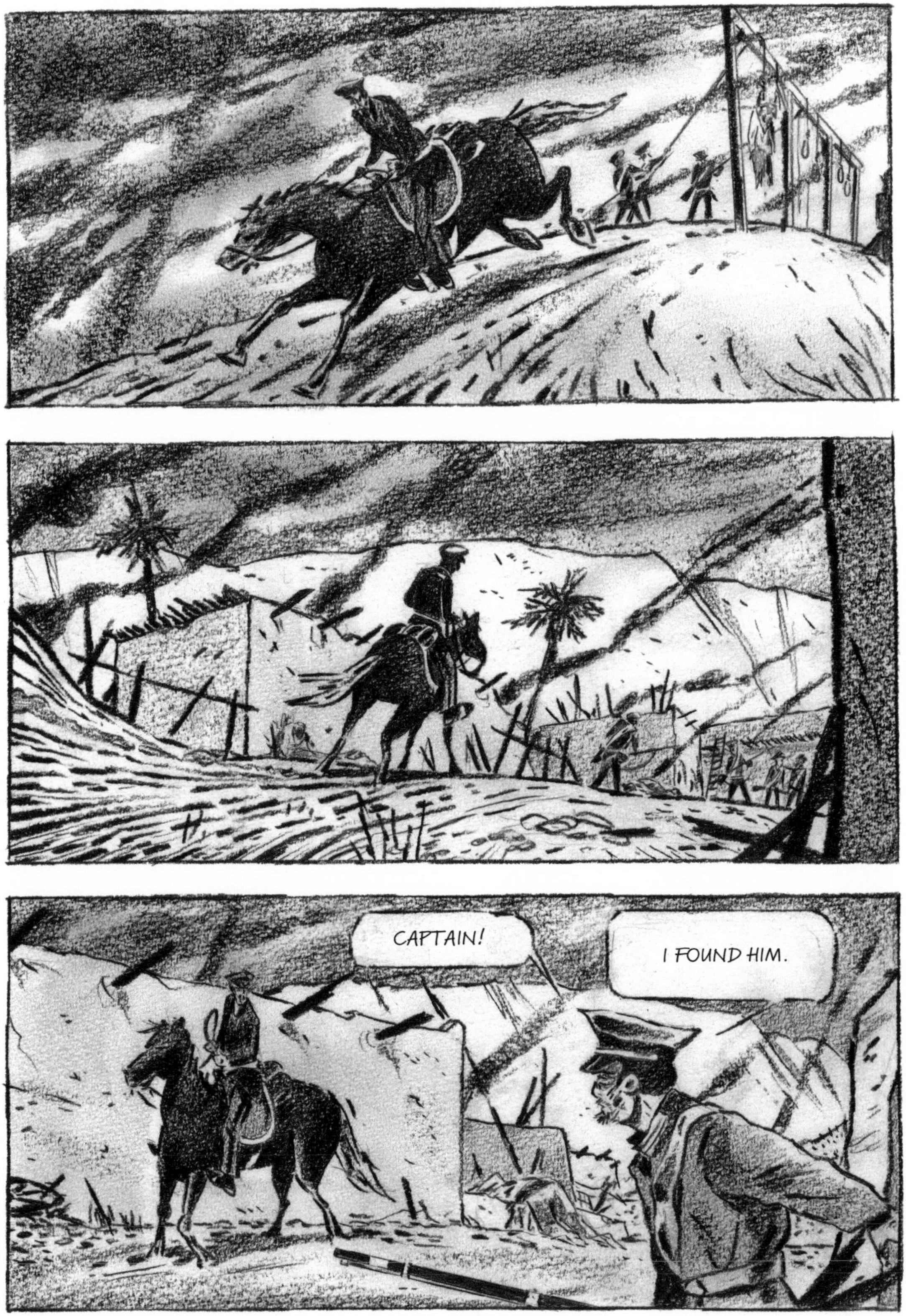
CAPTAIN!
I FOUND HIM.

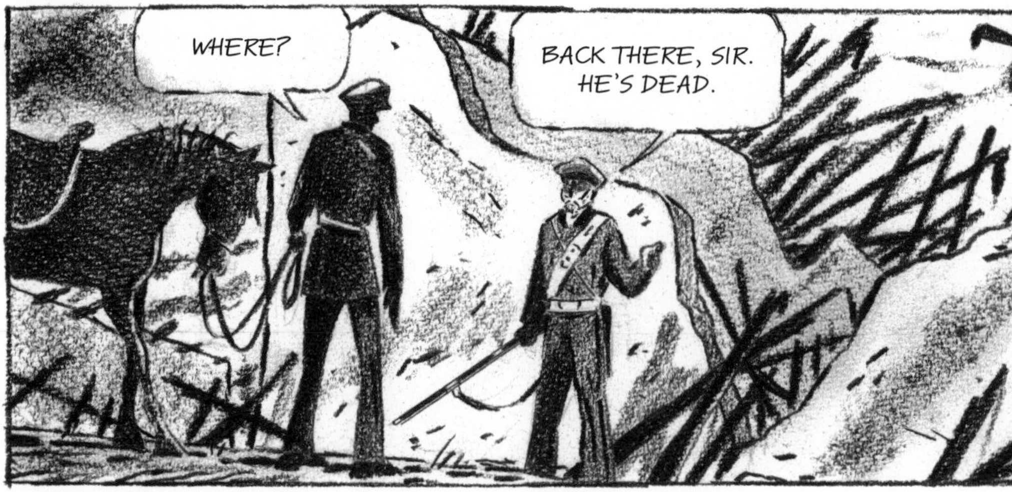
WHERE?
BACK THERE, SIR. HE'S DEAD.

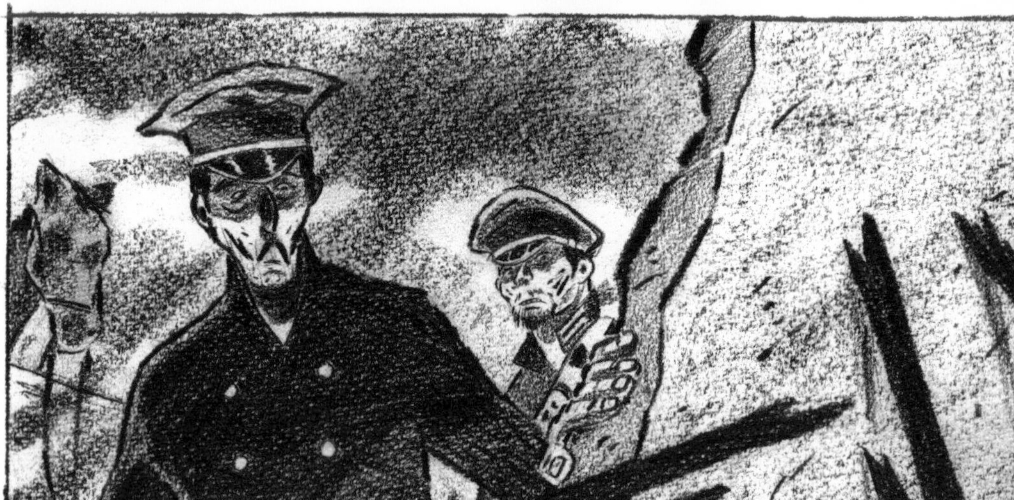

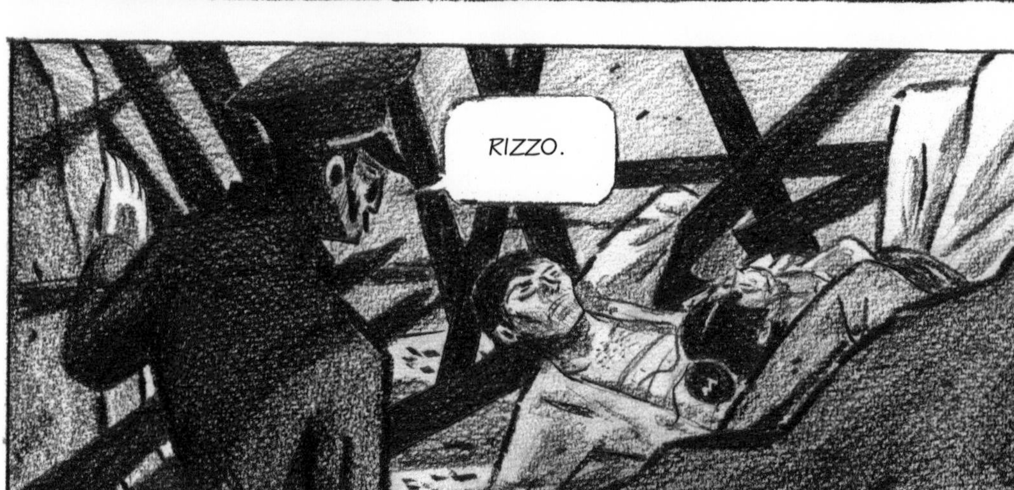
RIZZO.

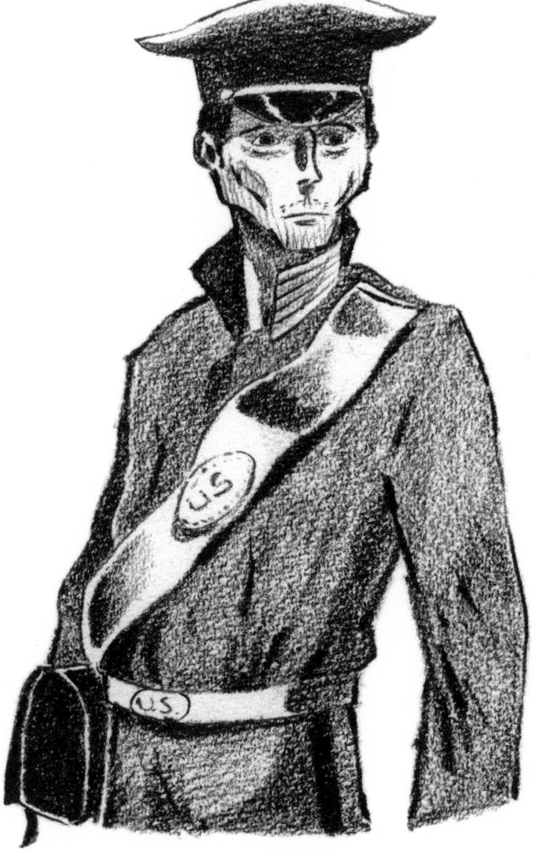
U.S.

CHAPTER TWO

RIZZO

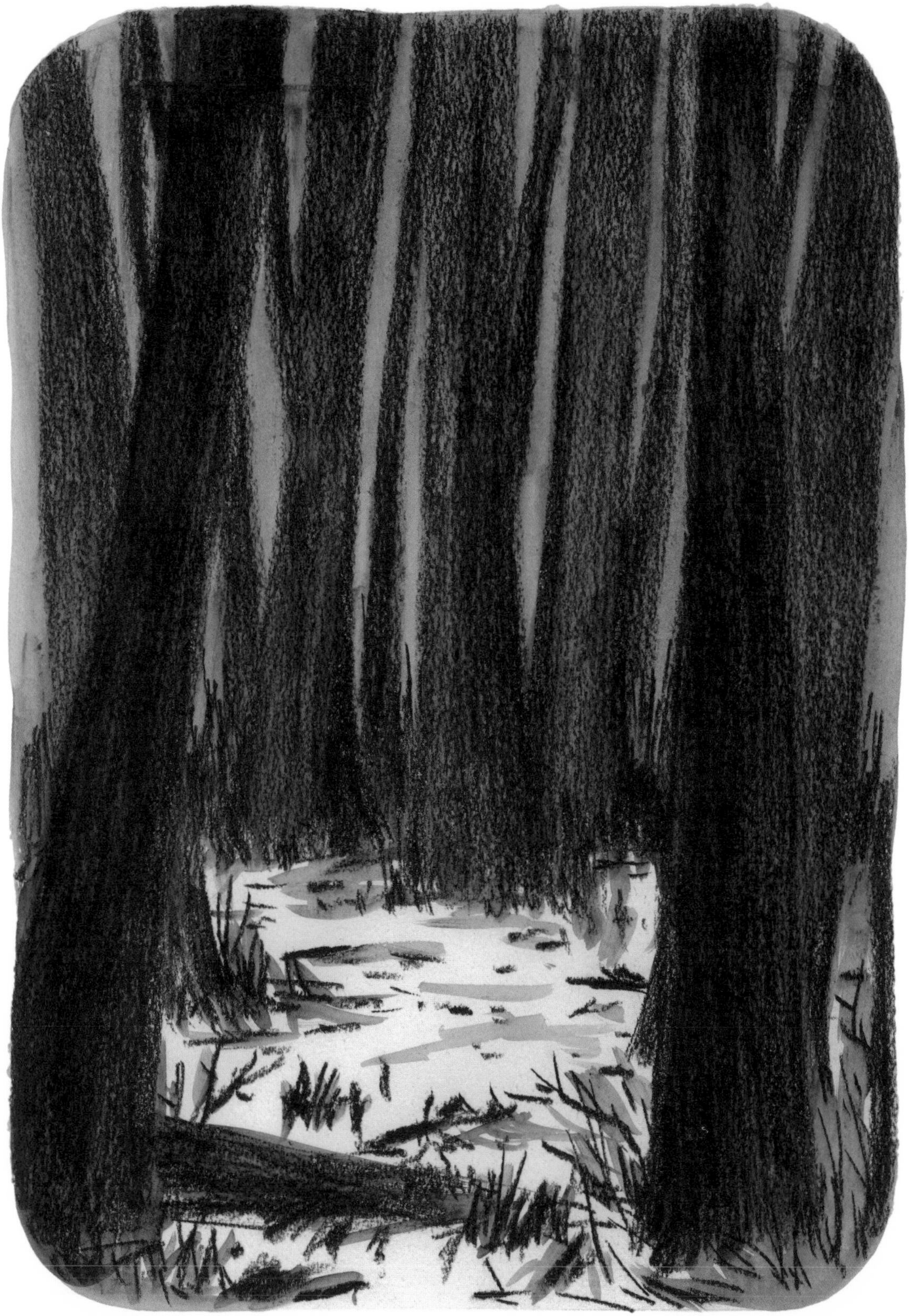

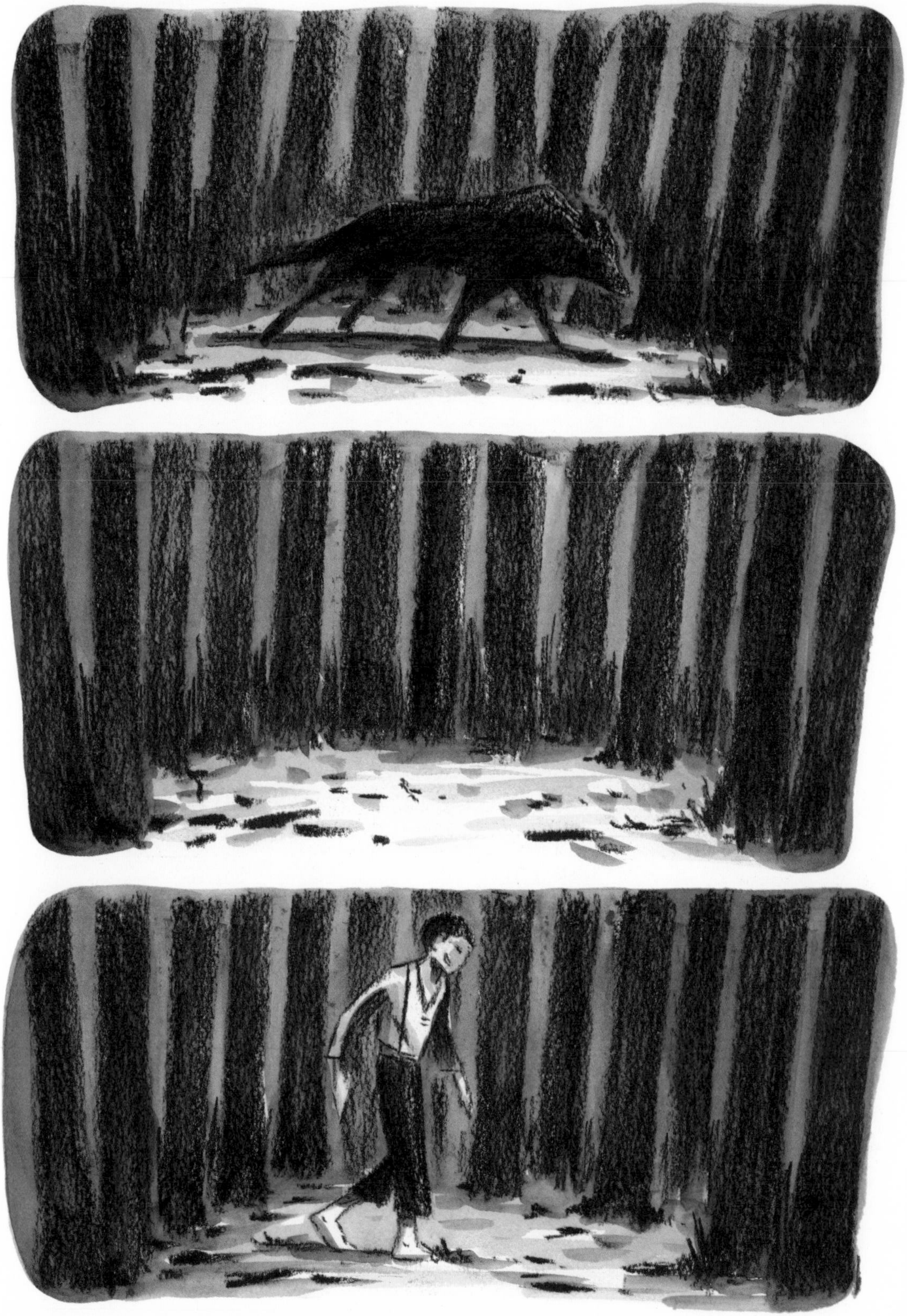

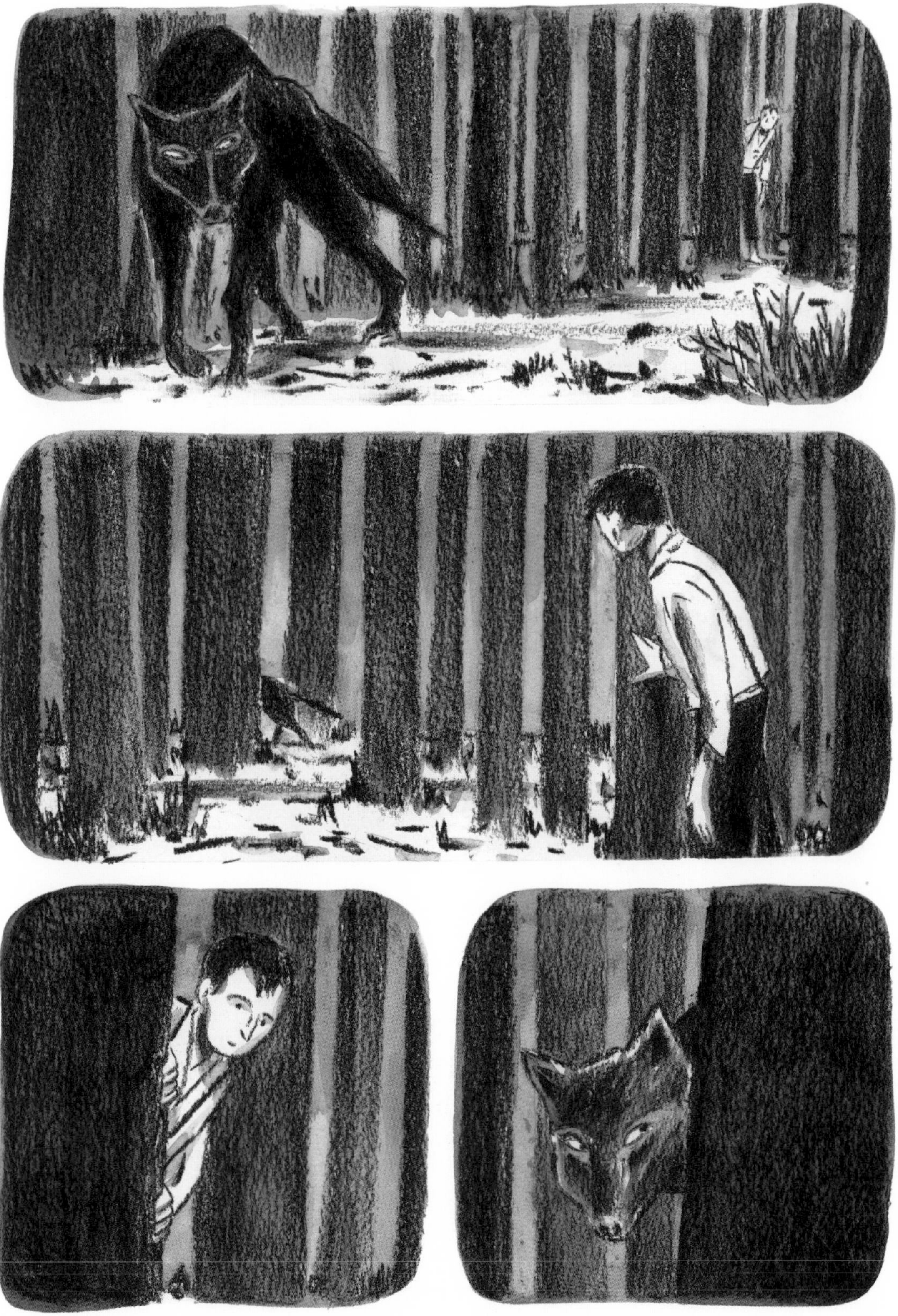

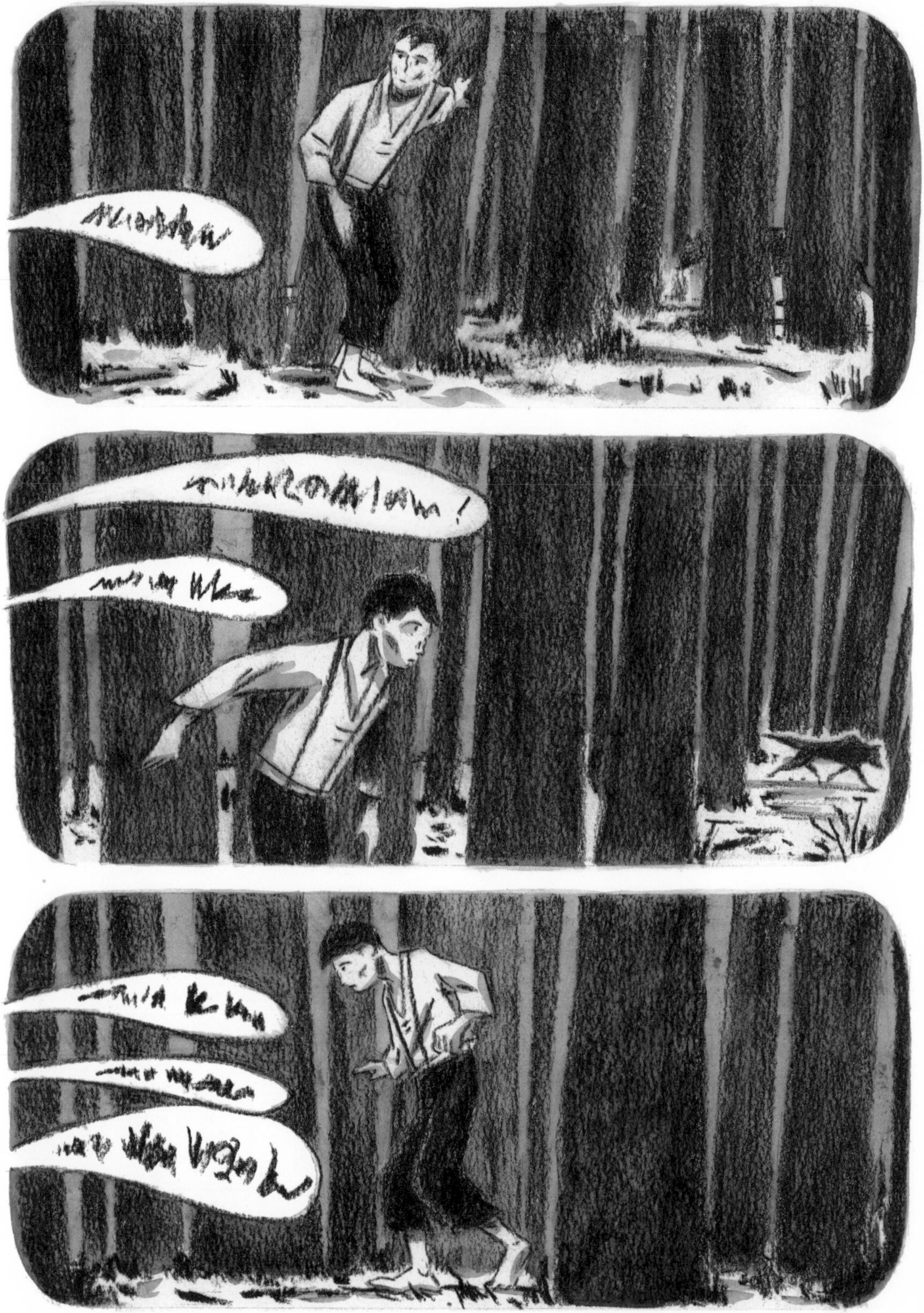

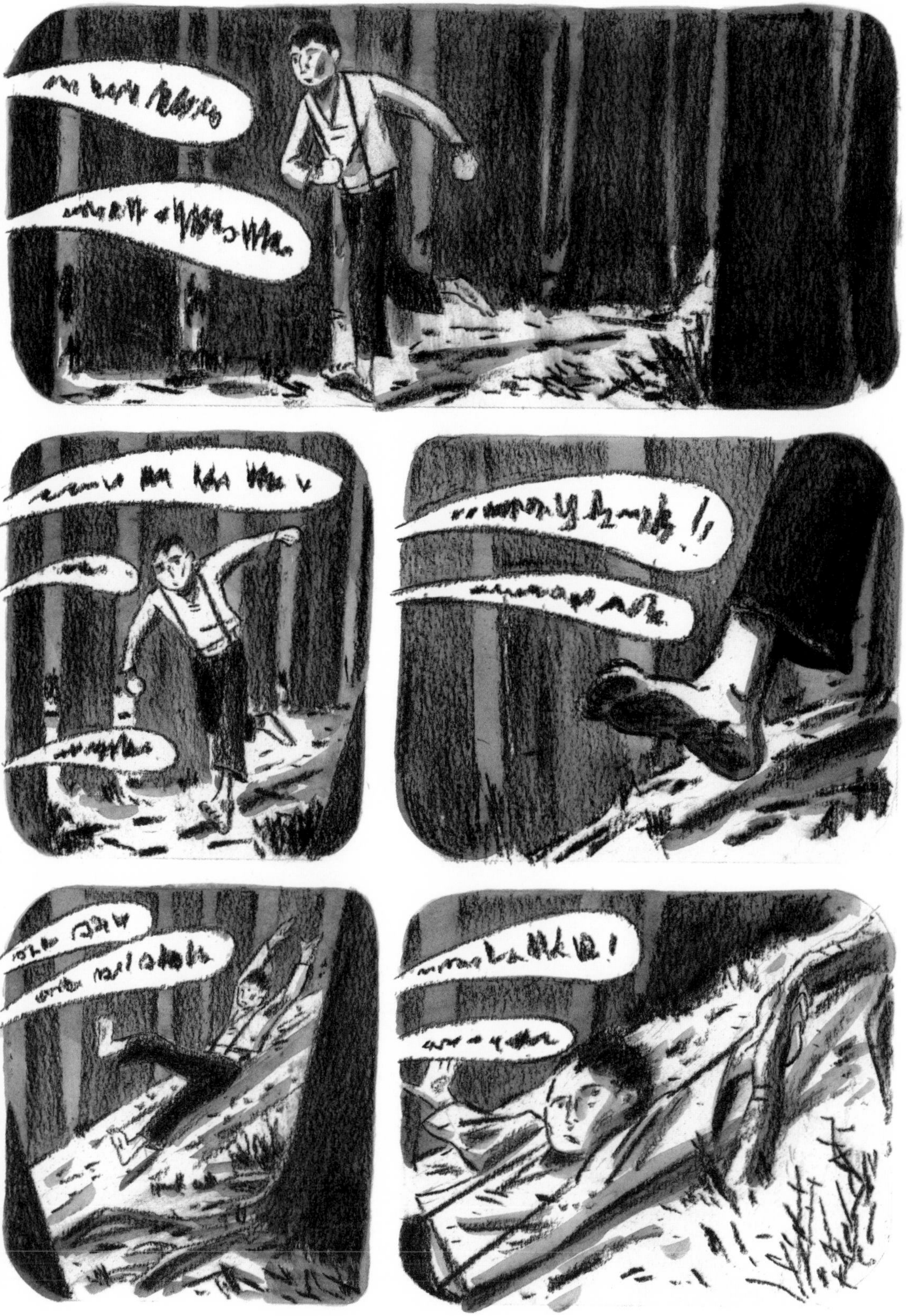

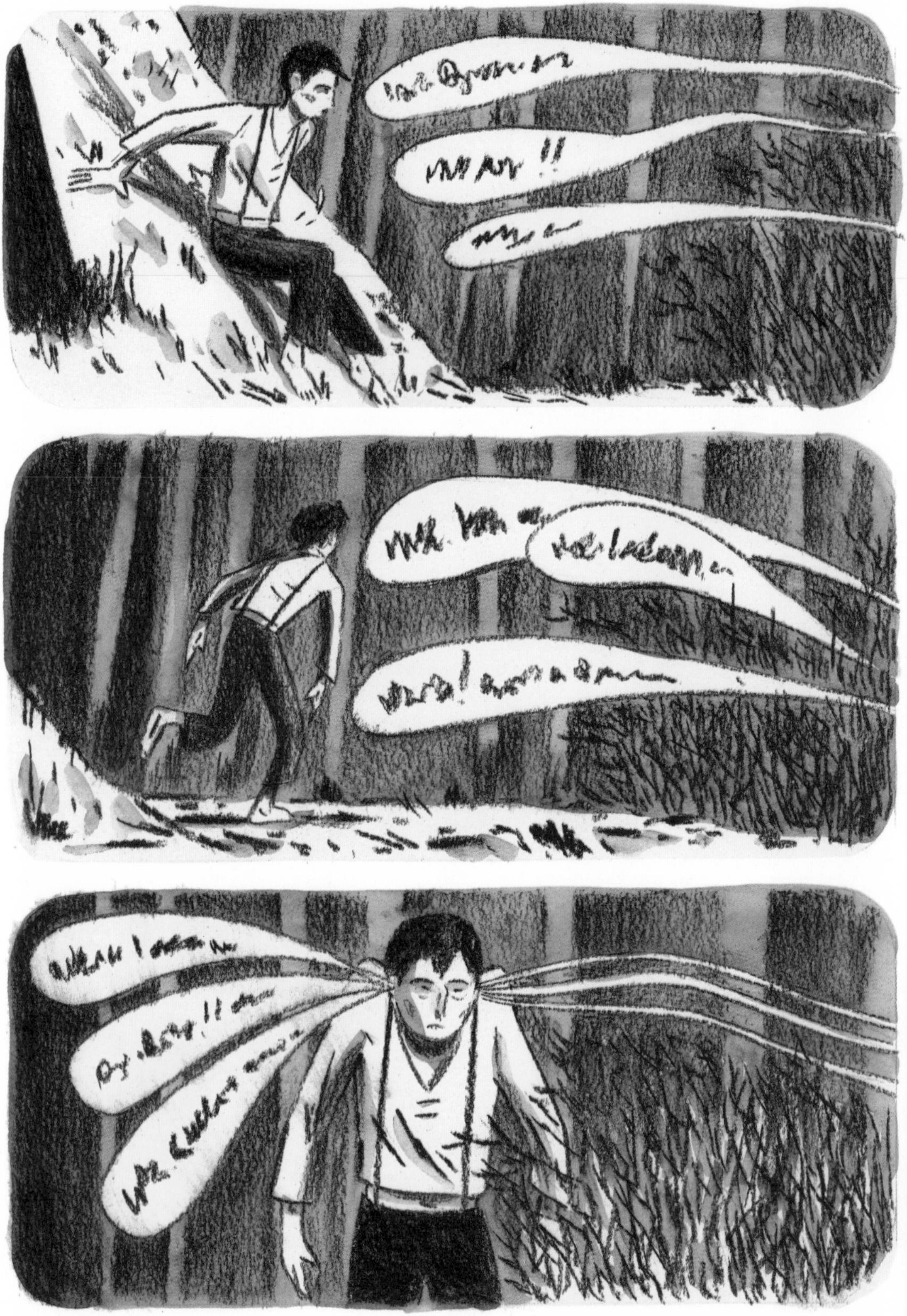

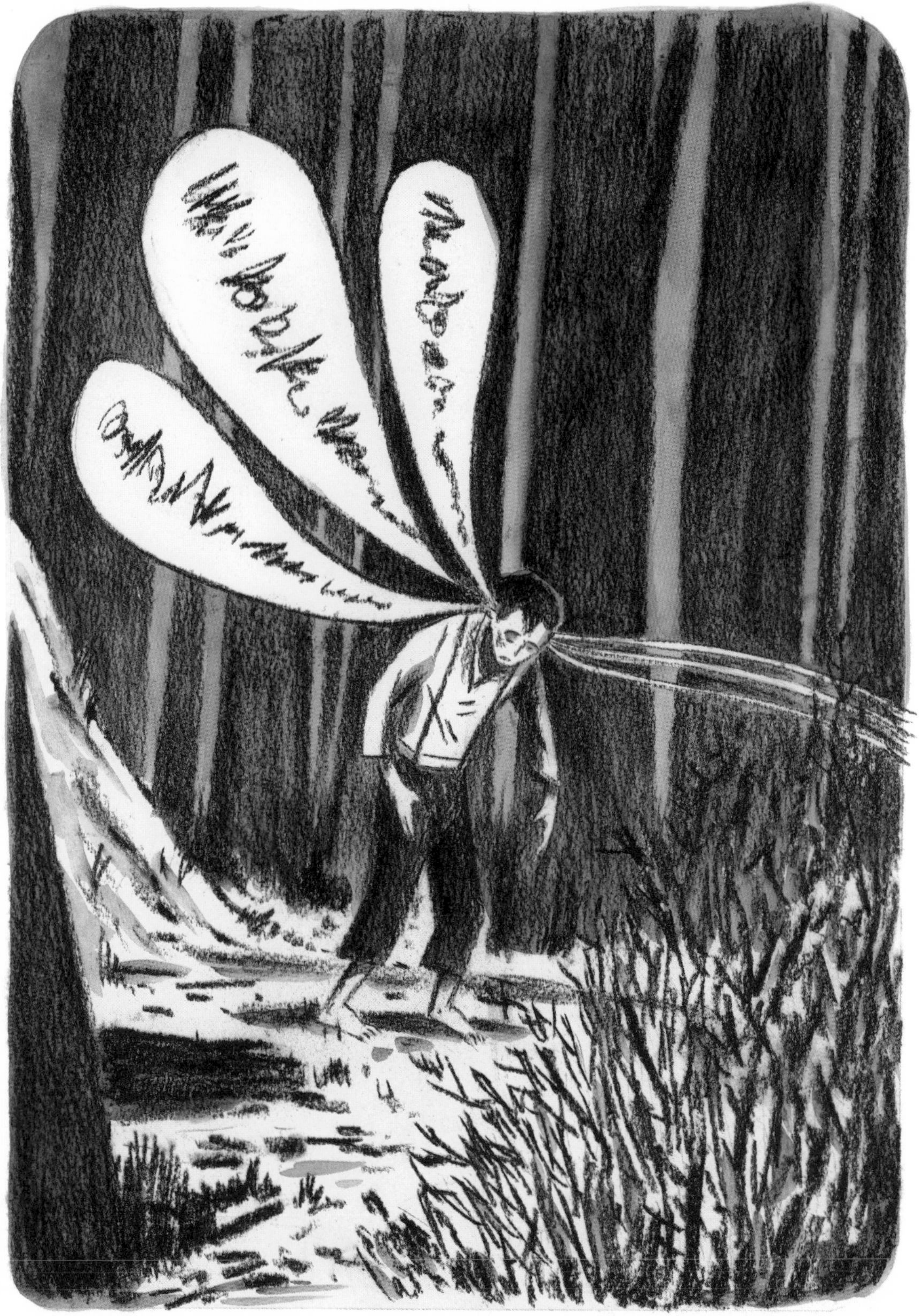

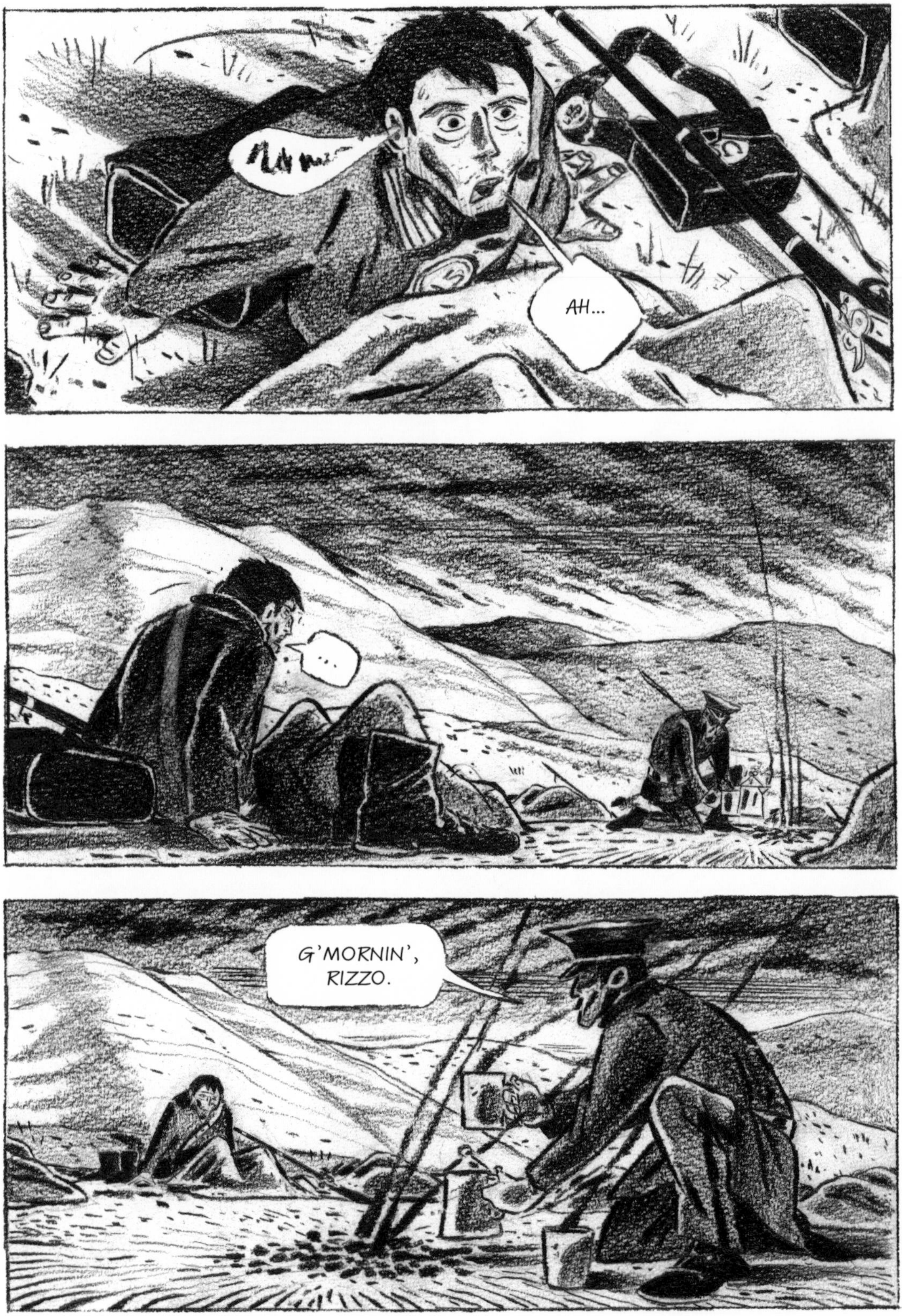
AH...
...
G'MORNIN', RIZZO.

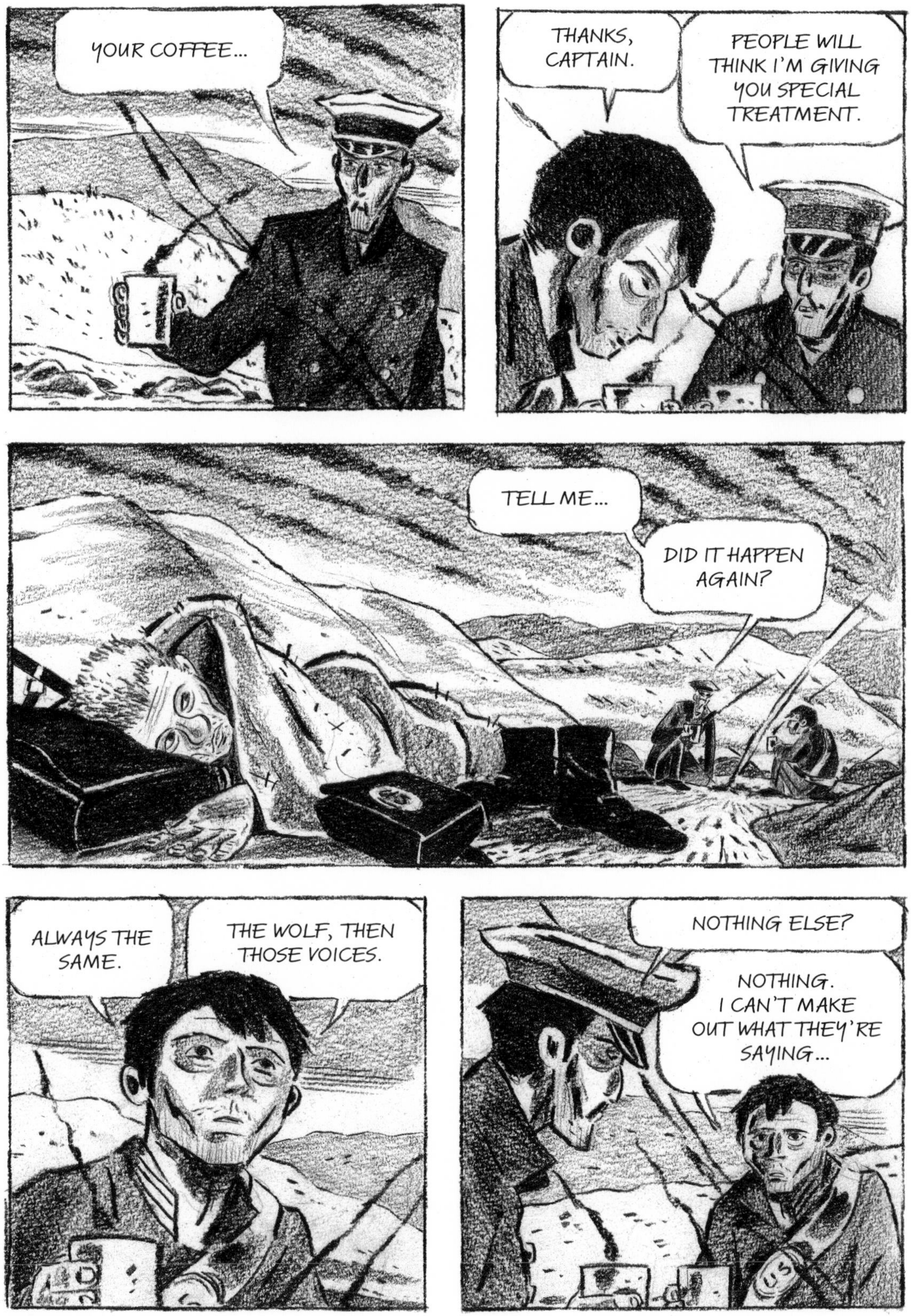
YOUR COFFEE...
THANKS, CAPTAIN.
PEOPLE WILL THINK I'M GIVING YOU SPECIAL TREATMENT.
TELL ME...
DID IT HAPPEN AGAIN?
ALWAYS THE SAME.
THE WOLF, THEN THOSE VOICES.
NOTHING ELSE?
NOTHING. I CAN'T MAKE OUT WHAT THEY'RE SAYING...

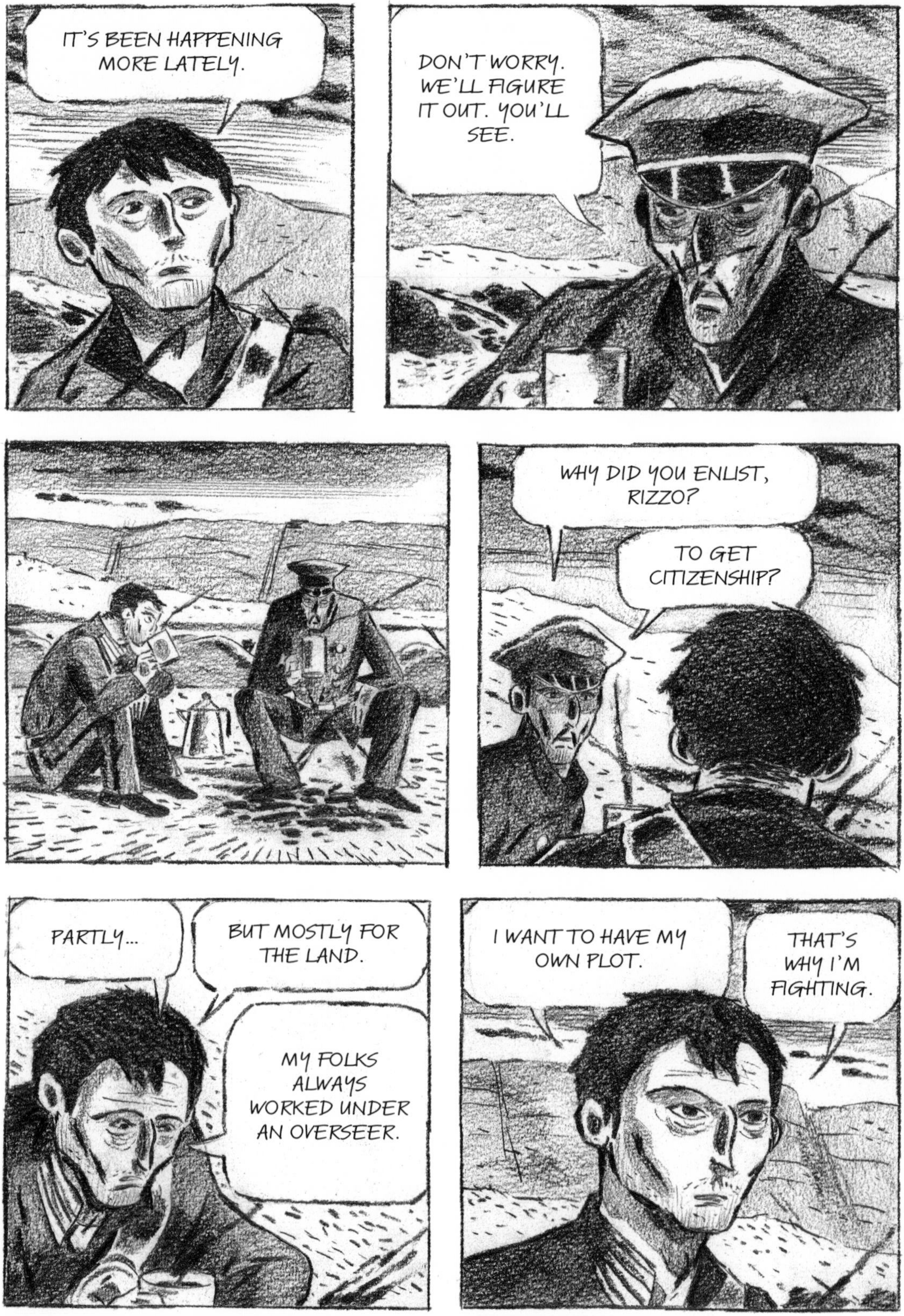
IT'S BEEN HAPPENING MORE LATELY.
DON'T WORRY. WE'LL FIGURE IT OUT. YOU'LL SEE.
WHY DID YOU ENLIST, RIZZO?
TO GET CITIZENSHIP?
PARTLY...
BUT MOSTLY FOR THE LAND.
MY FOLKS ALWAYS WORKED UNDER AN OVERSEER.
I WANT TO HAVE MY OWN PLOT.
THAT'S WHY I'M FIGHTING.

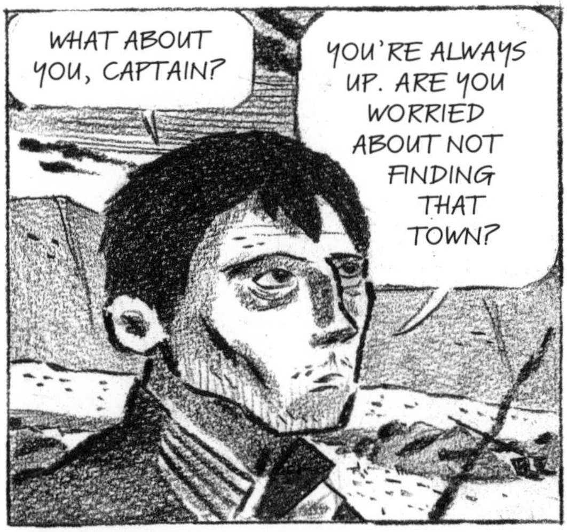
WHAT ABOUT YOU, CAPTAIN?
YOU'RE ALWAYS UP. ARE YOU WORRIED ABOUT NOT FINDING THAT TOWN?

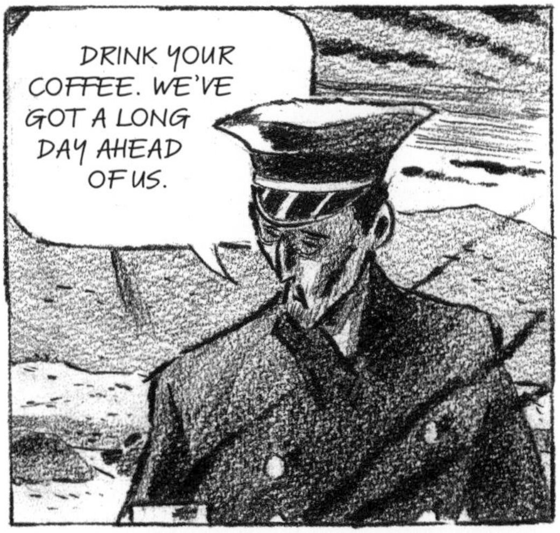
DRINK YOUR COFFEE. WE'VE GOT A LONG DAY AHEAD OF US.

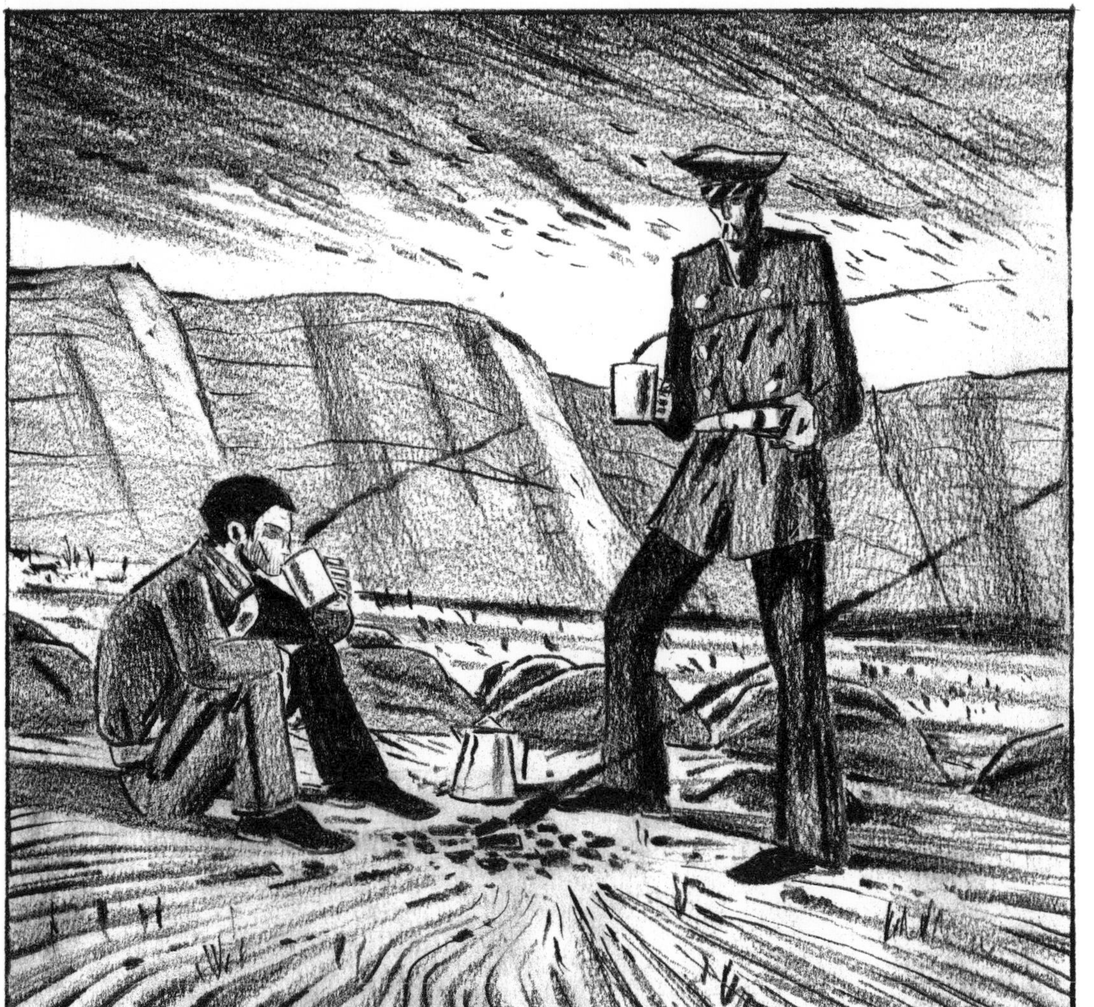

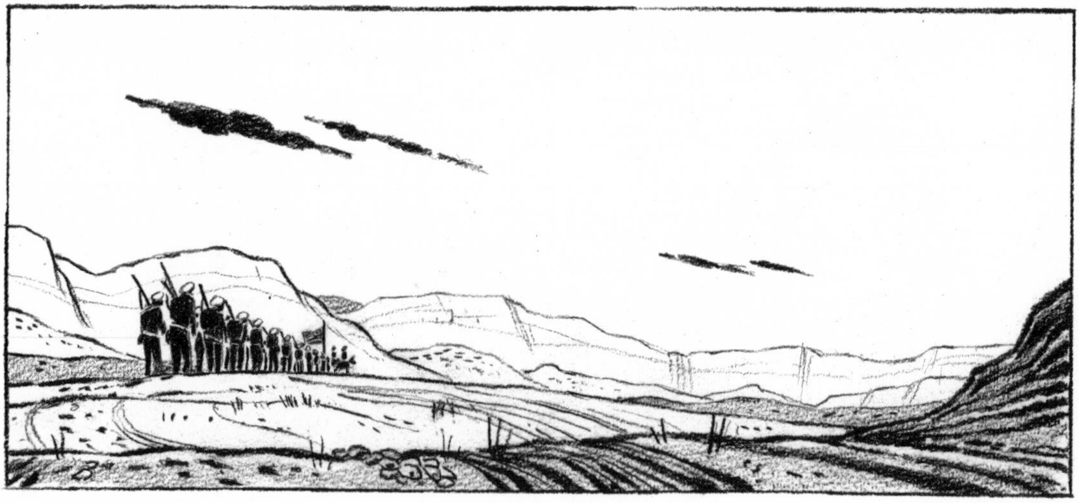

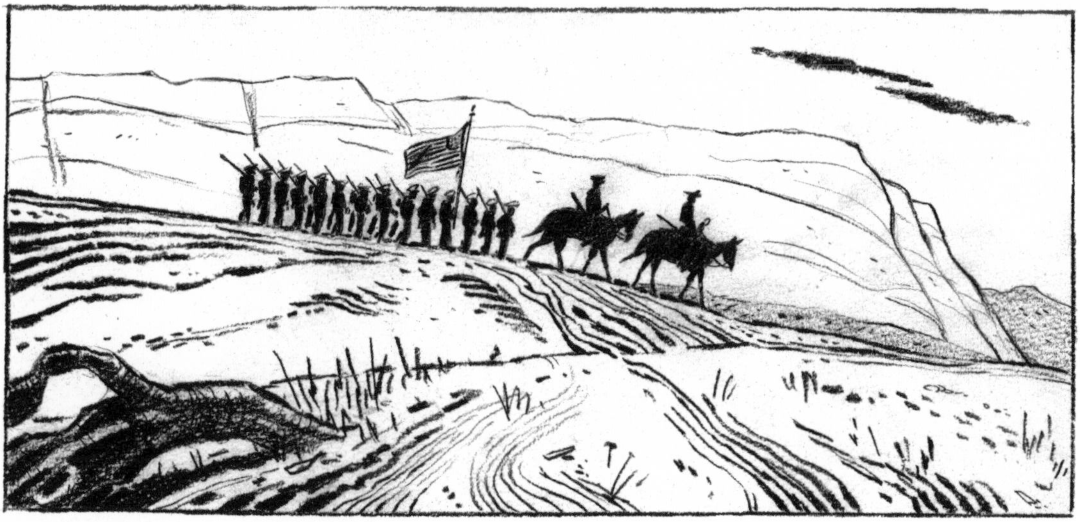

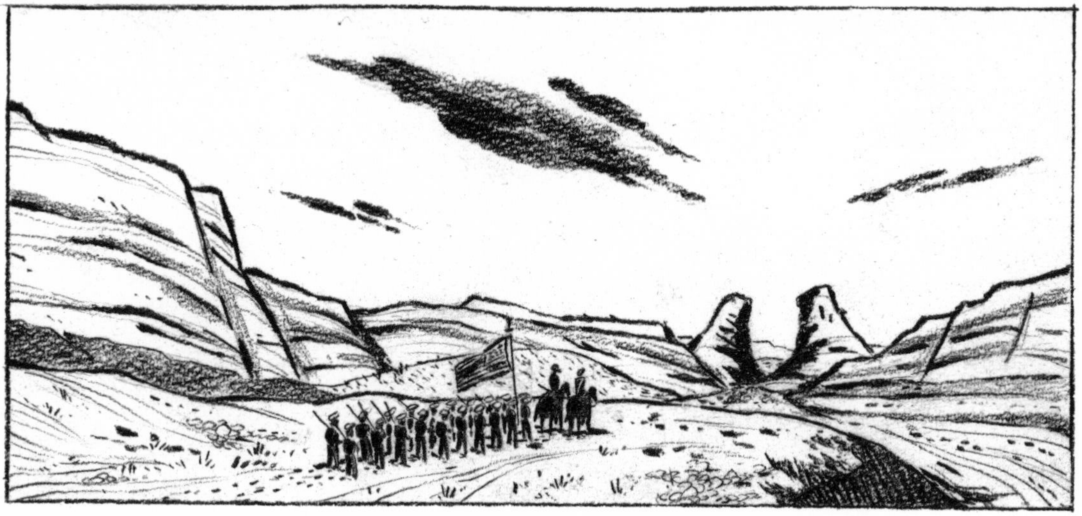

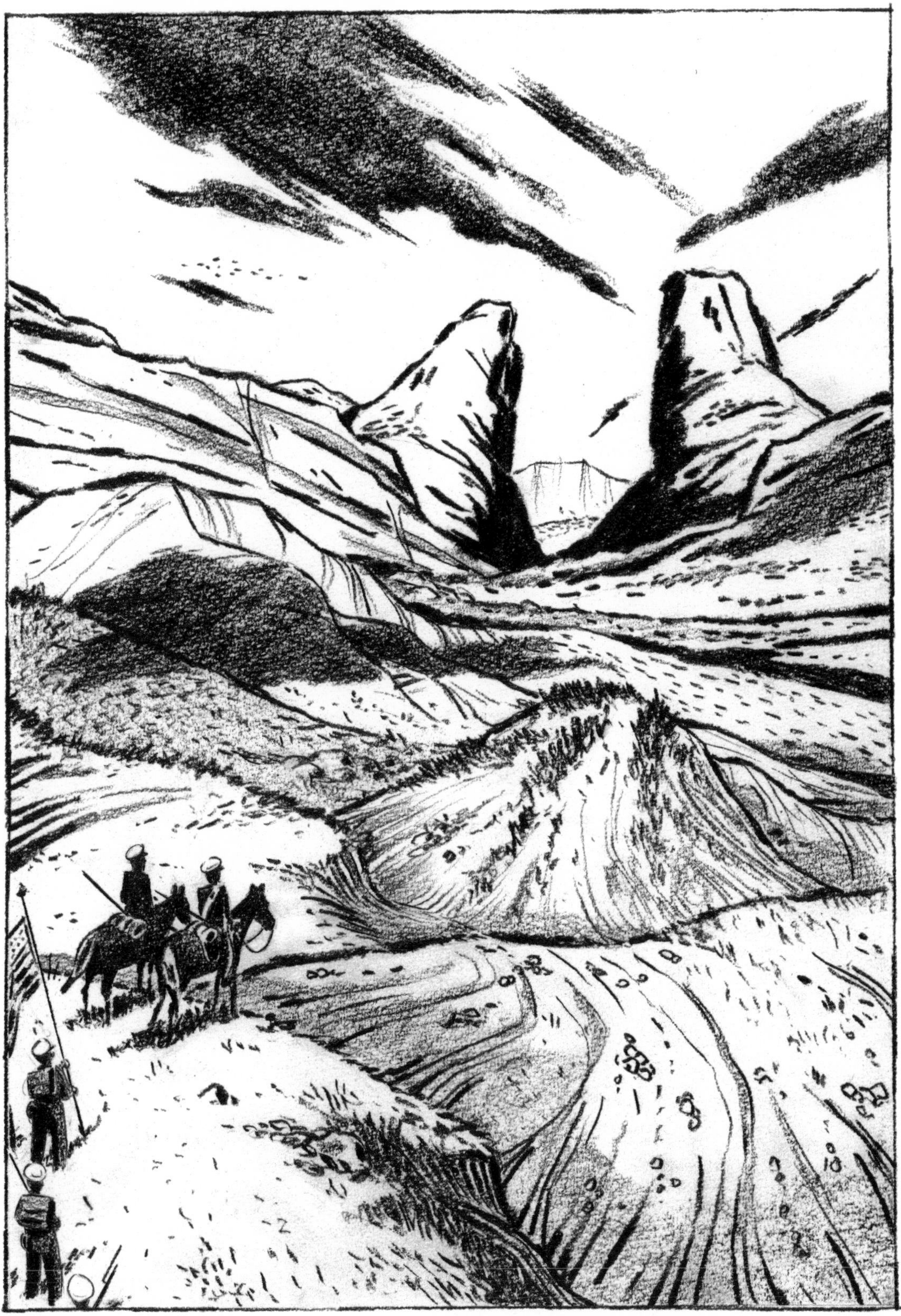

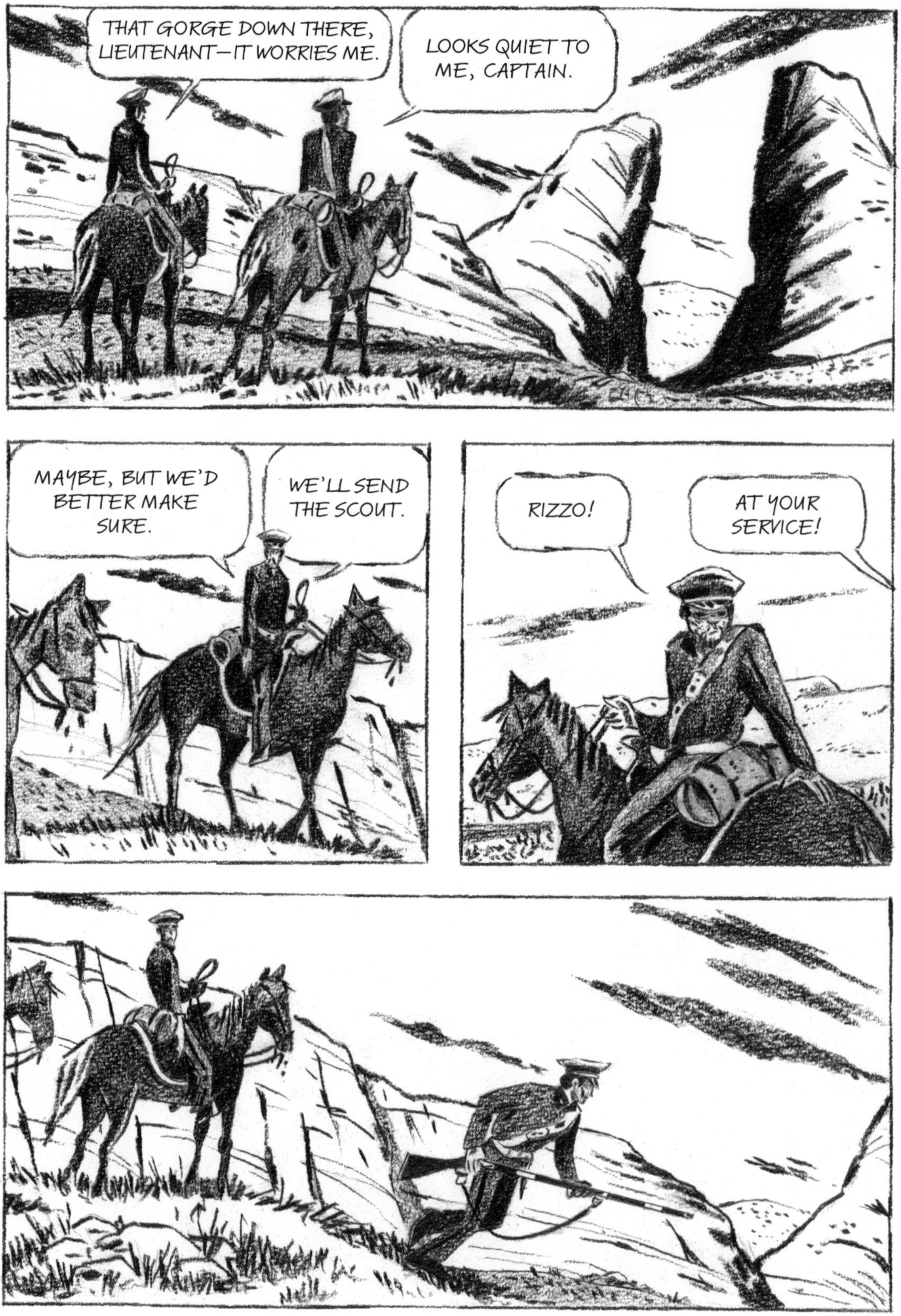
THAT GORGE DOWN THERE, LIEUTENANT—IT WORRIES ME.
LOOKS QUIET TO ME, CAPTAIN.
MAYBE, BUT WE'D BETTER MAKE SURE.
WE'LL SEND THE SCOUT.
RIZZO!
AT YOUR SERVICE!

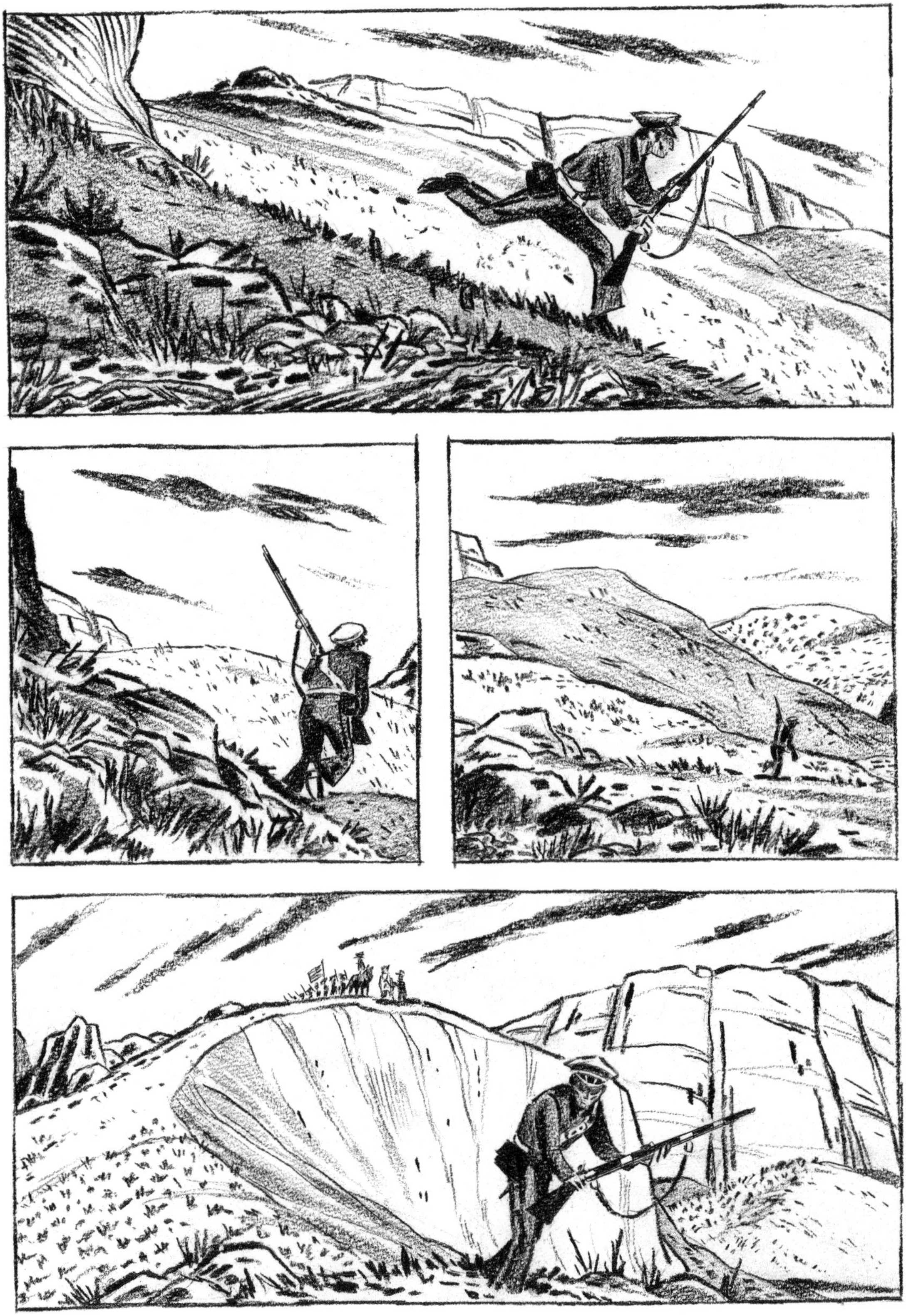

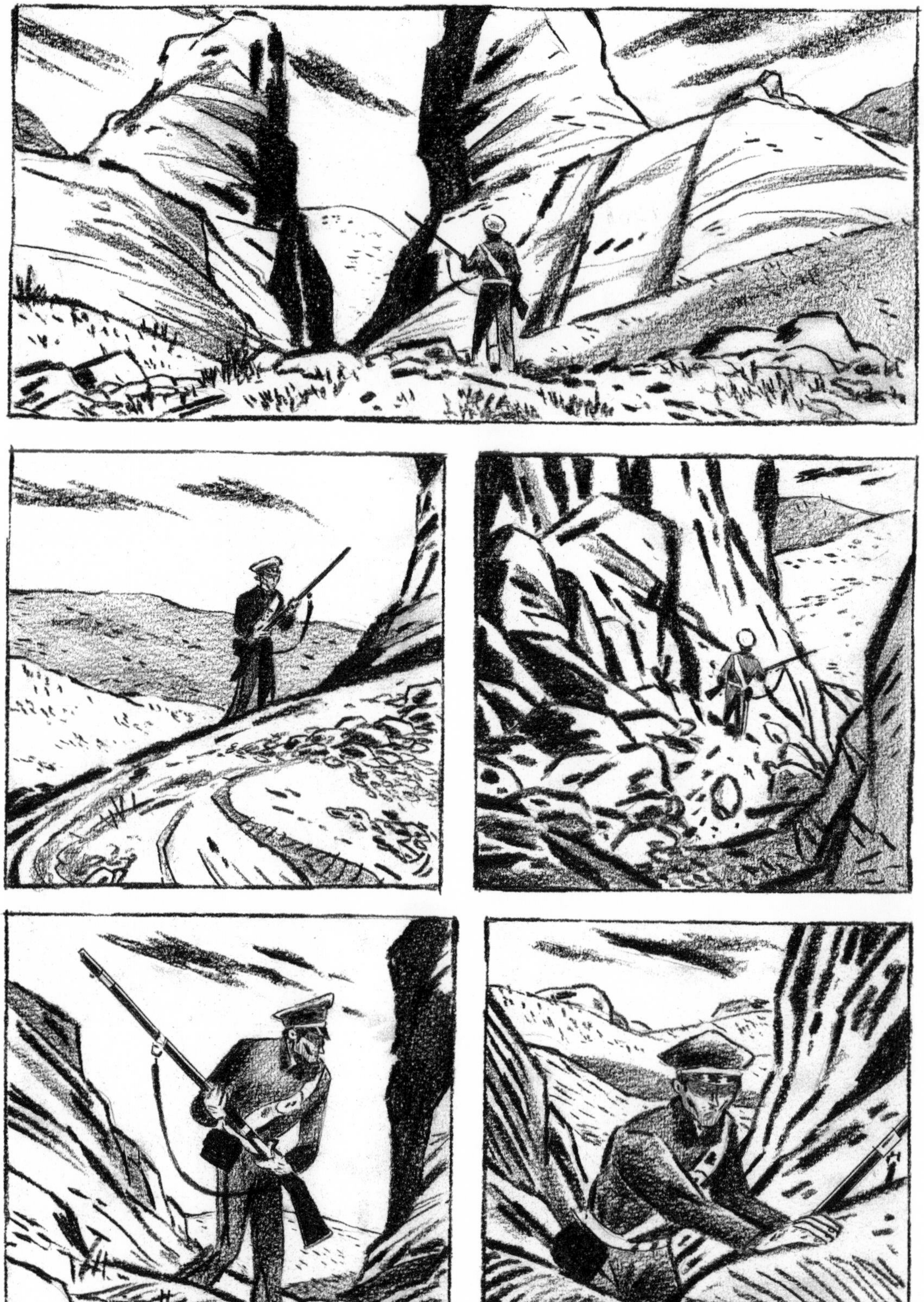

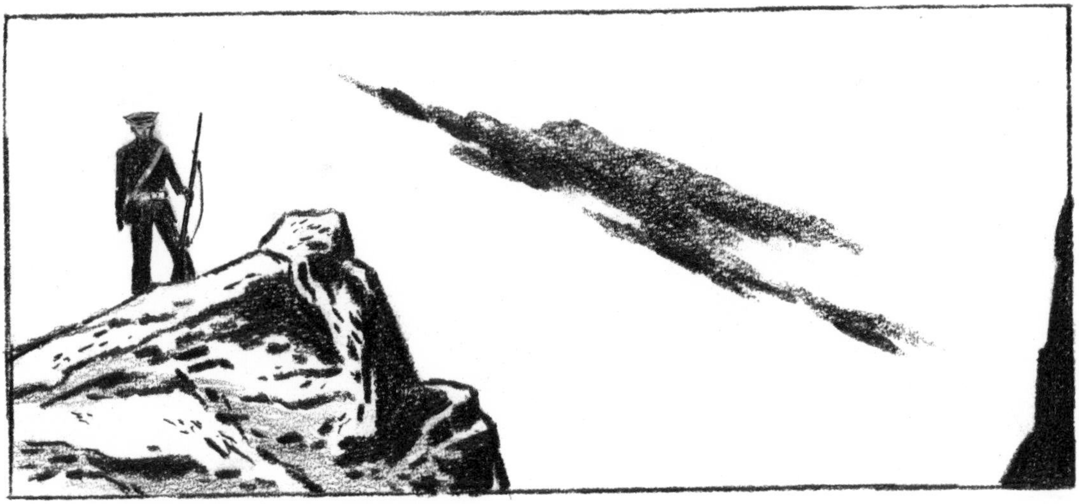

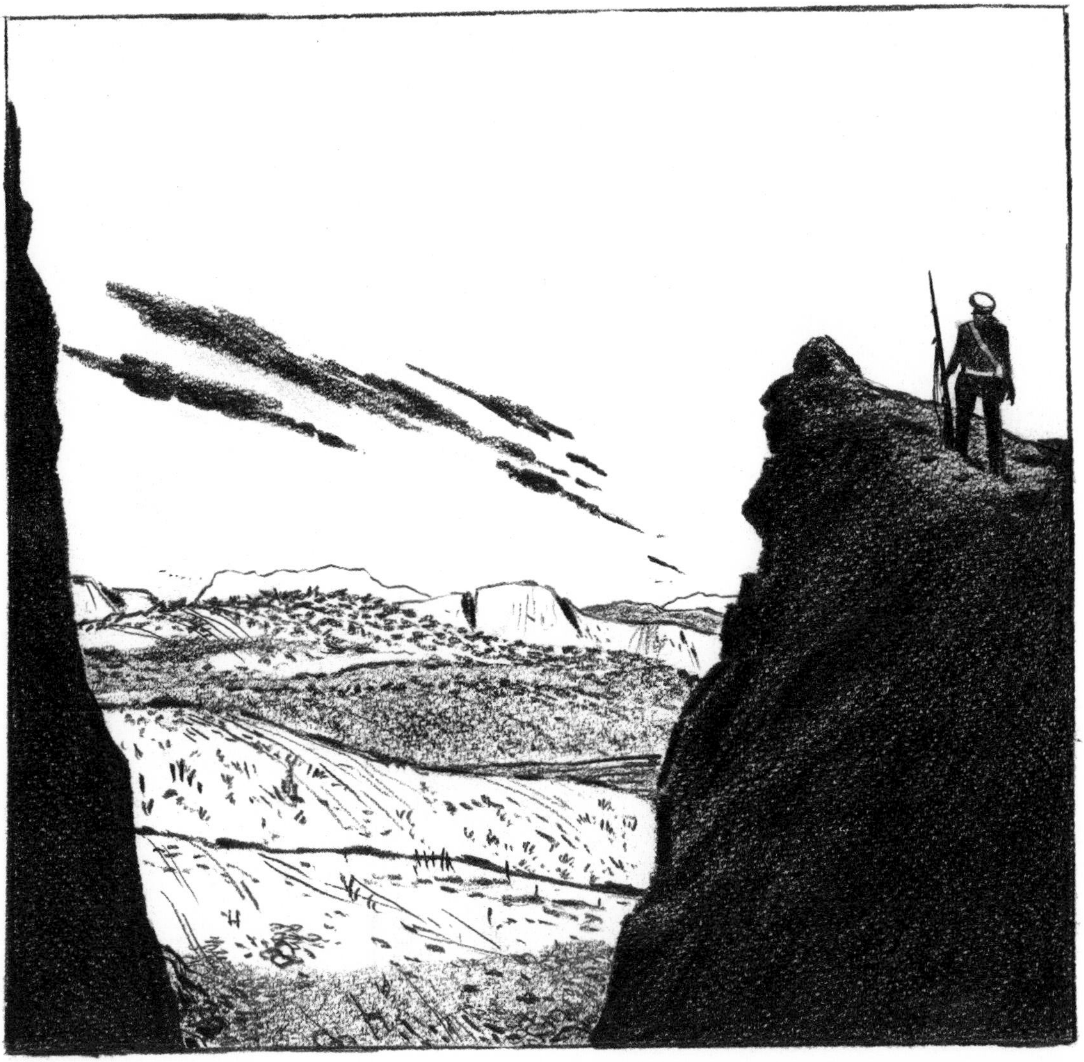

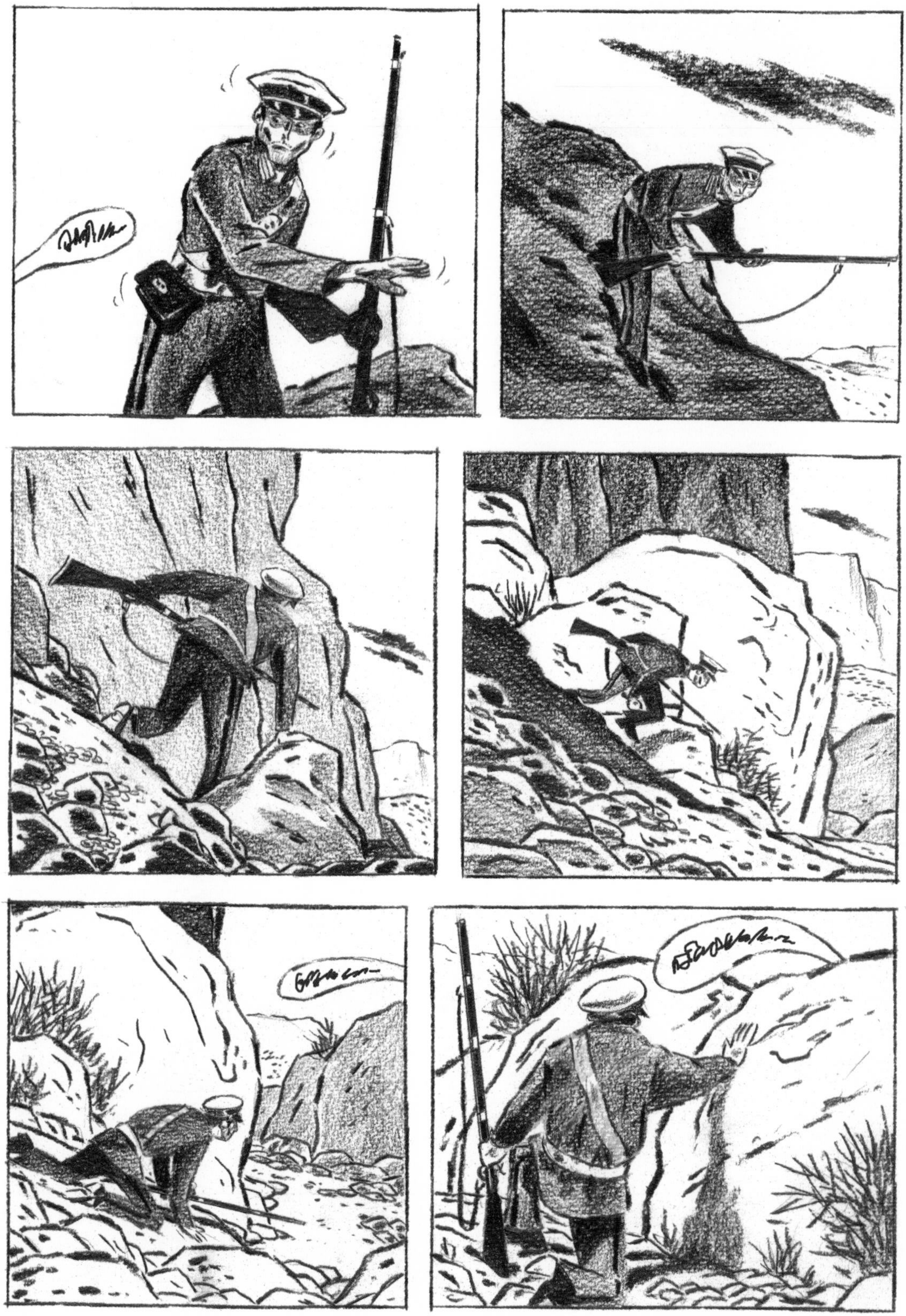

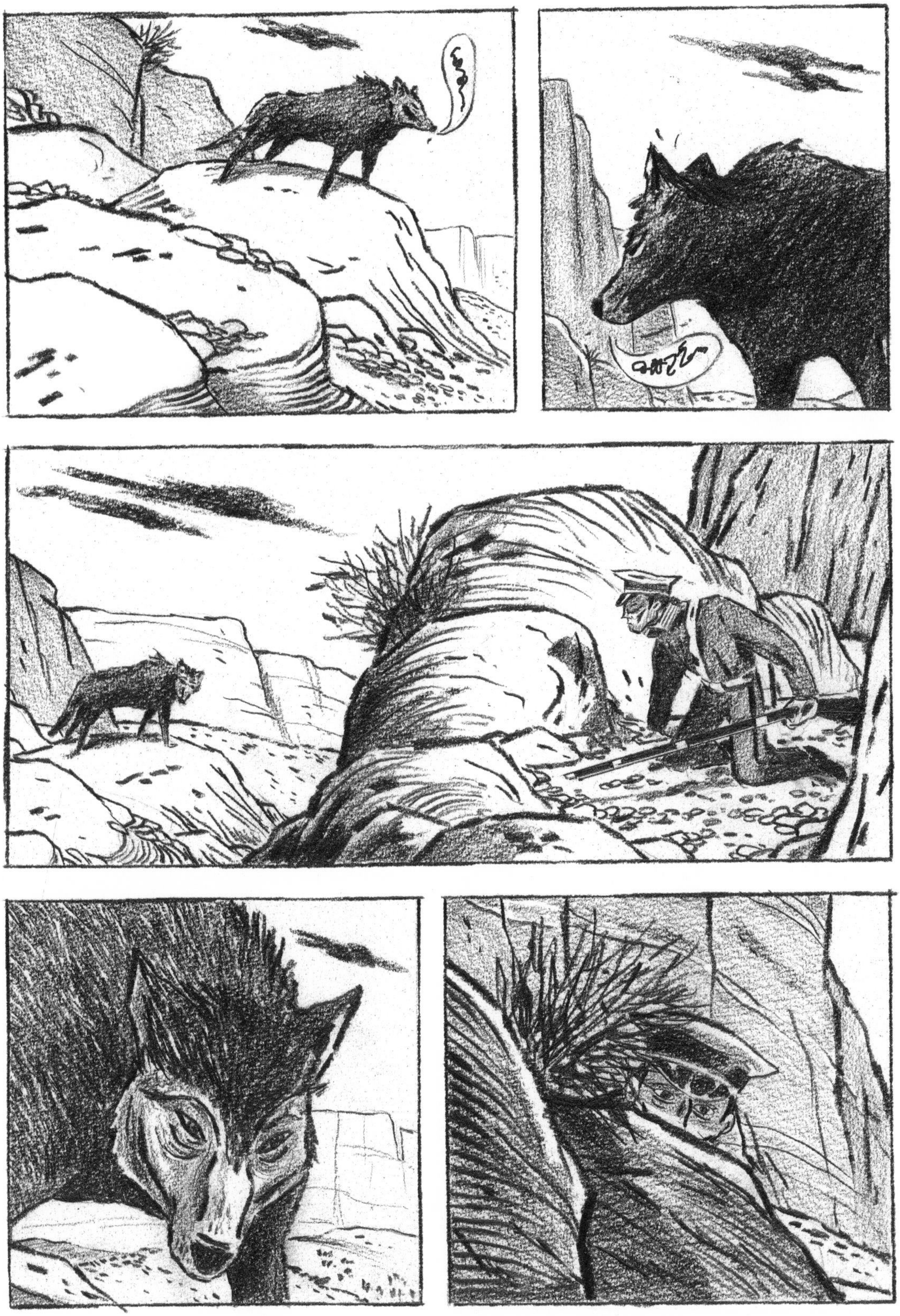

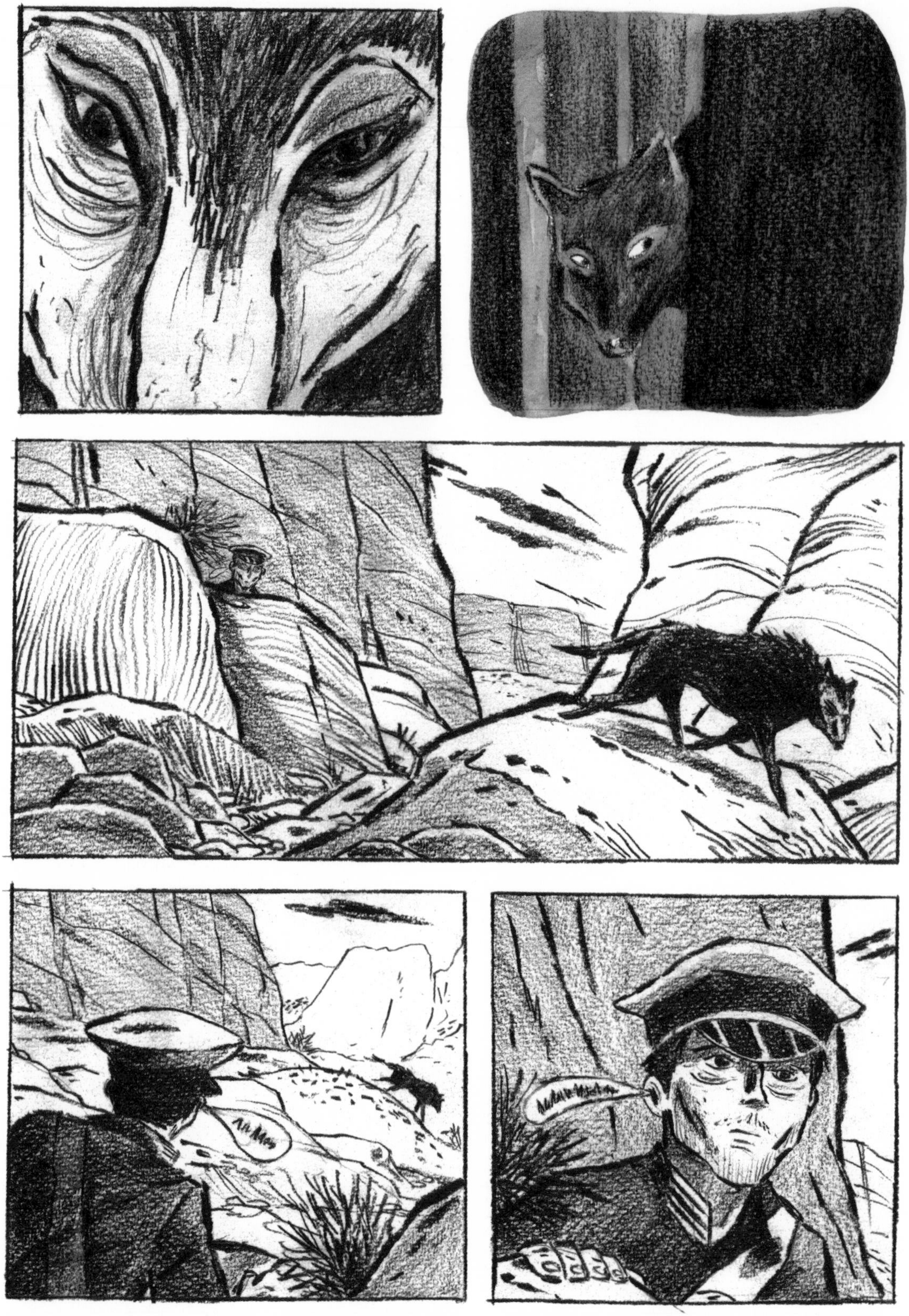

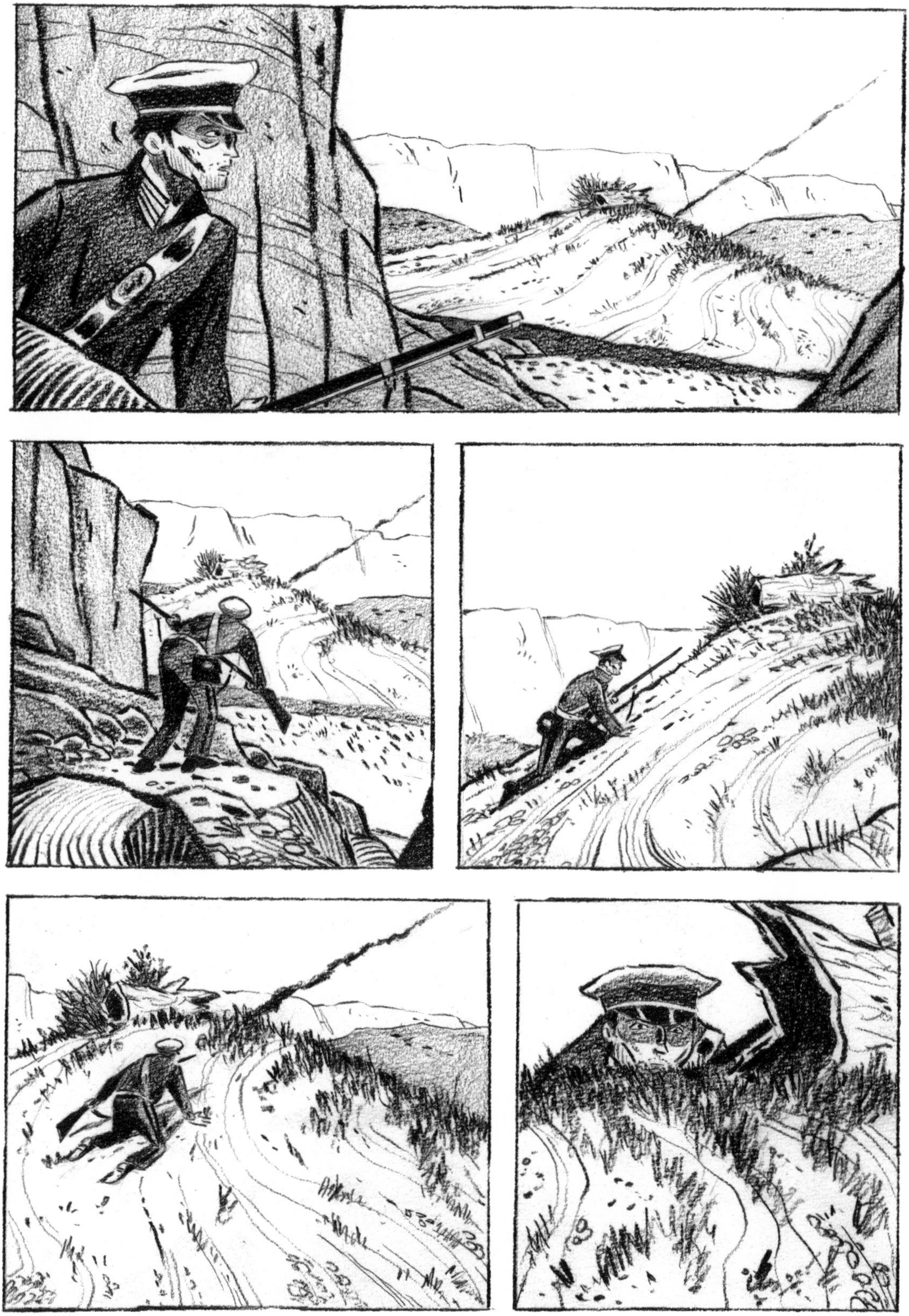

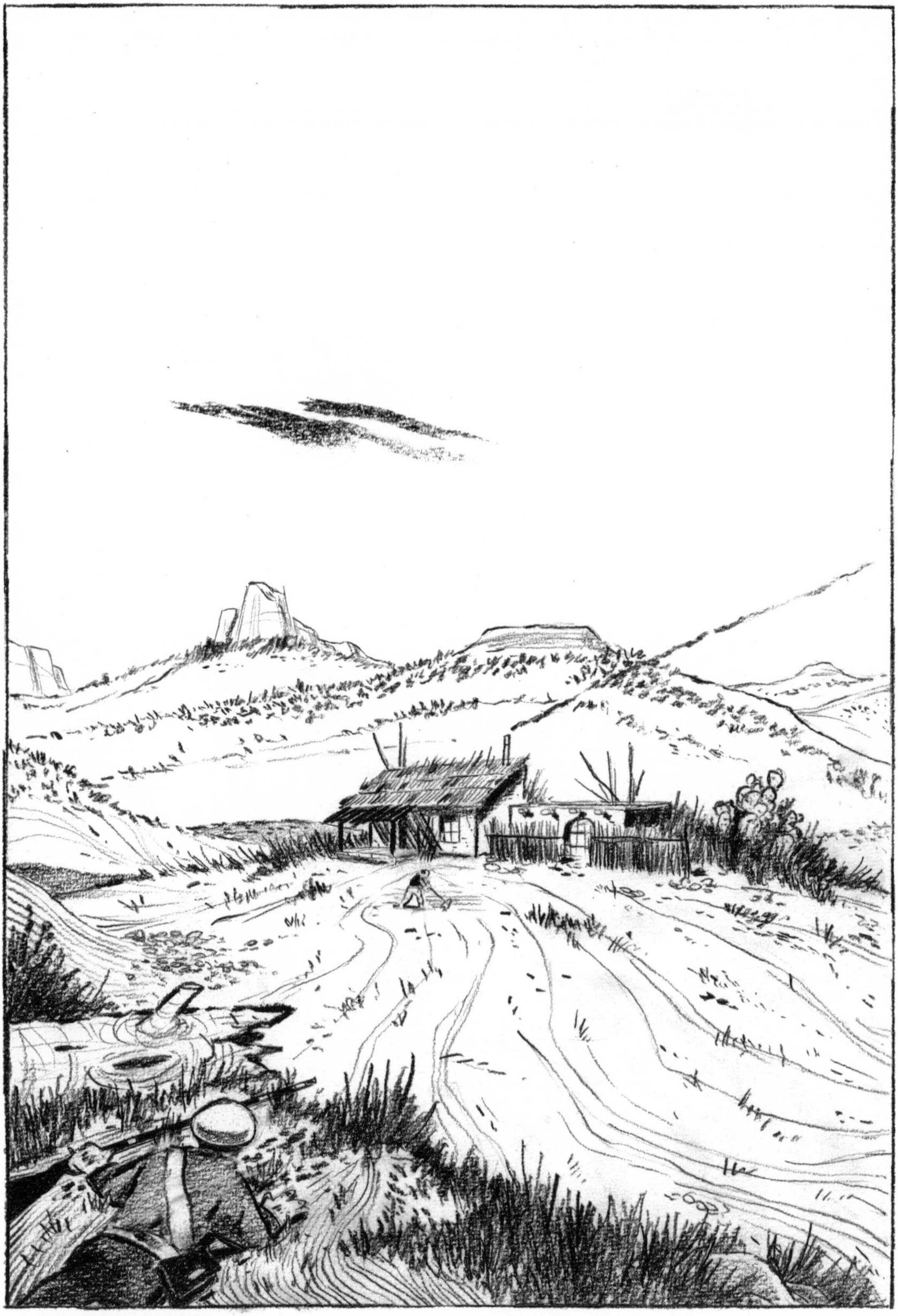

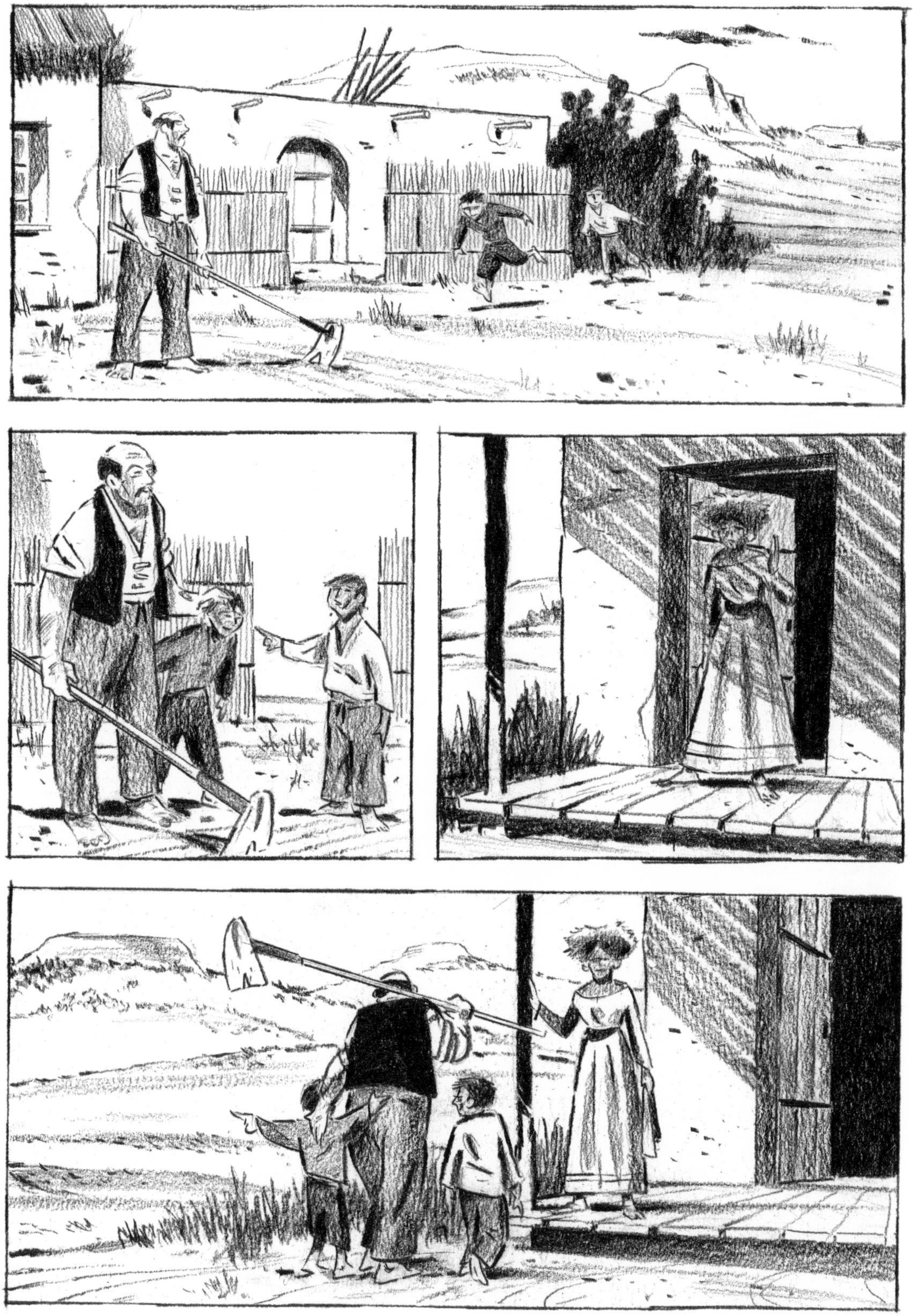

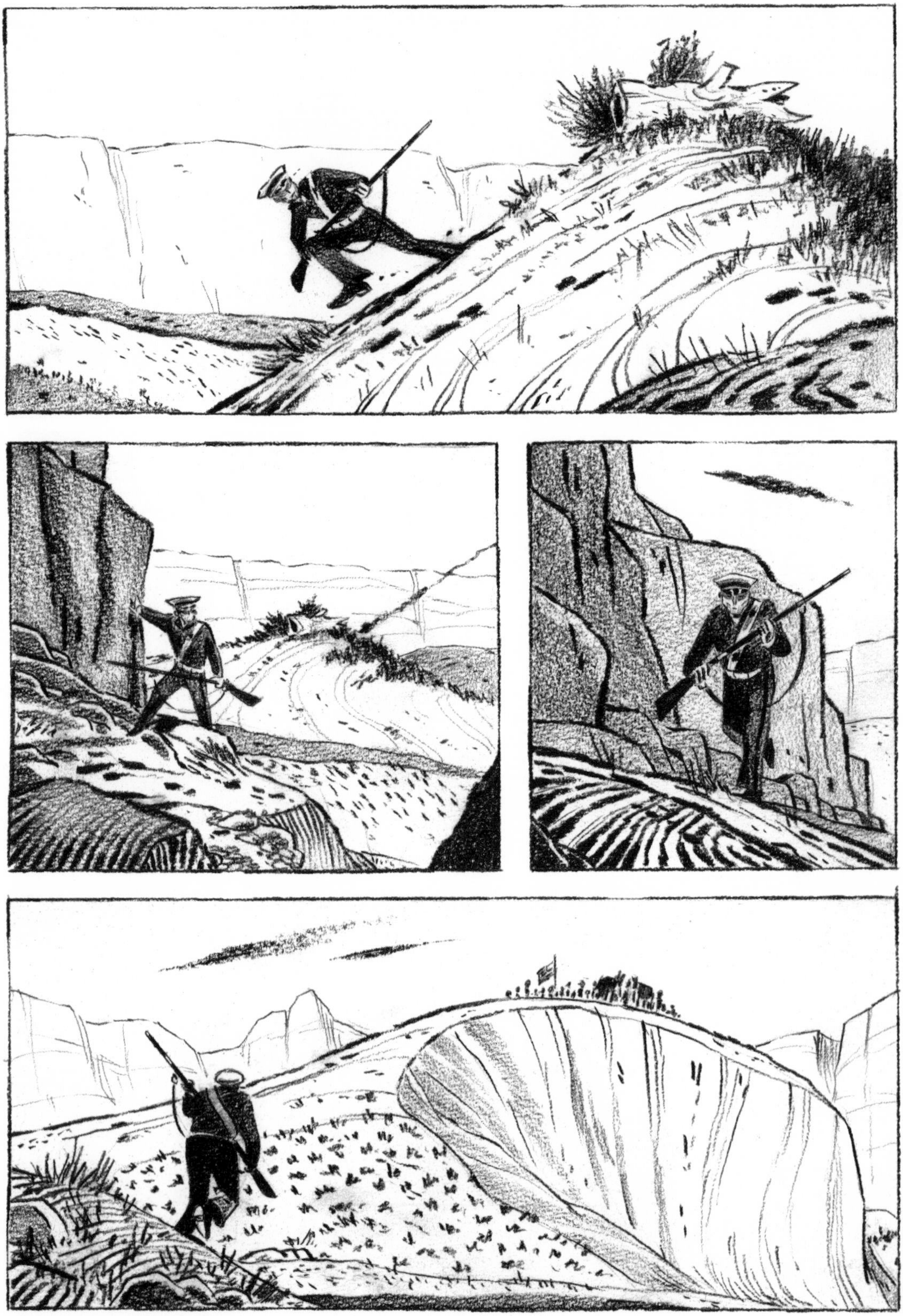

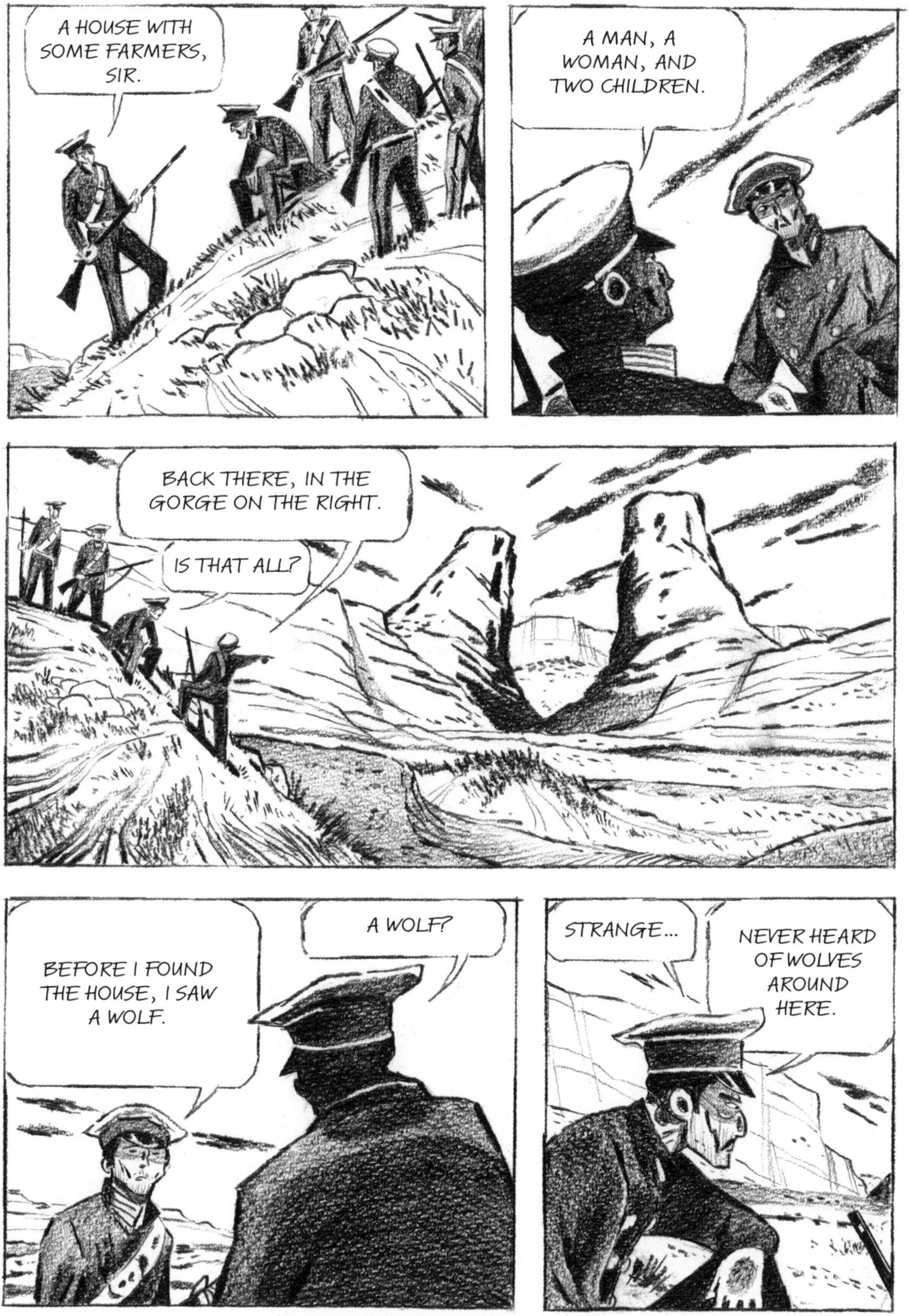
A HOUSE WITH SOME FARMERS, SIR.
A MAN, A WOMAN, AND TWO CHILDREN.
BACK THERE, IN THE GORGE ON THE RIGHT.
IS THAT ALL?
BEFORE I FOUND THE HOUSE, I SAW A WOLF.
A WOLF?
STRANGE...
NEVER HEARD OF WOLVES AROUND HERE.

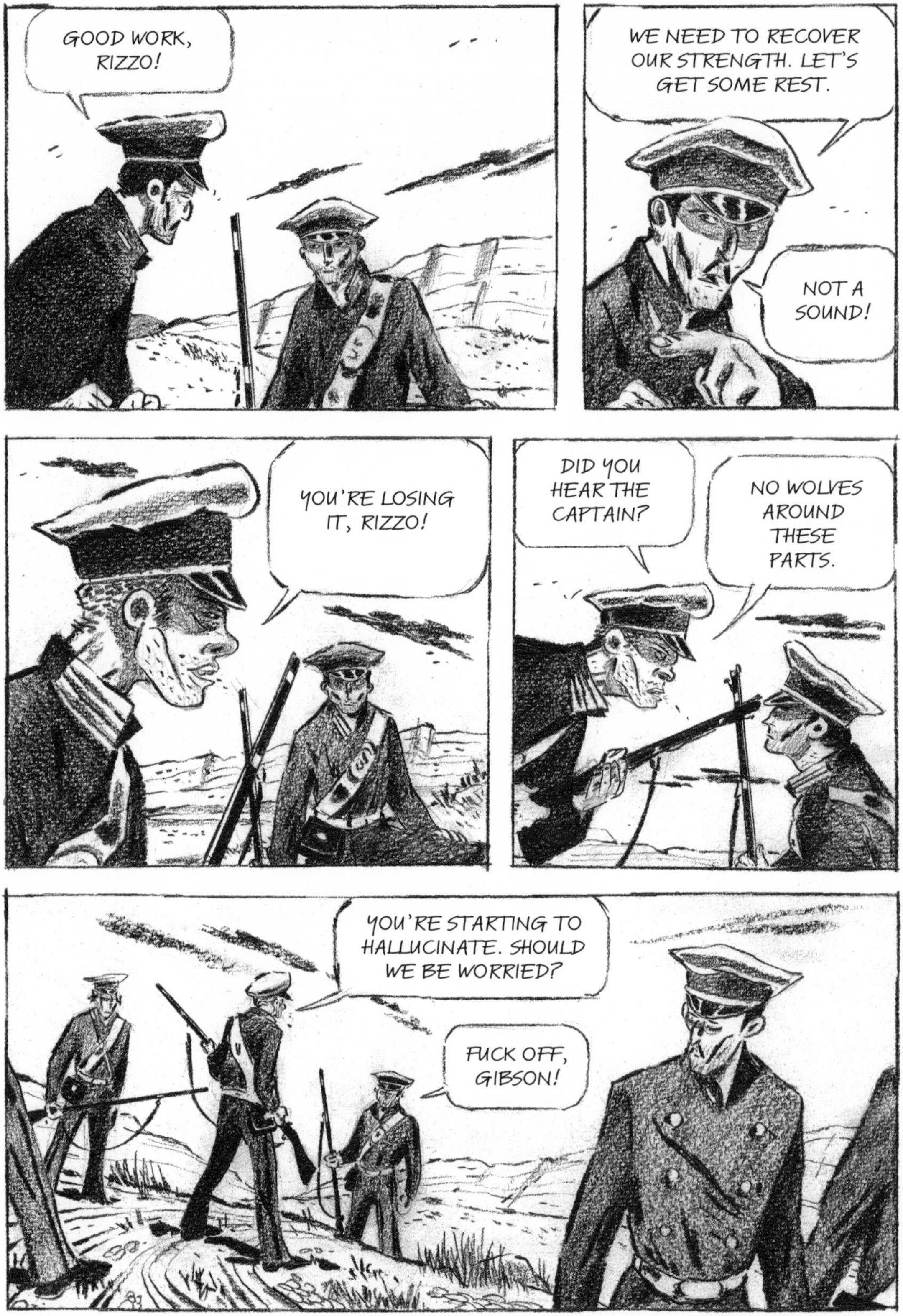
GOOD WORK, RIZZO!
WE NEED TO RECOVER OUR STRENGTH. LET'S GET SOME REST.
NOT A SOUND!
YOU'RE LOSING IT, RIZZO!
DID YOU HEAR THE CAPTAIN?
NO WOLVES AROUND THESE PARTS.
YOU'RE STARTING TO HALLUCINATE. SHOULD WE BE WORRIED?
FUCK OFF, GIBSON!

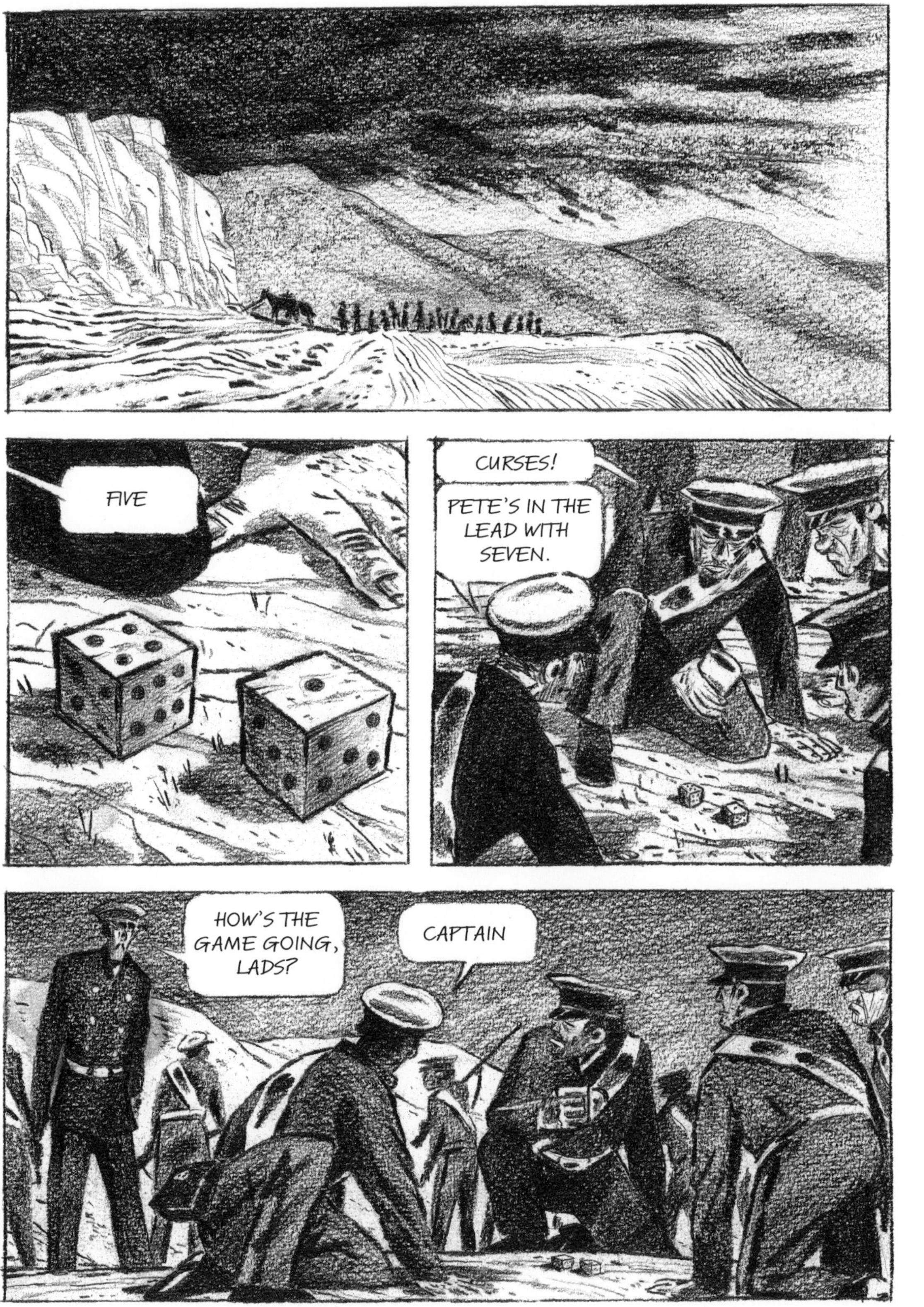
FIVE
CURSES!
PETE'S IN THE LEAD WITH SEVEN.
HOW'S THE GAME GOING, LADS?
CAPTAIN

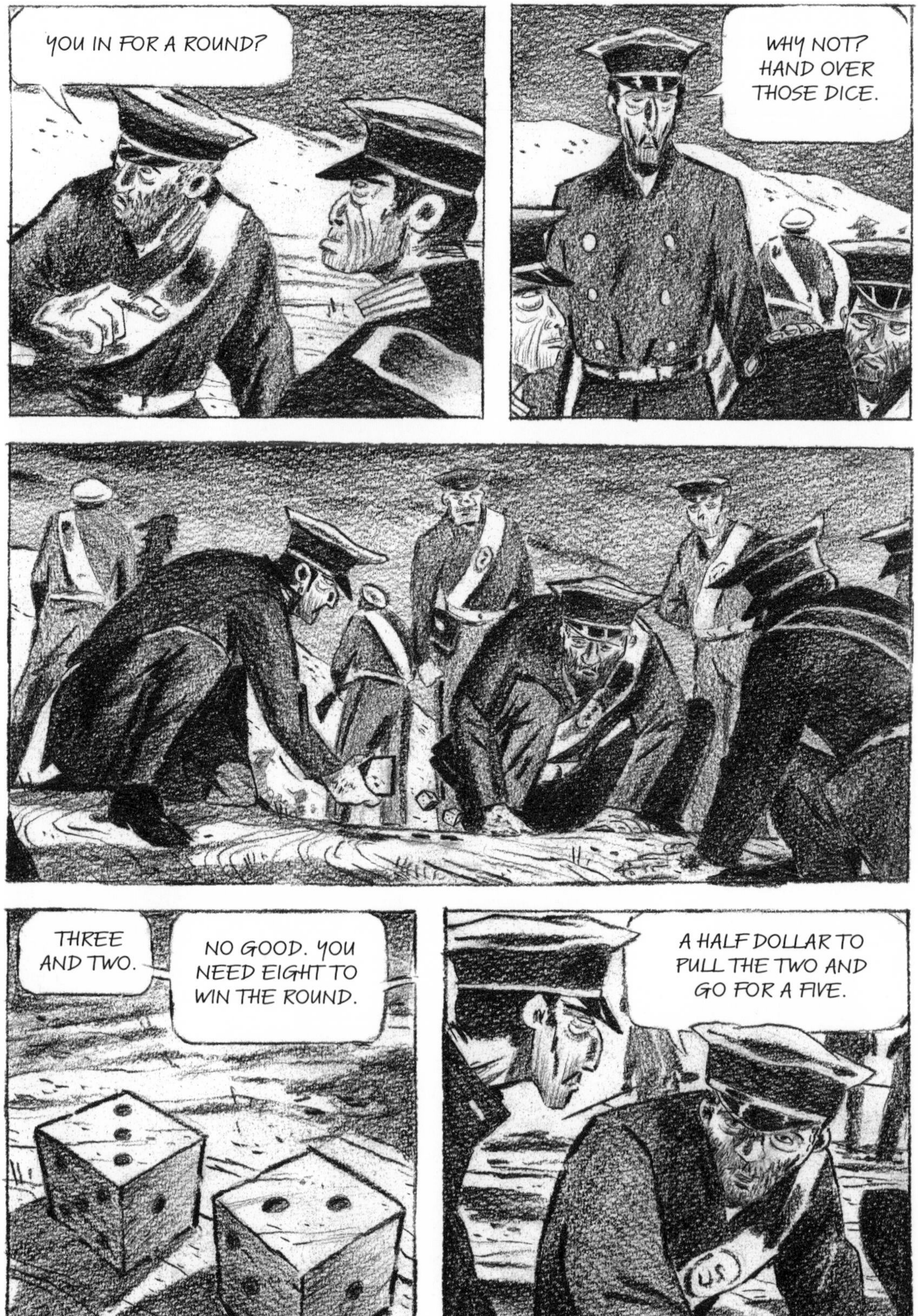
YOU IN FOR A ROUND?
WHY NOT? HAND OVER THOSE DICE.
THREE AND TWO.
NO GOOD. YOU NEED EIGHT TO WIN THE ROUND.
A HALF DOLLAR TO PULL THE TWO AND GO FOR A FIVE.

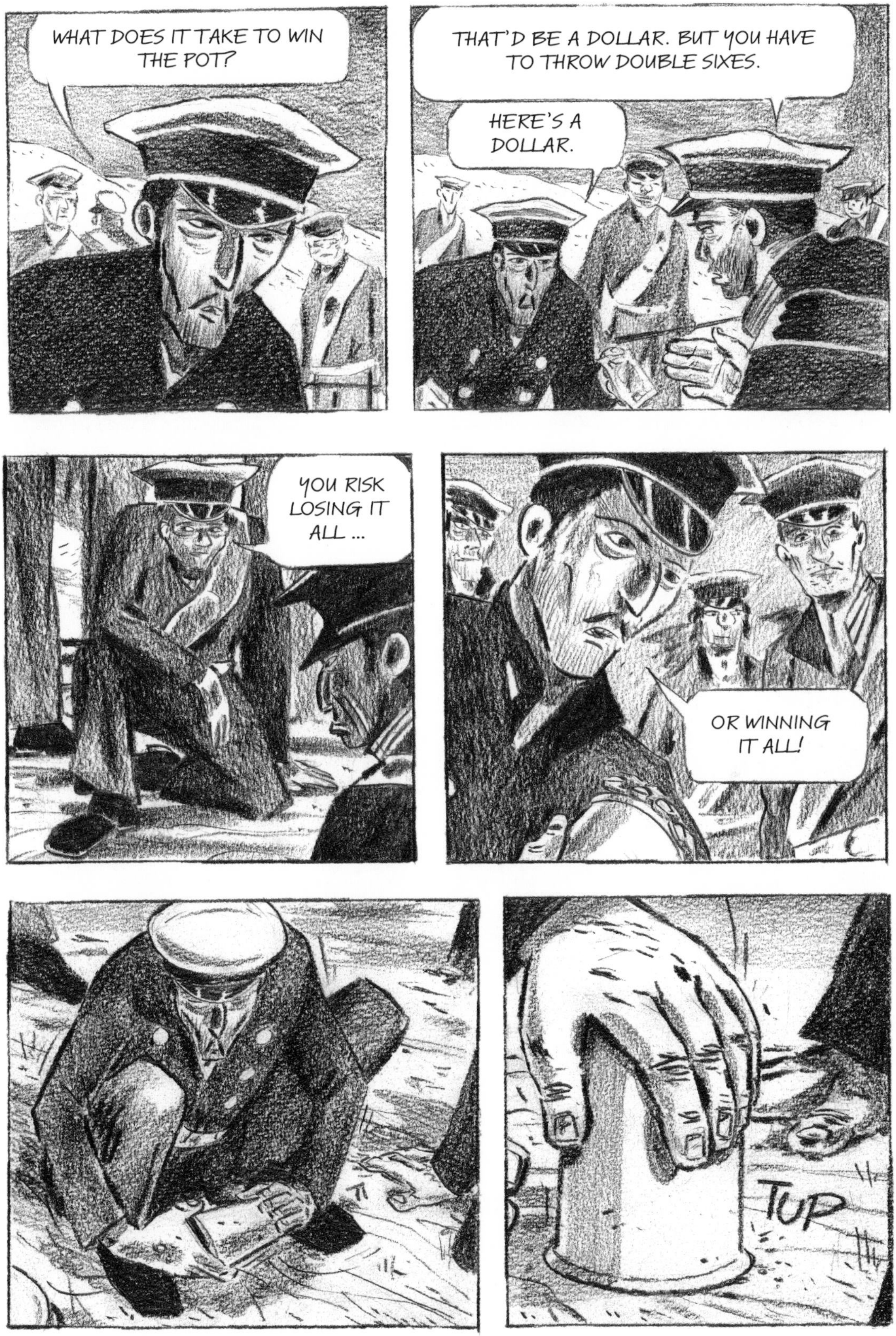
WHAT DOES IT TAKE TO WIN THE POT?
THAT'D BE A DOLLAR. BUT YOU HAVE TO THROW DOUBLE SIXES.
HERE'S A DOLLAR.
YOU RISK LOSING IT ALL ...
OR WINNING IT ALL!
TUP

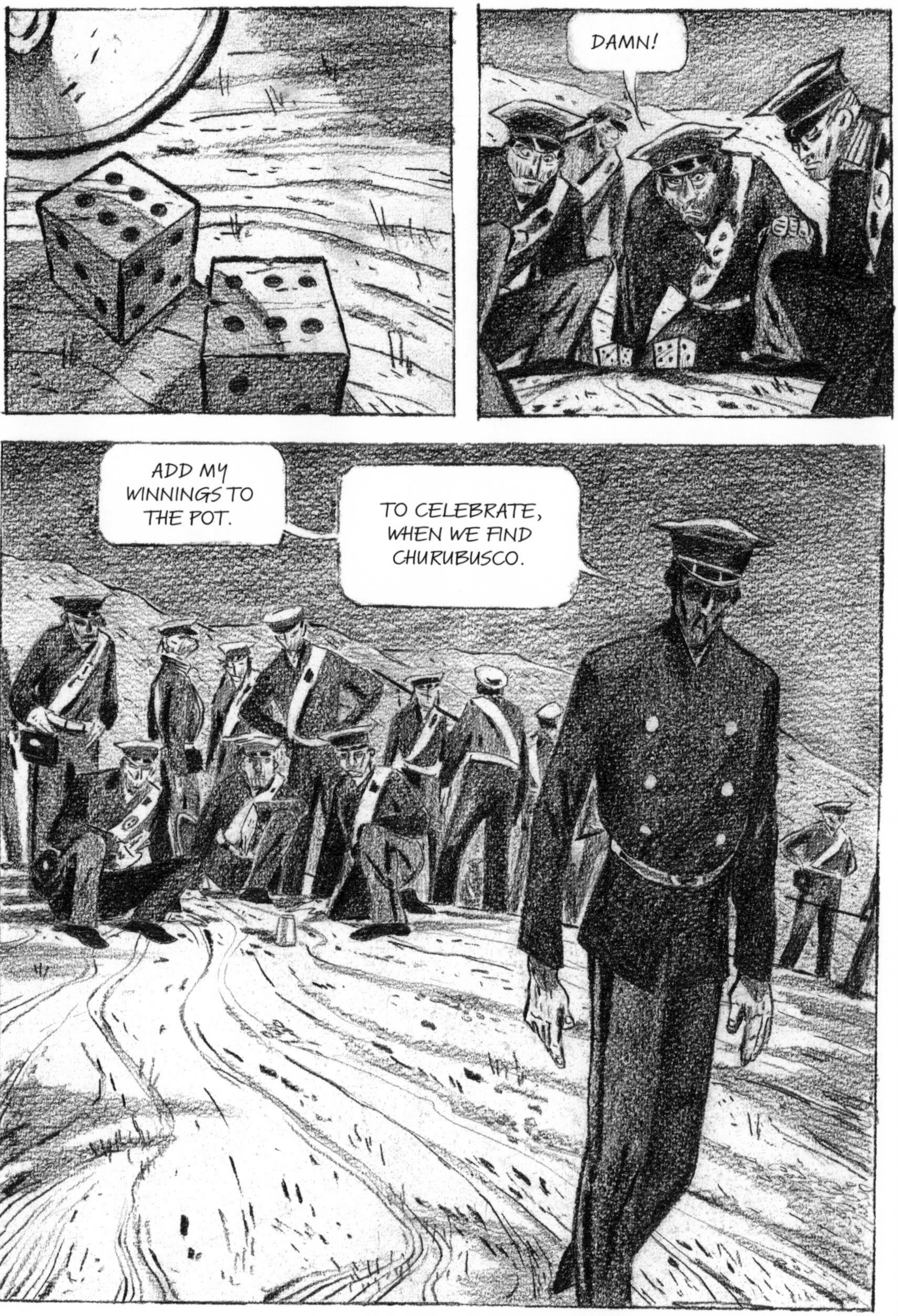
DAMN!
ADD MY WINNINGS TO THE POT.
TO CELEBRATE, WHEN WE FIND CHURUBUSCO.

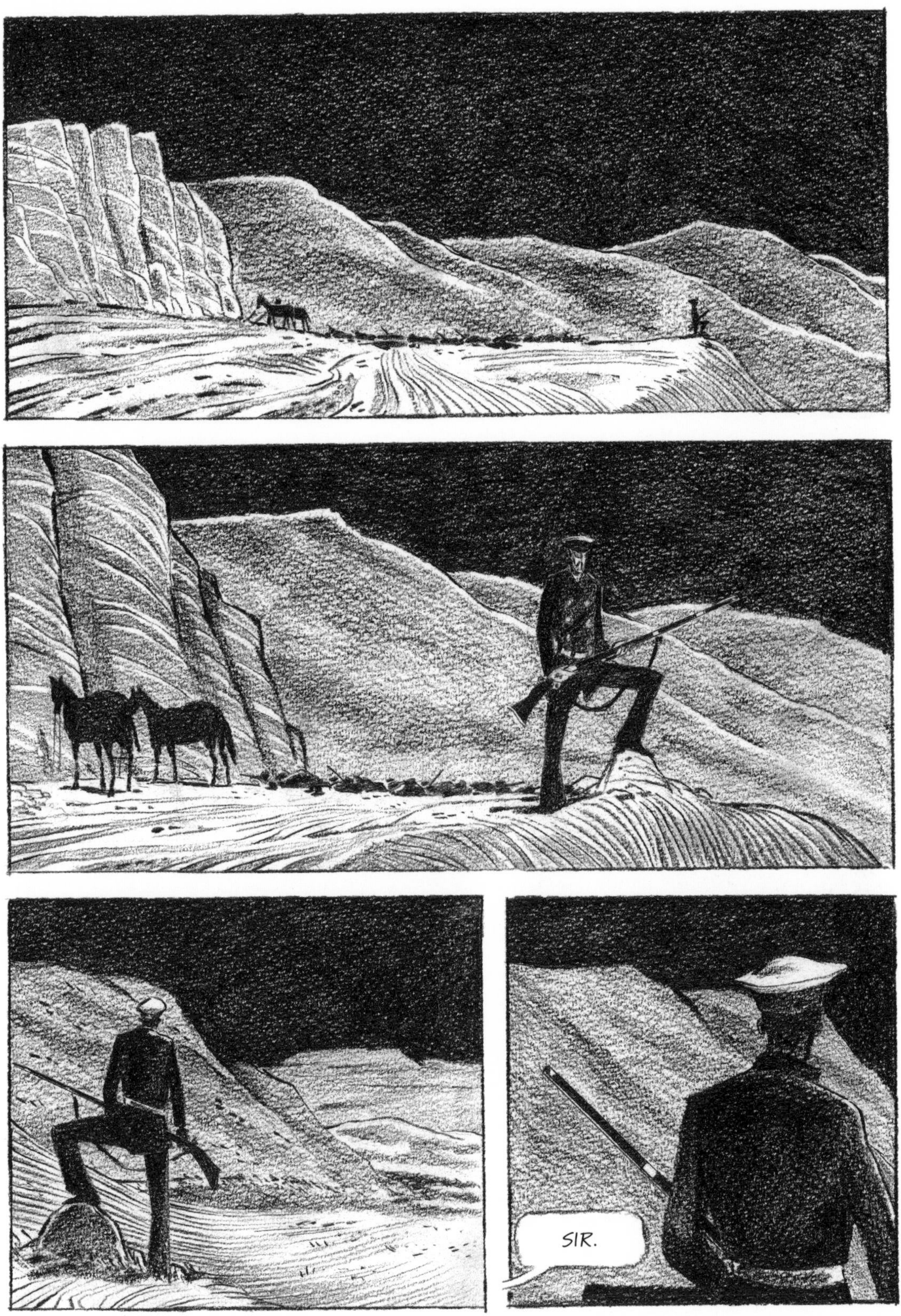
SIR.

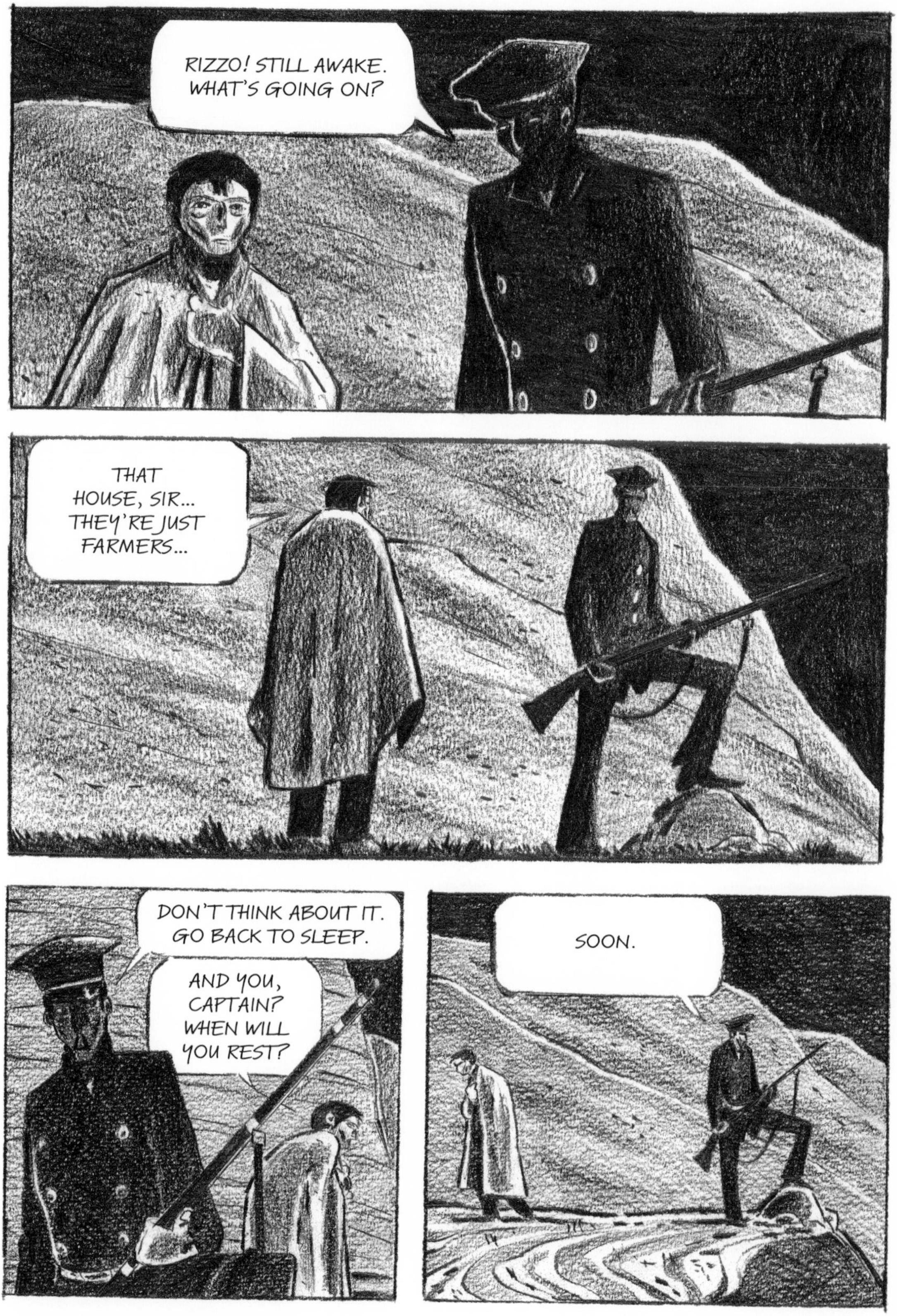
RIZZO! STILL AWAKE. WHAT'S GOING ON?
THAT HOUSE, SIR... THEY'RE JUST FARMERS...
DON'T THINK ABOUT IT. GO BACK TO SLEEP.
AND YOU, CAPTAIN? WHEN WILL YOU REST?
SOON.

CHAPTER THREE

THE IRISH
HARP

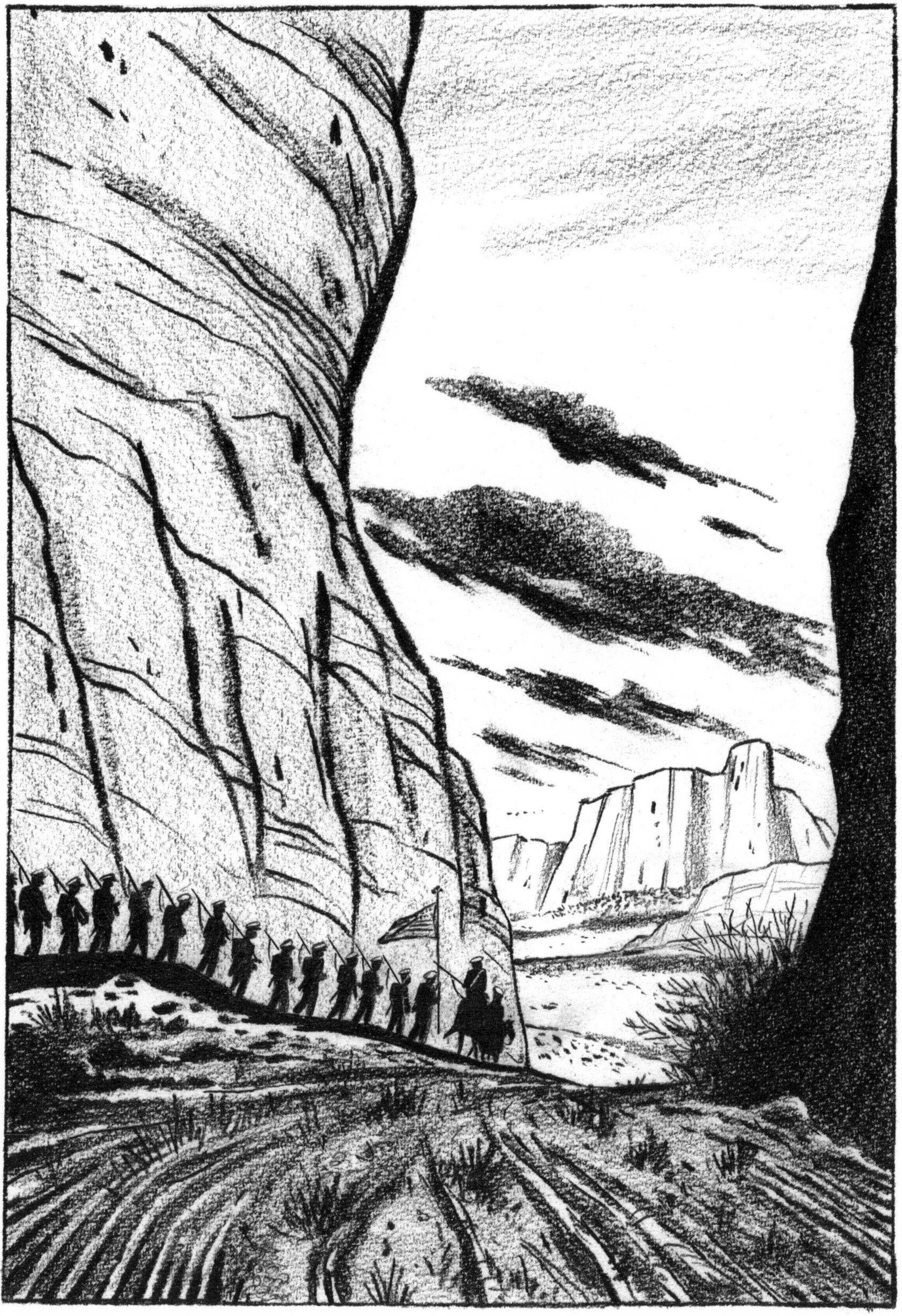

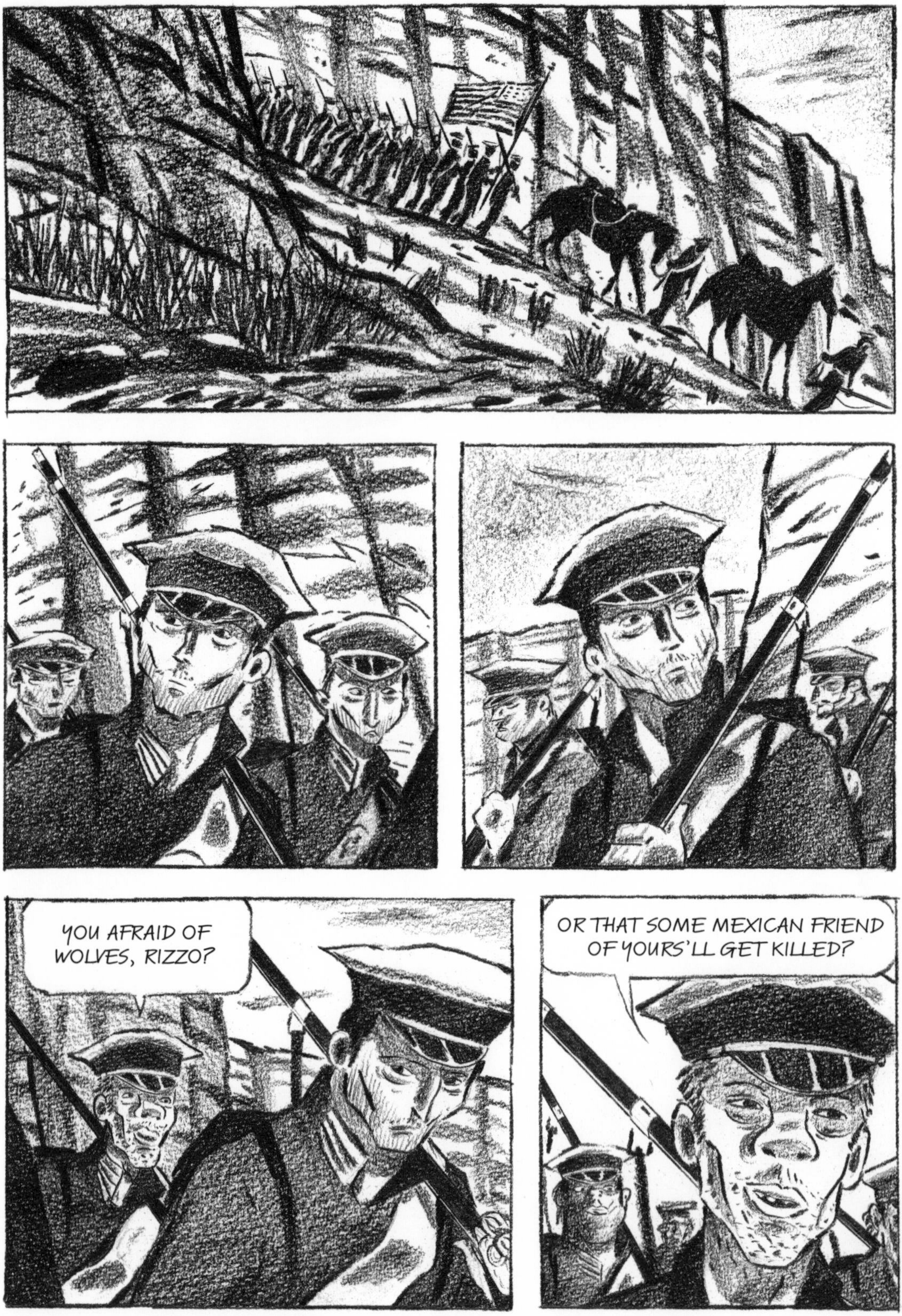
YOU AFRAID OF WOLVES, RIZZO?
OR THAT SOME MEXICAN FRIEND OF YOURS'LL GET KILLED?

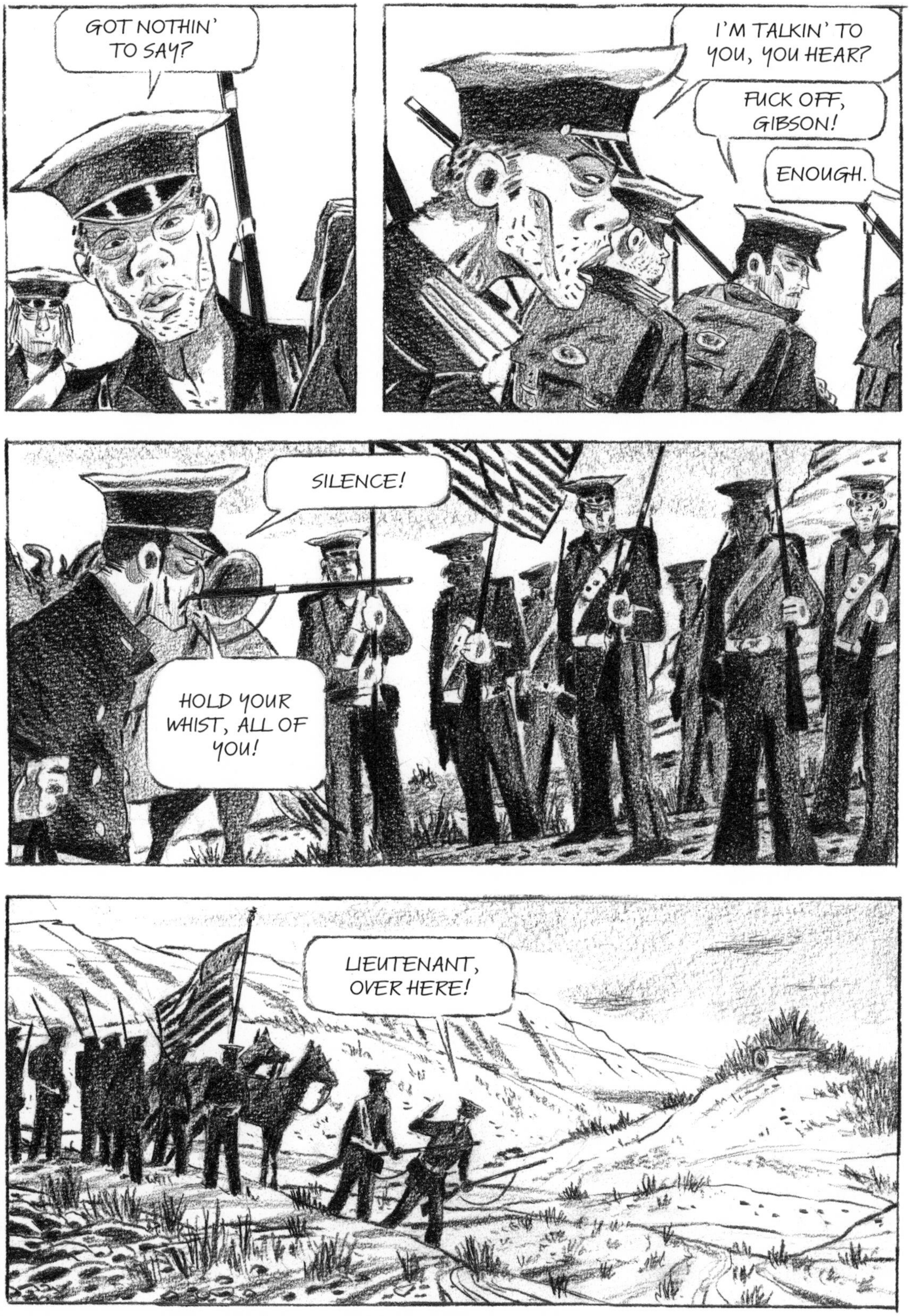
GOT NOTHIN' TO SAY?
I'M TALKIN' TO YOU, YOU HEAR?
FUCK OFF, GIBSON!
ENOUGH.
SILENCE!
HOLD YOUR WHIST, ALL OF YOU!
LIEUTENANT, OVER HERE!

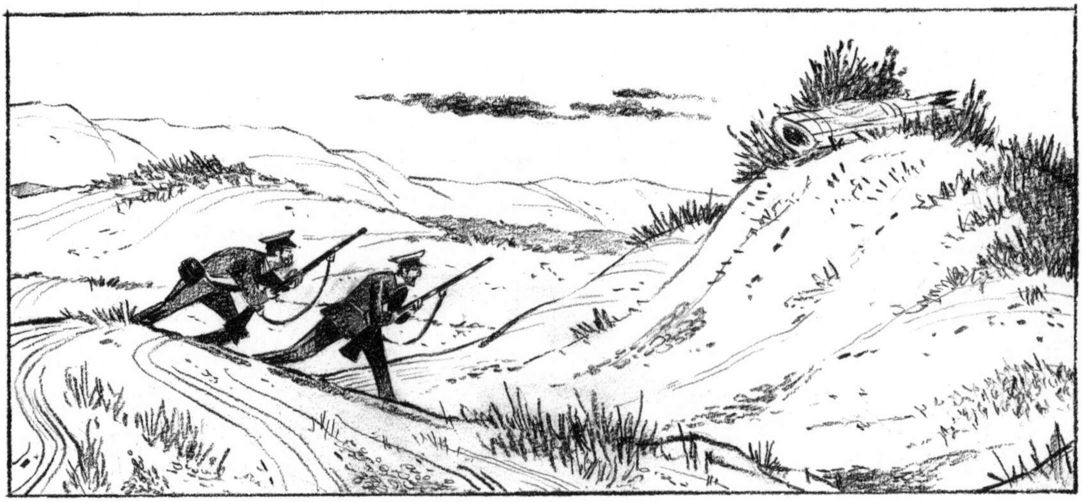

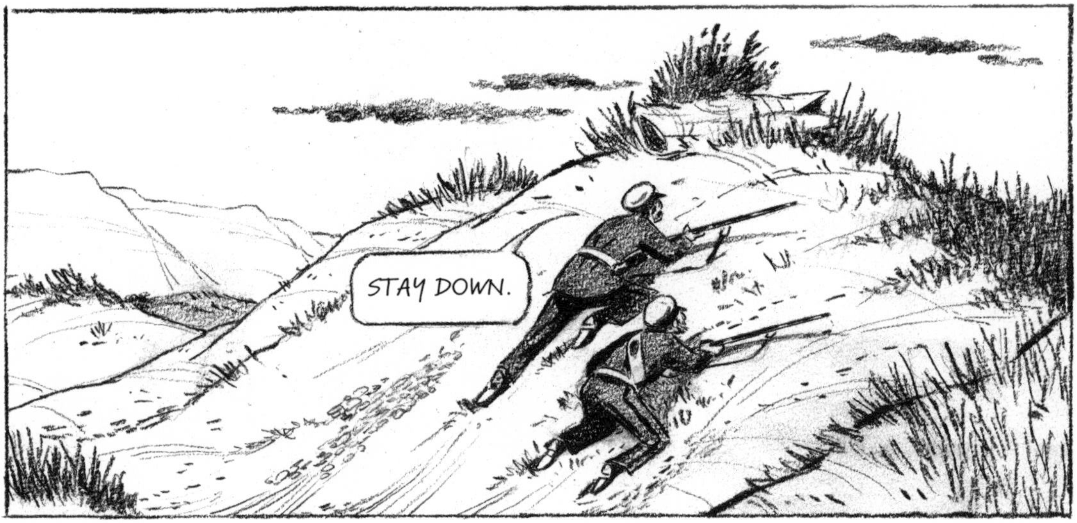
STAY DOWN.

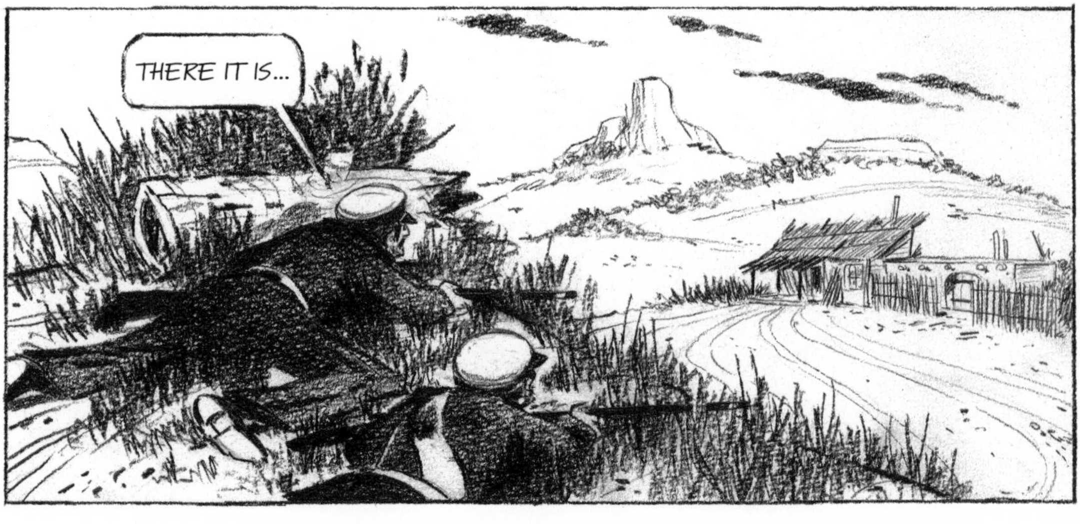
THERE IT IS...

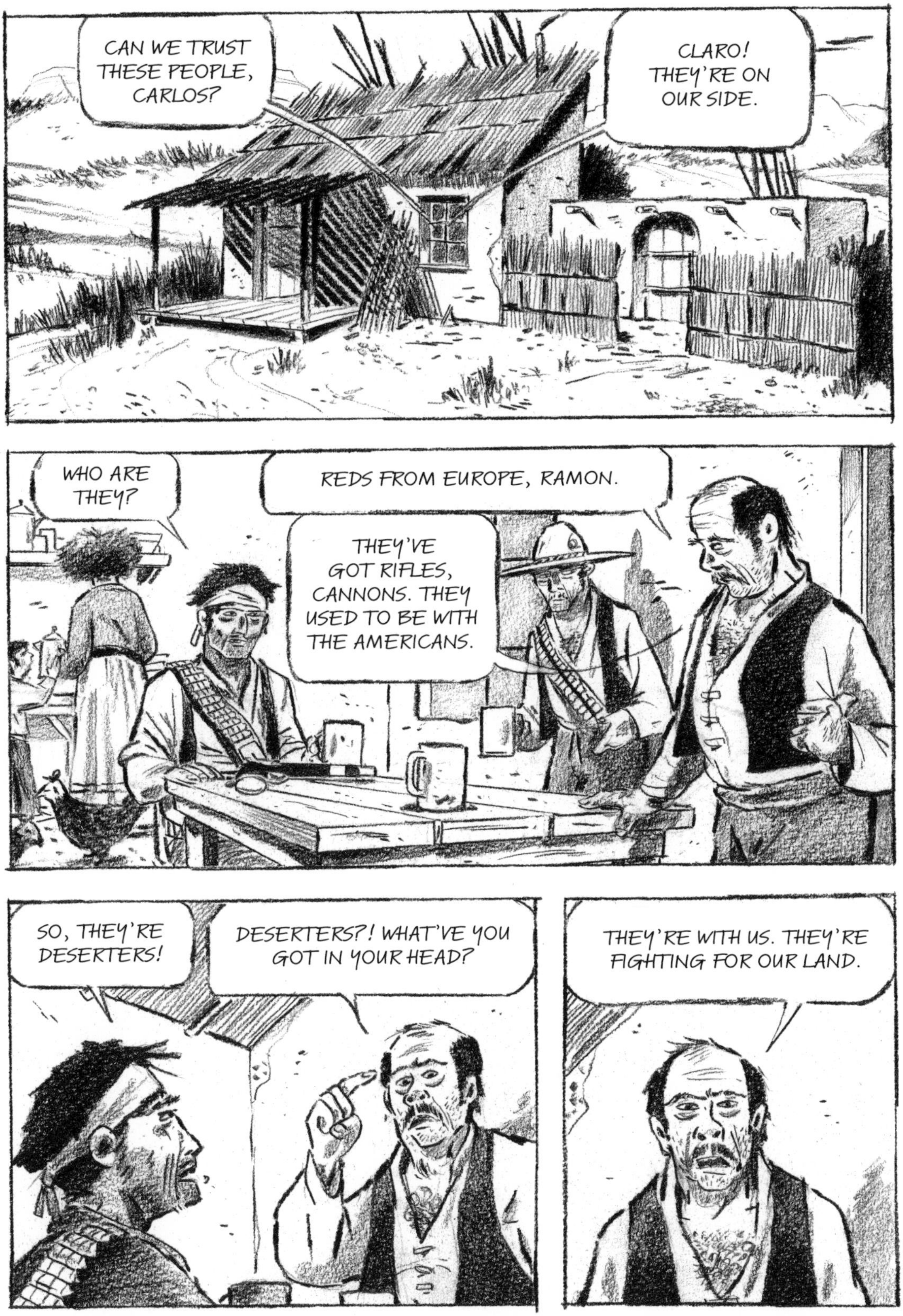
CAN WE TRUST THESE PEOPLE, CARLOS?
CLARO! THEY'RE ON OUR SIDE.
WHO ARE THEY?
REDS FROM EUROPE, RAMON.
THEY'VE GOT RIFLES, CANNONS. THEY USED TO BE WITH THE AMERICANS.
SO, THEY'RE DESERTERS!
DESERTERS?! WHAT'VE YOU GOT IN YOUR HEAD?
THEY'RE WITH US. THEY'RE FIGHTING FOR OUR LAND.

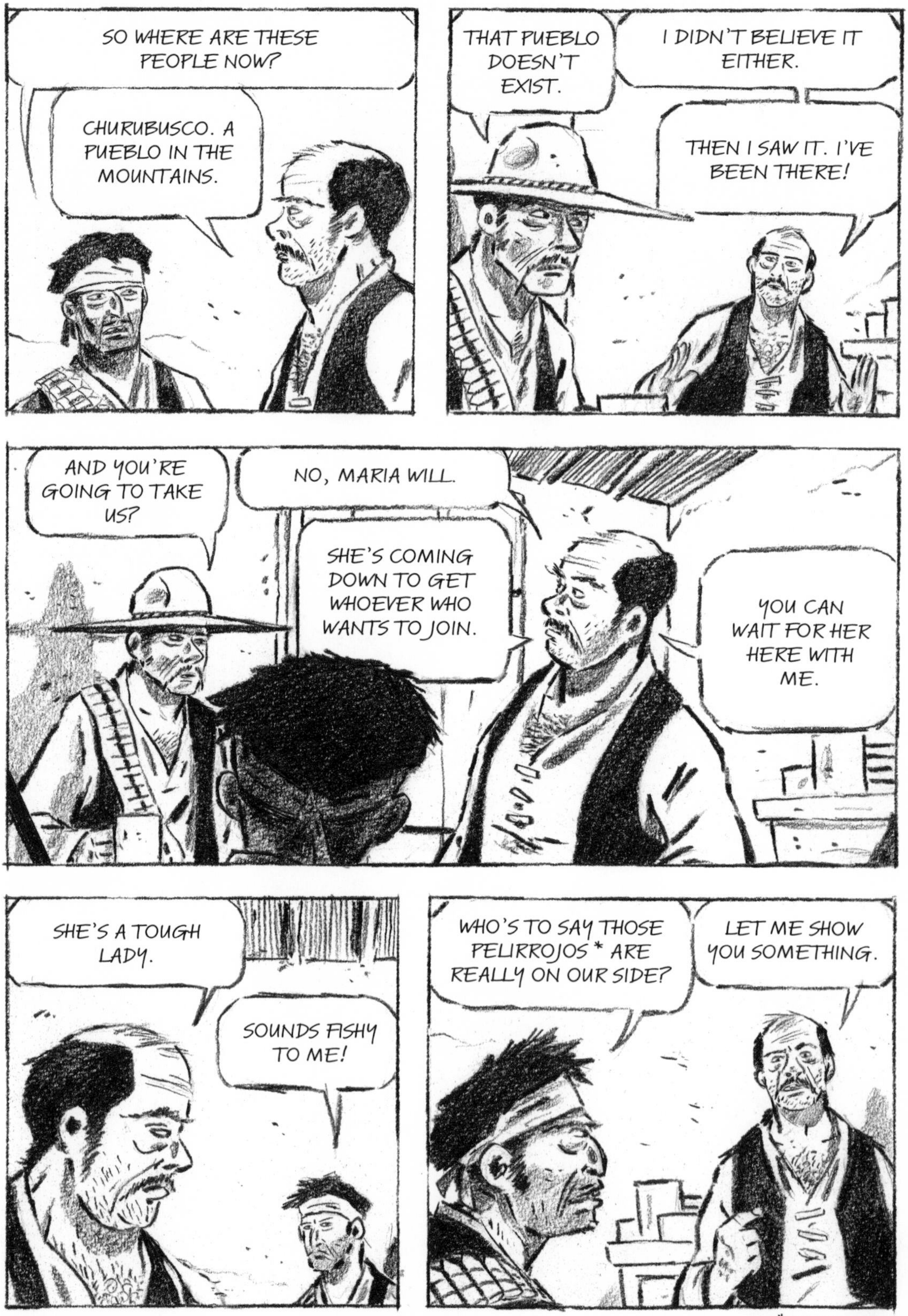
SO WHERE ARE THESE PEOPLE NOW?
CHURUBUSCO. A PUEBLO IN THE MOUNTAINS.
THAT PUEBLO DOESN'T EXIST.
I DIDN'T BELIEVE IT EITHER.
THEN I SAW IT. I'VE BEEN THERE!
AND YOU'RE GOING TO TAKE US?
NO, MARIA WILL.
SHE'S COMING DOWN TO GET WHOEVER WHO WANTS TO JOIN.
YOU CAN WAIT FOR HER HERE WITH ME.
SHE'S A TOUGH LADY.
SOUNDS FISHY TO ME!
WHO'S TO SAY THOSE PELIRROJOS* ARE REALLY ON OUR SIDE?
LET ME SHOW YOU SOMETHING.

*REDHEADS

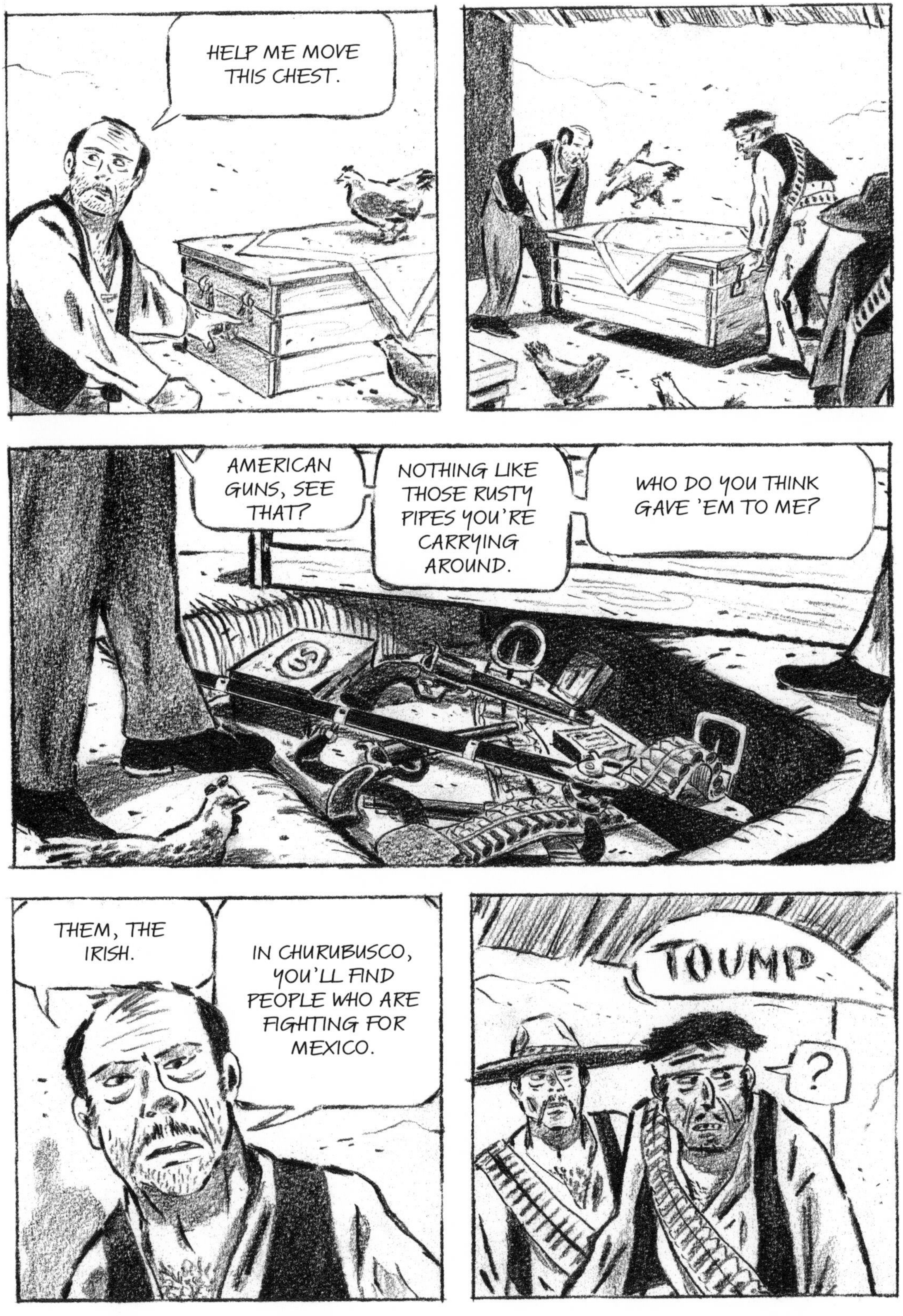
HELP ME MOVE THIS CHEST.
AMERICAN GUNS, SEE THAT?
NOTHING LIKE THOSE RUSTY PIPES YOU'RE CARRYING AROUND.
WHO DO YOU THINK GAVE 'EM TO ME?
THEM, THE IRISH.
IN CHURUBUSCO, YOU'LL FIND PEOPLE WHO ARE FIGHTING FOR MEXICO.
TOUMP
?

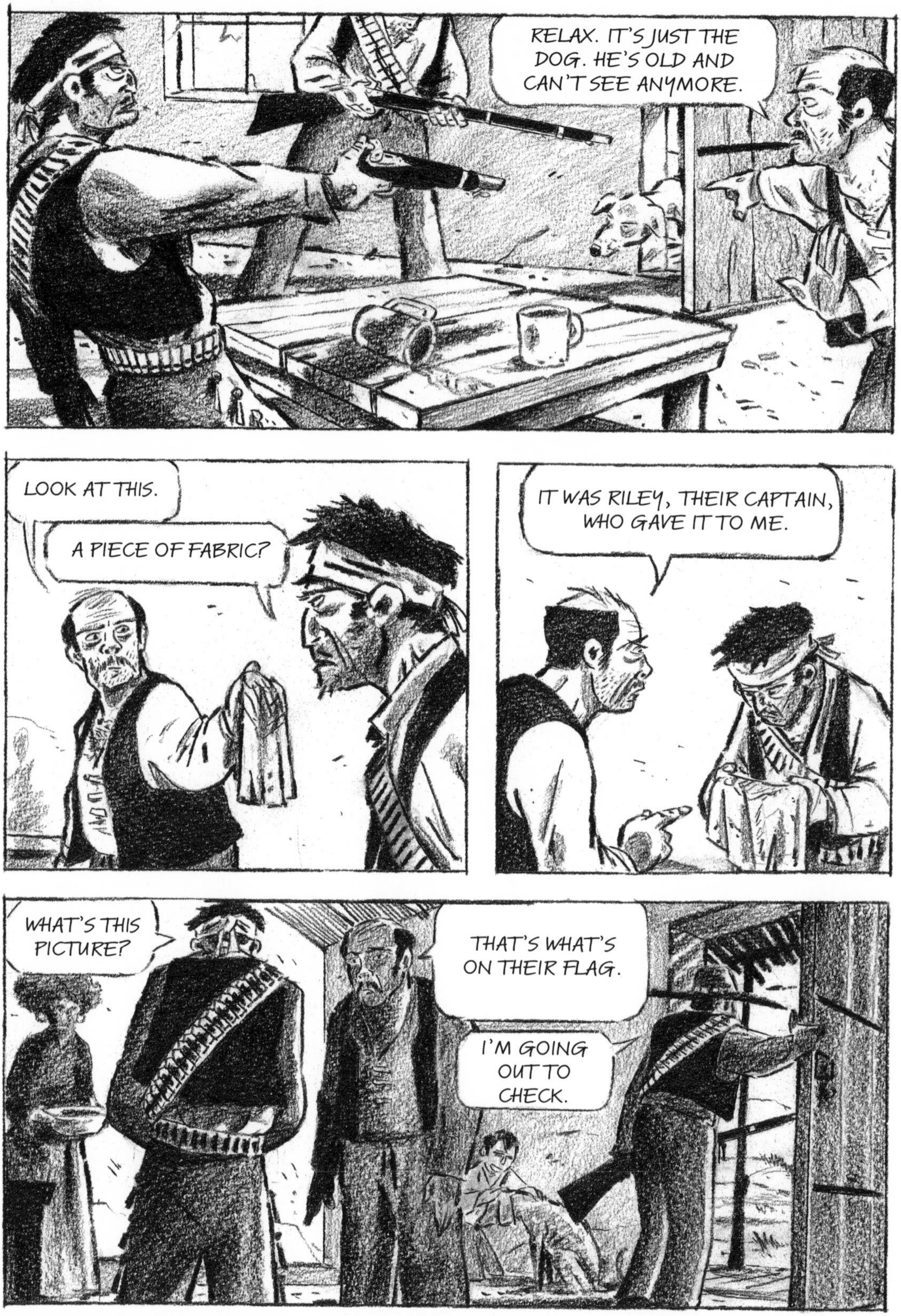
RELAX. IT'S JUST THE DOG. HE'S OLD AND CAN'T SEE ANYMORE.
LOOK AT THIS.
A PIECE OF FABRIC?
IT WAS RILEY, THEIR CAPTAIN, WHO GAVE IT TO ME.
WHAT'S THIS PICTURE?
THAT'S WHAT'S ON THEIR FLAG.
I'M GOING OUT TO CHECK.

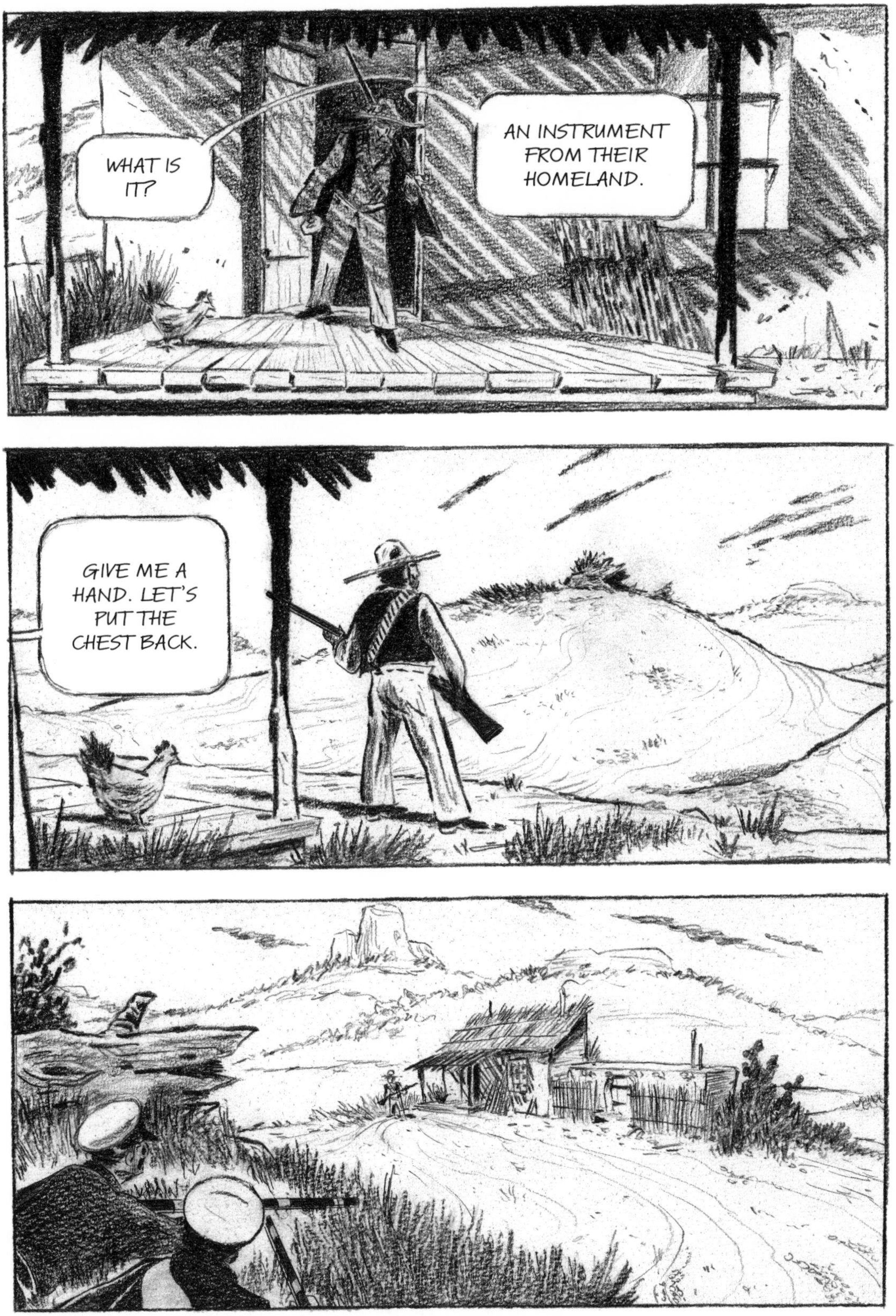
WHAT IS IT?
AN INSTRUMENT FROM THEIR HOMELAND.
GIVE ME A HAND. LET'S PUT THE CHEST BACK.

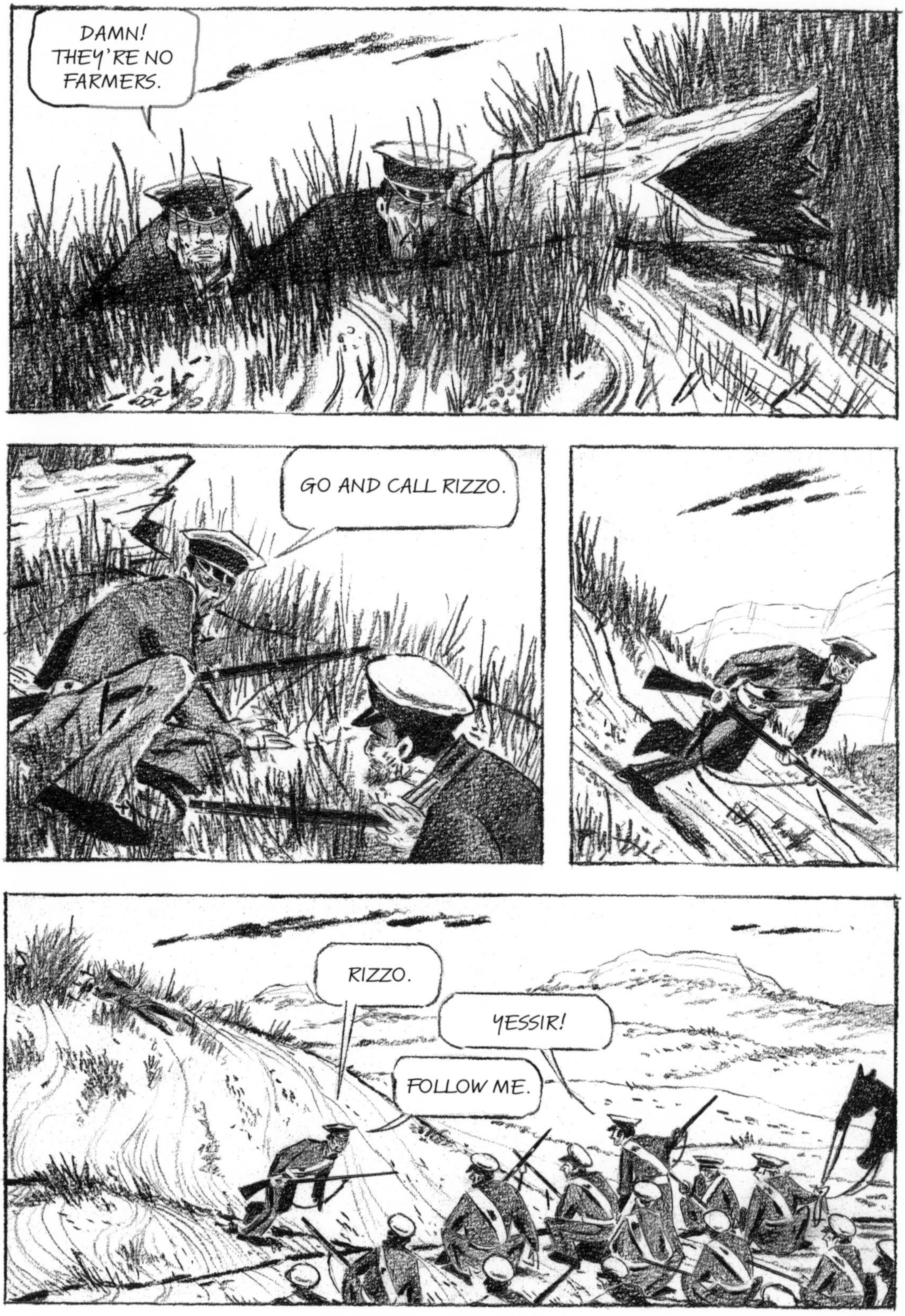
DAMN! THEY'RE NO FARMERS.
GO AND CALL RIZZO.
RIZZO.
YESSIR!
FOLLOW ME.

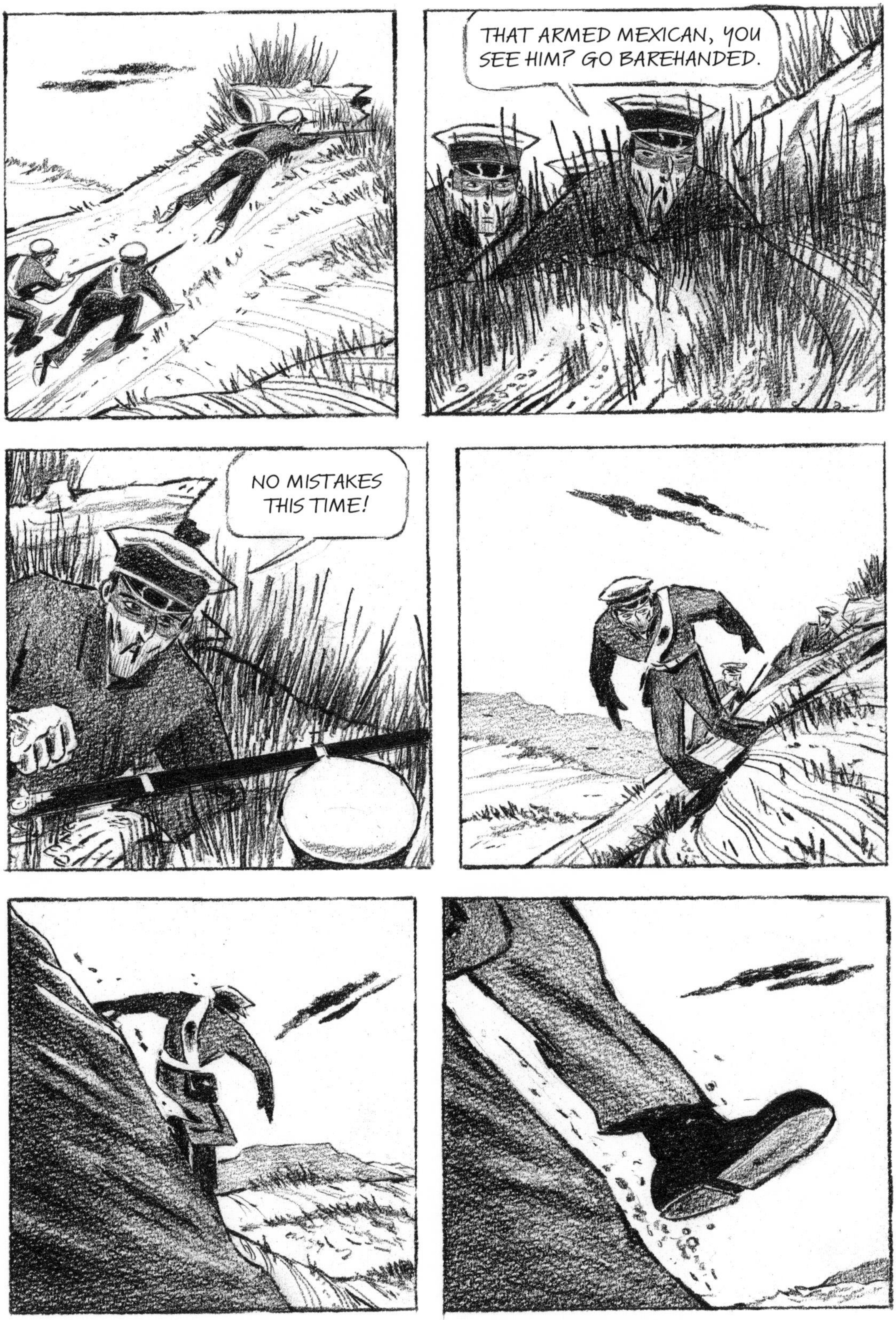
THAT ARMED MEXICAN, YOU SEE HIM? GO BAREHANDED.
NO MISTAKES THIS TIME!

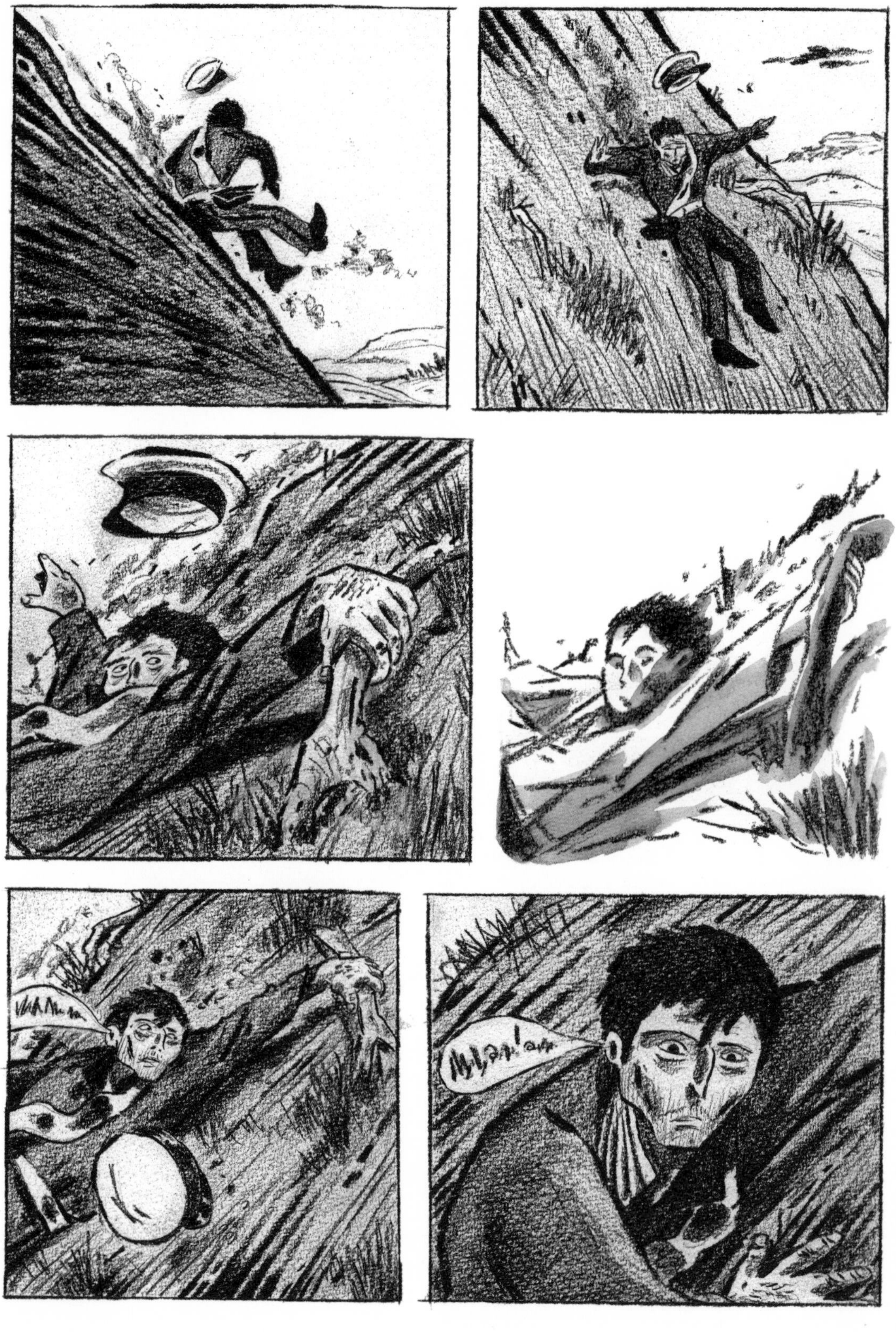

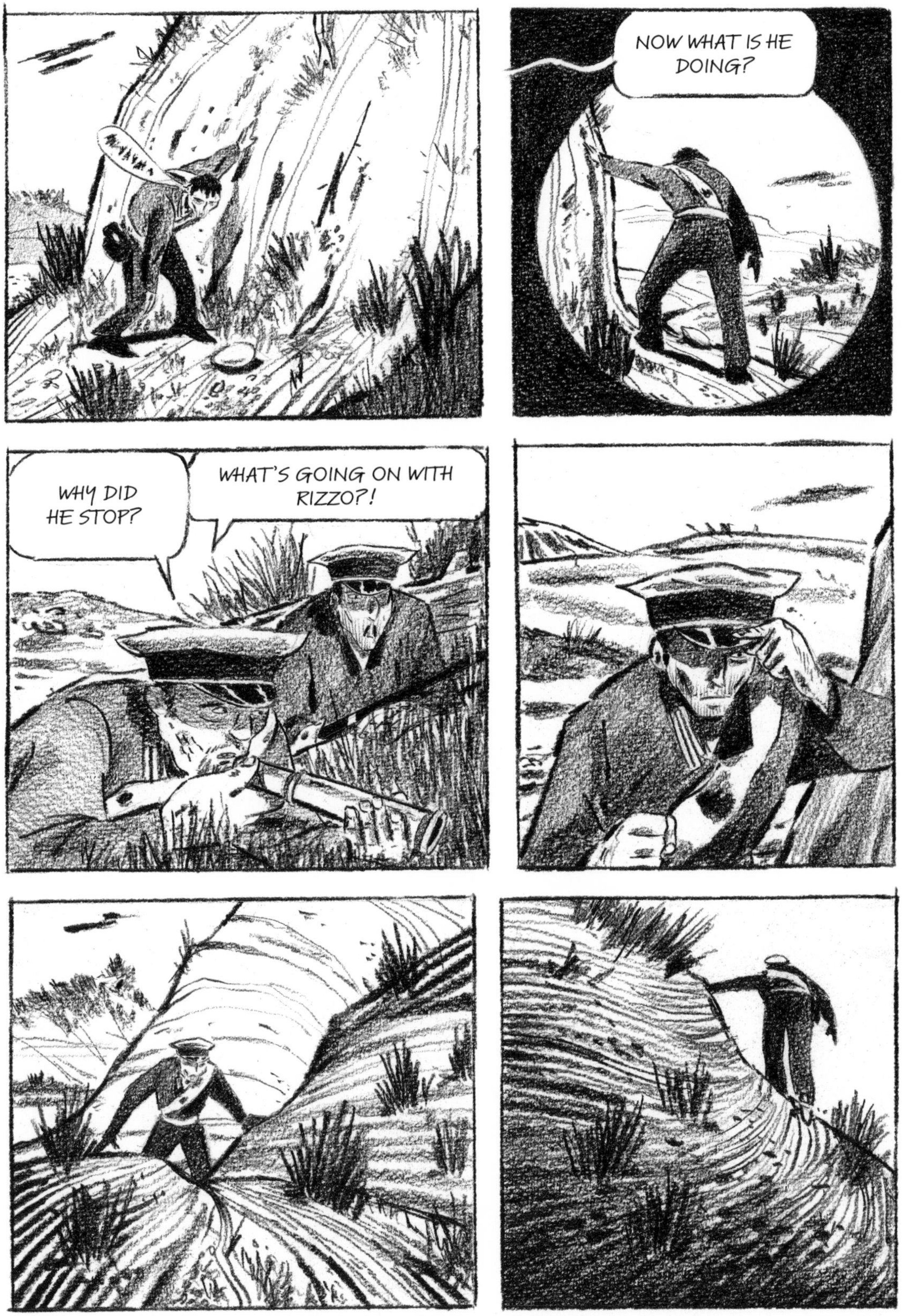
NOW WHAT IS HE DOING?
WHY DID HE STOP?
WHAT'S GOING ON WITH RIZZO?!

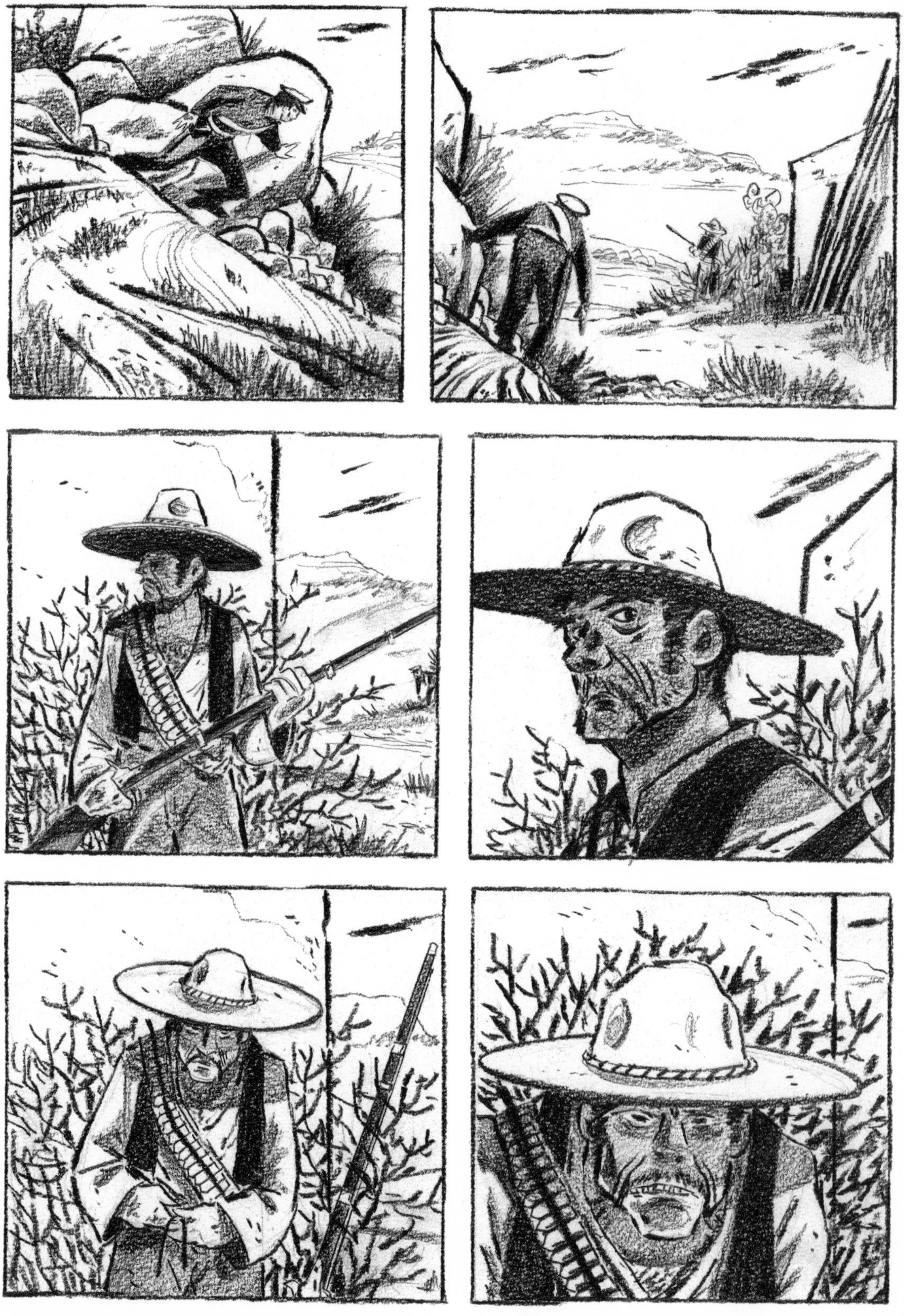

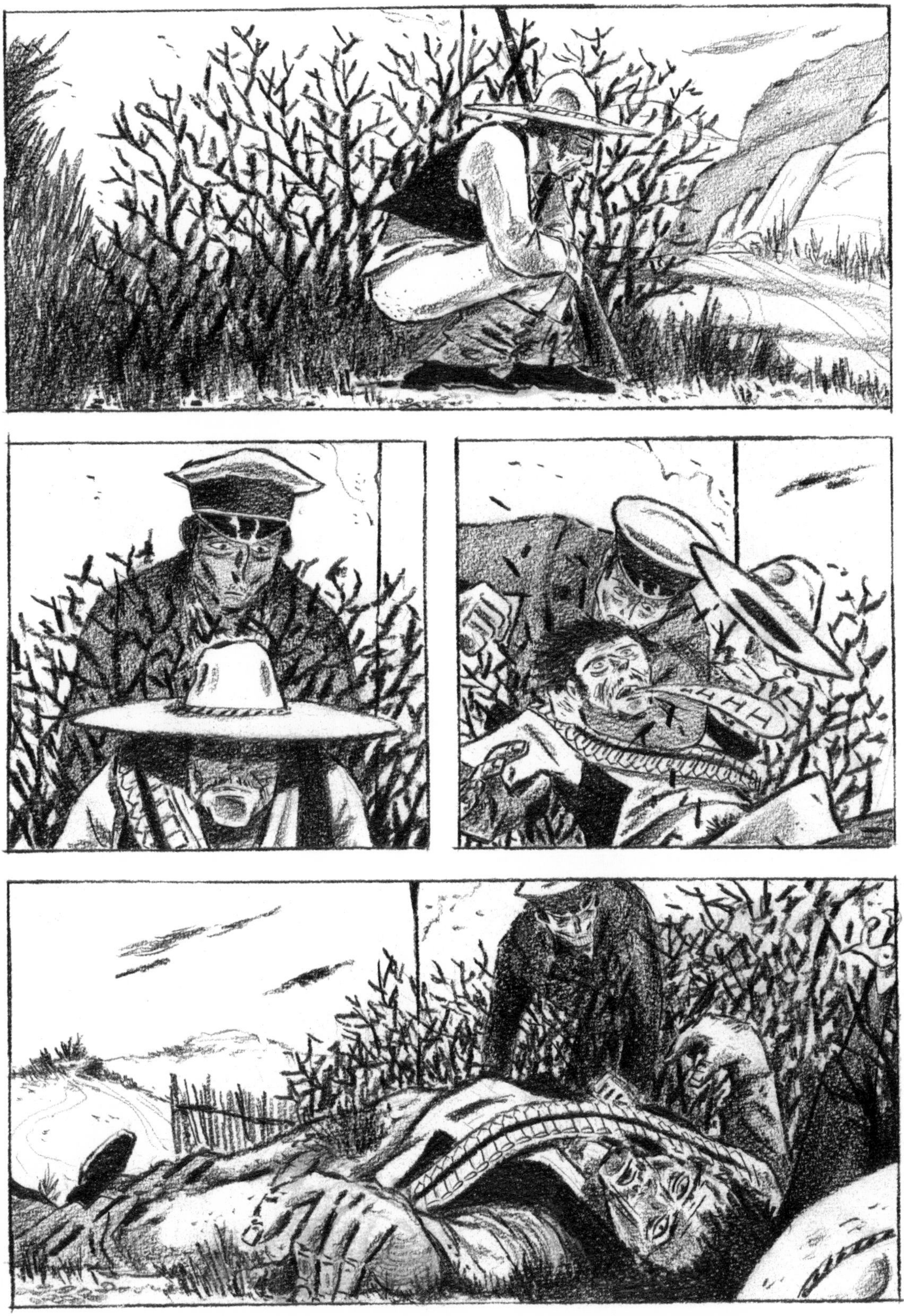
HHH

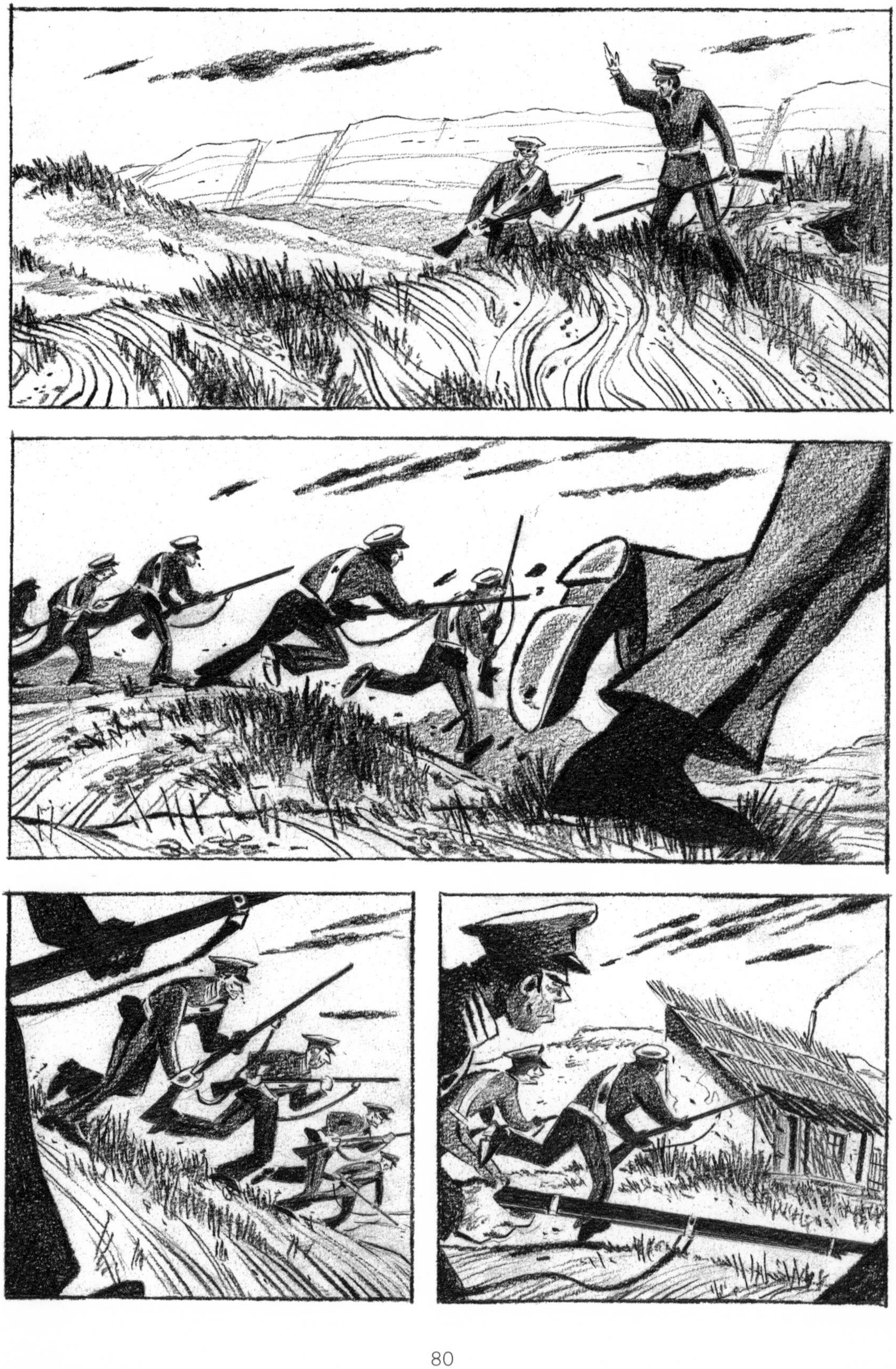

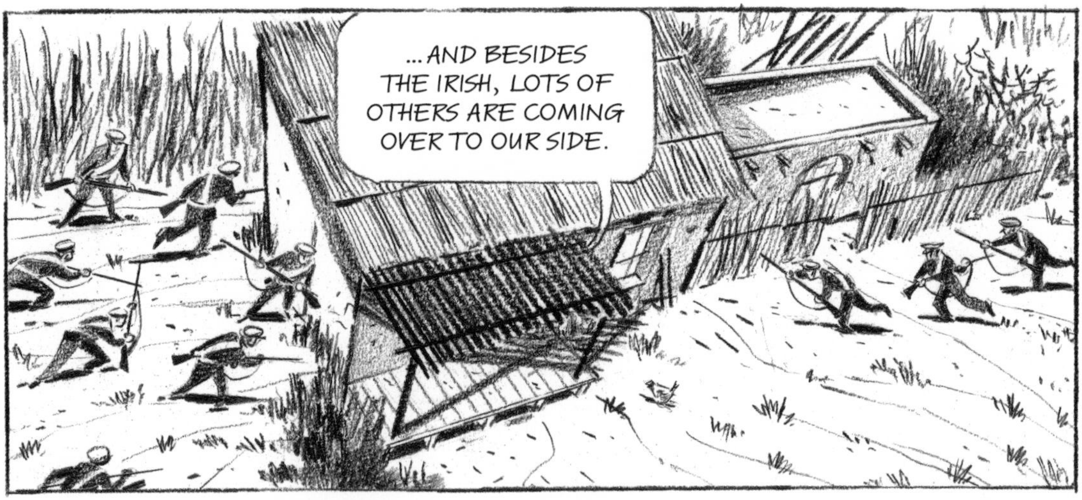
...AND BESIDES THE IRISH, LOTS OF OTHERS ARE COMING OVER TO OUR SIDE.

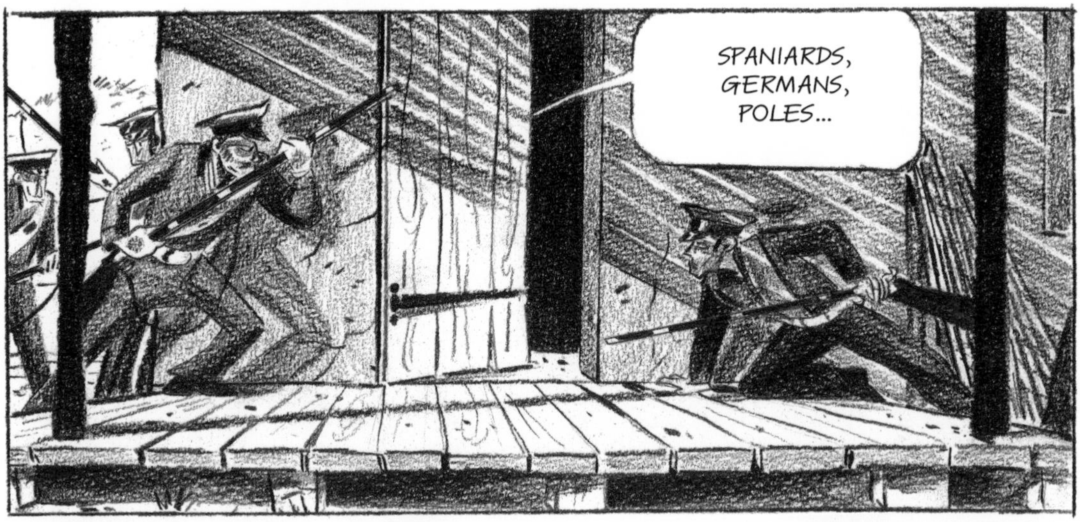
SPANIARDS, GERMANS, POLES...

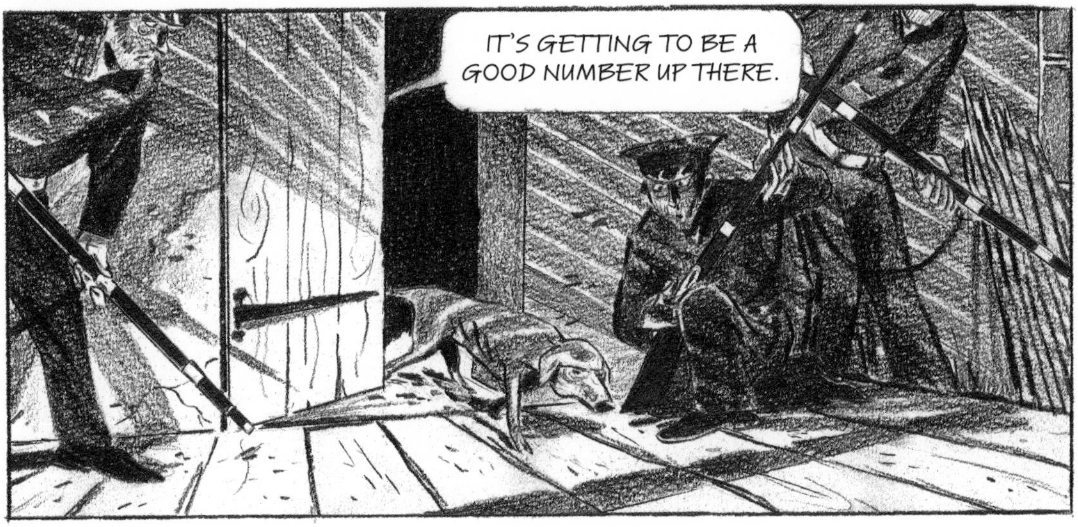
IT'S GETTING TO BE A GOOD NUMBER UP THERE.

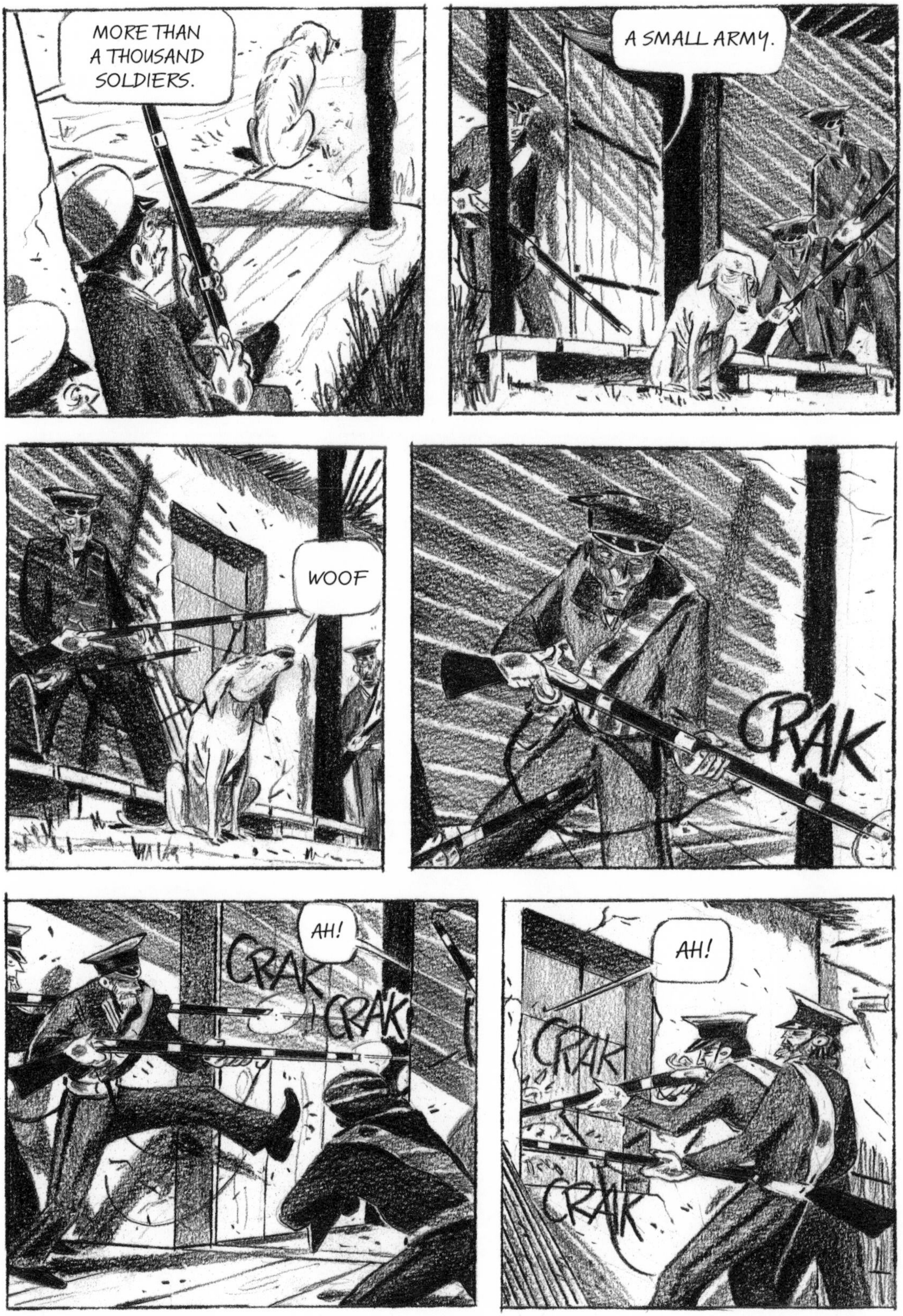
MORE THAN A THOUSAND SOLDIERS.
A SMALL ARMY.
WOOF
CRAK
AH!
CRAK
CRAK
AH!
CRAK
CRAK

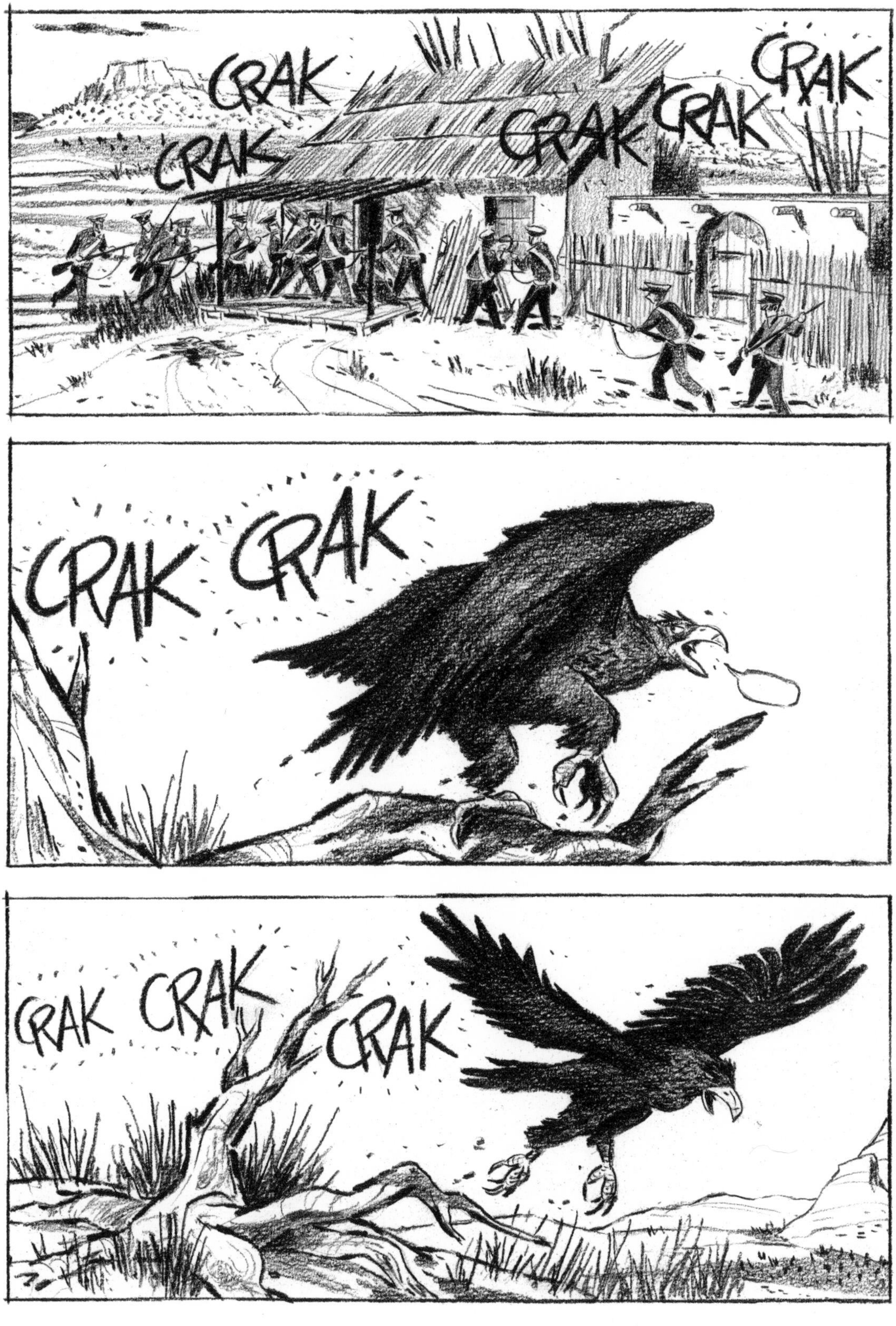
CRAK
CRAK
CRAK
CRAK
CRAK
CRAK
CRAK
CRAK
CRAK
CRAK

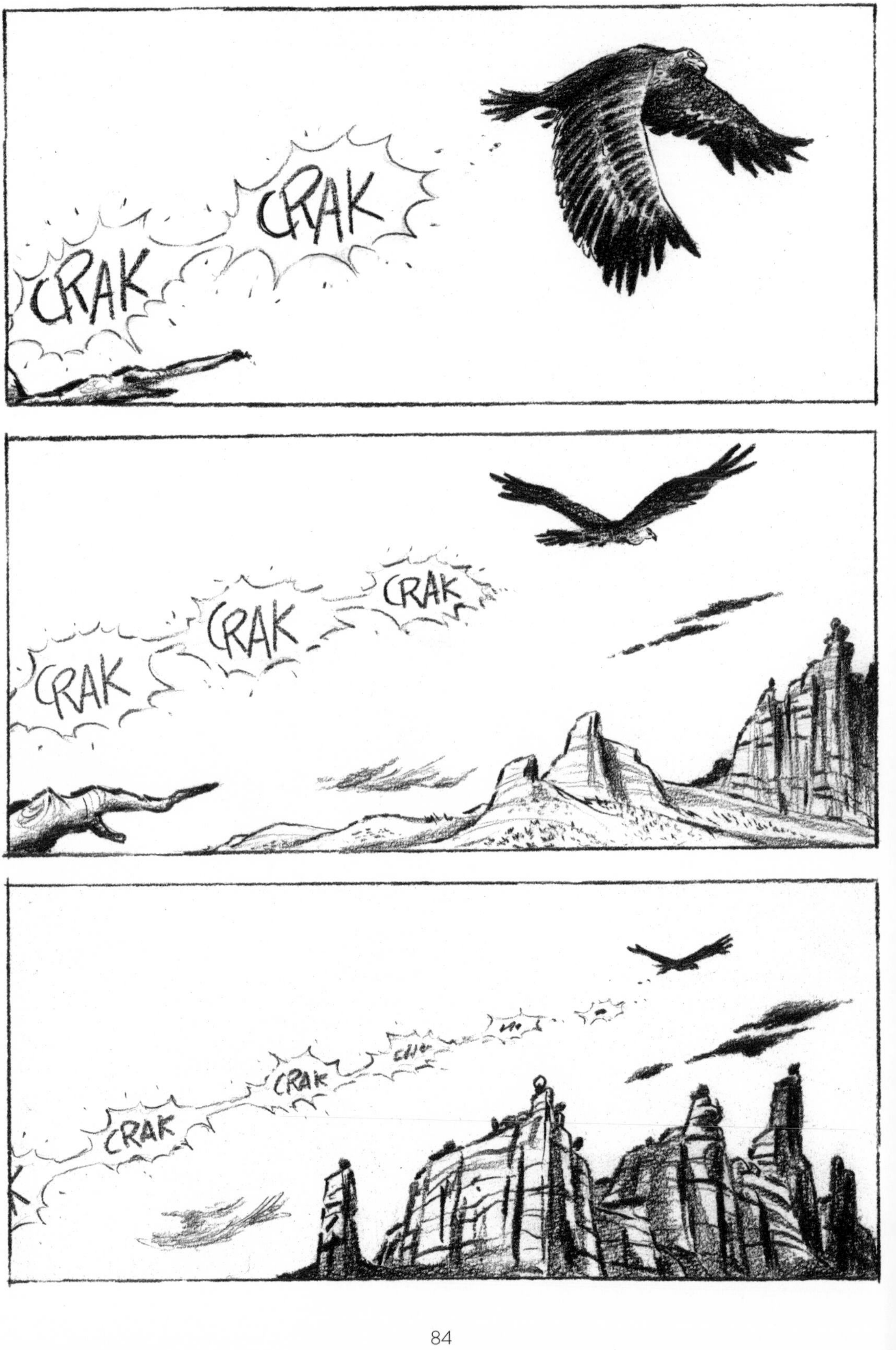
CRAK
CRAK
CRAK
CRAK
CRAK
CRAK
CRAK

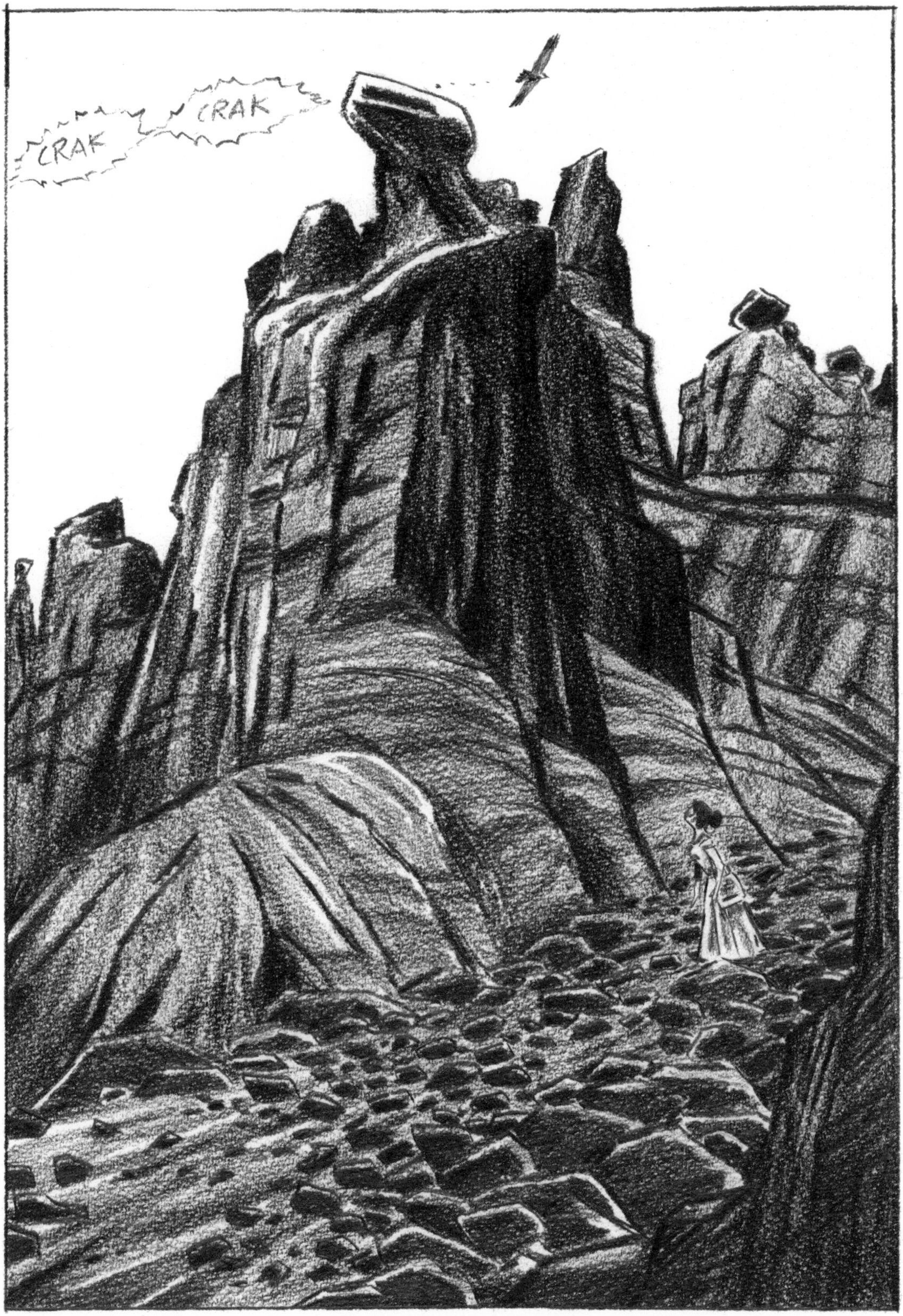
CRAK
CRAK

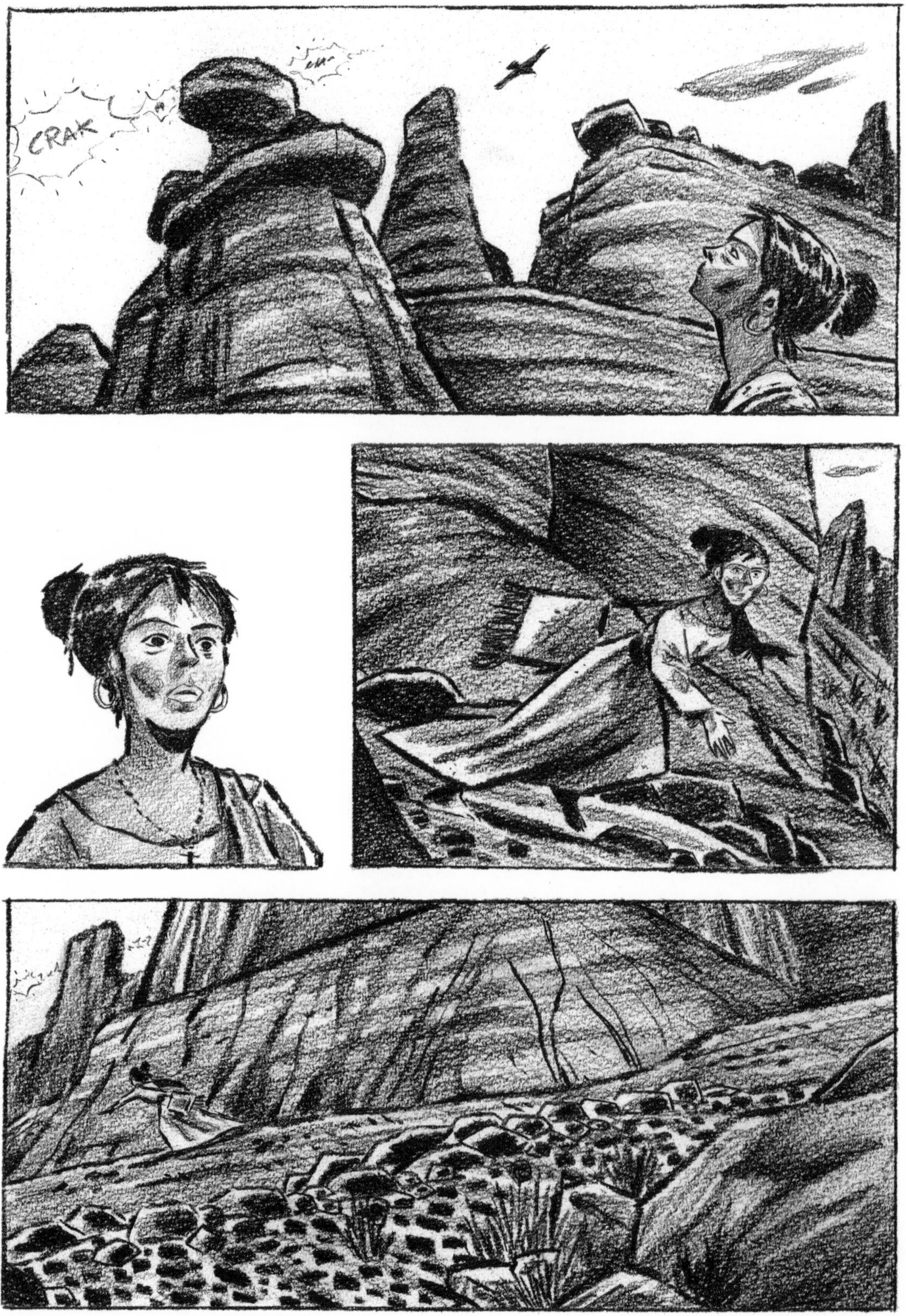
CRAK

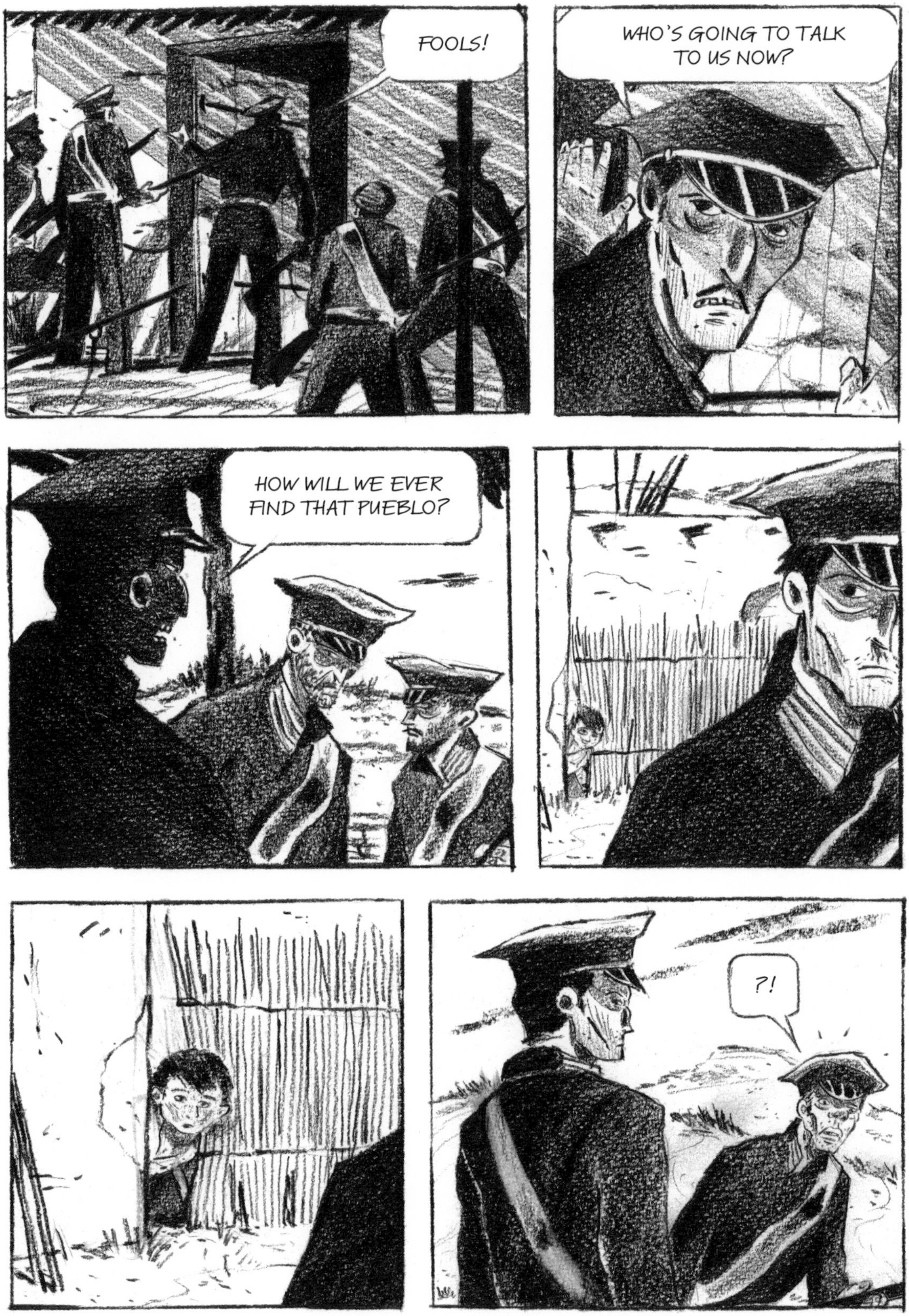
FOOLS!
WHO'S GOING TO TALK TO US NOW?
HOW WILL WE EVER FIND THAT PUEBLO?
?!

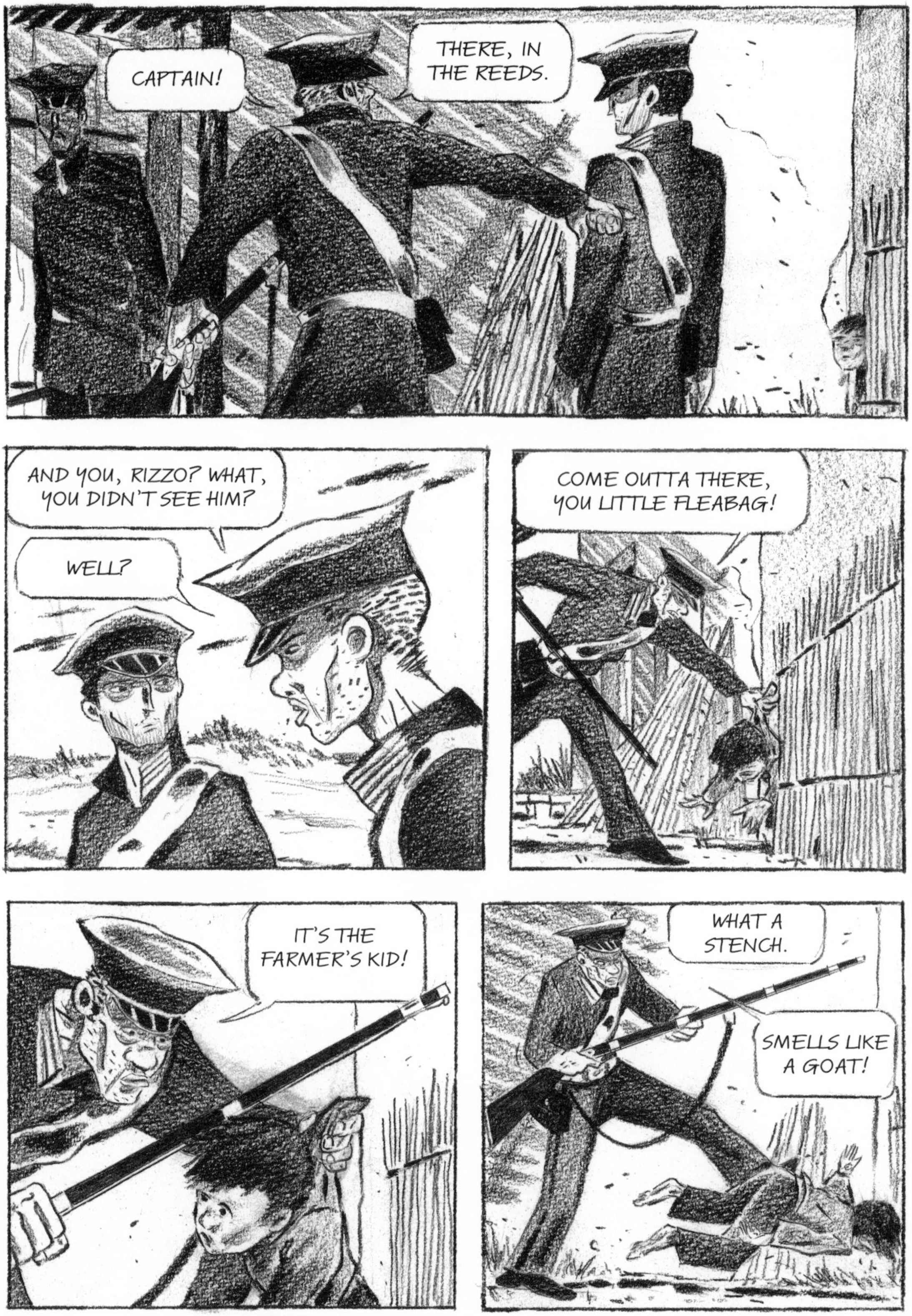
CAPTAIN!
THERE, IN THE REEDS.
AND YOU, RIZZO? WHAT, YOU DIDN'T SEE HIM?
WELL?
COME OUTTA THERE, YOU LITTLE FLEABAG!
IT'S THE FARMER'S KID!
WHAT A STENCH.
SMELLS LIKE A GOAT!

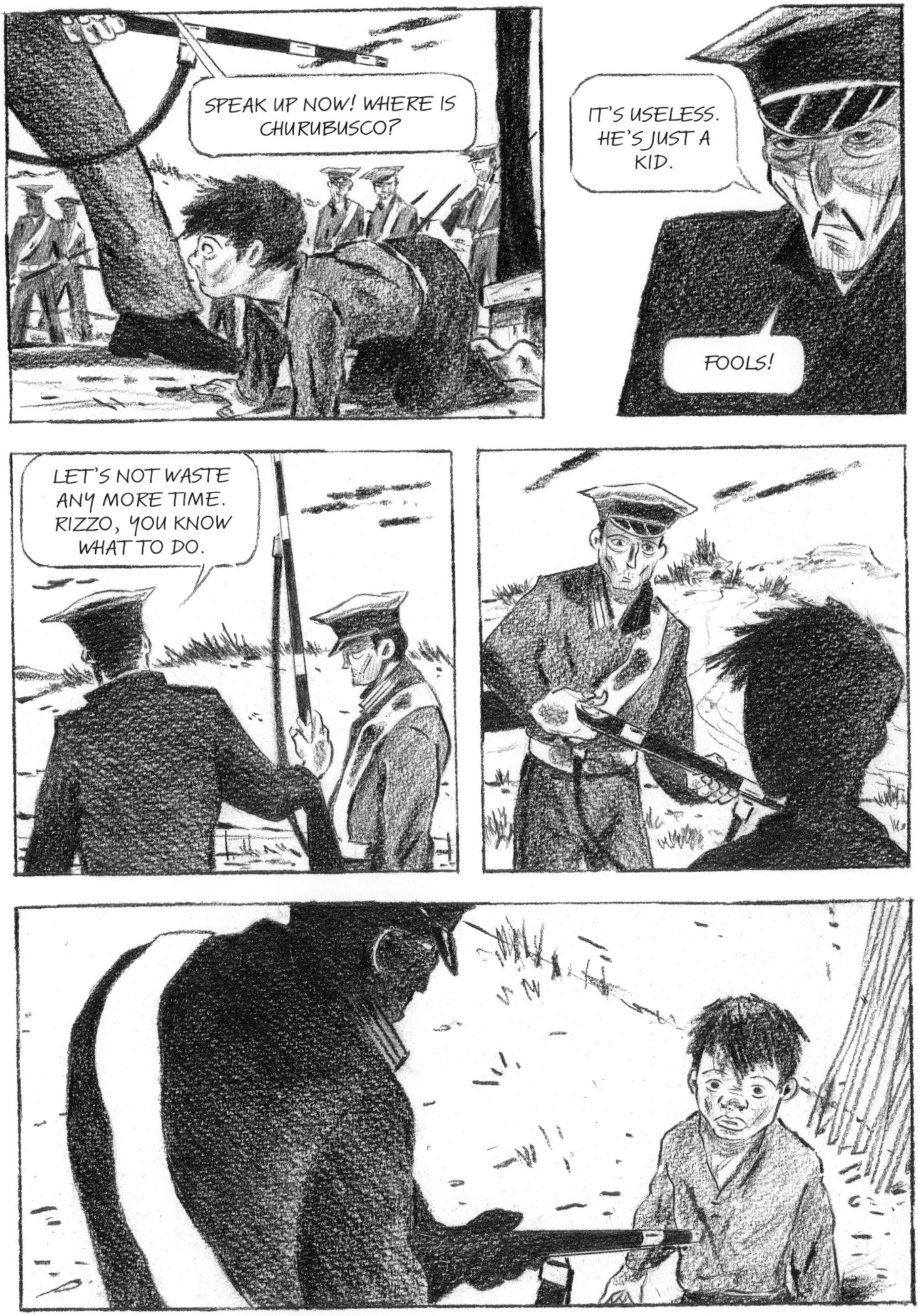
SPEAK UP NOW! WHERE IS CHURUBUSCO?
IT'S USELESS. HE'S JUST A KID.
FOOLS!
LET'S NOT WASTE ANY MORE TIME. RIZZO, YOU KNOW WHAT TO DO.

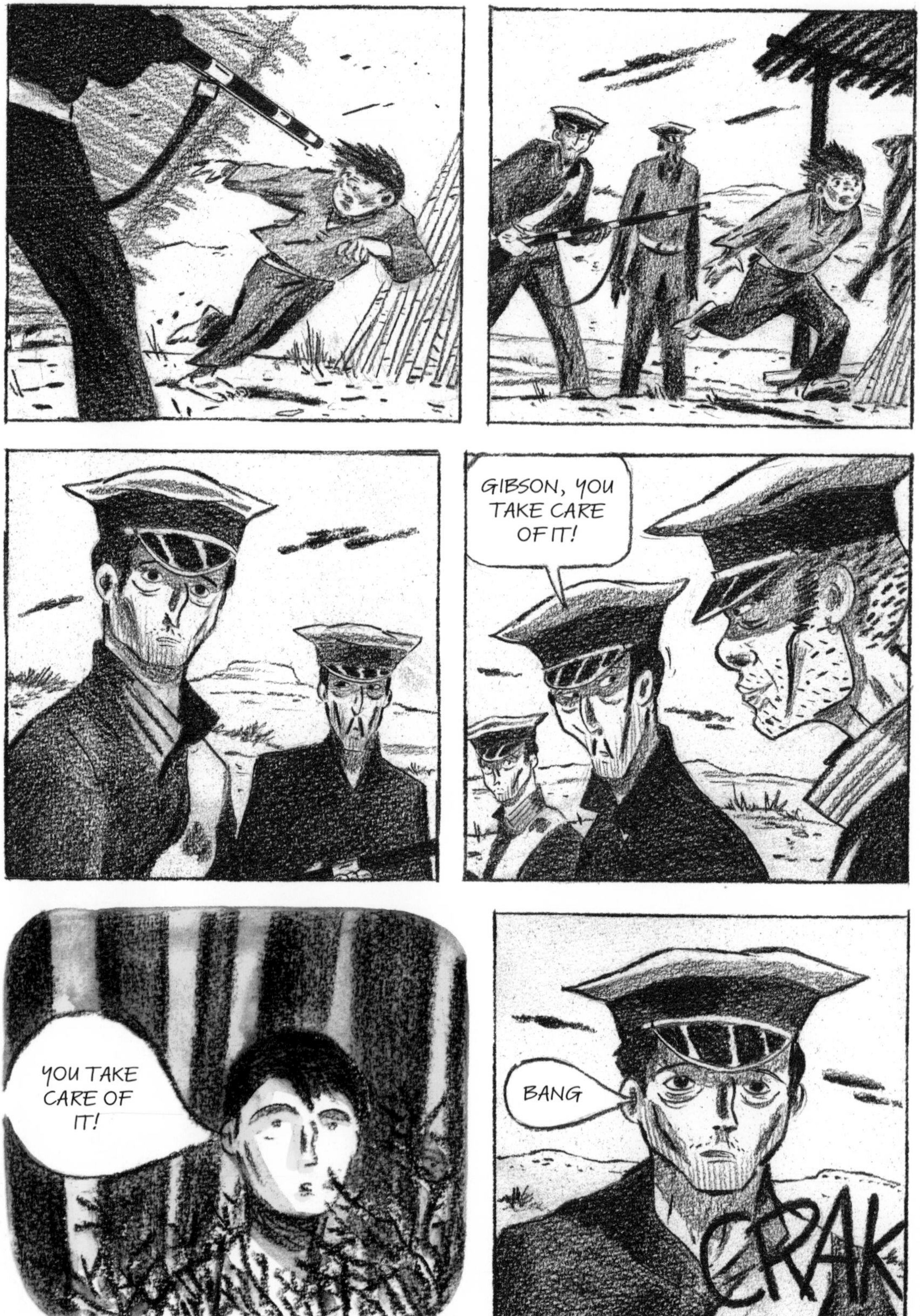
GIBSON, YOU TAKE CARE OF IT!
YOU TAKE CARE OF IT!
BANG
CRAK

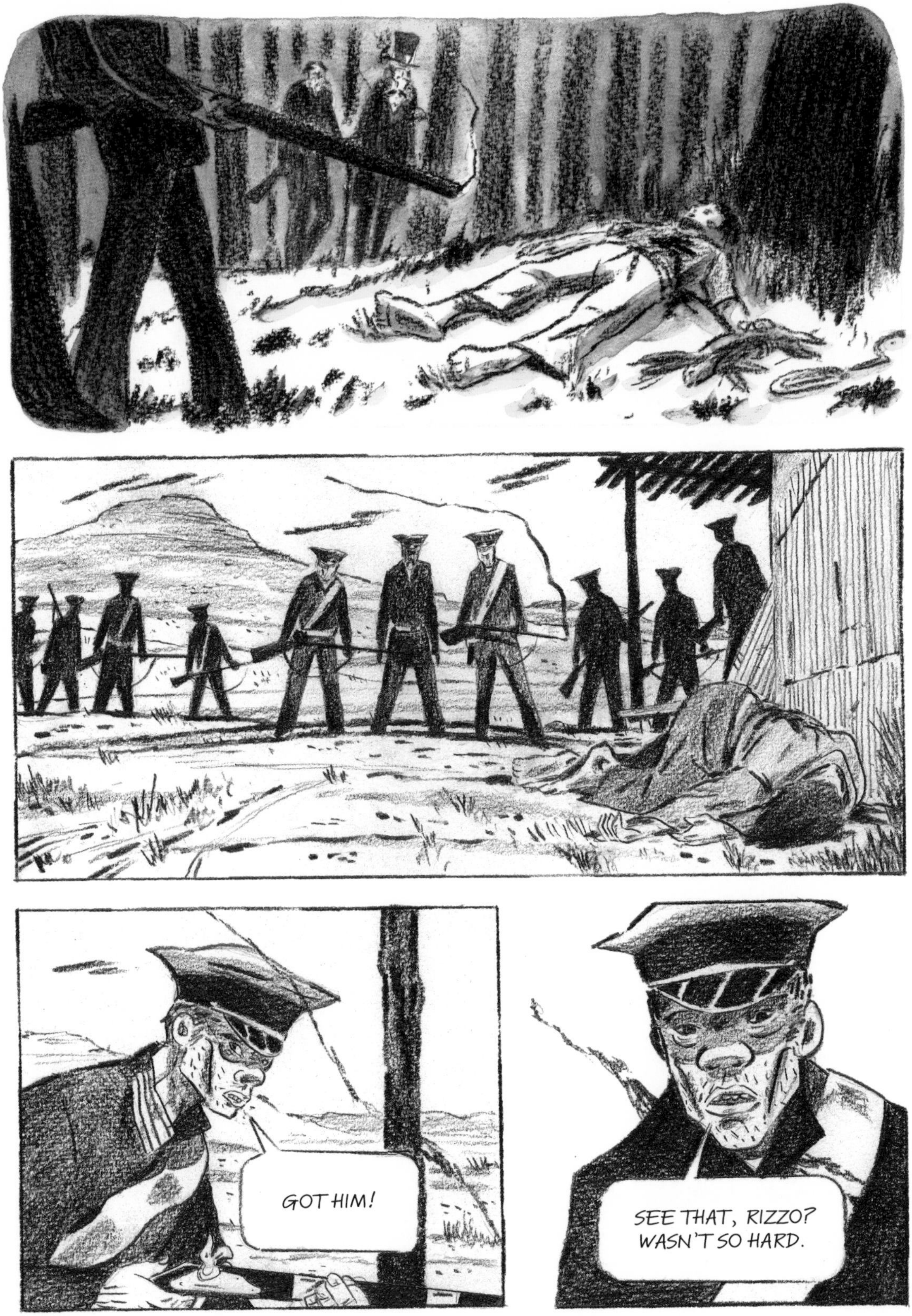
GOT HIM!
SEE THAT, RIZZO? WASN'T SO HARD.

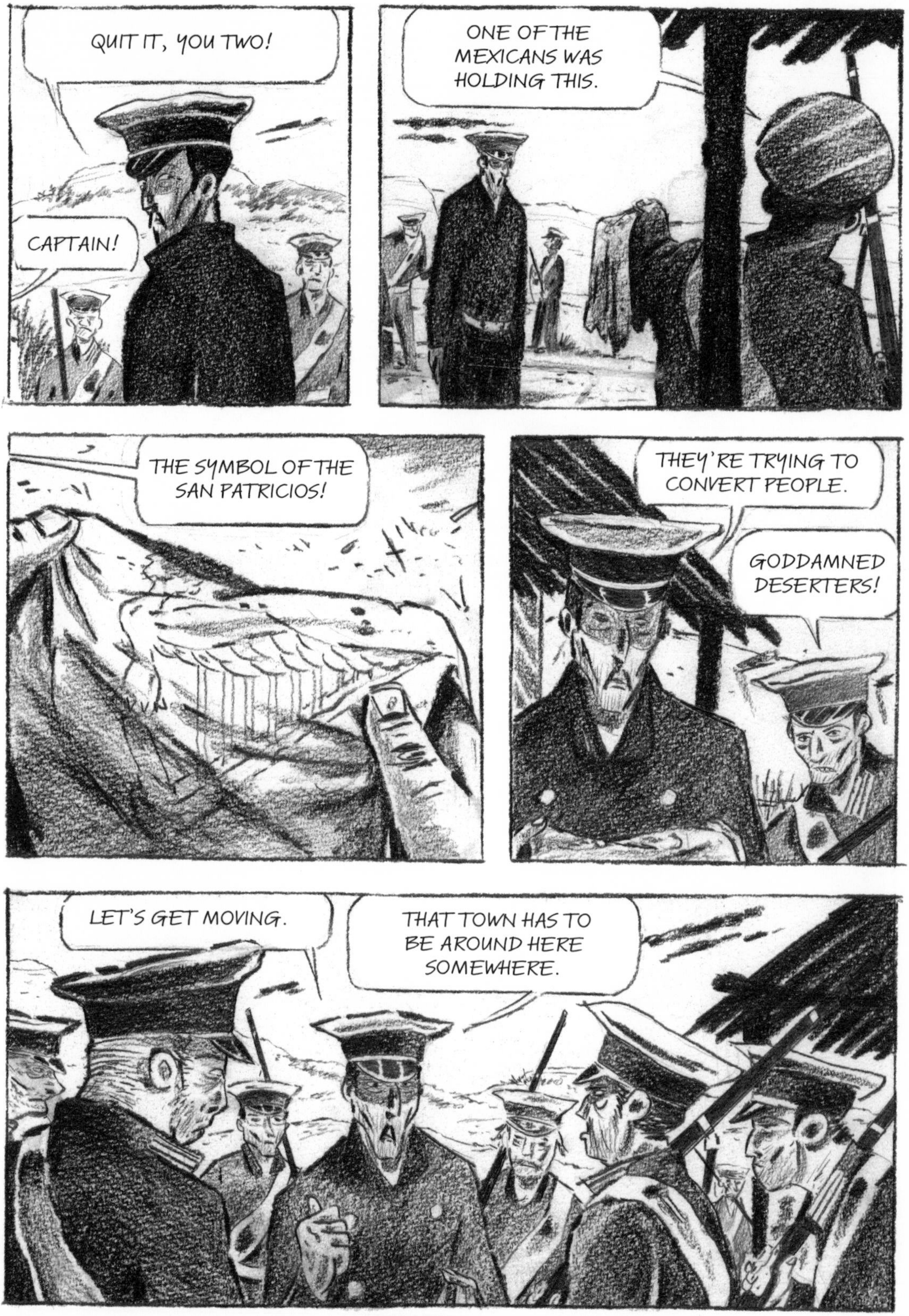
QUIT IT, YOU TWO!
CAPTAIN!
ONE OF THE MEXICANS WAS HOLDING THIS.
THE SYMBOL OF THE SAN PATRICIOS!
THEY'RE TRYING TO CONVERT PEOPLE.
GODDAMNED DESERTERS!
LET'S GET MOVING.
THAT TOWN HAS TO BE AROUND HERE SOMEWHERE.

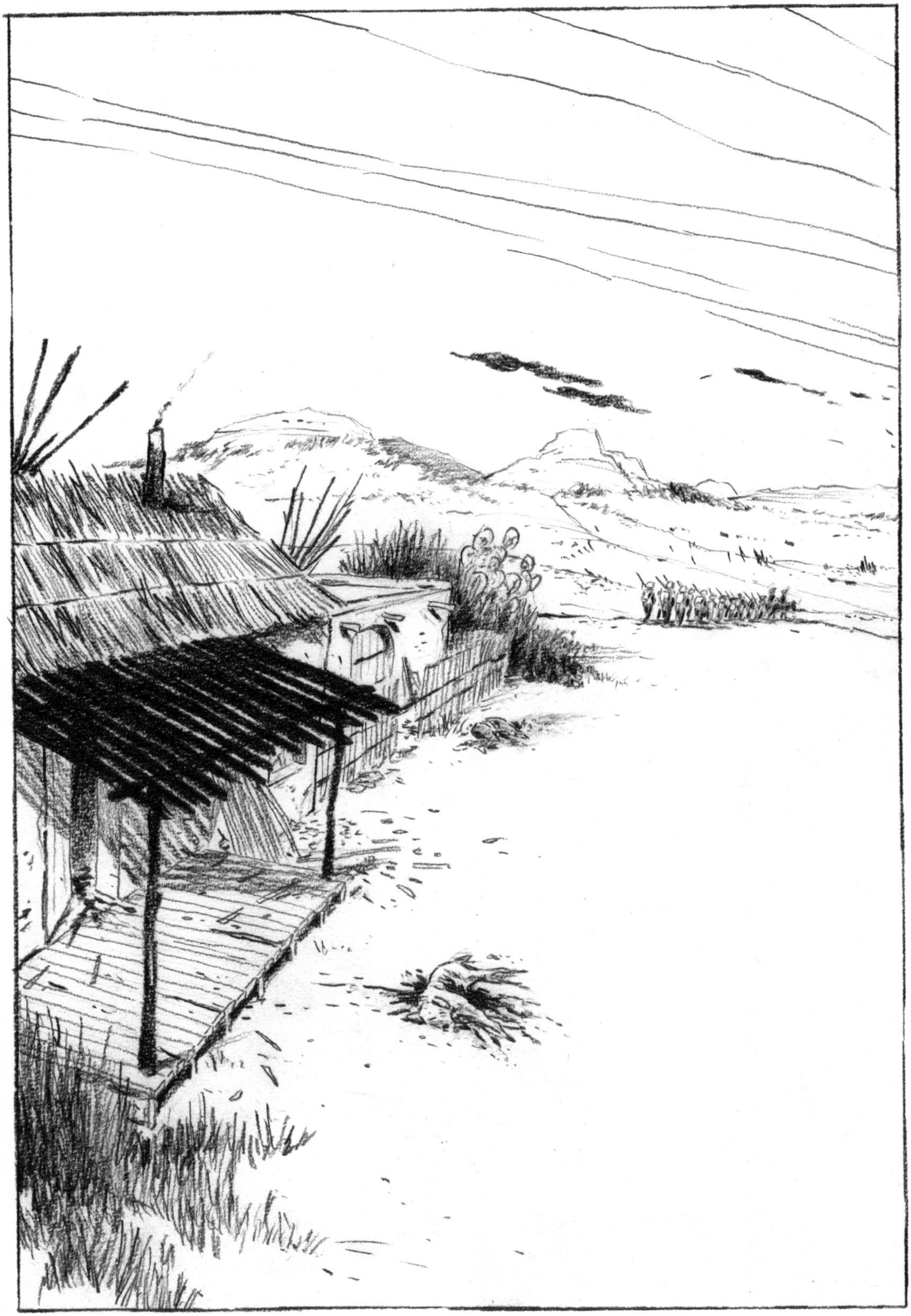

CHAPTER FOUR

LUZ DE
LUNA

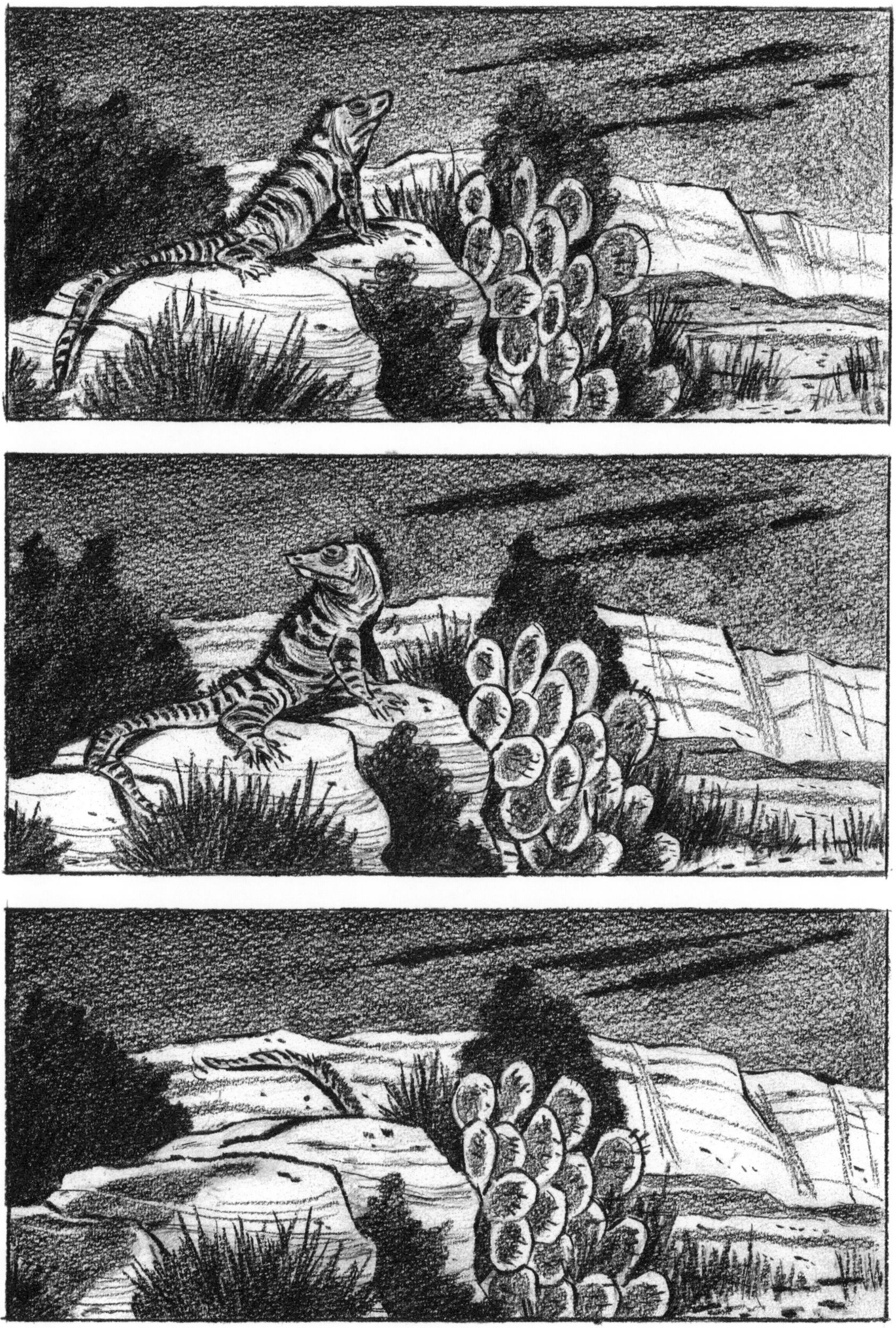

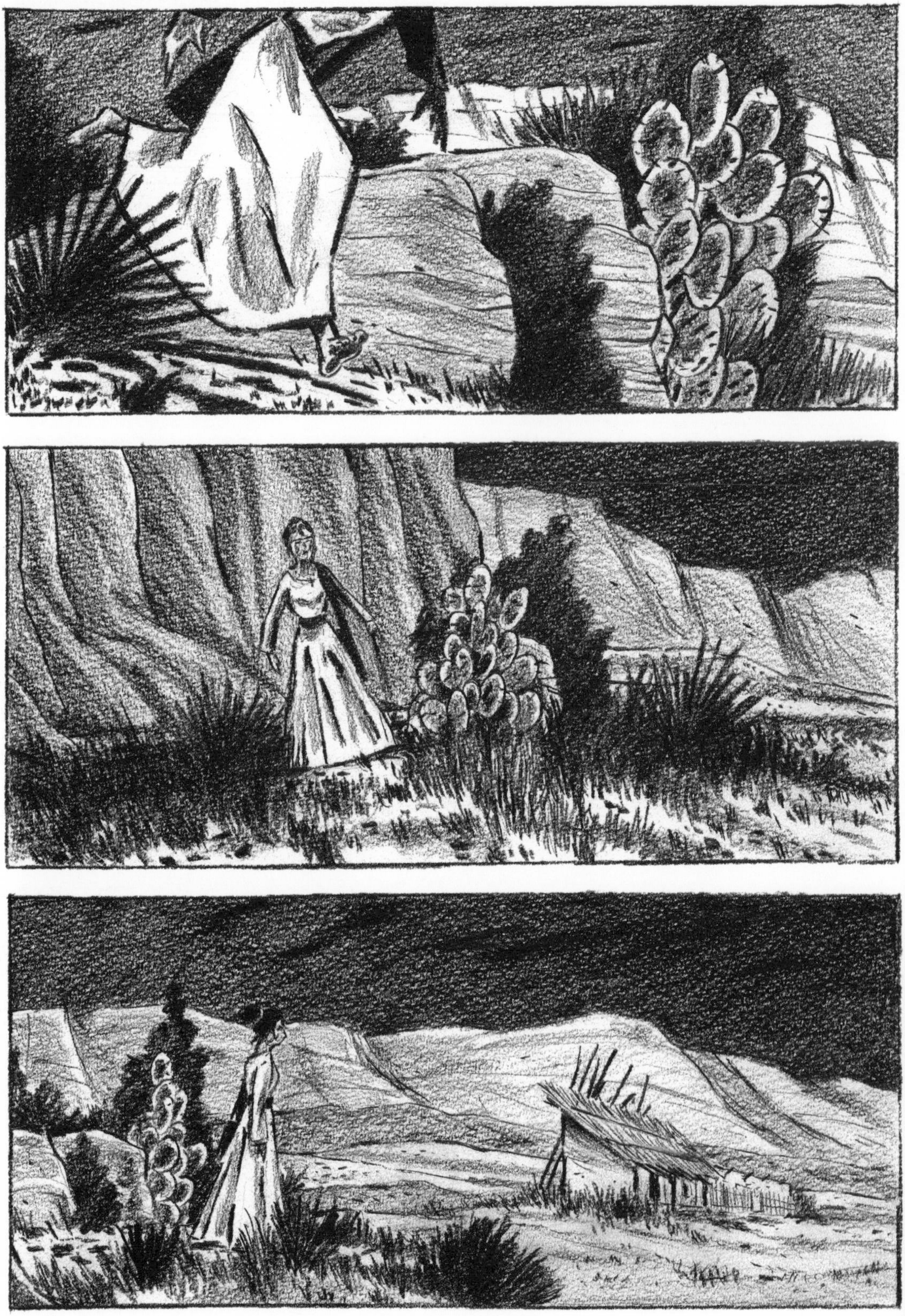

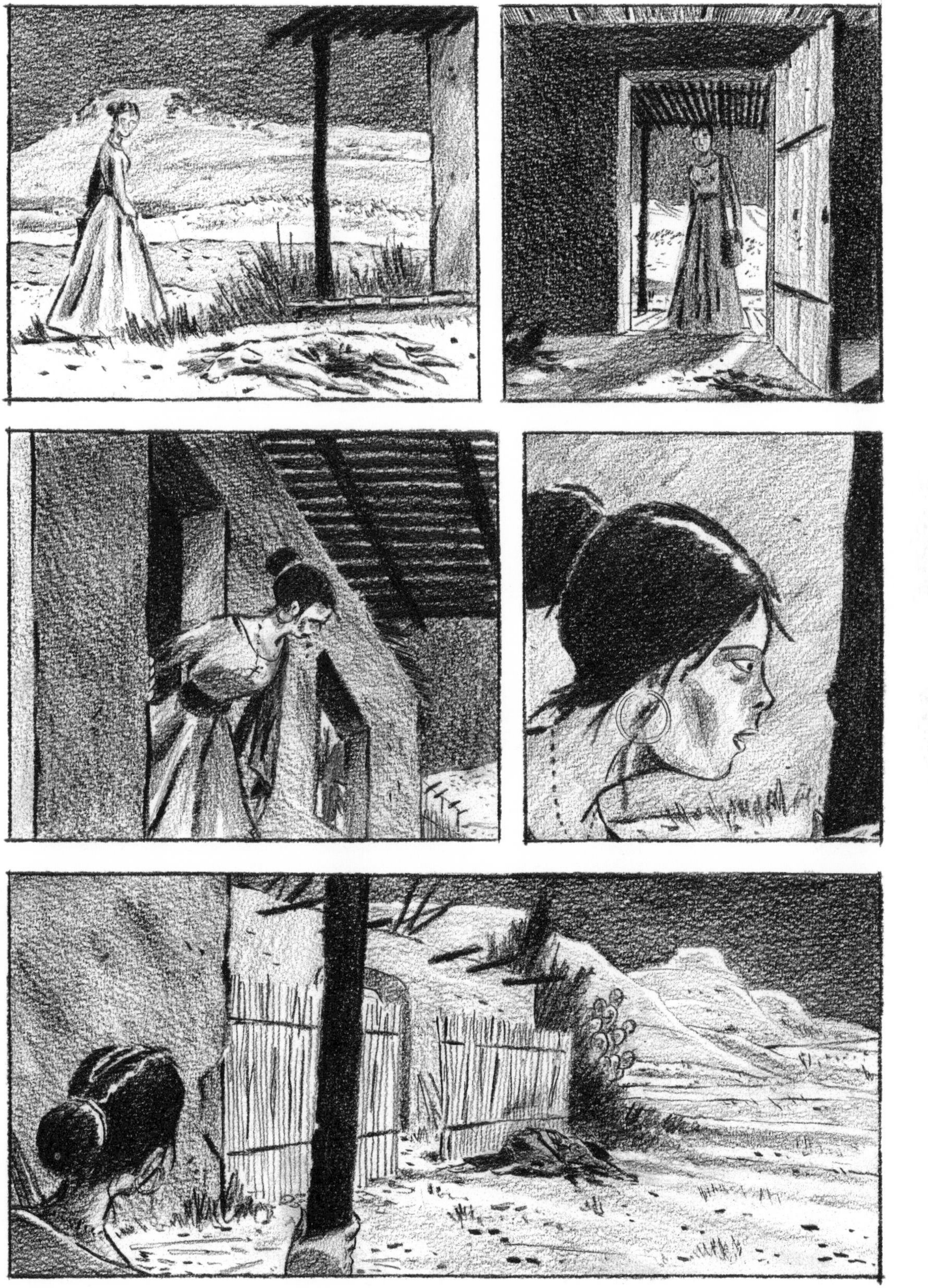

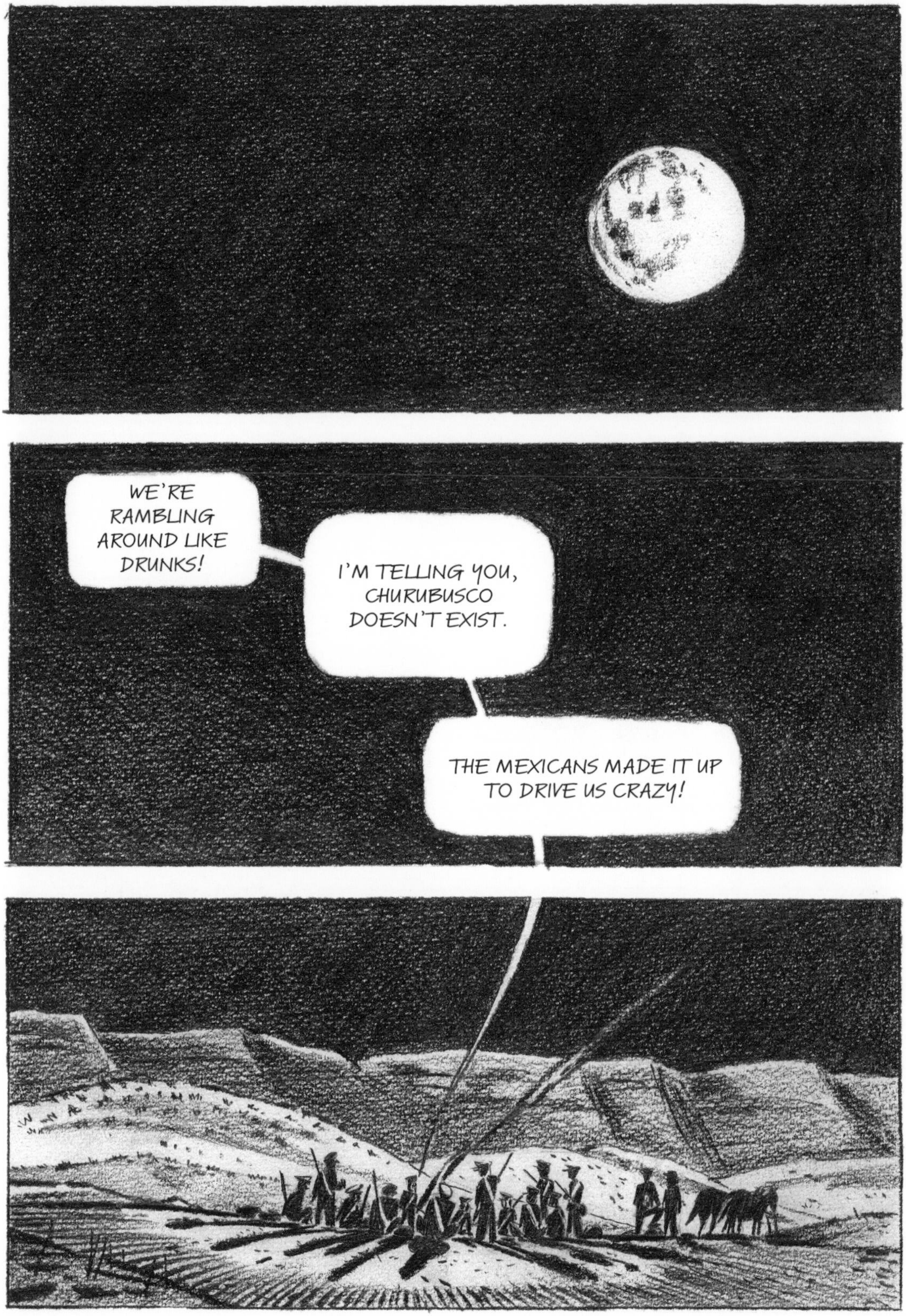
WE'RE RAMBLING AROUND LIKE DRUNKS!
I'M TELLING YOU, CHURUBUSCO DOESN'T EXIST.
THE MEXICANS MADE IT UP TO DRIVE US CRAZY!

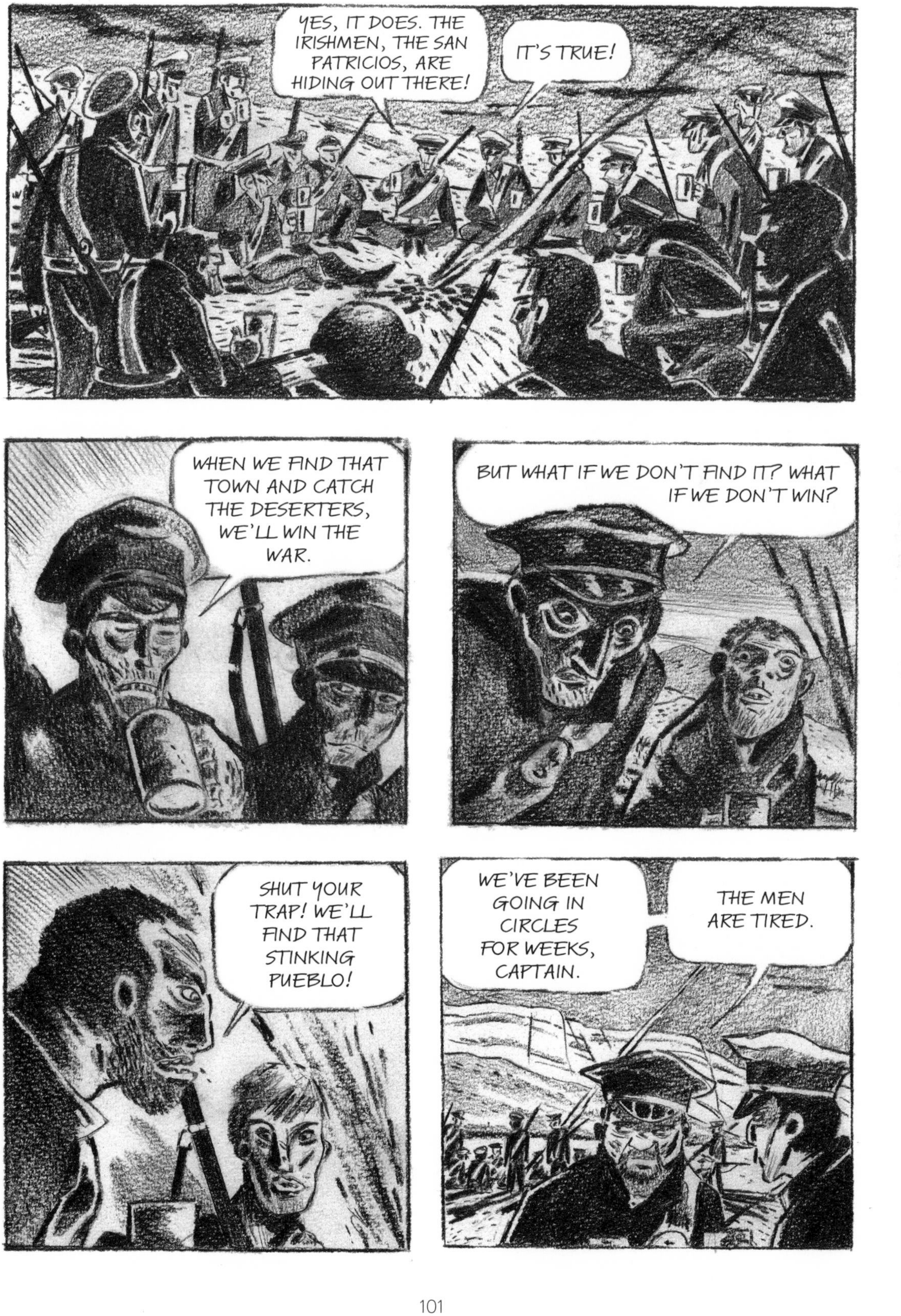
YES, IT DOES. THE IRISHMEN, THE SAN PATRICIOS, ARE HIDING OUT THERE!
IT'S TRUE!
WHEN WE FIND THAT TOWN AND CATCH THE DESERTERS, WE'LL WIN THE WAR.
BUT WHAT IF WE DON'T FIND IT? WHAT IF WE DON'T WIN?
SHUT YOUR TRAP! WE'LL FIND THAT STINKING PUEBLO!
WE'VE BEEN GOING IN CIRCLES FOR WEEKS, CAPTAIN.
THE MEN ARE TIRED.

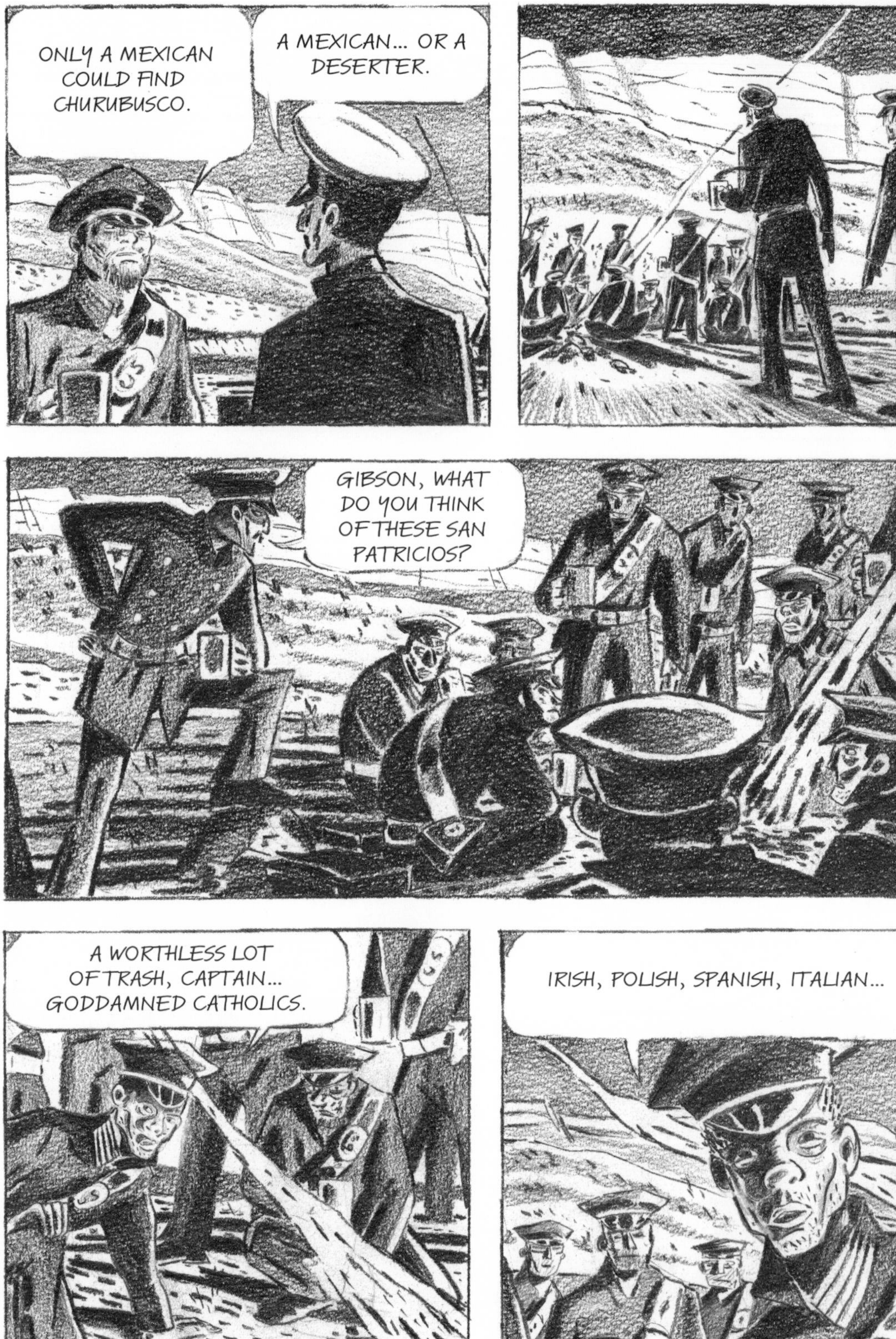

ONLY A MEXICAN COULD FIND CHURUBUSCO.
A MEXICAN... OR A DESERTER.
GIBSON, WHAT DO YOU THINK OF THESE SAN PATRICIOS?
A WORTHLESS LOT OF TRASH, CAPTAIN... GODDAMNED CATHOLICS.
IRISH, POLISH, SPANISH, ITALIAN...

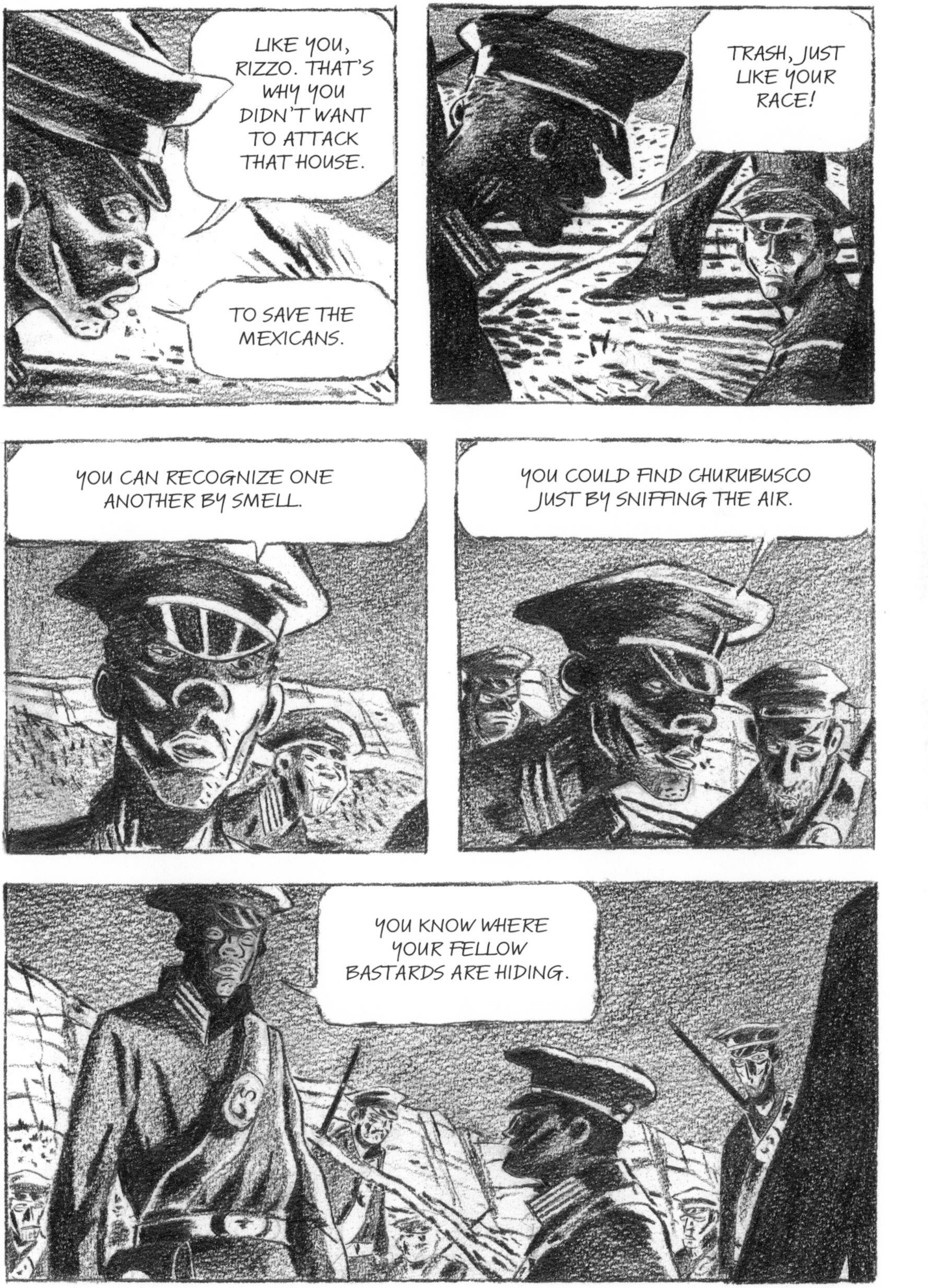
LIKE YOU, RIZZO. THAT'S WHY YOU DIDN'T WANT TO ATTACK THAT HOUSE.
TO SAVE THE MEXICANS.
TRASH, JUST LIKE YOUR RACE!
YOU CAN RECOGNIZE ONE ANOTHER BY SMELL.
YOU COULD FIND CHURUBUSCO JUST BY SNIFFING THE AIR.
YOU KNOW WHERE YOUR FELLOW BASTARDS ARE HIDING.

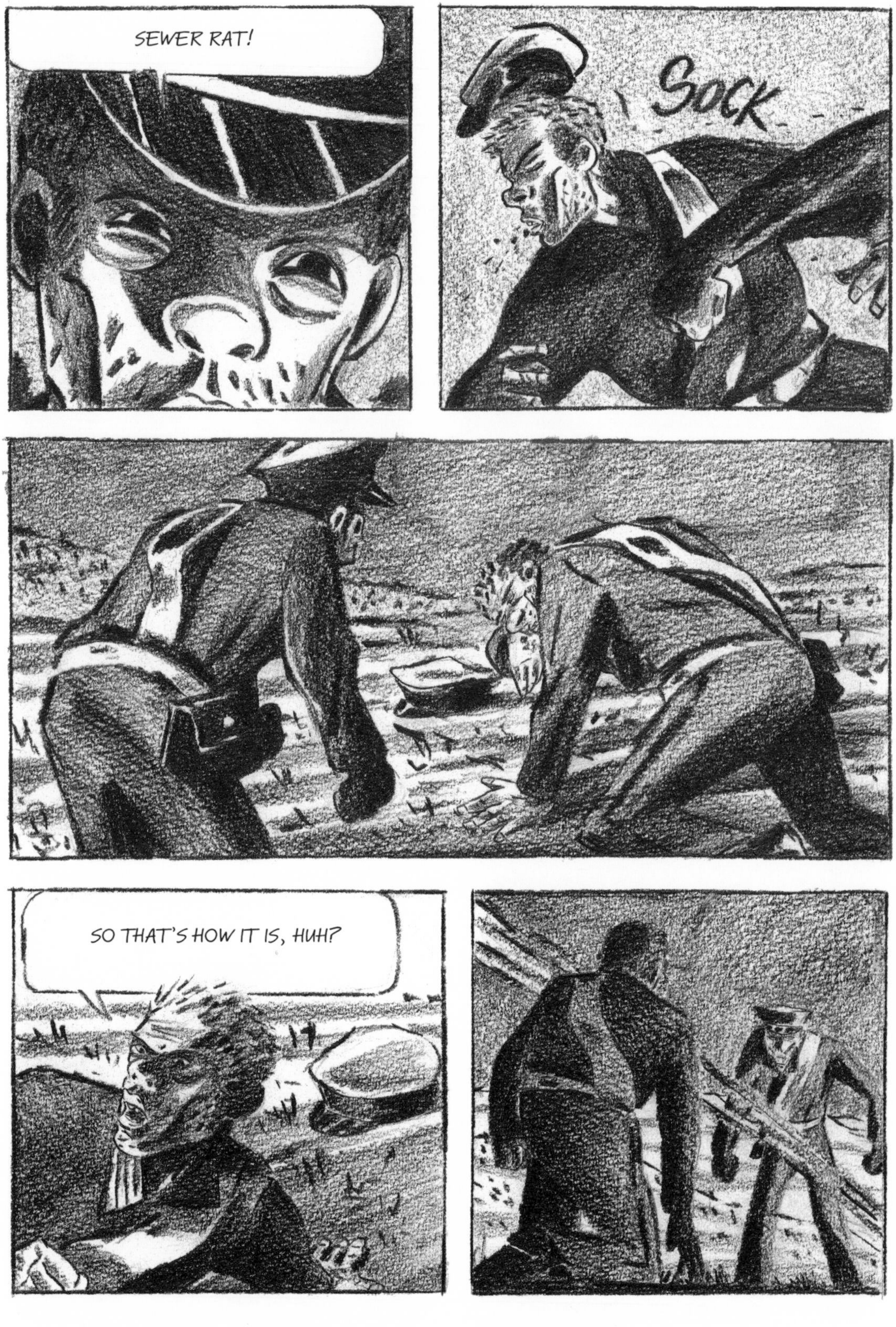
SEWER RAT!
SOCK
SO THAT'S HOW IT IS, HUH?

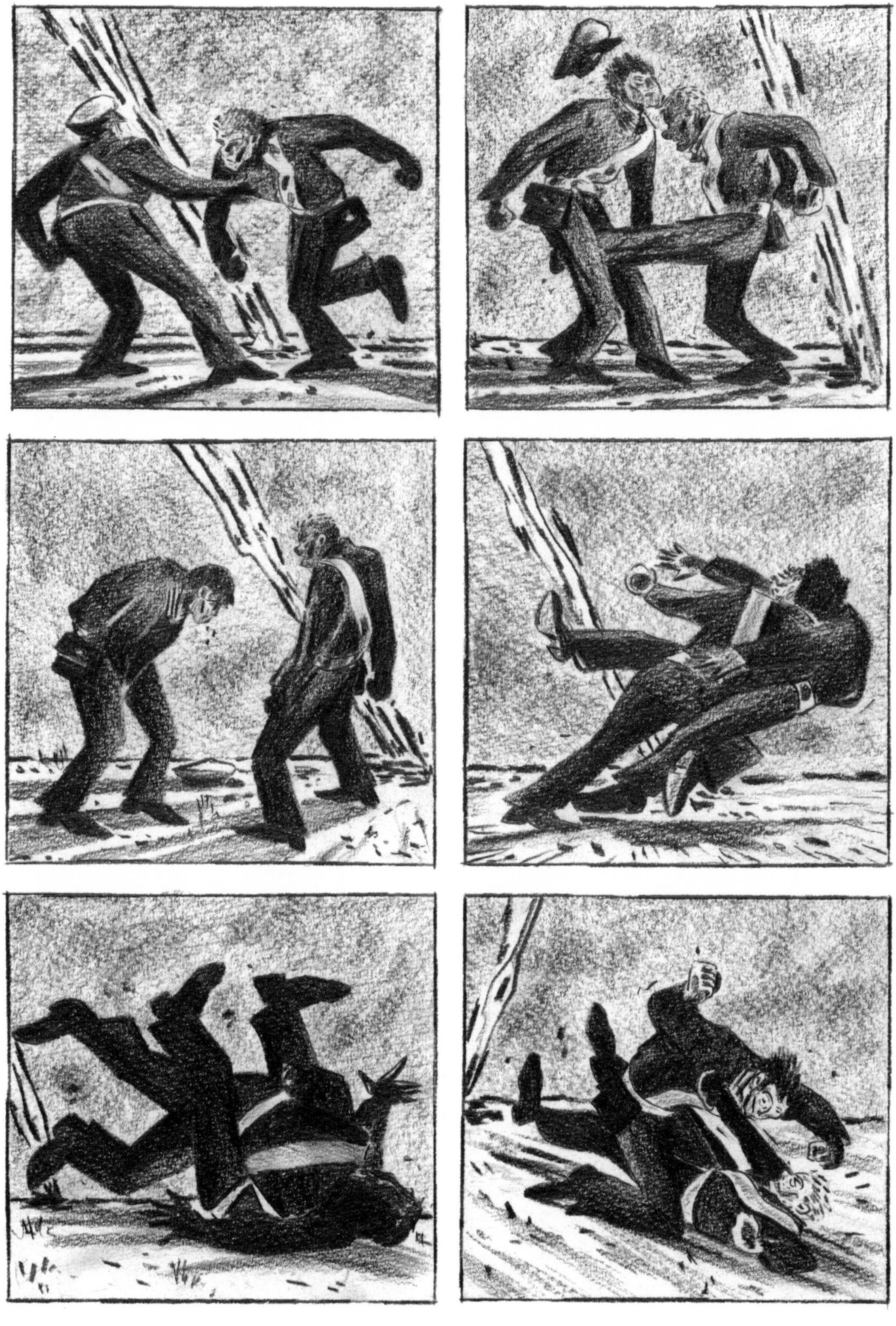

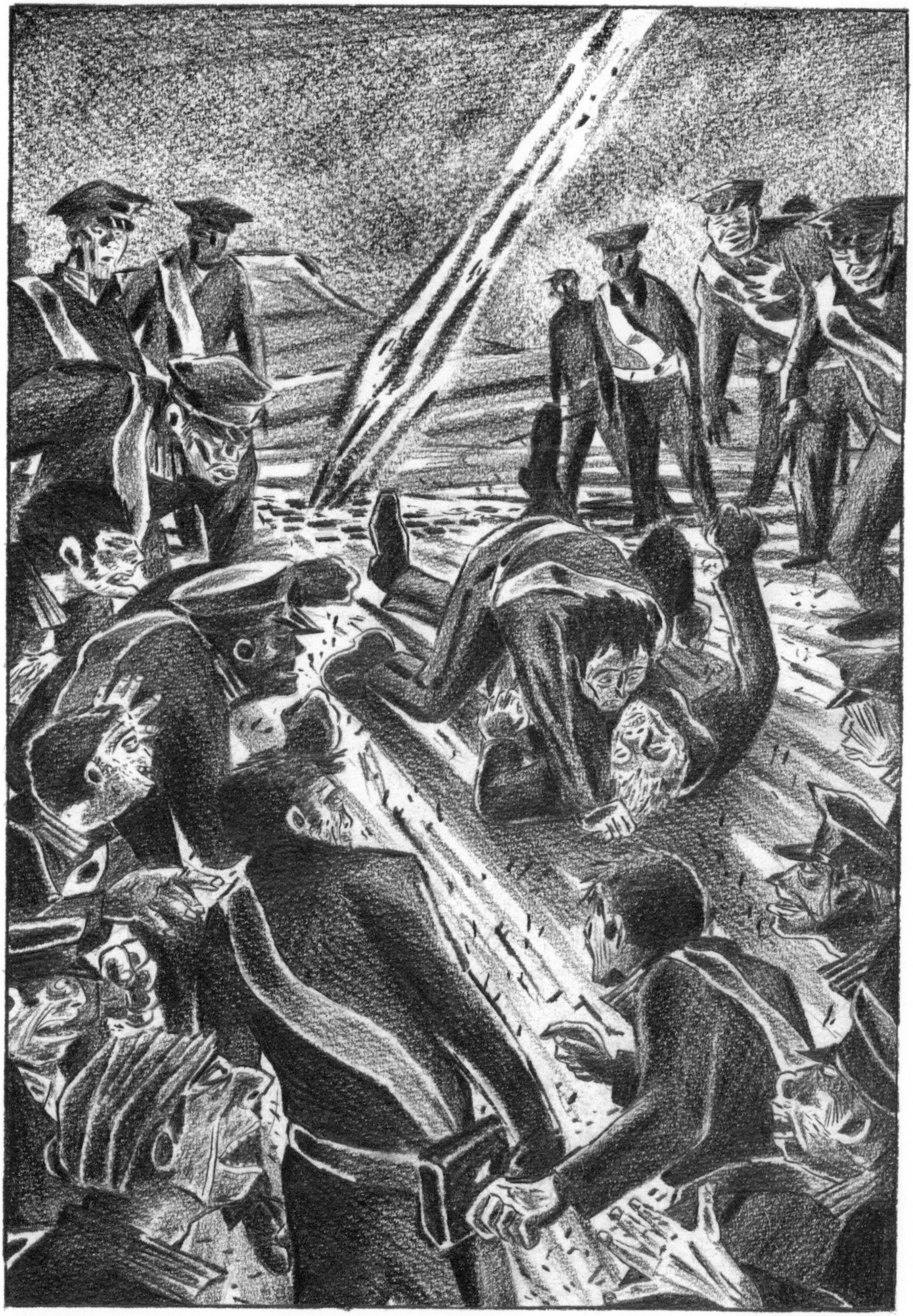

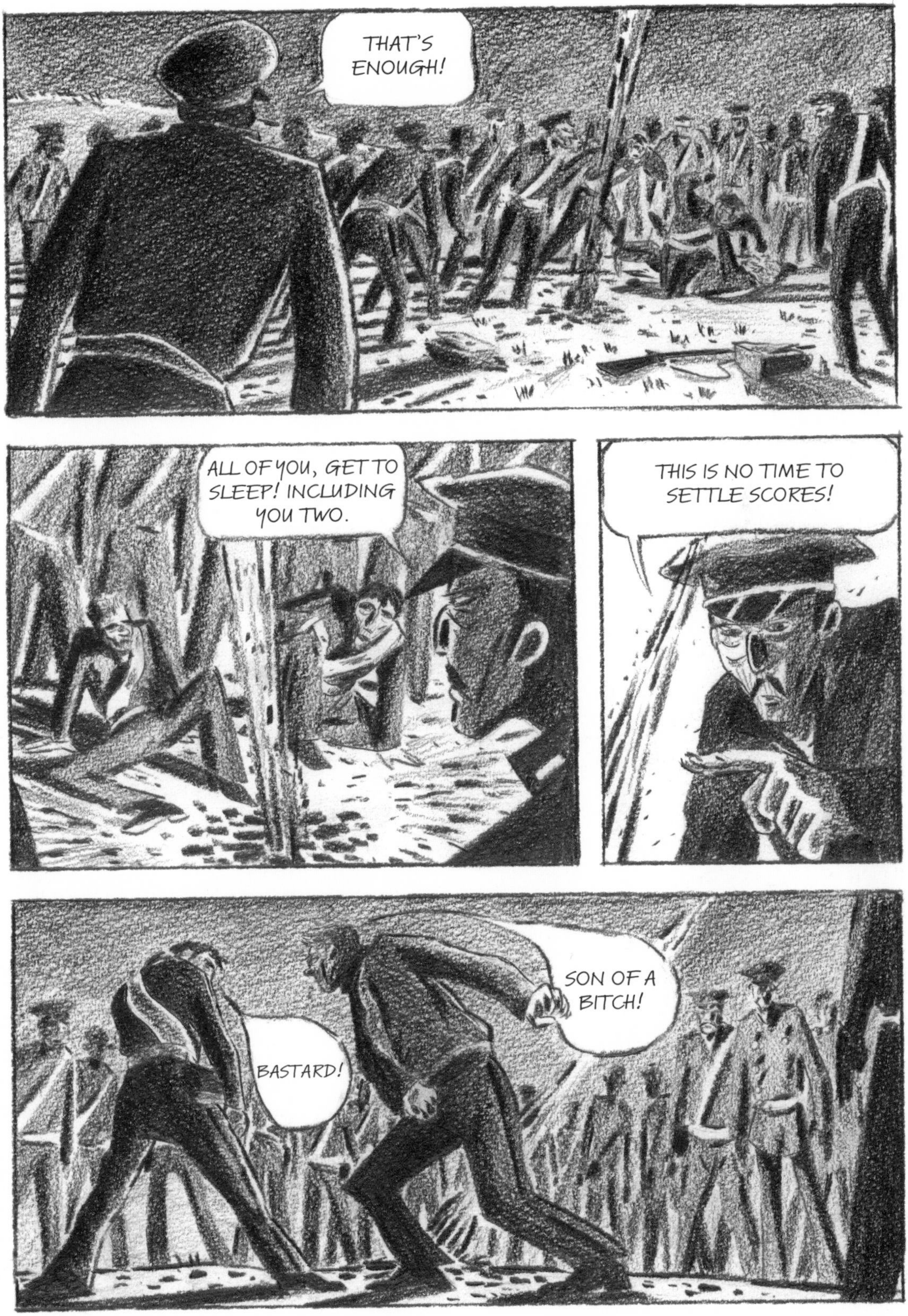
THAT'S ENOUGH!
ALL OF YOU, GET TO SLEEP! INCLUDING YOU TWO.
THIS IS NO TIME TO SETTLE SCORES!
SON OF A BITCH!
BASTARD!

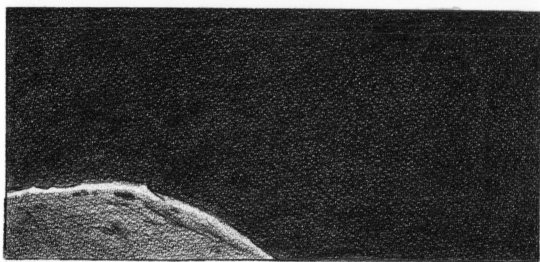

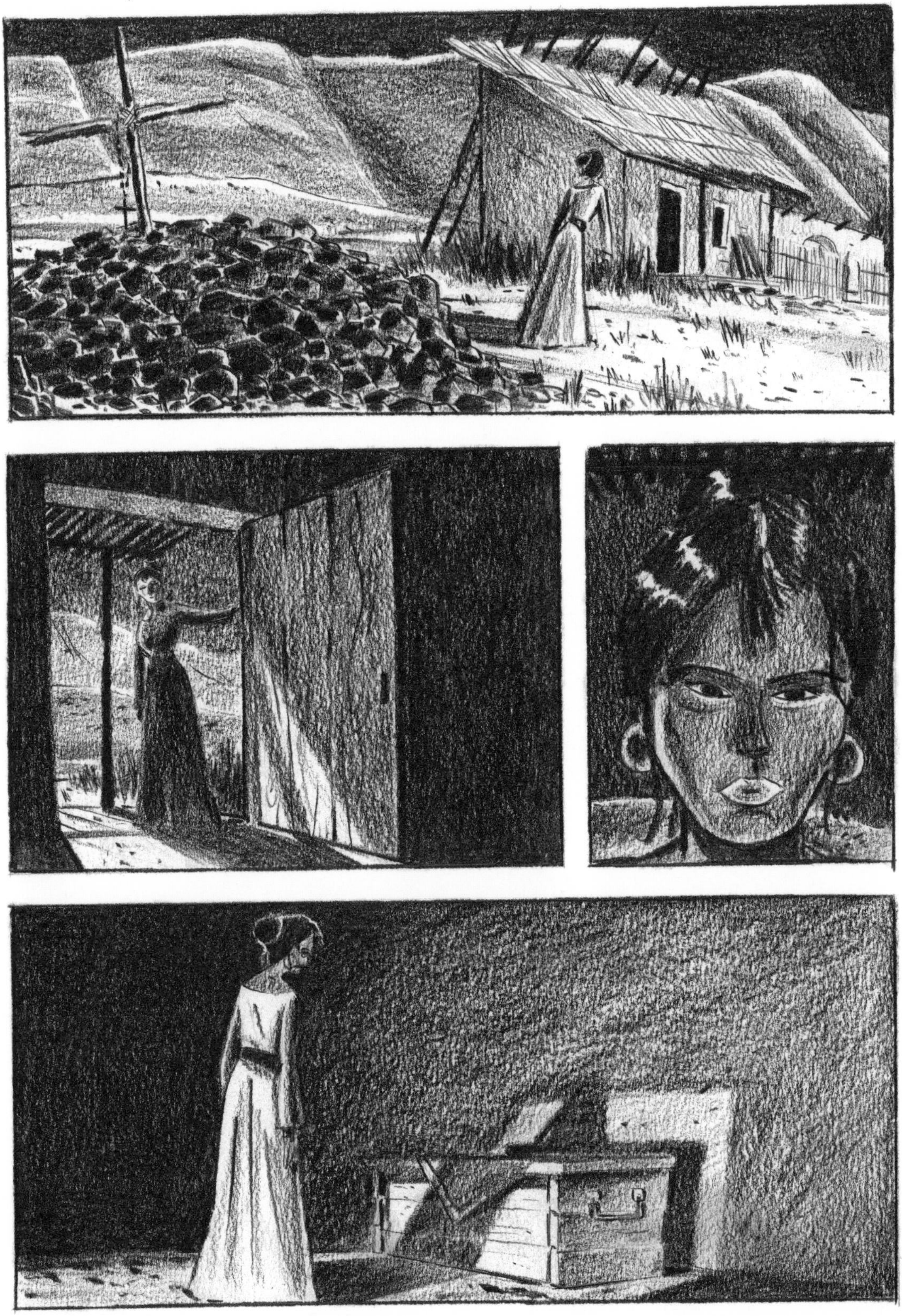

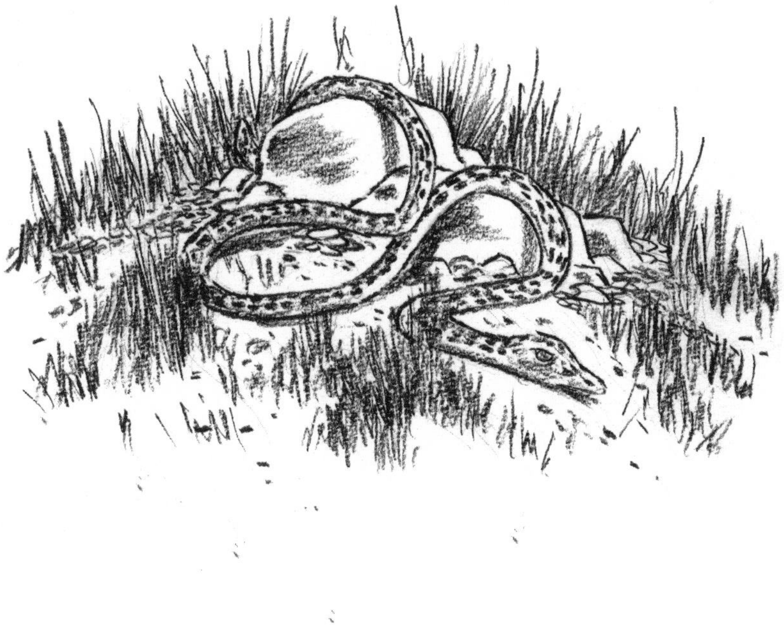

CHAPTER FIVE

DOUBLE SIXES

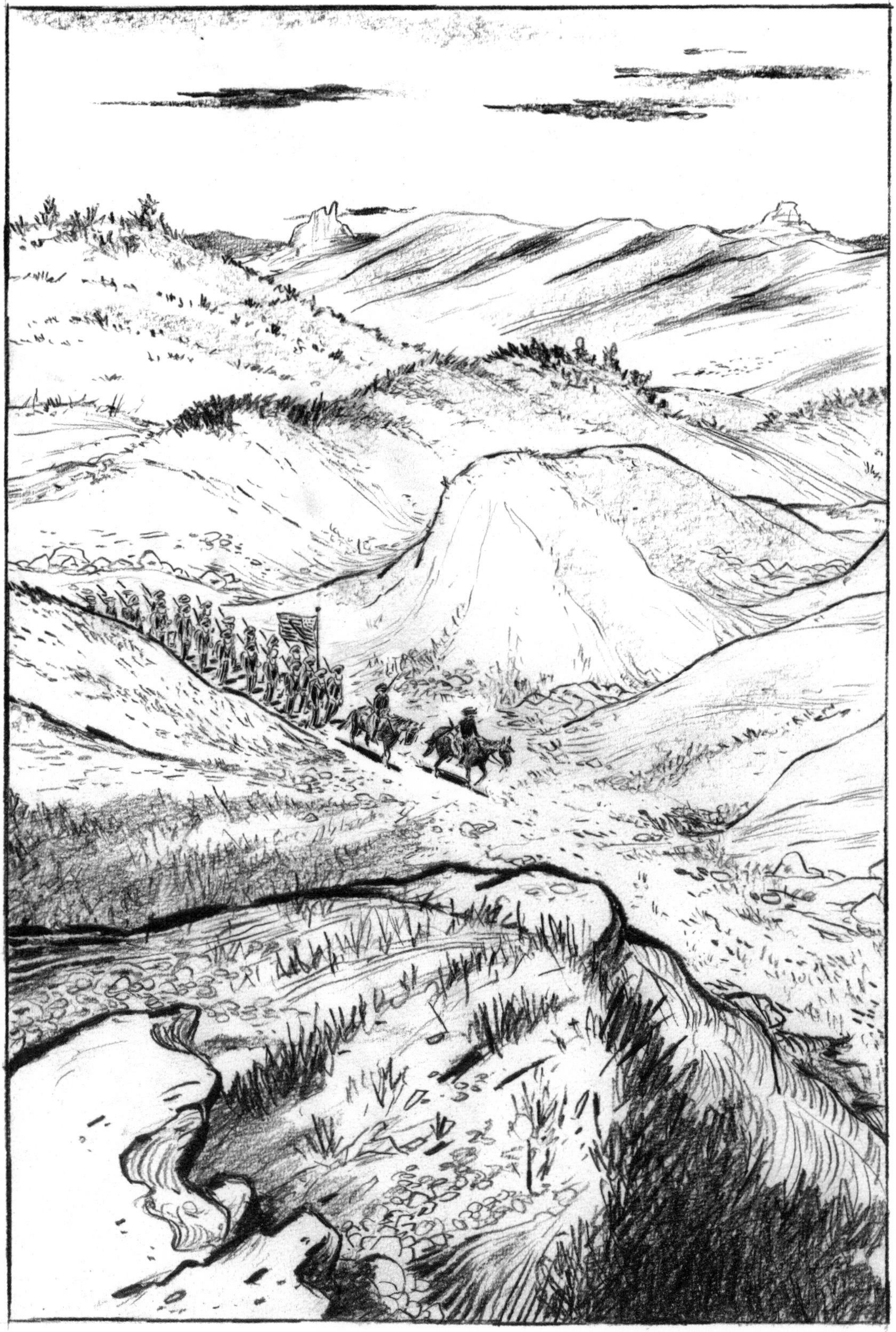

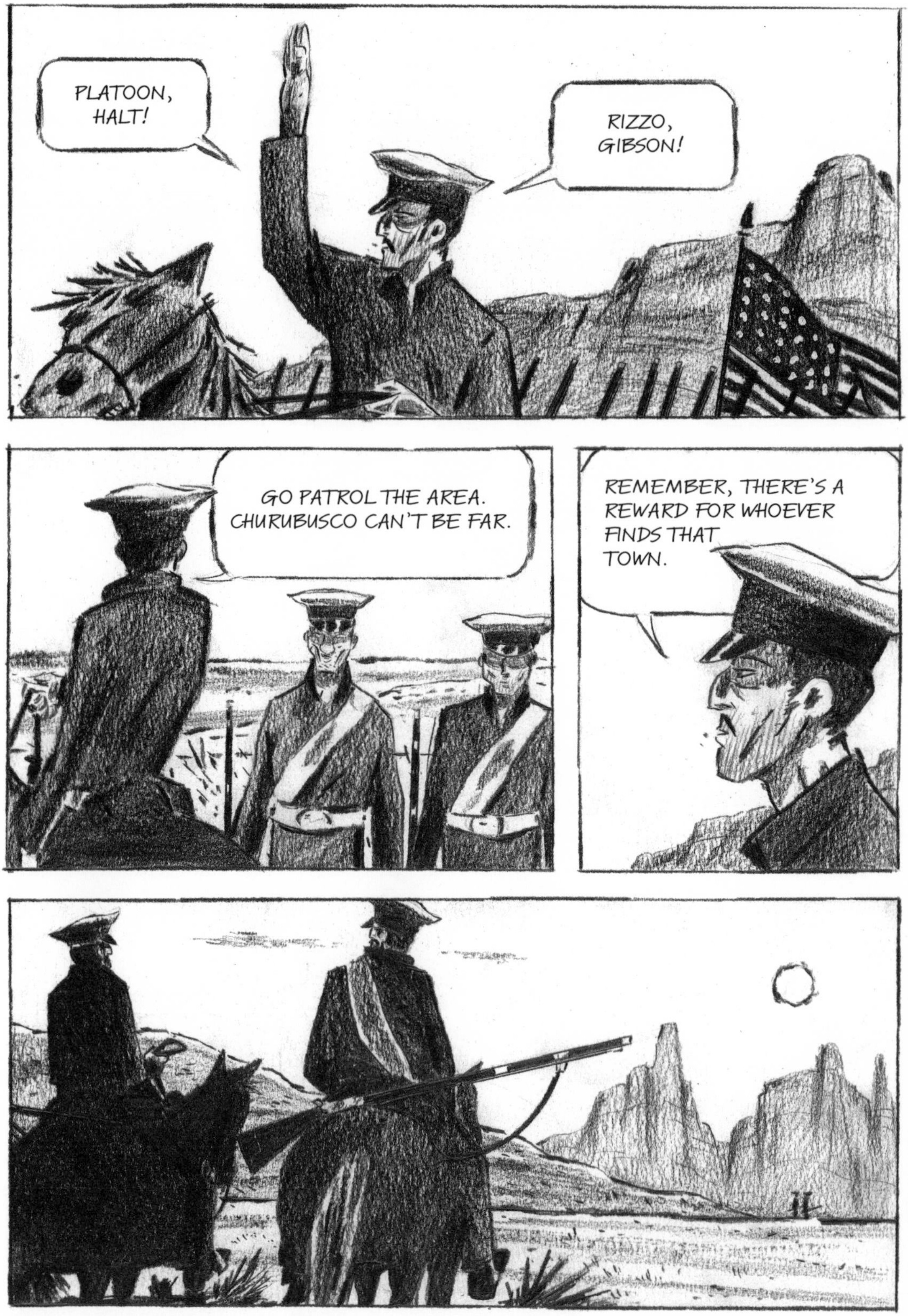
PLATOON, HALT!
RIZZO, GIBSON!
GO PATROL THE AREA. CHURUBUSCO CAN'T BE FAR.
REMEMBER, THERE'S A REWARD FOR WHOEVER FINDS THAT TOWN.

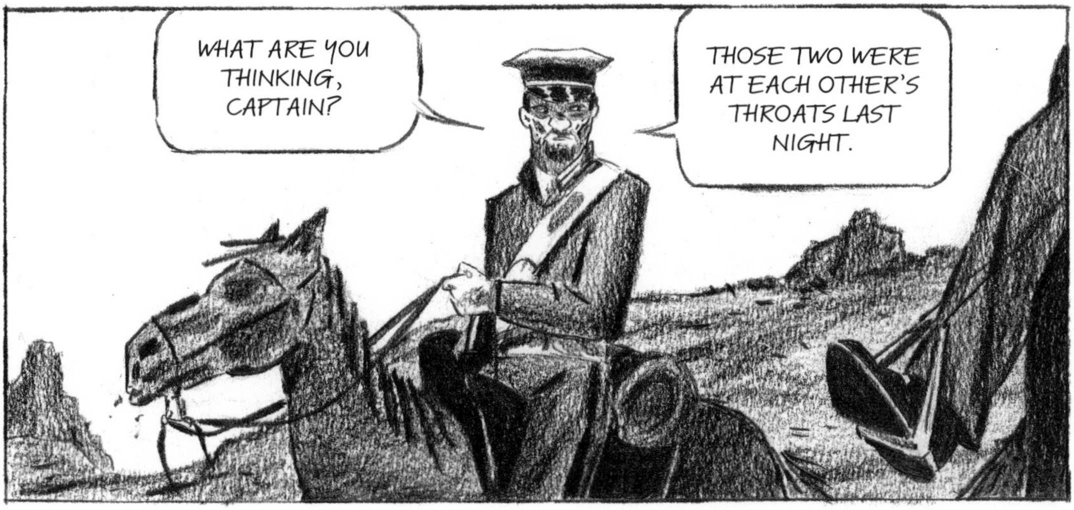
WHAT ARE YOU THINKING, CAPTAIN?
THOSE TWO WERE AT EACH OTHER'S THROATS LAST NIGHT.

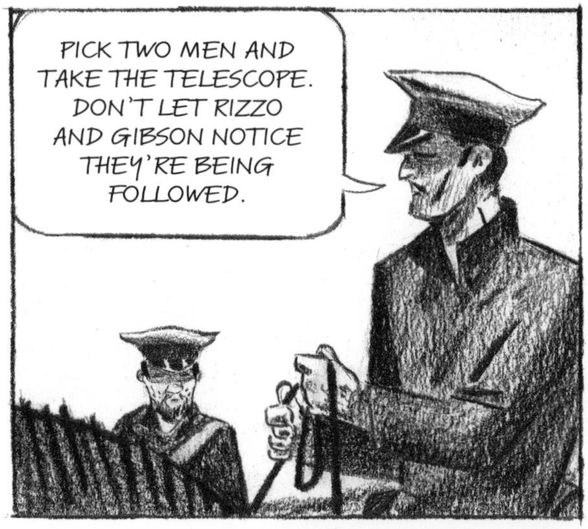
PICK TWO MEN AND TAKE THE TELESCOPE. DON'T LET RIZZO AND GIBSON NOTICE THEY'RE BEING FOLLOWED.

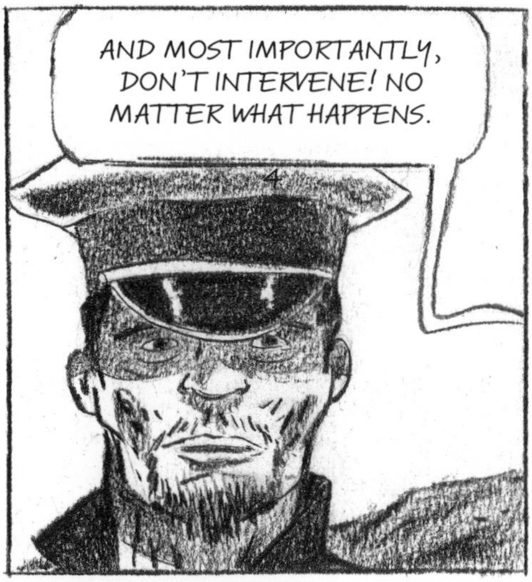
AND MOST IMPORTANTLY, DON'T INTERVENE! NO MATTER WHAT HAPPENS.

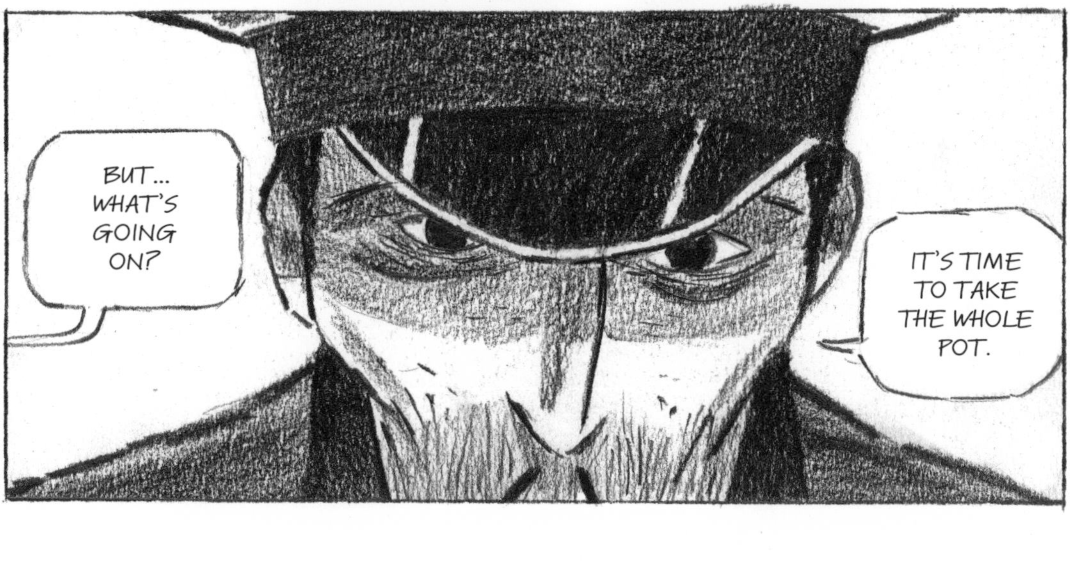
BUT... WHAT'S GOING ON?
IT'S TIME TO TAKE THE WHOLE POT.

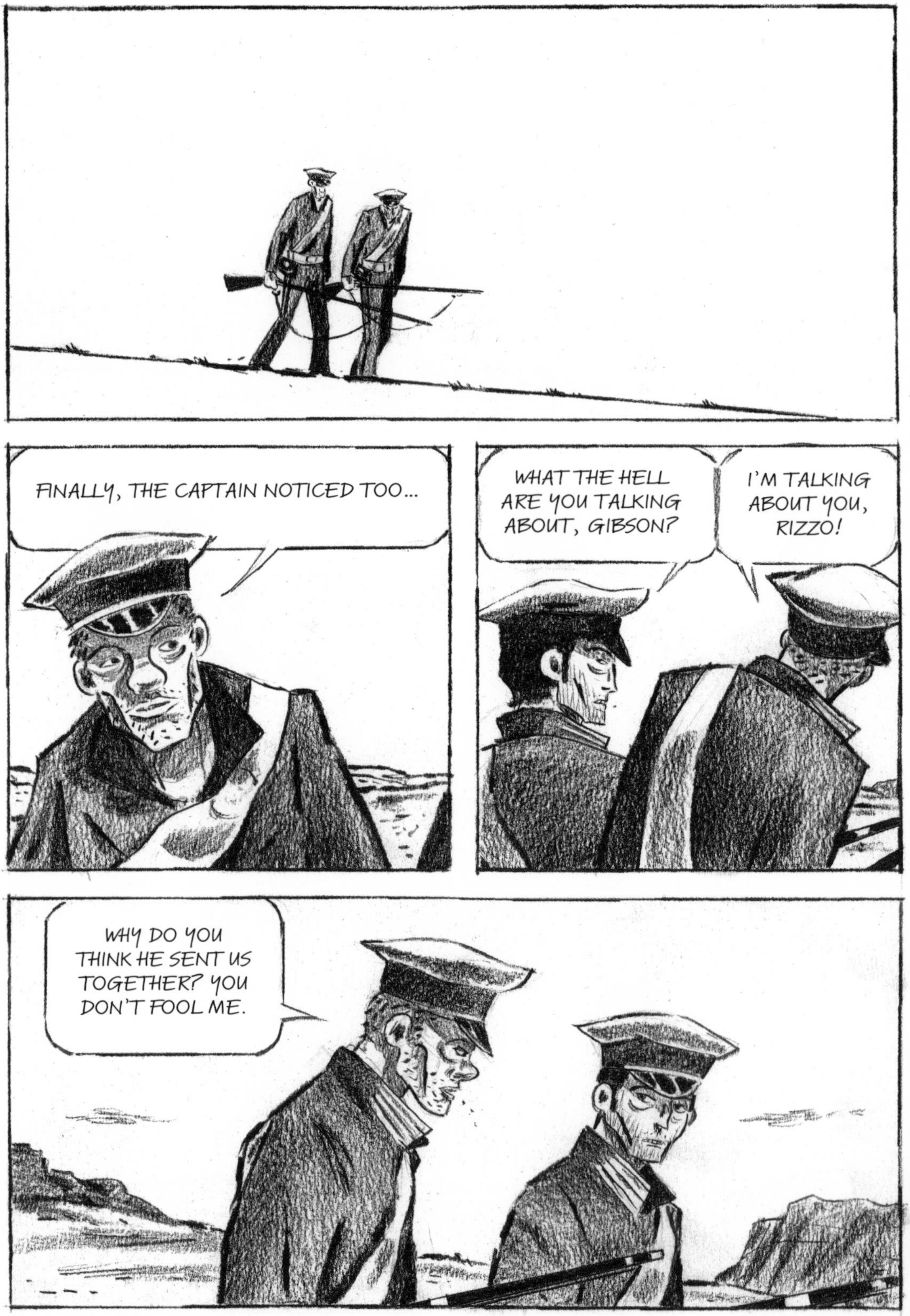
FINALLY, THE CAPTAIN NOTICED TOO...
WHAT THE HELL ARE YOU TALKING ABOUT, GIBSON?
I'M TALKING ABOUT YOU, RIZZO!
WHY DO YOU THINK HE SENT US TOGETHER? YOU DON'T FOOL ME.

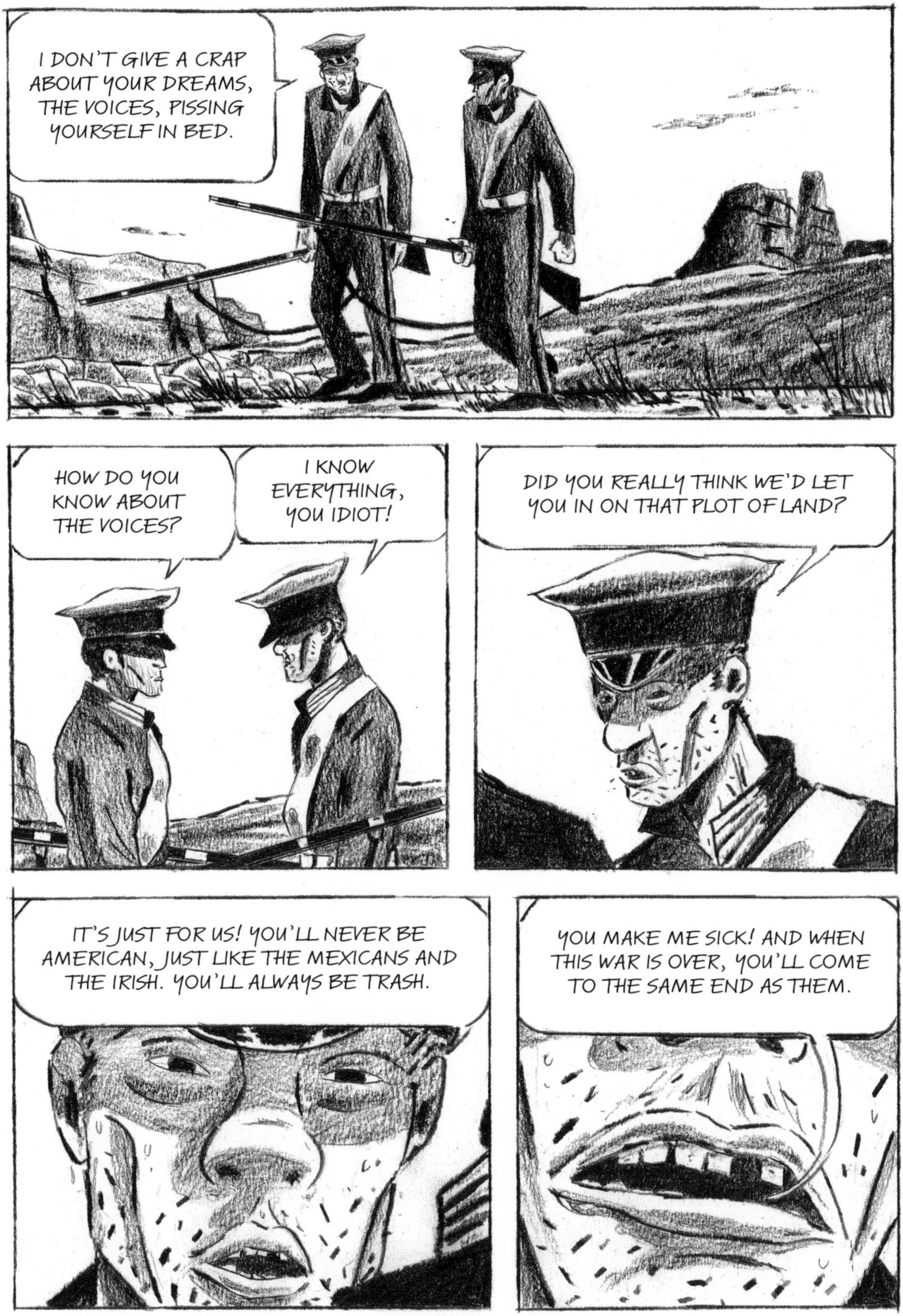
I DON'T GIVE A CRAP ABOUT YOUR DREAMS, THE VOICES, PISSING YOURSELF IN BED.
HOW DO YOU KNOW ABOUT THE VOICES?
I KNOW EVERYTHING, YOU IDIOT!
DID YOU REALLY THINK WE'D LET YOU IN ON THAT PLOT OF LAND?
IT'S JUST FOR US! YOU'LL NEVER BE AMERICAN, JUST LIKE THE MEXICANS AND THE IRISH. YOU'LL ALWAYS BE TRASH.
YOU MAKE ME SICK! AND WHEN THIS WAR IS OVER, YOU'LL COME TO THE SAME END AS THEM.

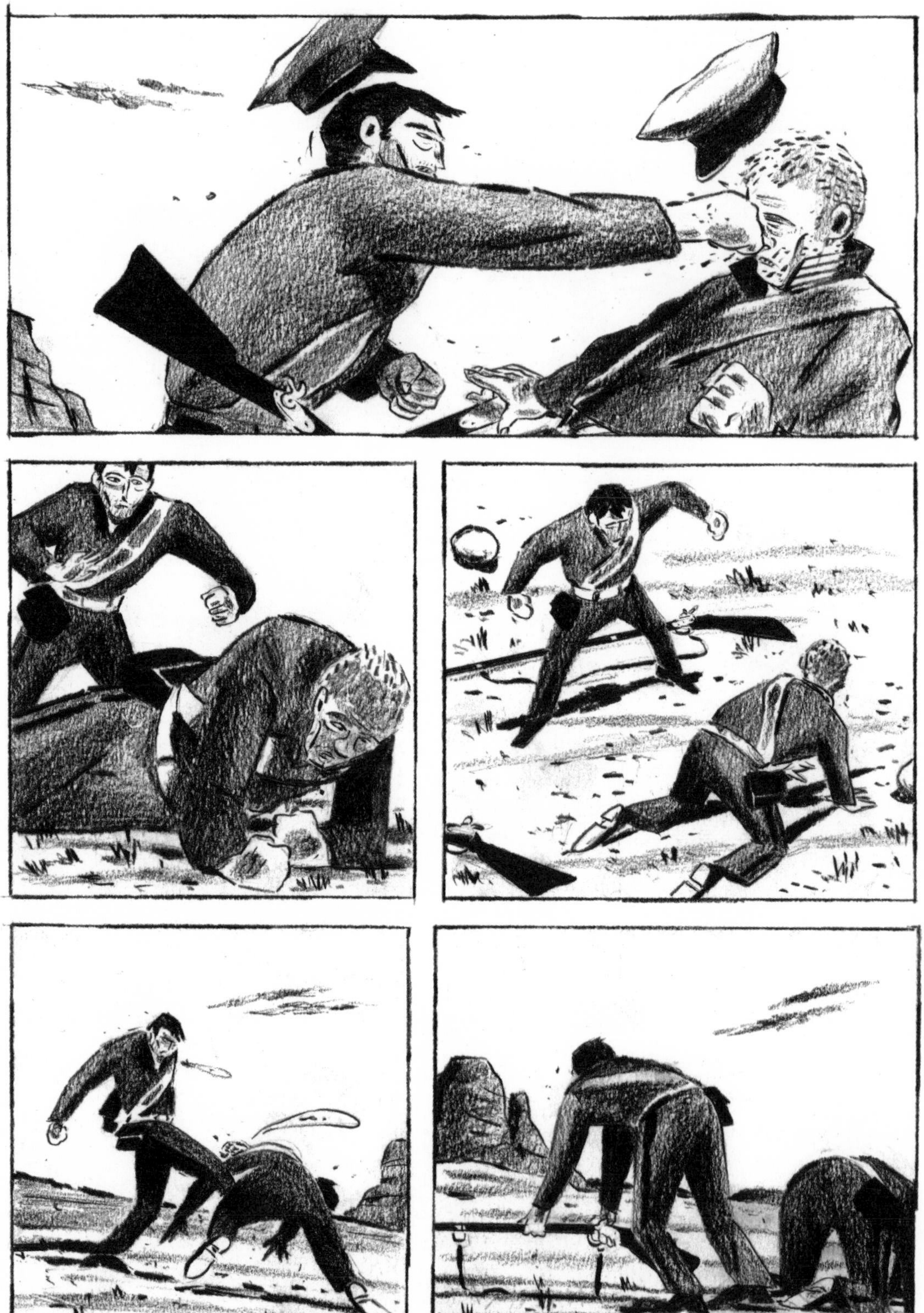

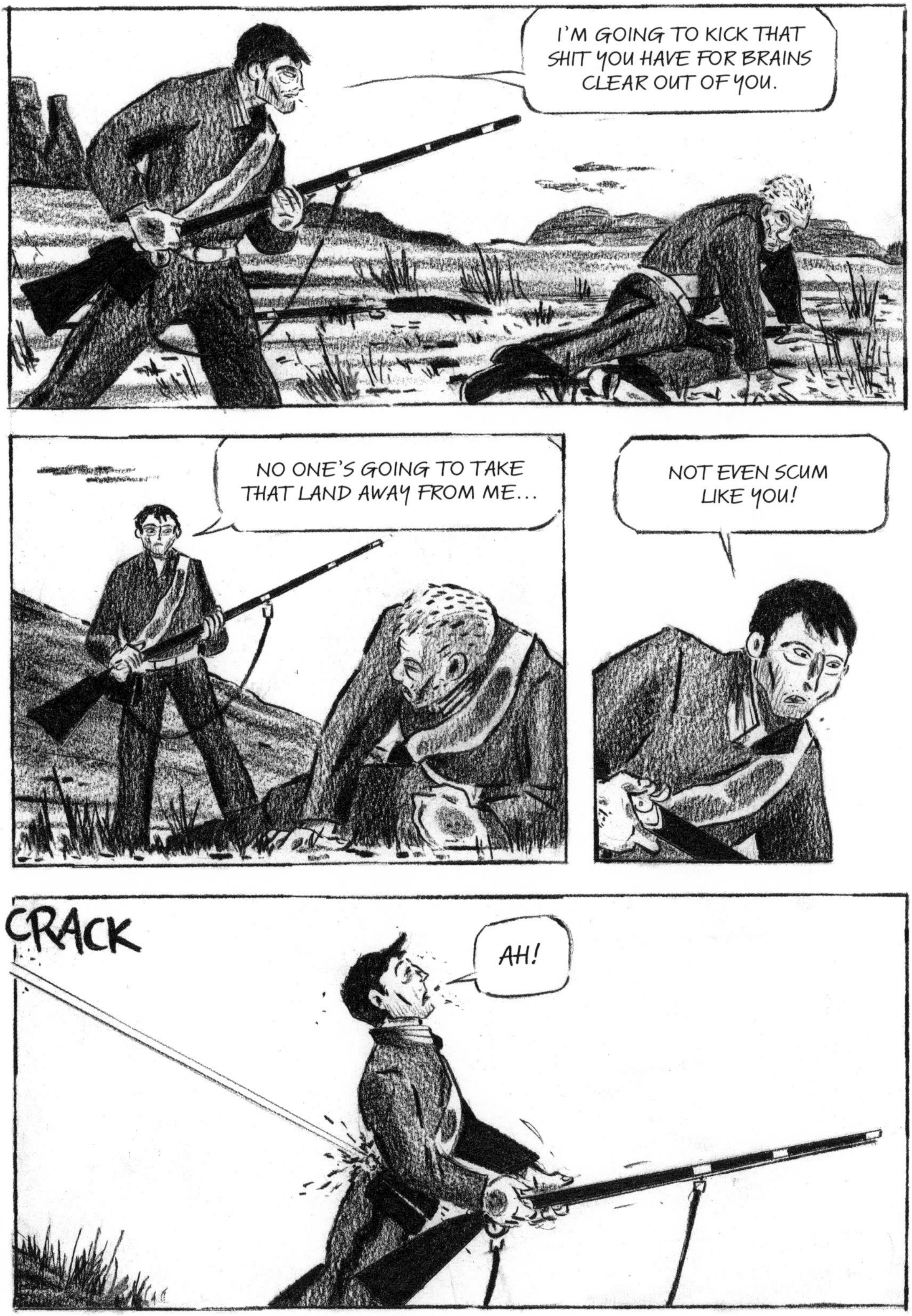
I'M GOING TO KICK THAT SHIT YOU HAVE FOR BRAINS CLEAR OUT OF YOU.
NO ONE'S GOING TO TAKE THAT LAND AWAY FROM ME...
NOT EVEN SCUM LIKE YOU!
CRACK
AH!

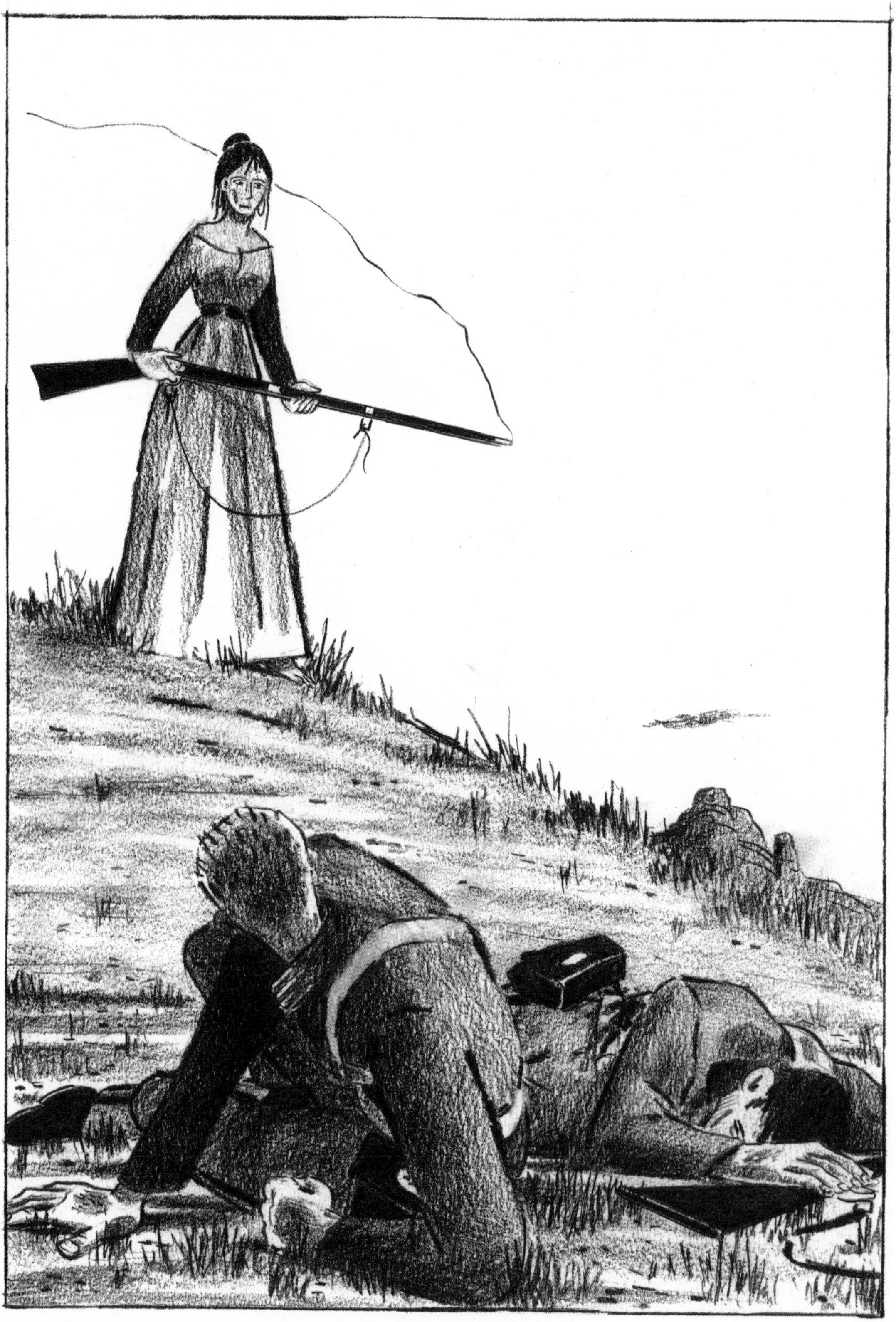

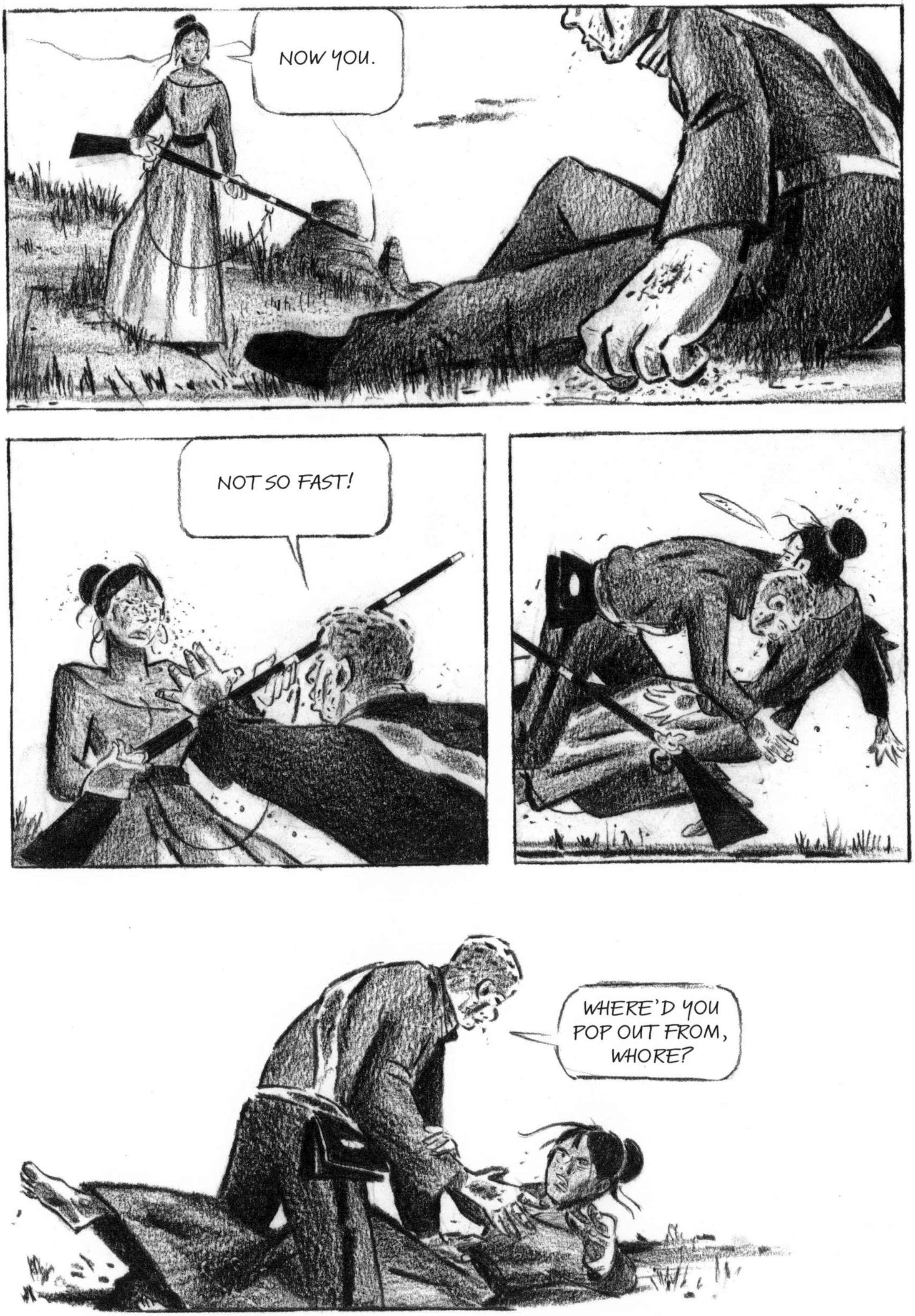
NOW YOU.
NOT SO FAST!
WHERE'D YOU POP OUT FROM, WHORE?

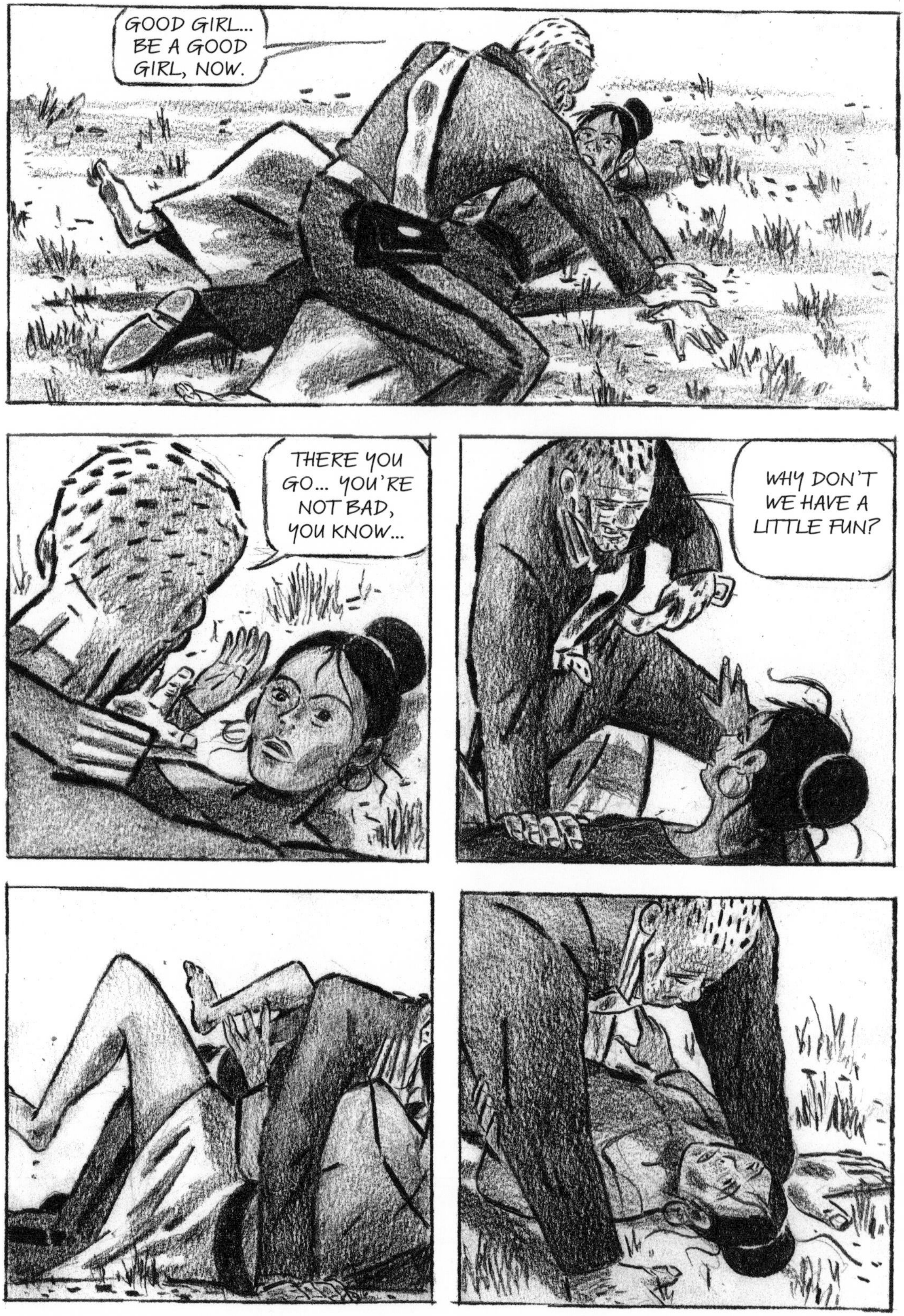
GOOD GIRL... BE A GOOD GIRL, NOW.
THERE YOU GO... YOU'RE NOT BAD, YOU KNOW...
WHY DON'T WE HAVE A LITTLE FUN?

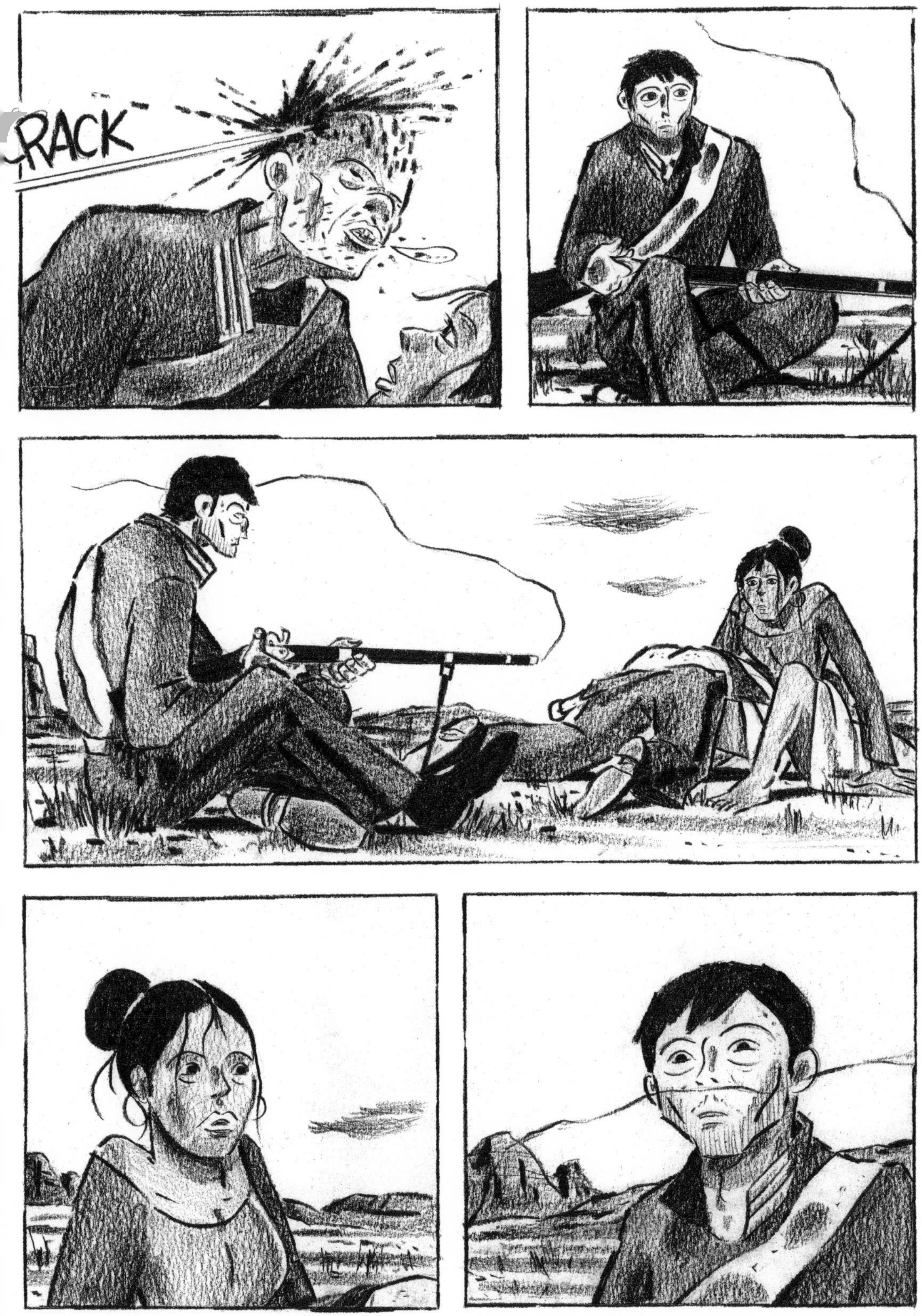
CRACK

CHAPTER SIX

THE FORBIDDEN
GARDEN

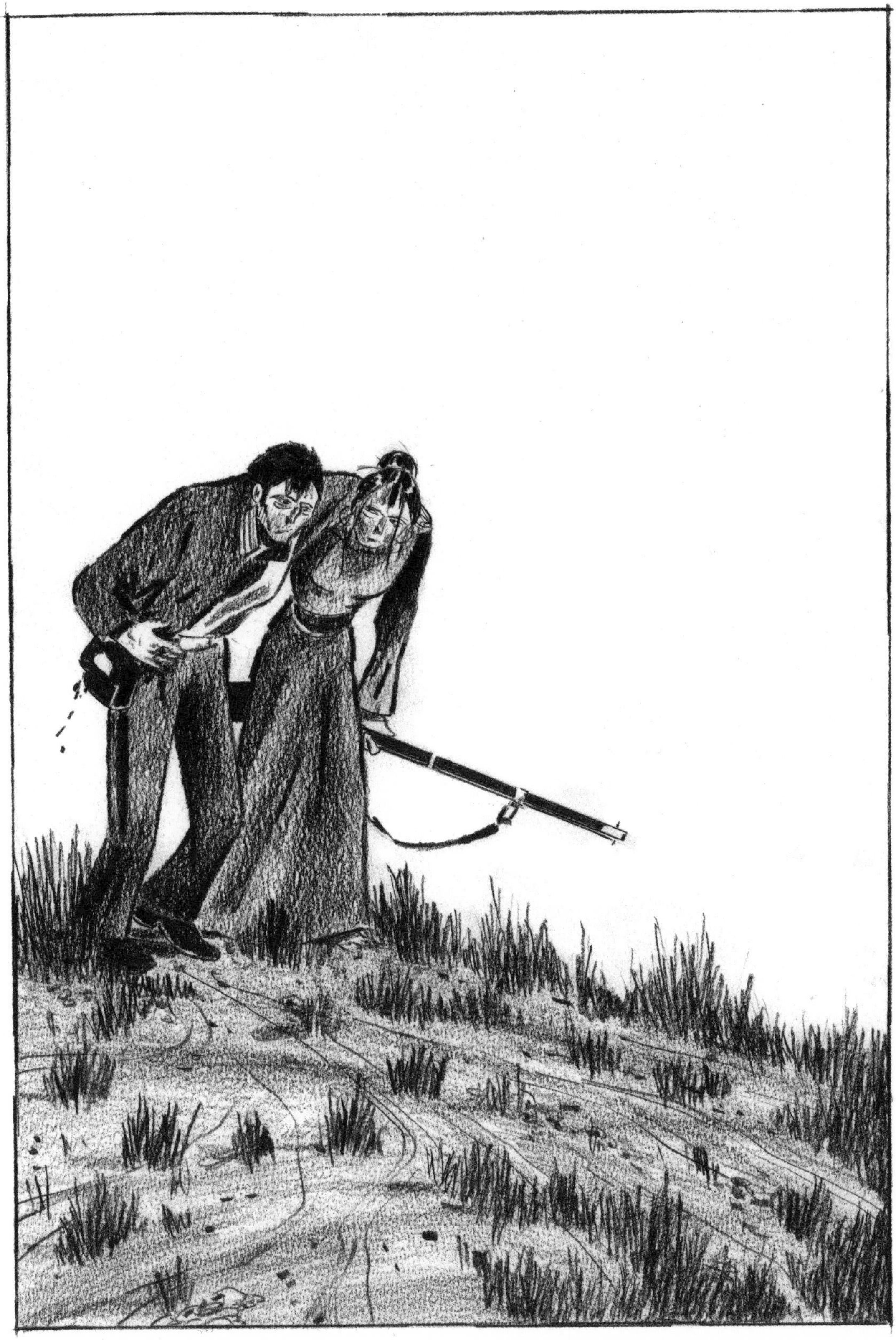

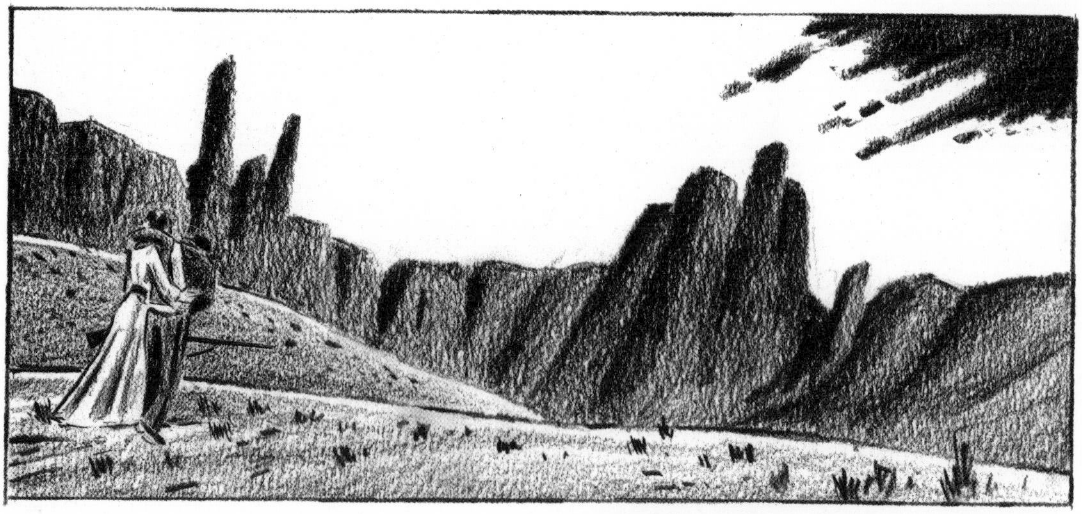
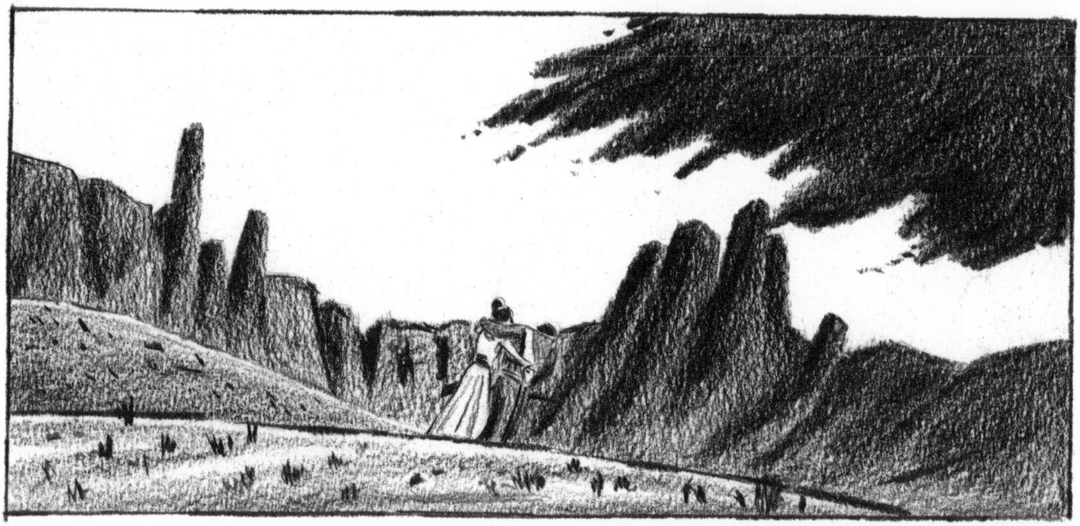
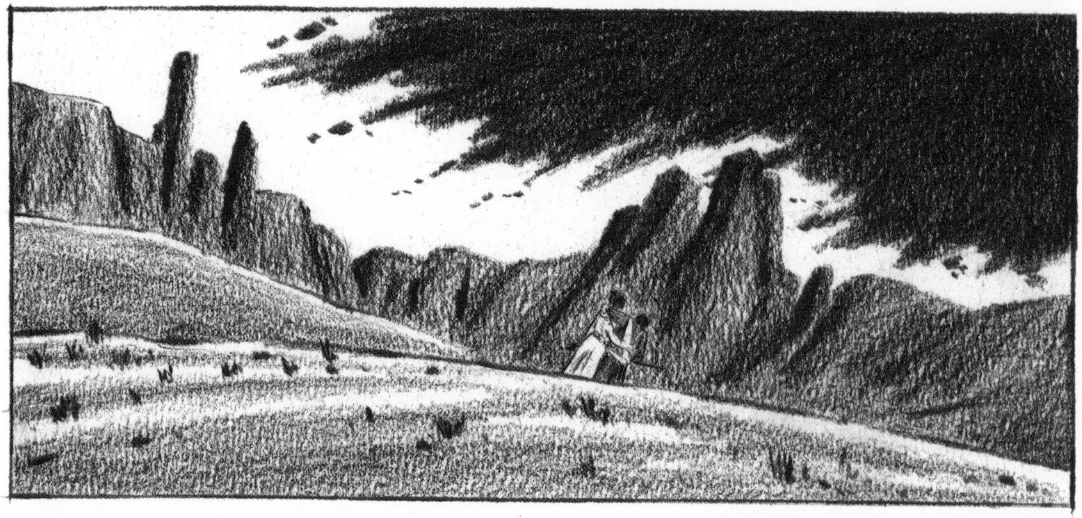

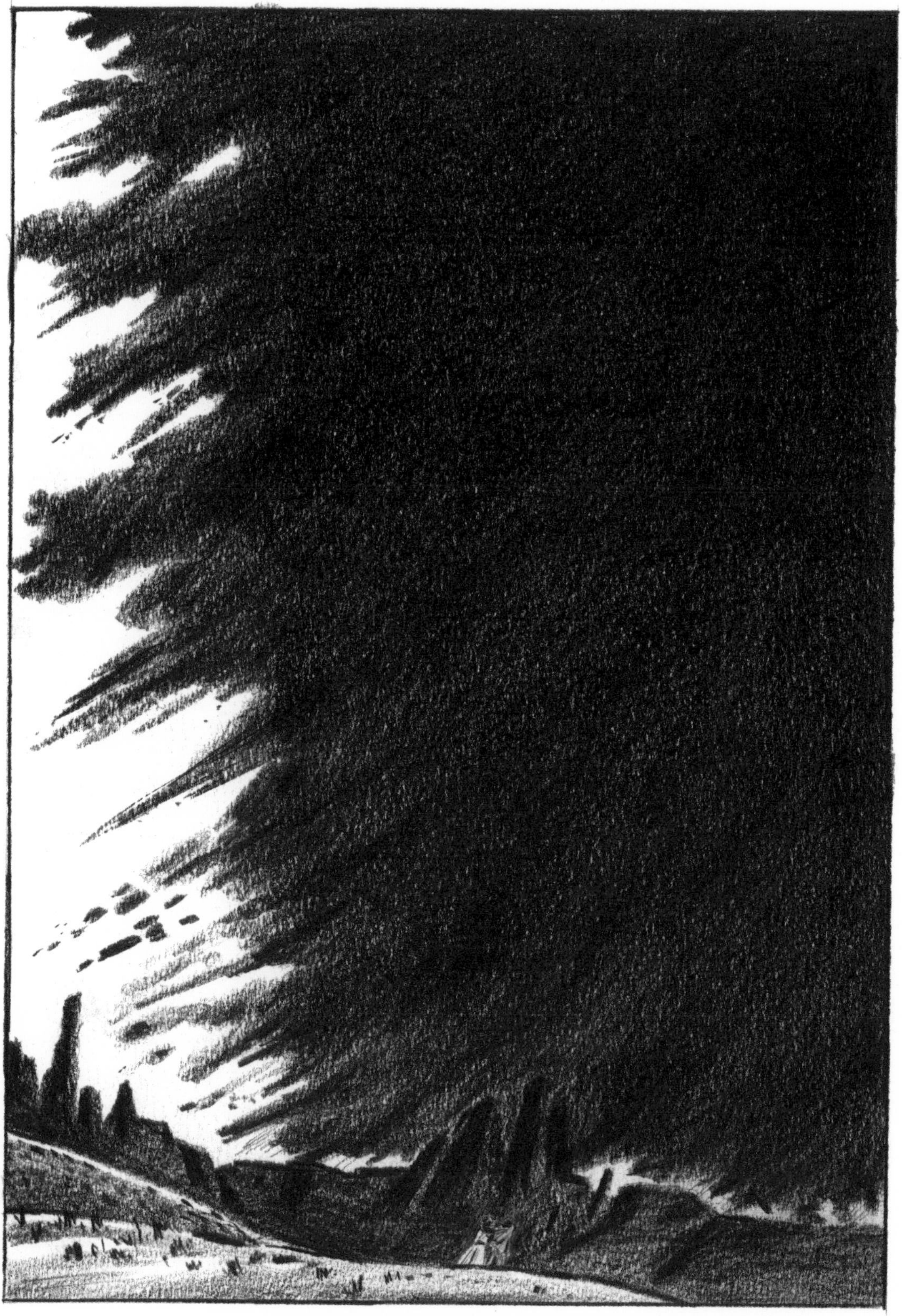

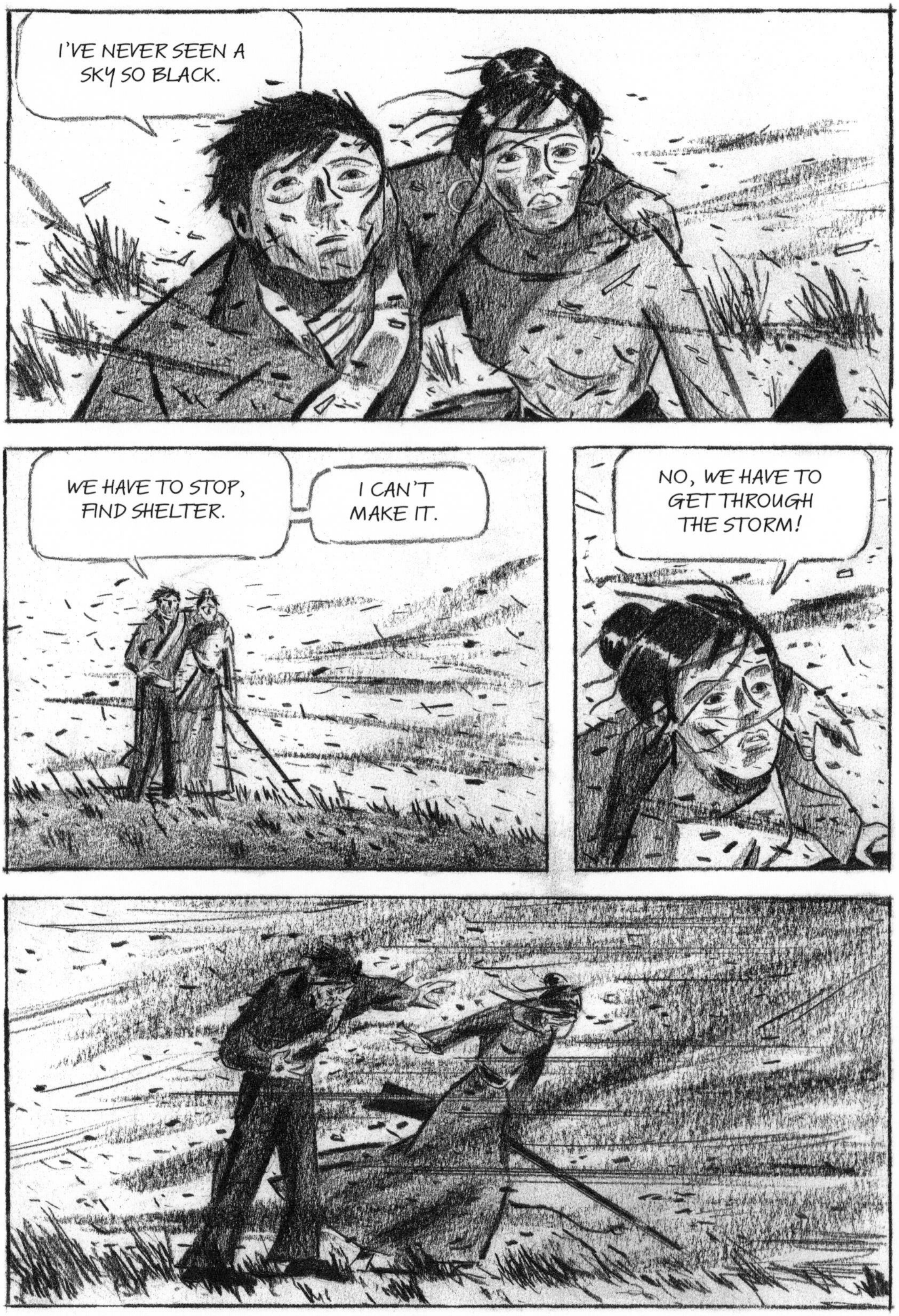
I'VE NEVER SEEN A SKY SO BLACK.
WE HAVE TO STOP, FIND SHELTER.
I CAN'T MAKE IT.
NO, WE HAVE TO GET THROUGH THE STORM!

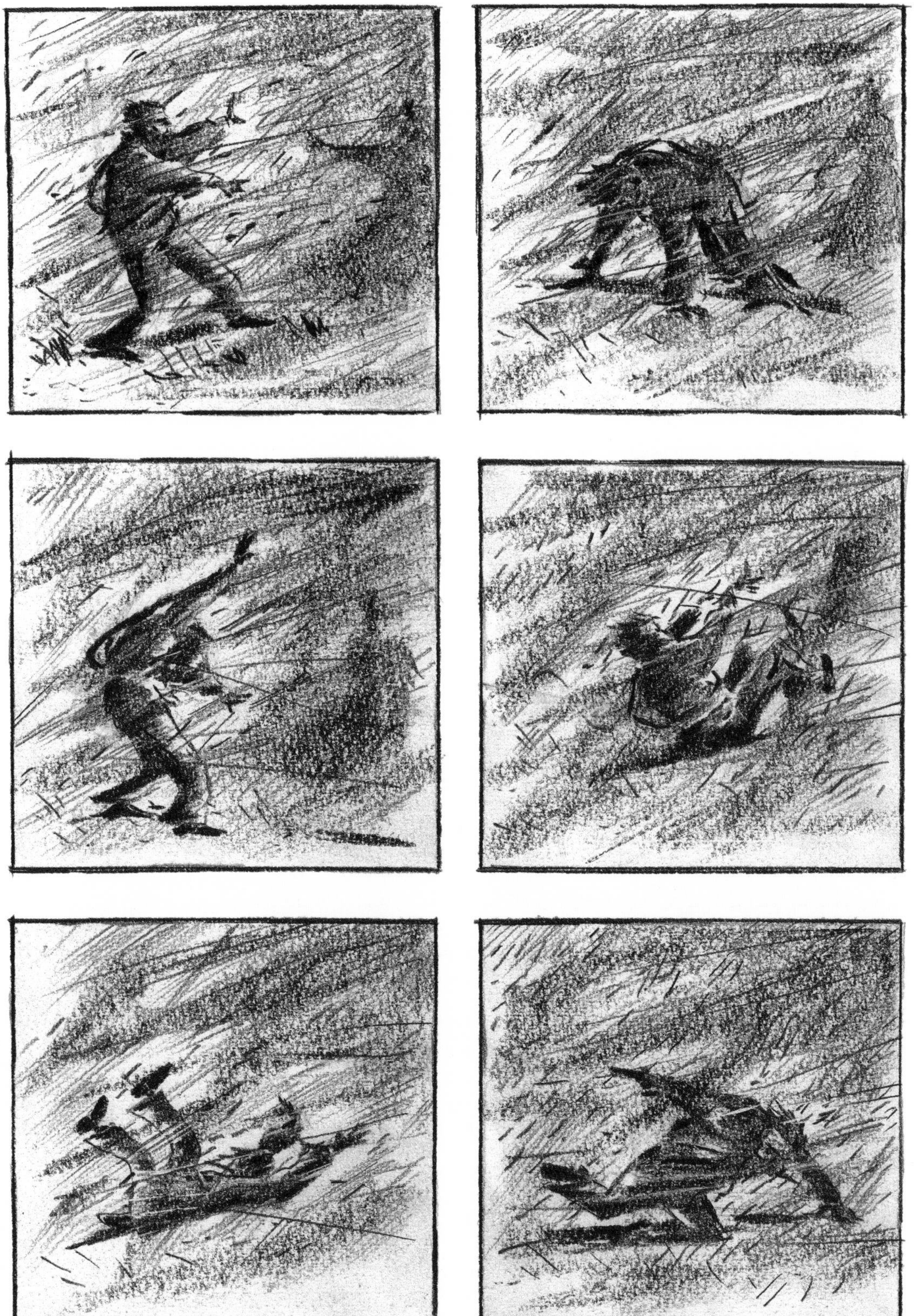

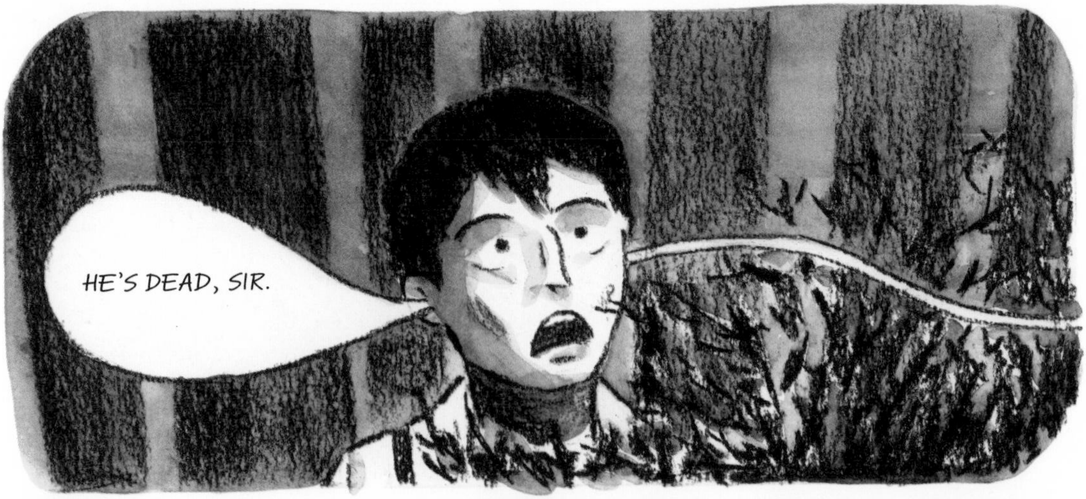
HE'S DEAD, SIR.

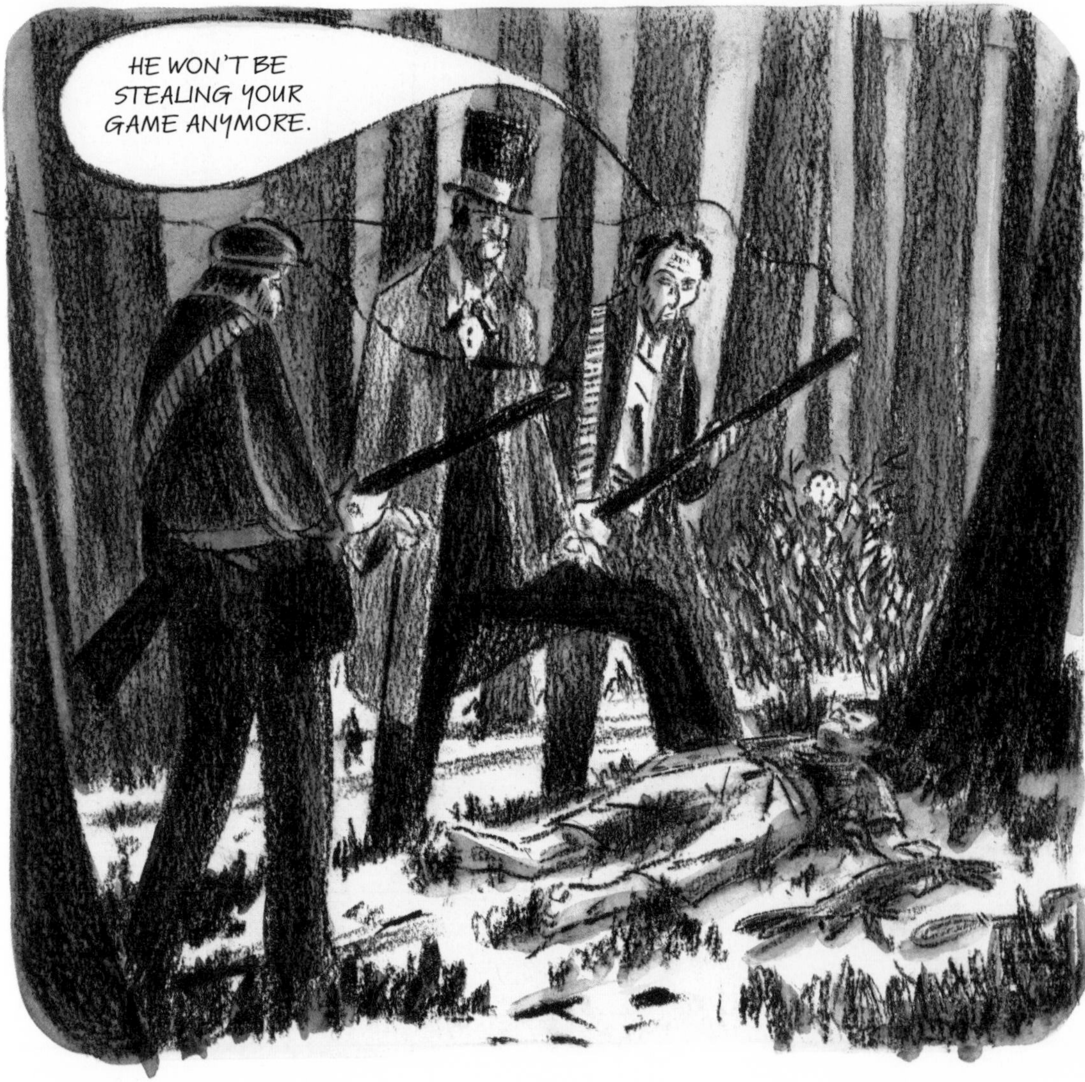
HE WON'T BE STEALING YOUR GAME ANYMORE.

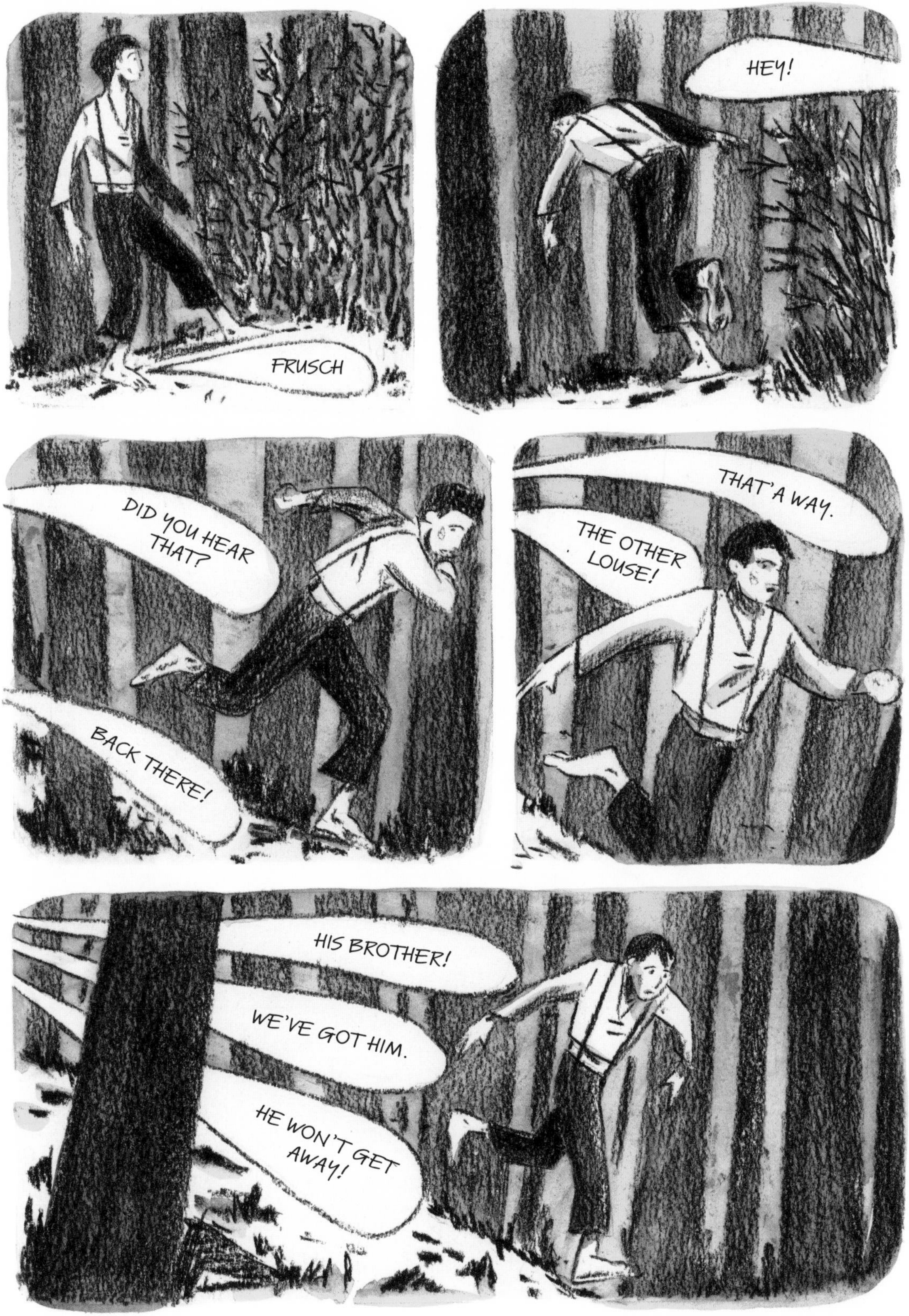
FRUSCH
HEY!
DID YOU HEAR THAT?
BACK THERE!
THAT'A WAY.
THE OTHER LOUSE!
HIS BROTHER!
WE'VE GOT HIM.
HE WON'T GET AWAY!

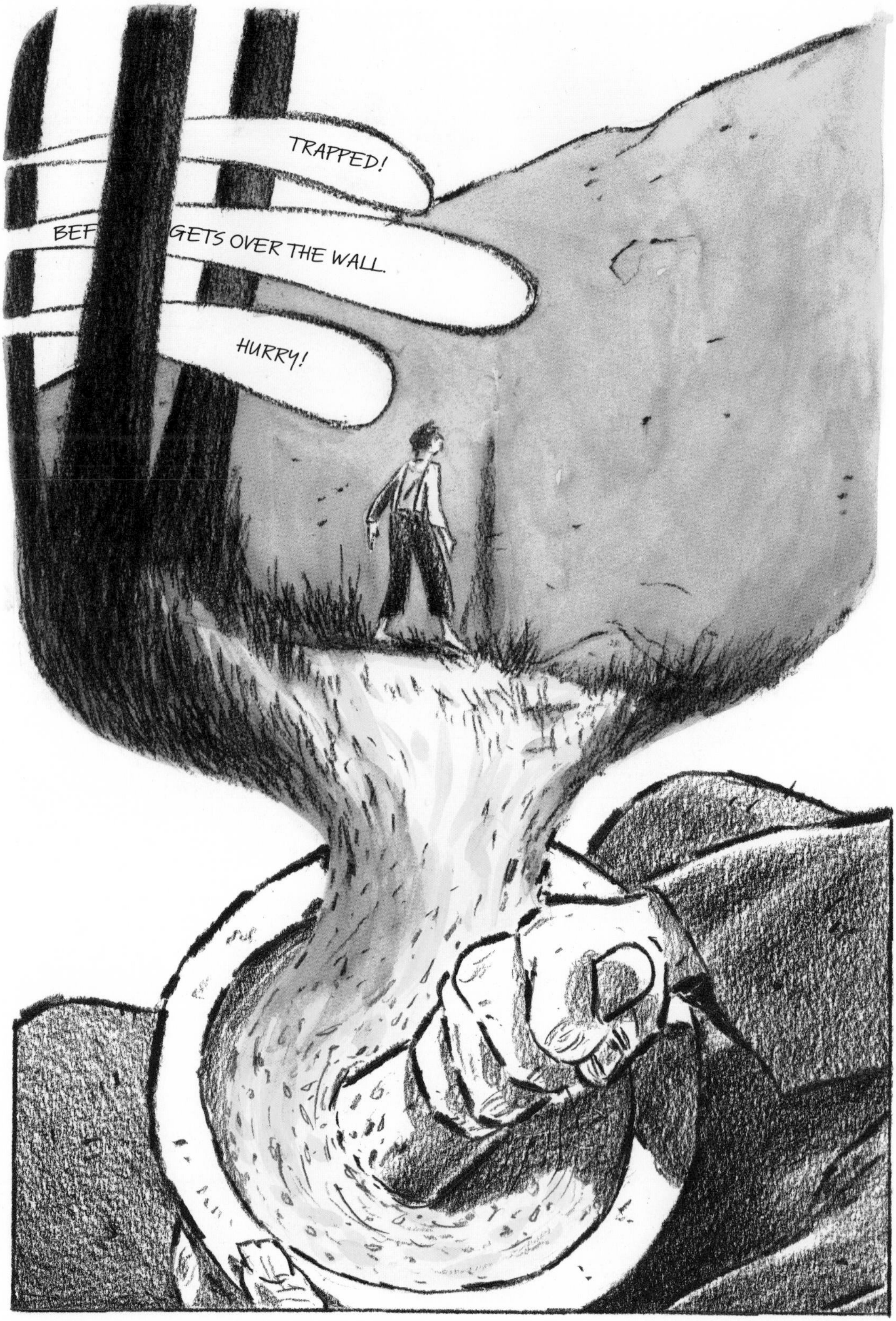
TRAPPED!
BEF GETS OVER THE WALL.
HURRY!

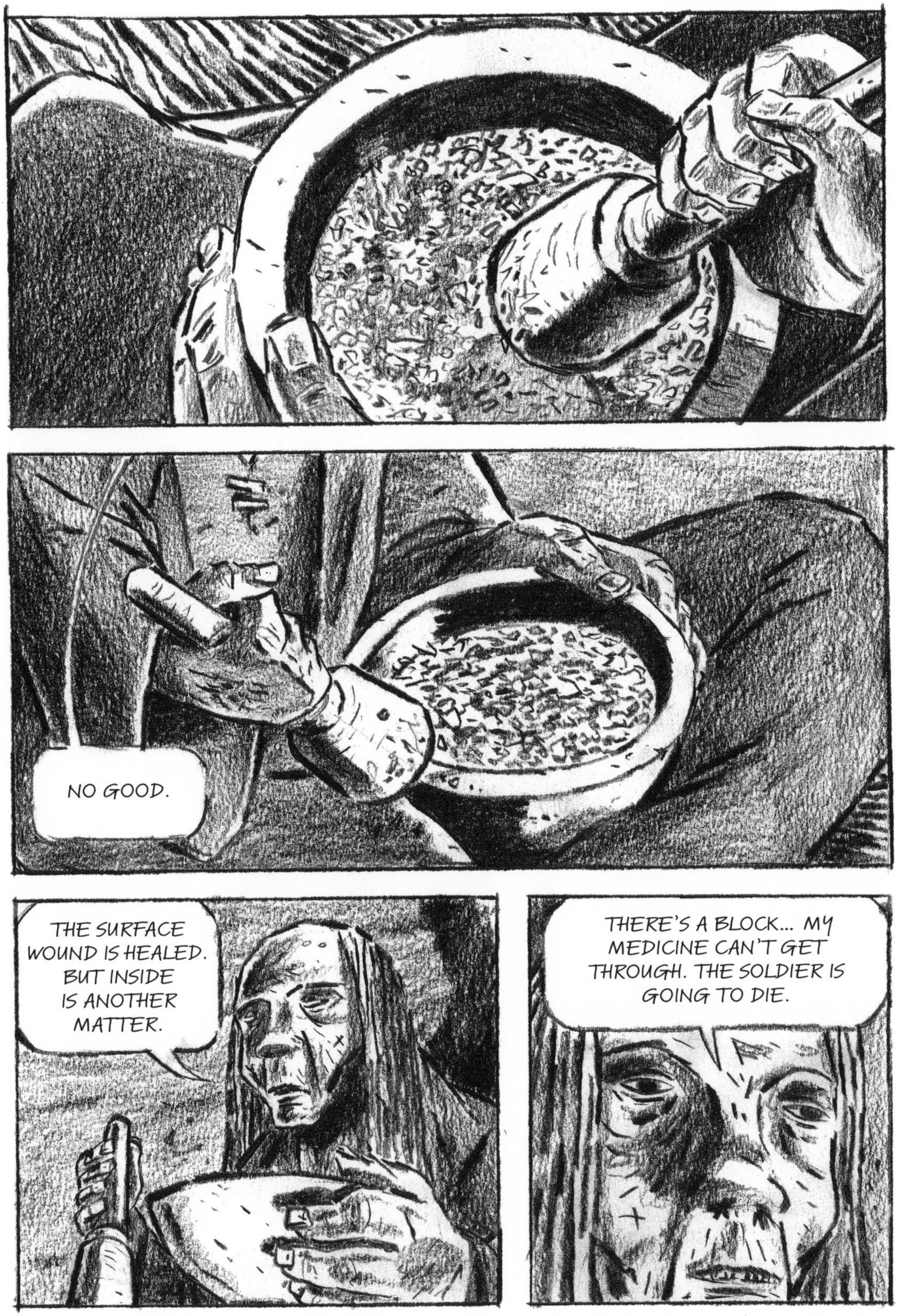
NO GOOD.
THE SURFACE WOUND IS HEALED. BUT INSIDE IS ANOTHER MATTER.
THERE'S A BLOCK... MY MEDICINE CAN'T GET THROUGH. THE SOLDIER IS GOING TO DIE.

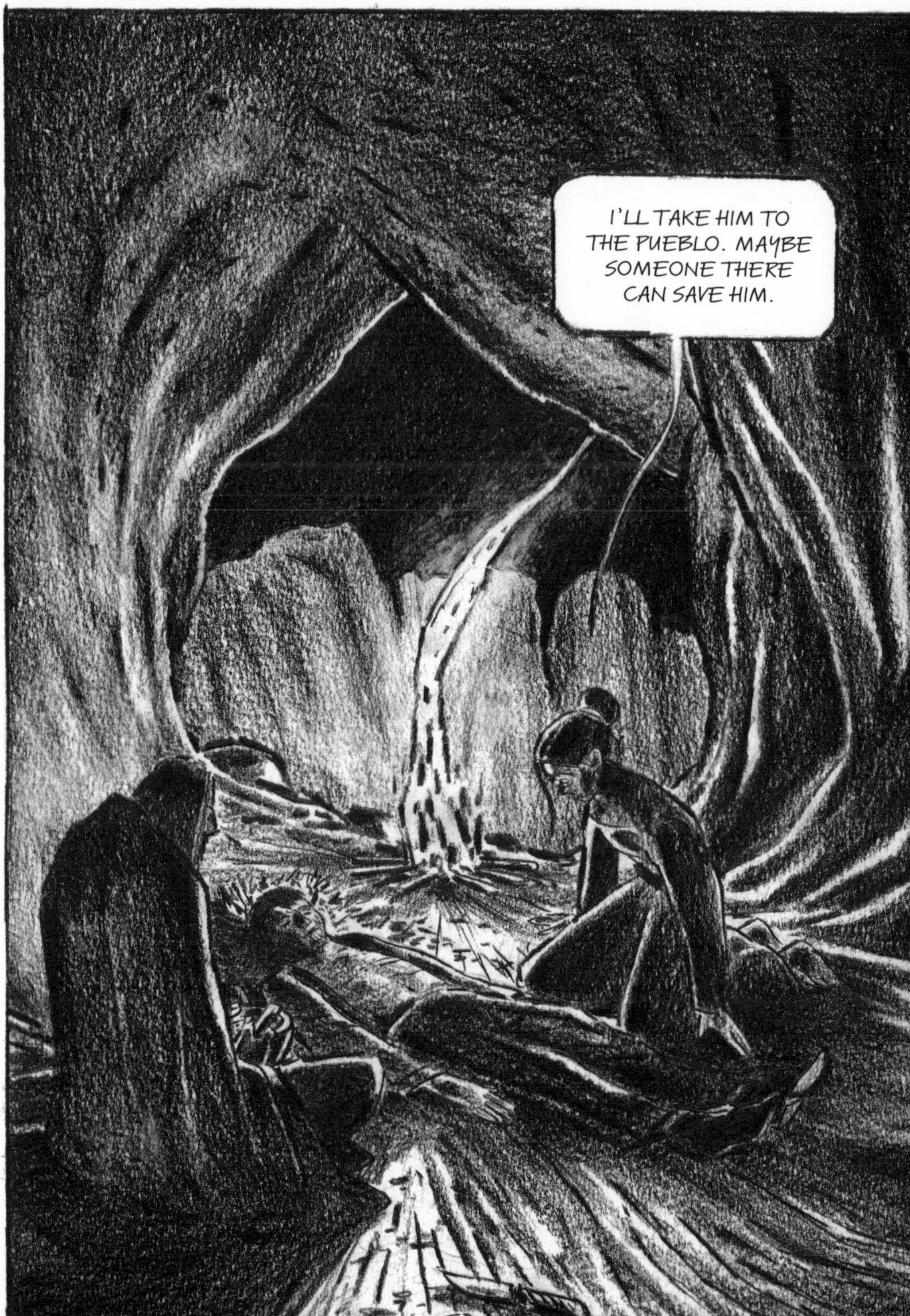
I'LL TAKE HIM TO THE PUEBLO. MAYBE SOMEONE THERE CAN SAVE HIM.

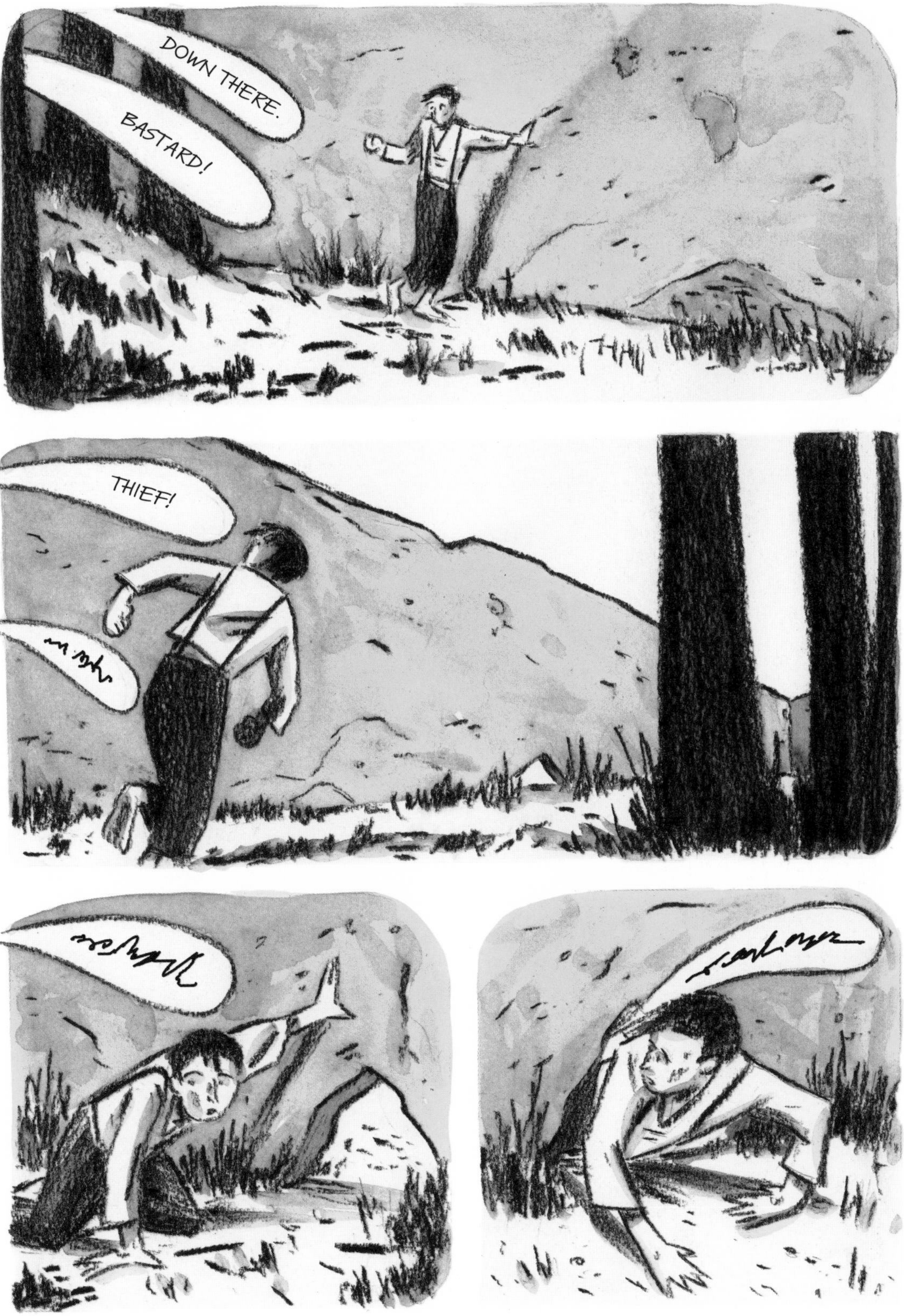
DOWN THERE.
BASTARD!
THIEF!

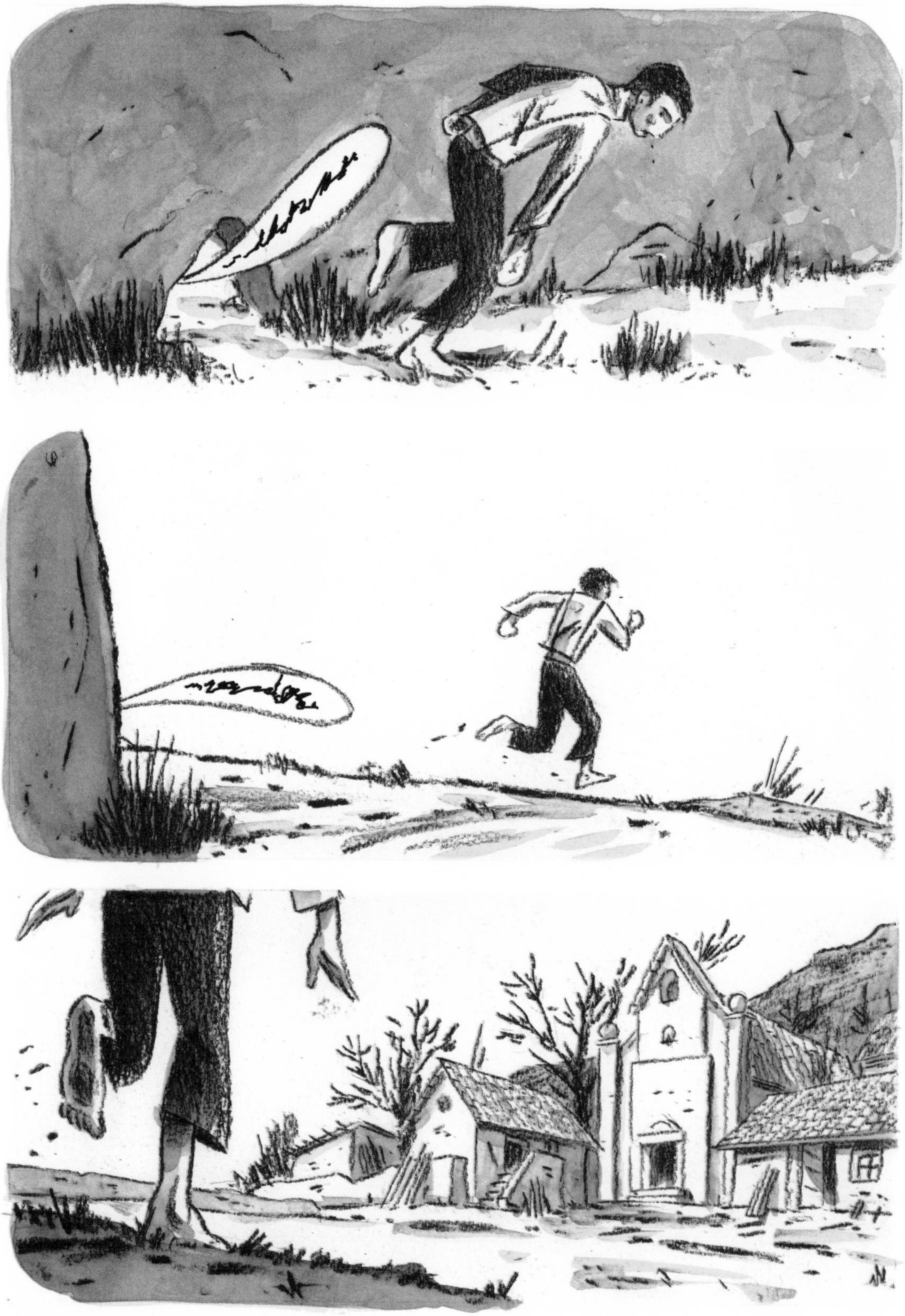

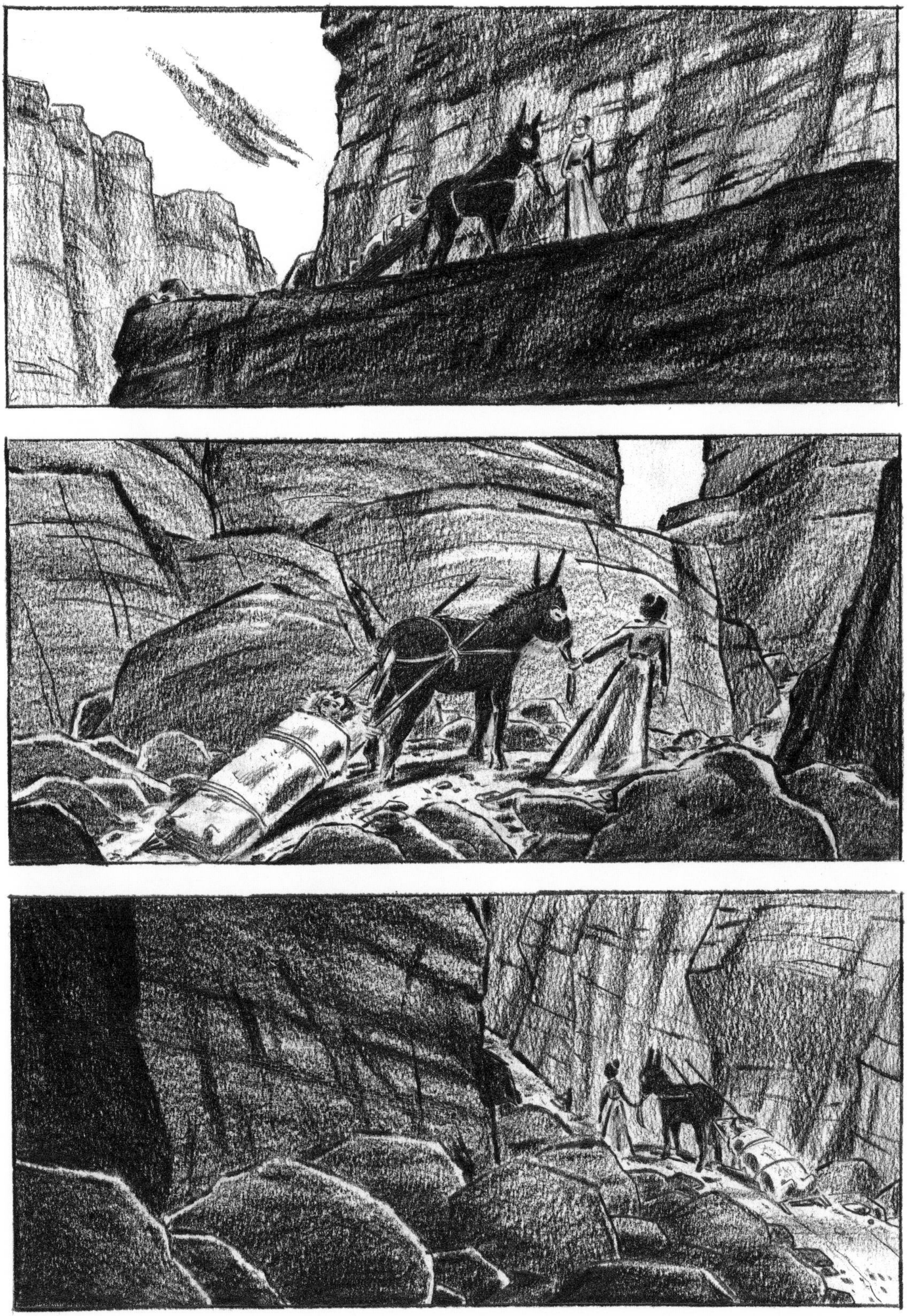

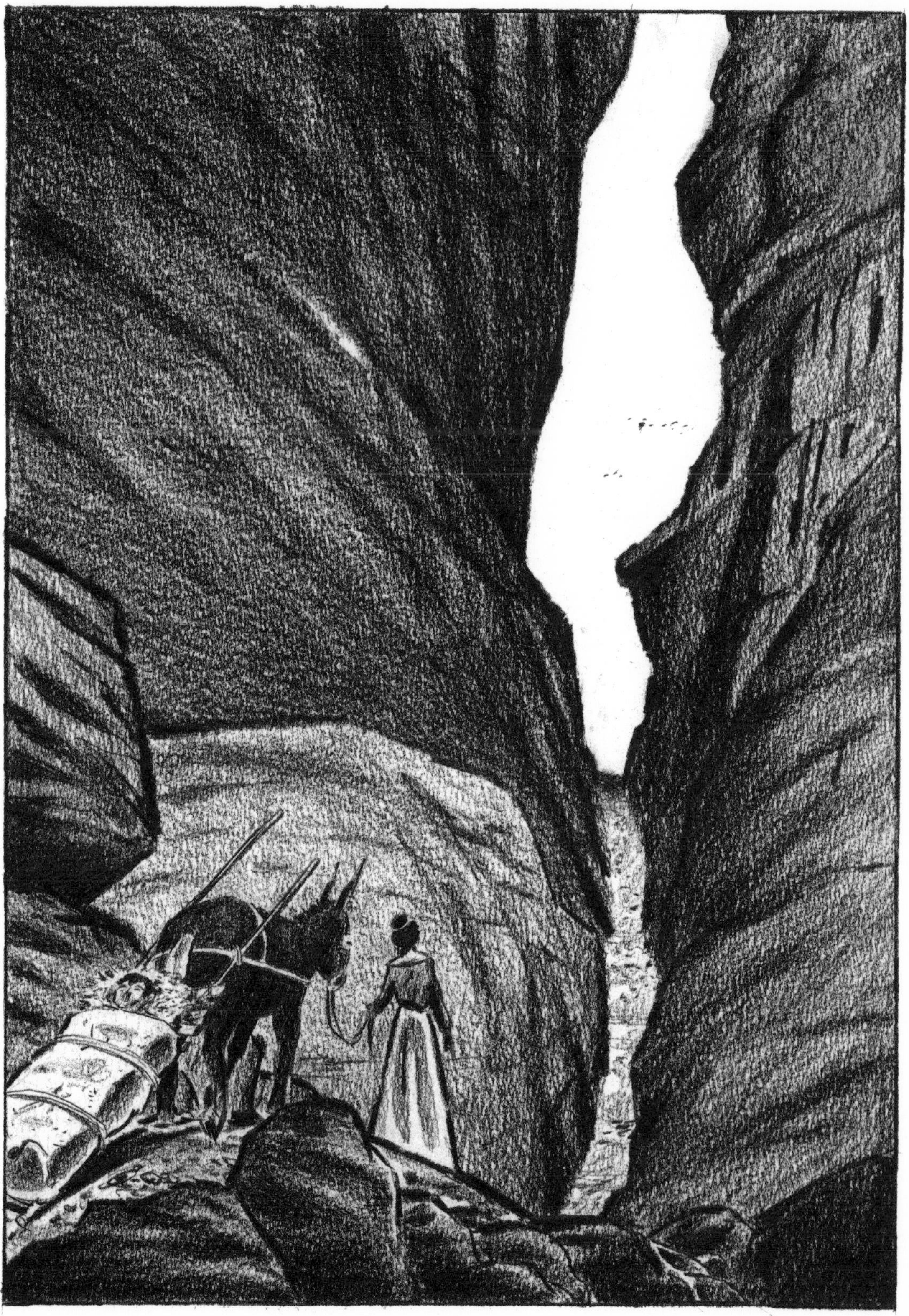

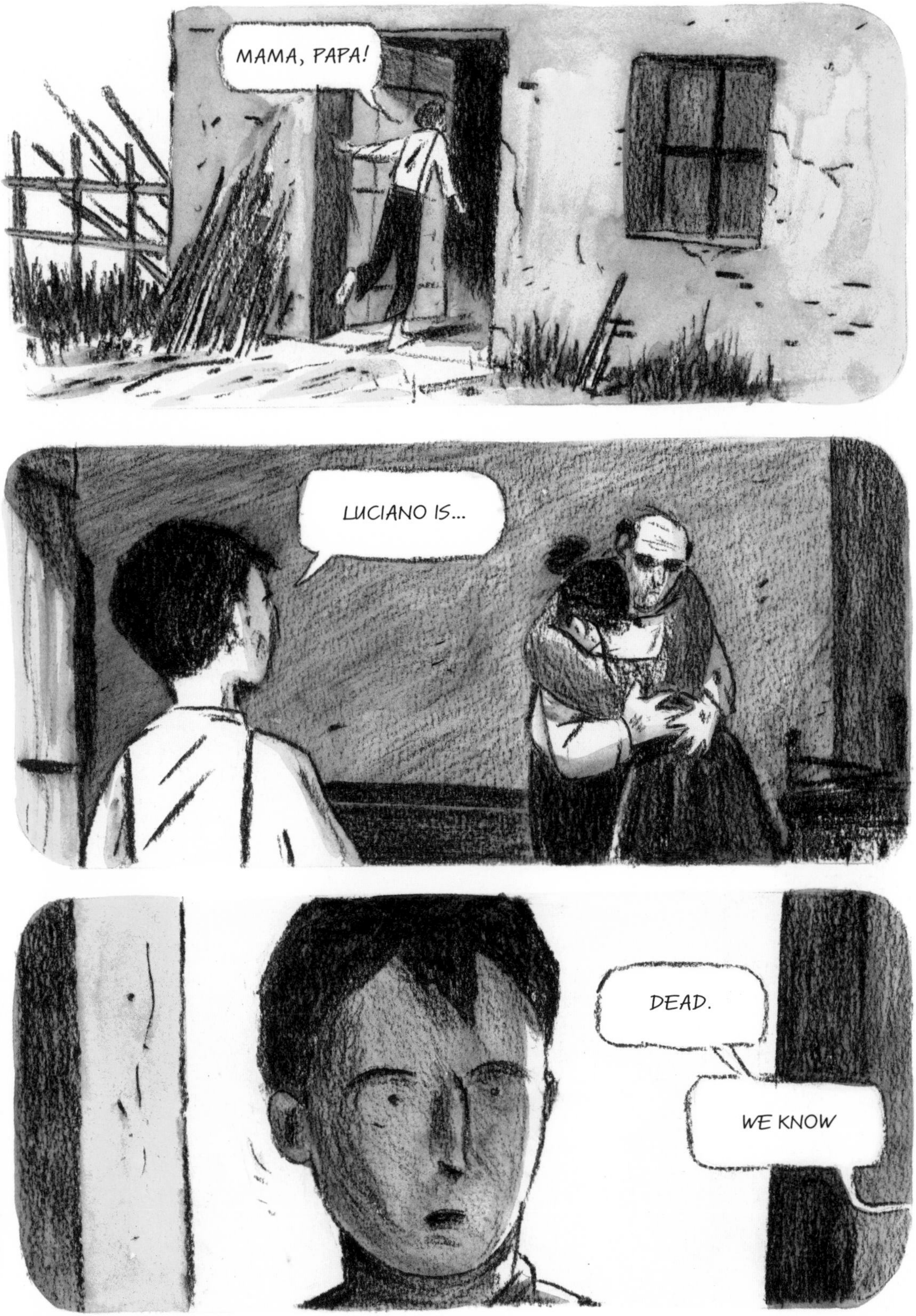
MAMA, PAPA!
LUCIANO IS...
DEAD.
WE KNOW

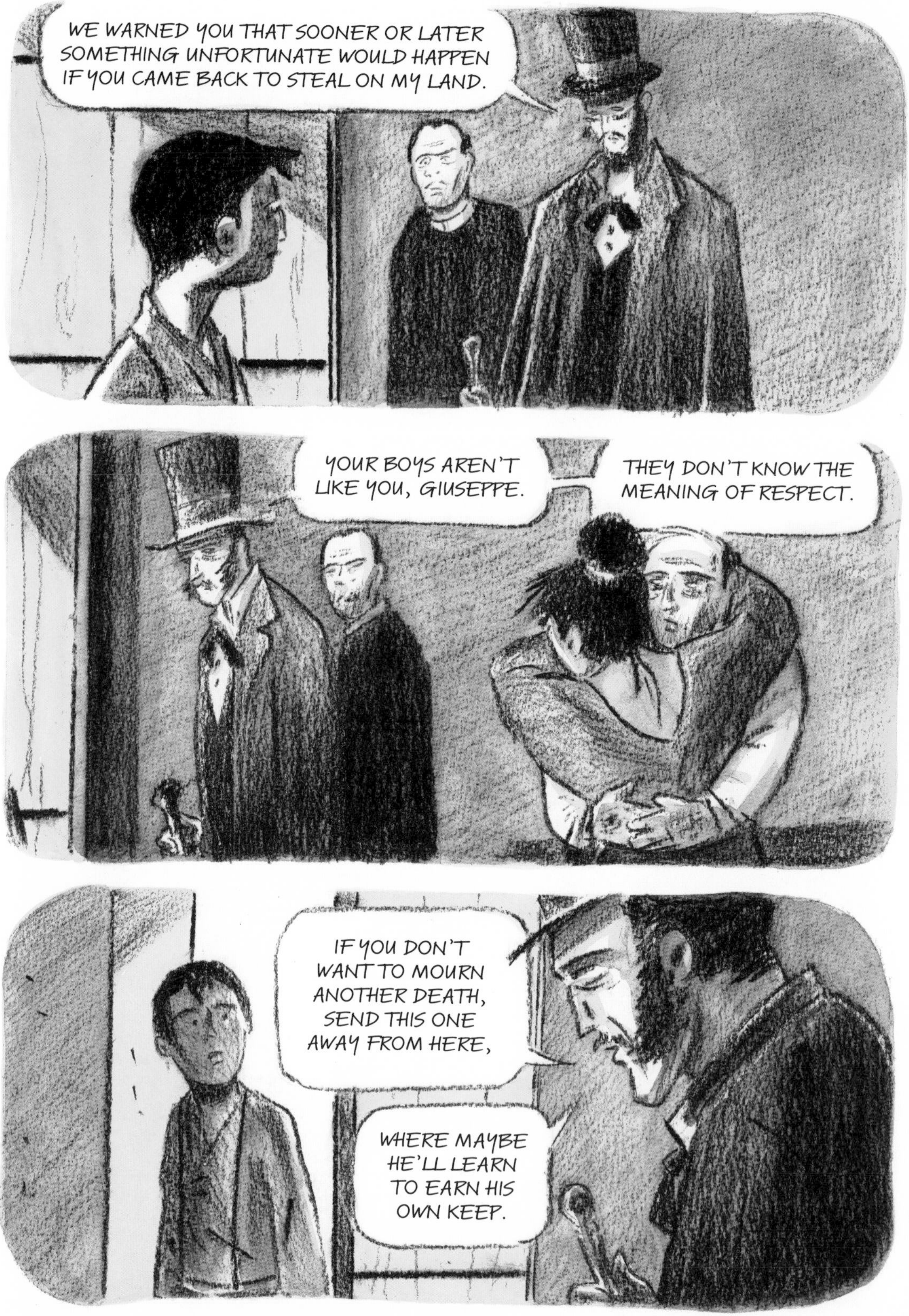
WE WARNED YOU THAT SOONER OR LATER SOMETHING UNFORTUNATE WOULD HAPPEN IF YOU CAME BACK TO STEAL ON MY LAND.
YOUR BOYS AREN'T LIKE YOU, GIUSEPPE.
THEY DON'T KNOW THE MEANING OF RESPECT.
IF YOU DON'T WANT TO MOURN ANOTHER DEATH, SEND THIS ONE AWAY FROM HERE,
WHERE MAYBE HE'LL LEARN TO EARN HIS OWN KEEP.

CHAPTER SEVEN

CHURUBUSCO

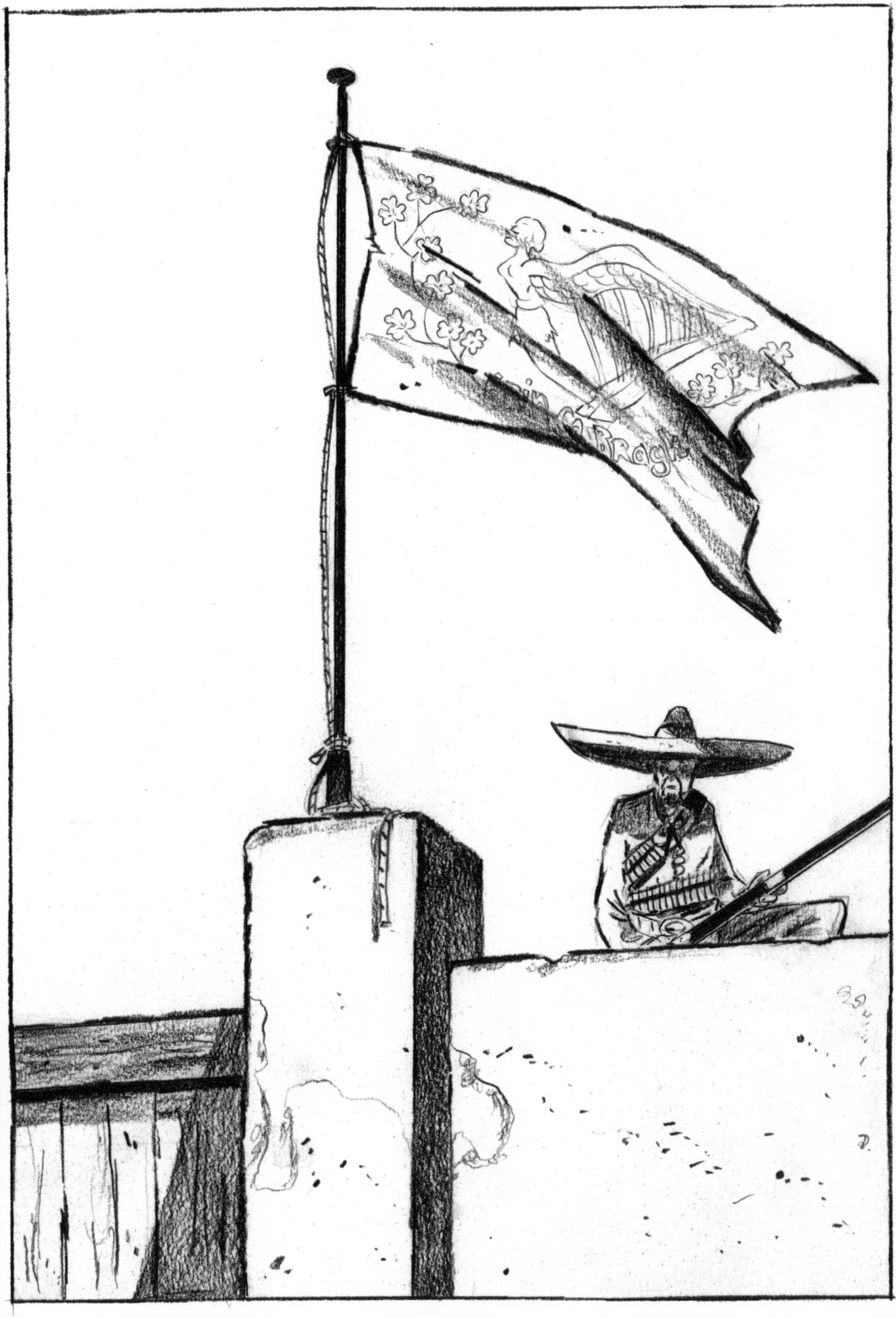

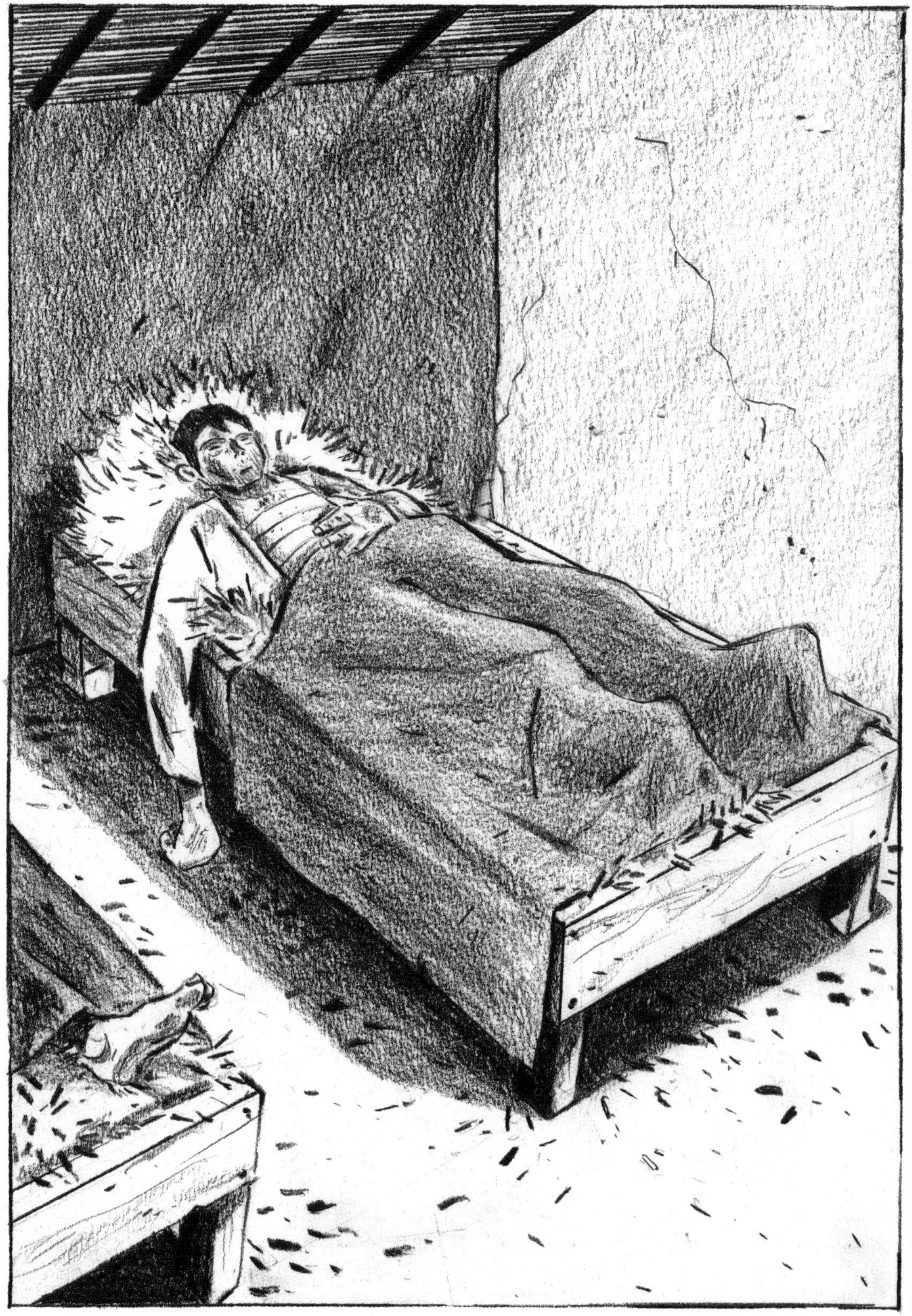

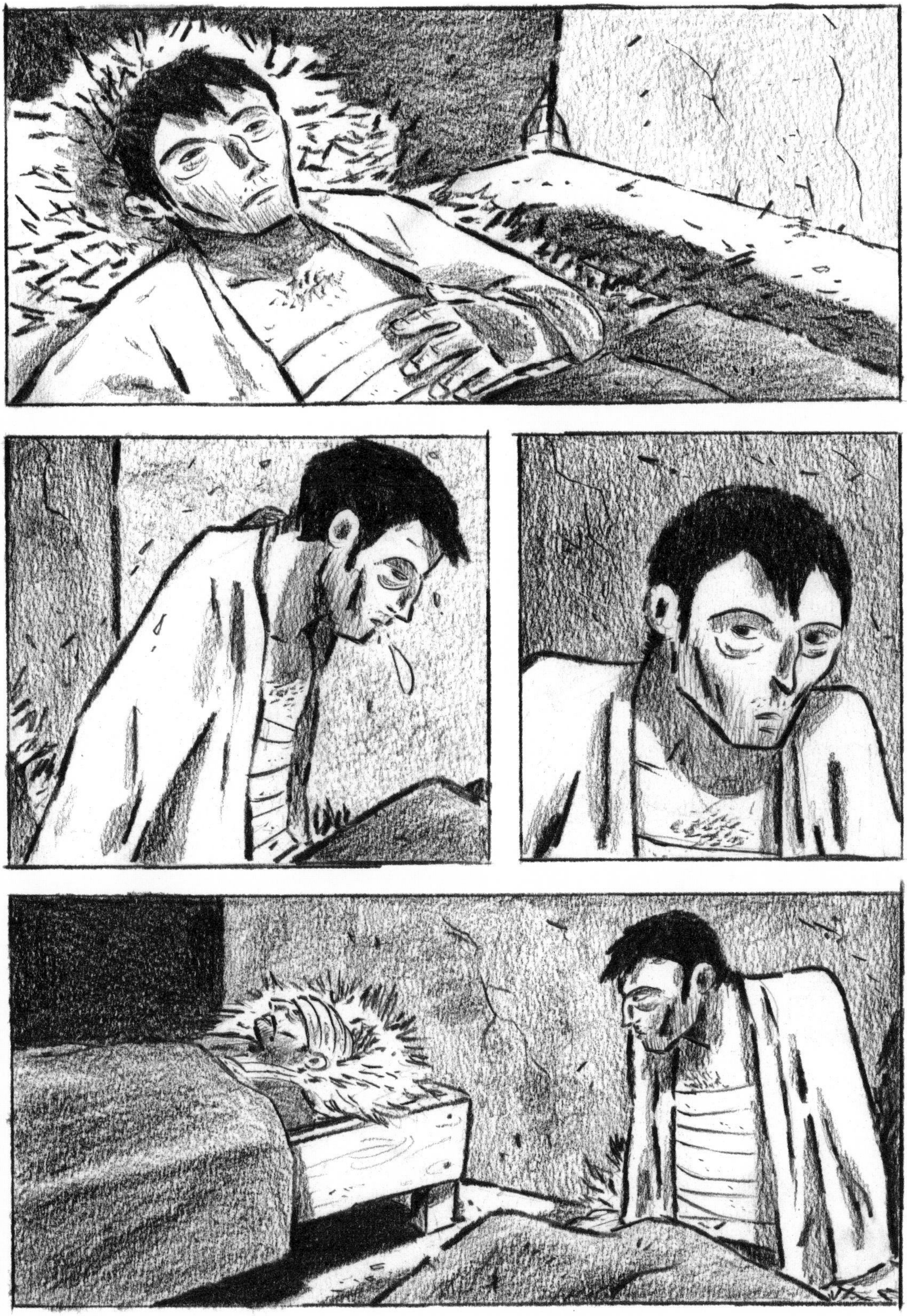

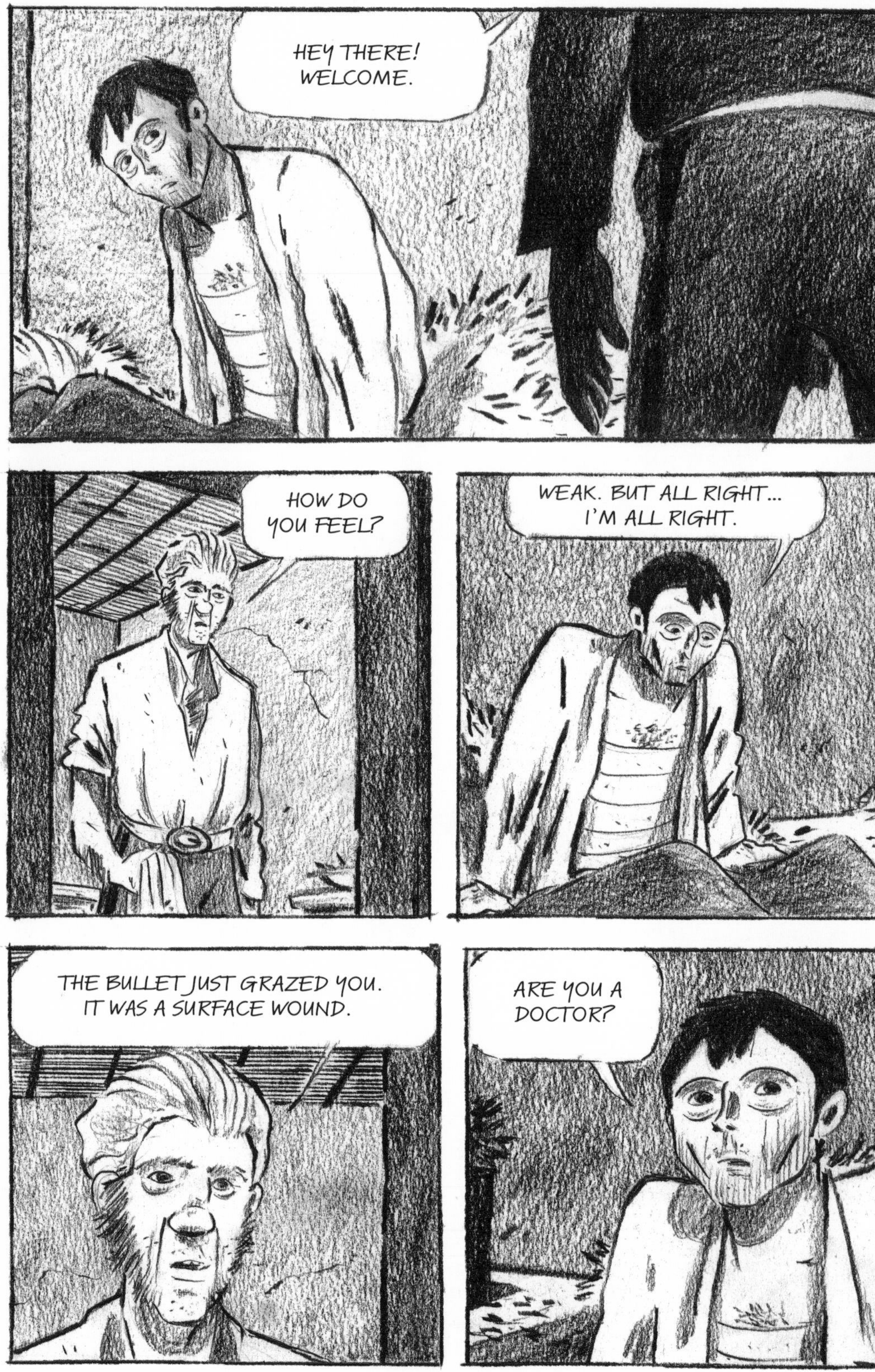
HEY THERE!
WELCOME.
HOW DO
YOU FEEL?
WEAK. BUT ALL RIGHT...
I'M ALL RIGHT.
THE BULLET JUST GRAZED YOU.
IT WAS A SURFACE WOUND.
ARE YOU A
DOCTOR?

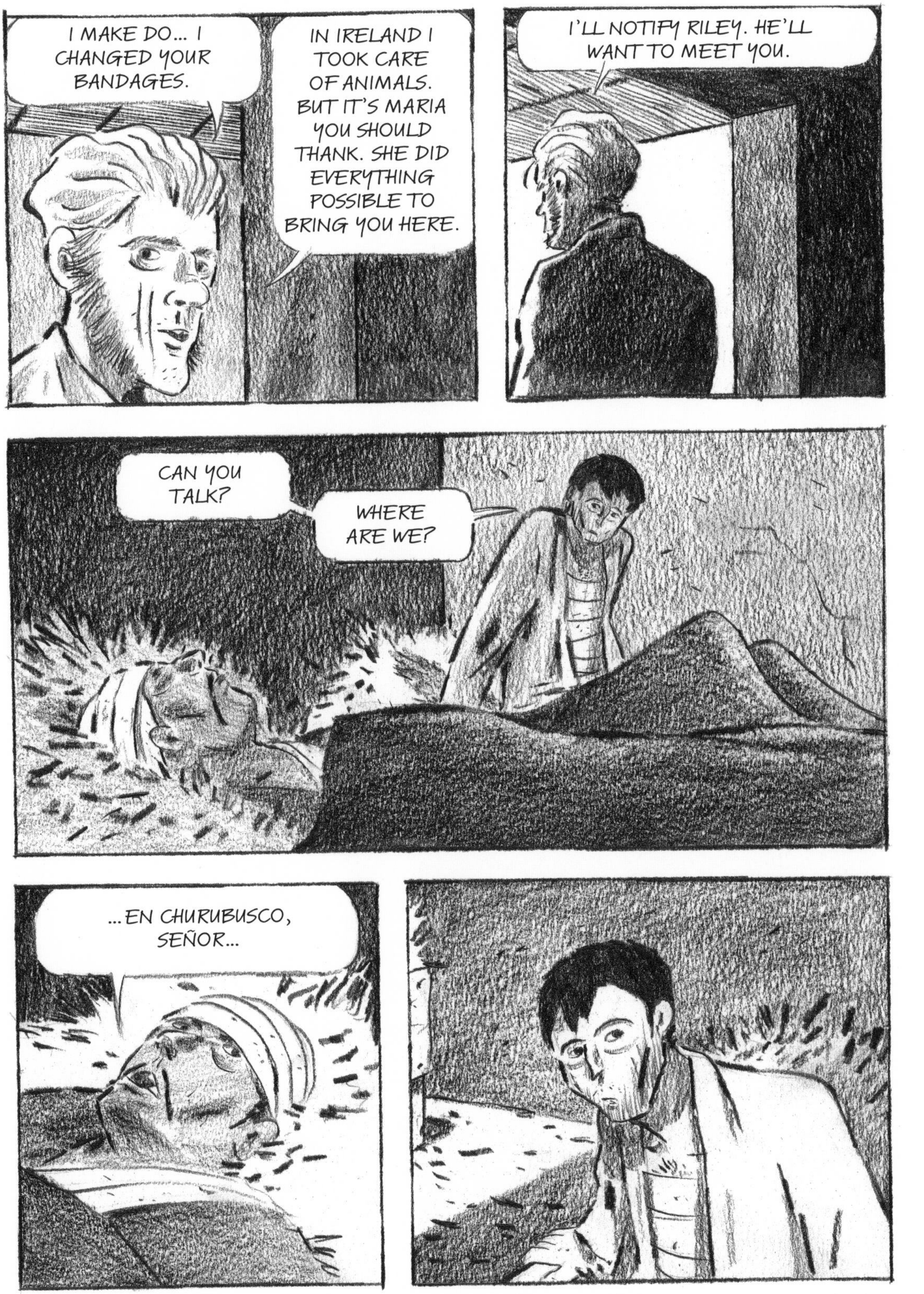
I MAKE DO... I CHANGED YOUR BANDAGES.
IN IRELAND I TOOK CARE OF ANIMALS. BUT IT'S MARIA YOU SHOULD THANK. SHE DID EVERYTHING POSSIBLE TO BRING YOU HERE.
I'LL NOTIFY RILEY. HE'LL WANT TO MEET YOU.
CAN YOU TALK?
WHERE ARE WE?
...EN CHURUBUSCO, SEÑOR...

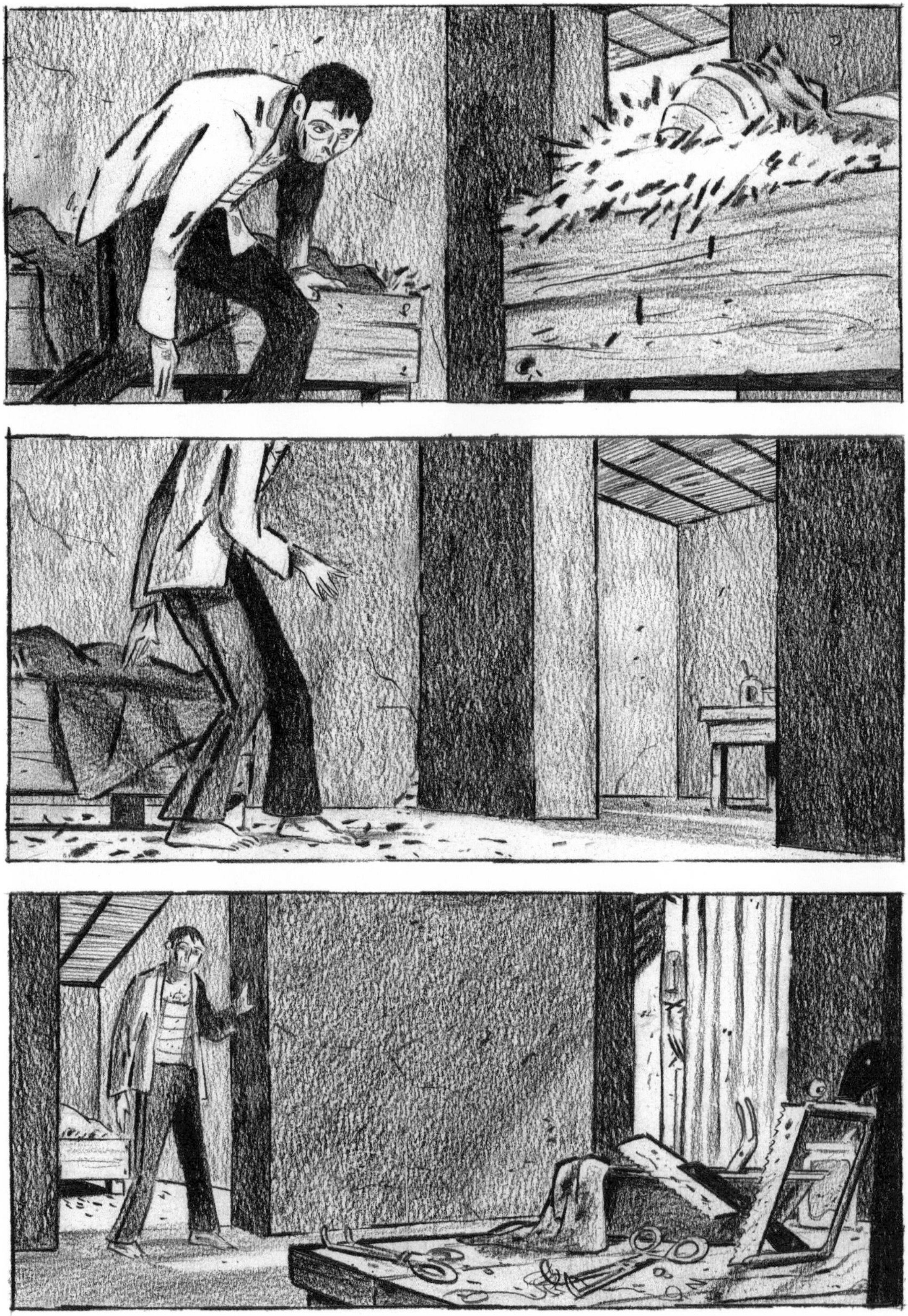

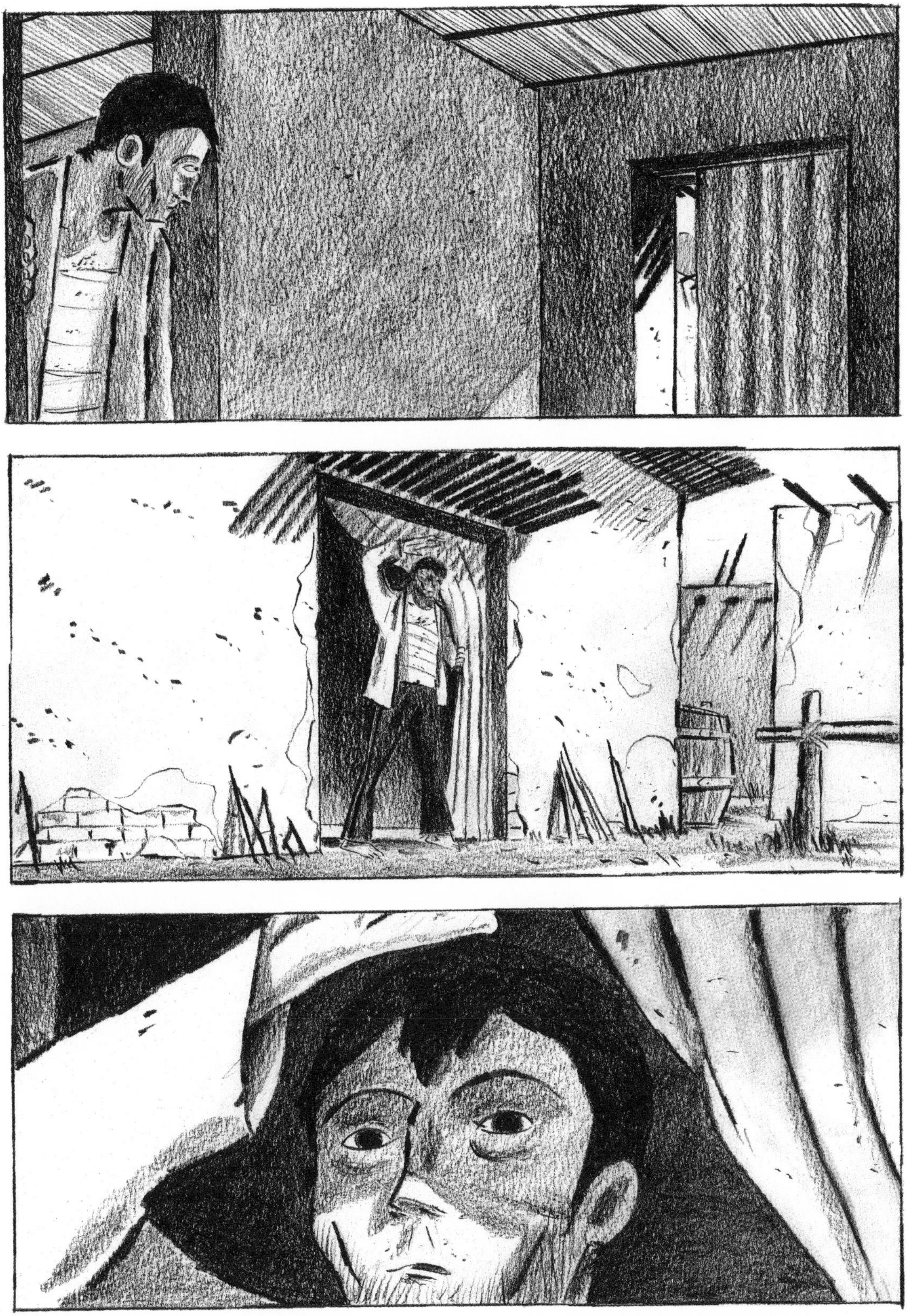

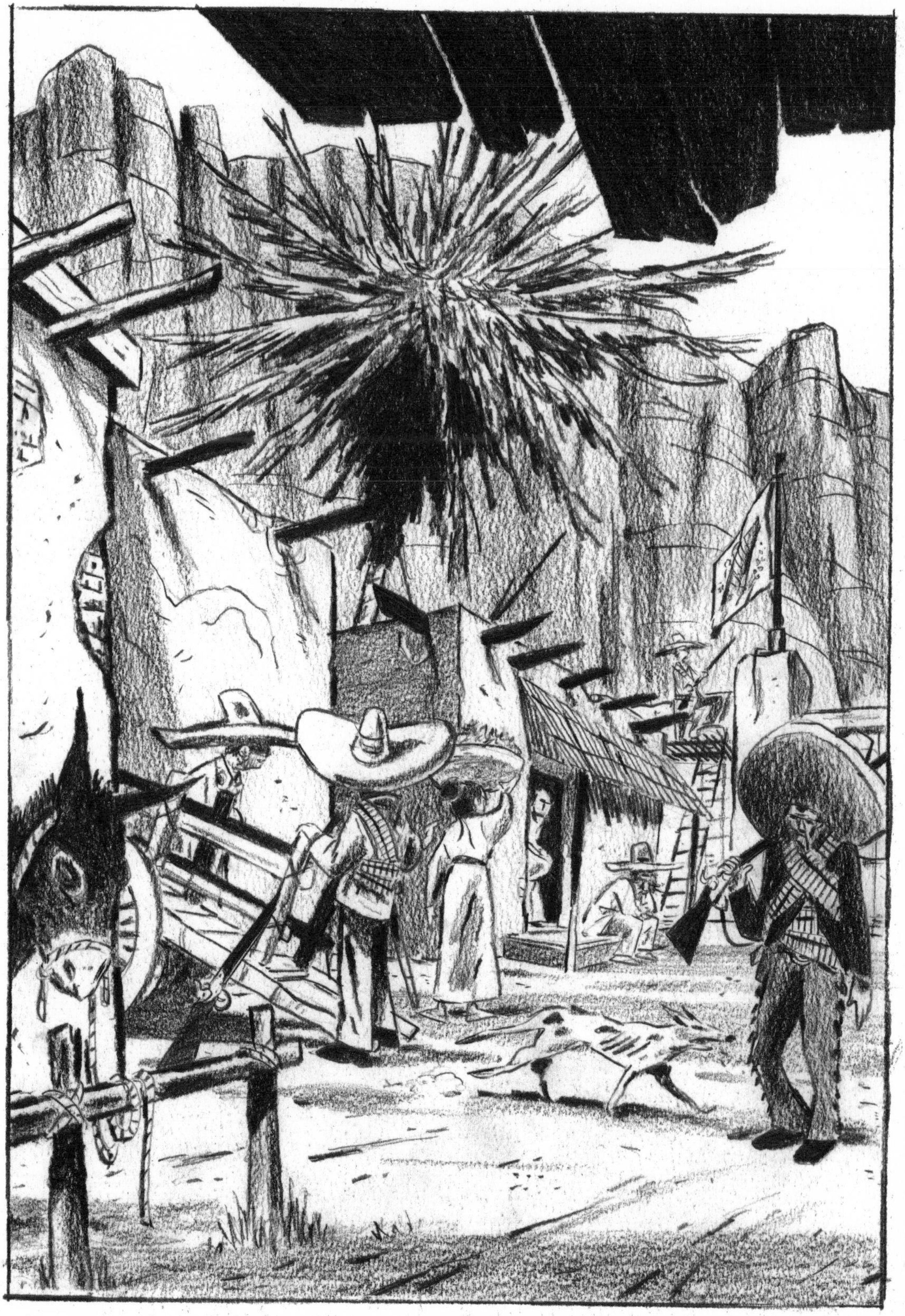

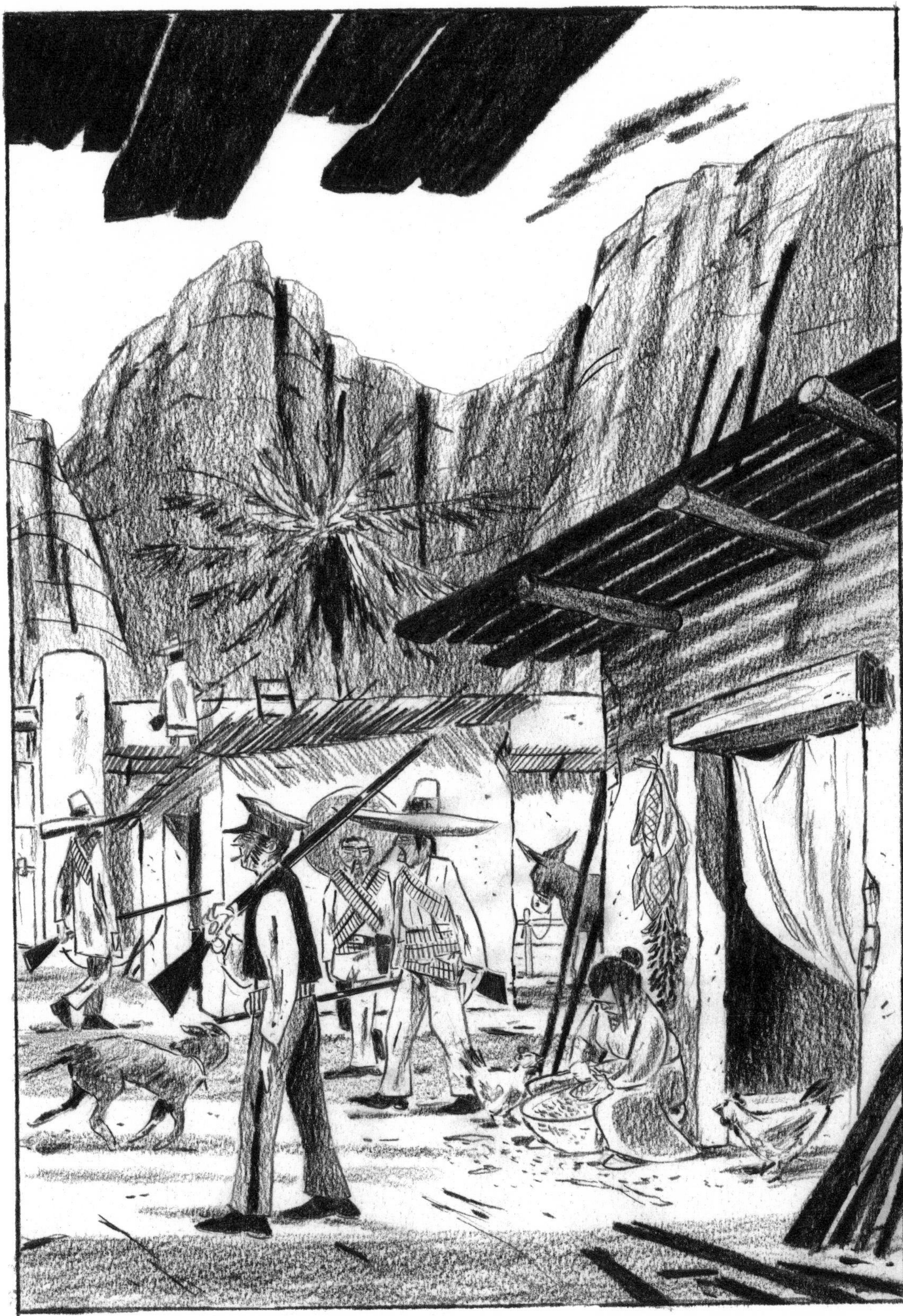

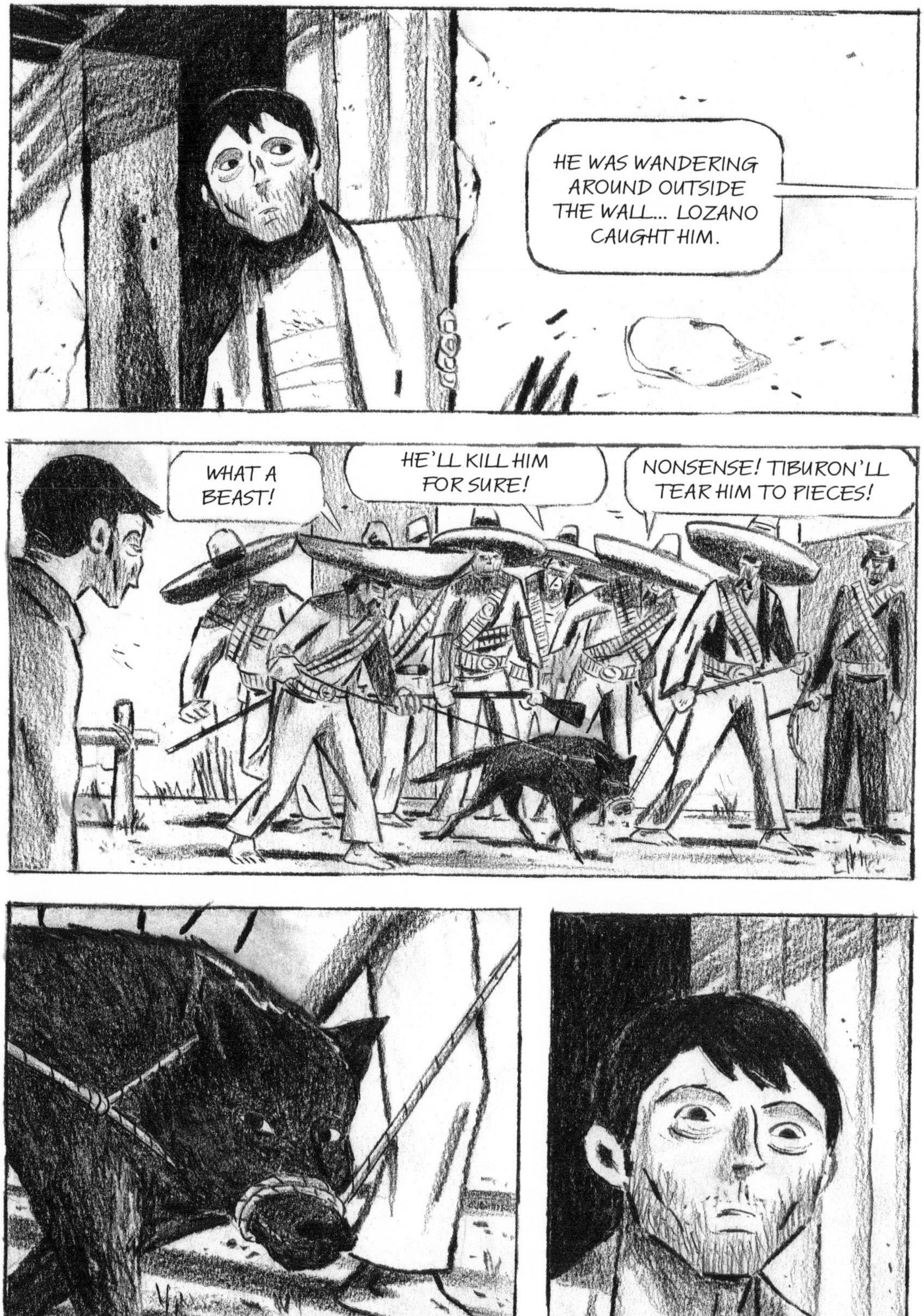
HE WAS WANDERING AROUND OUTSIDE THE WALL... LOZANO CAUGHT HIM.
WHAT A BEAST!
HE'LL KILL HIM FOR SURE!
NONSENSE! TIBURON'LL TEAR HIM TO PIECES!

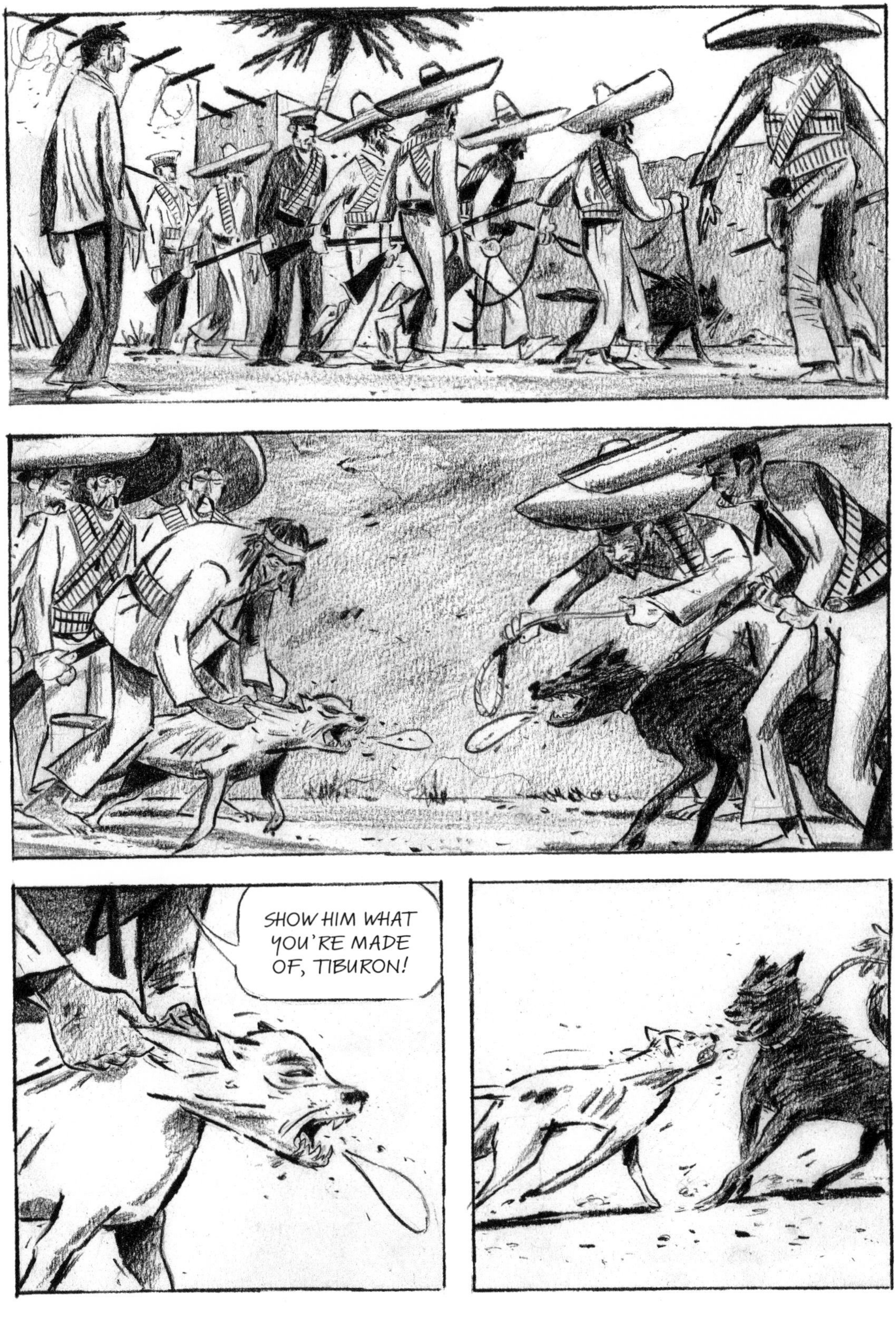
SHOW HIM WHAT YOU'RE MADE OF, TIBURON!

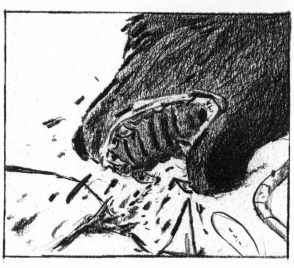

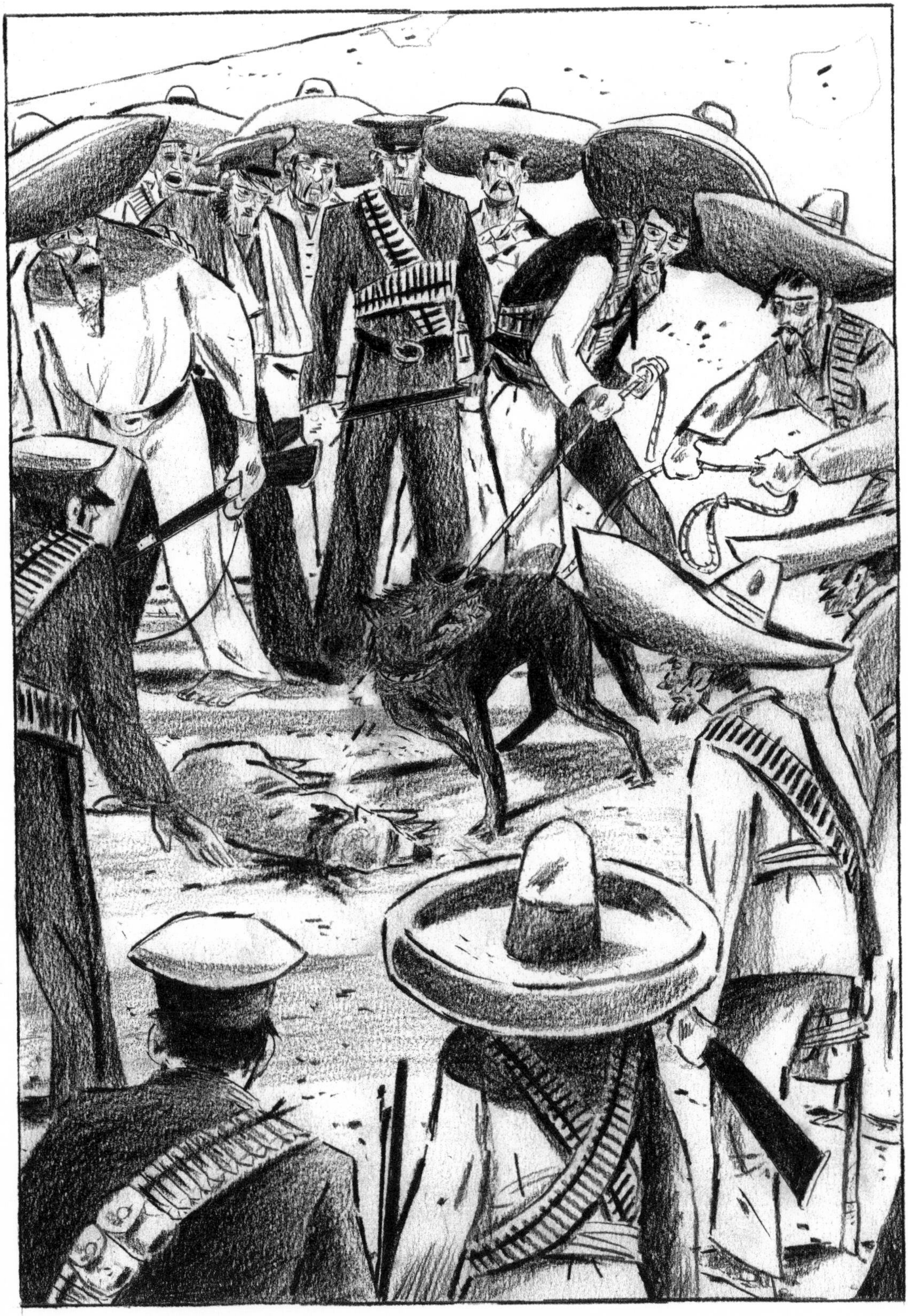

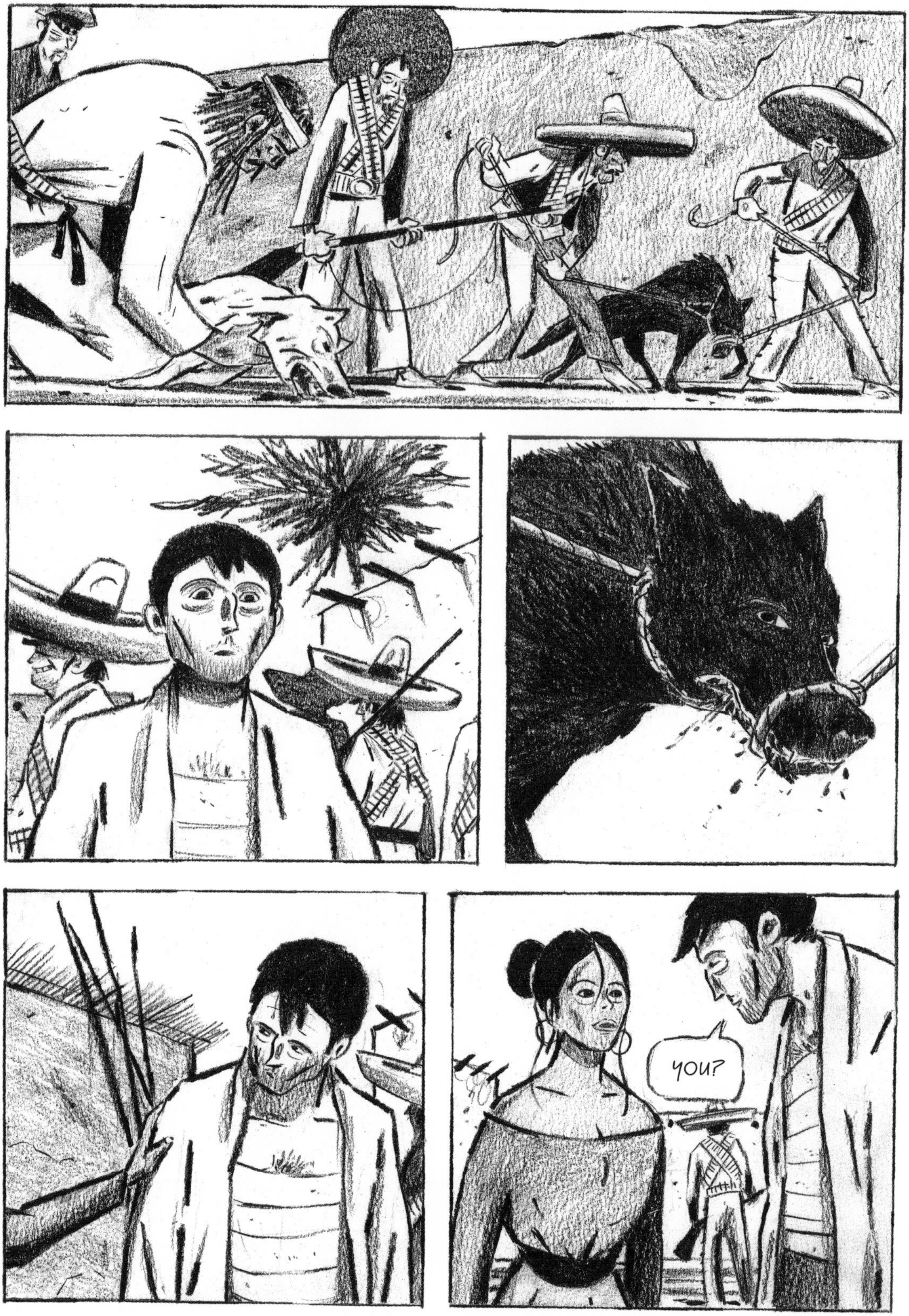
YOU?

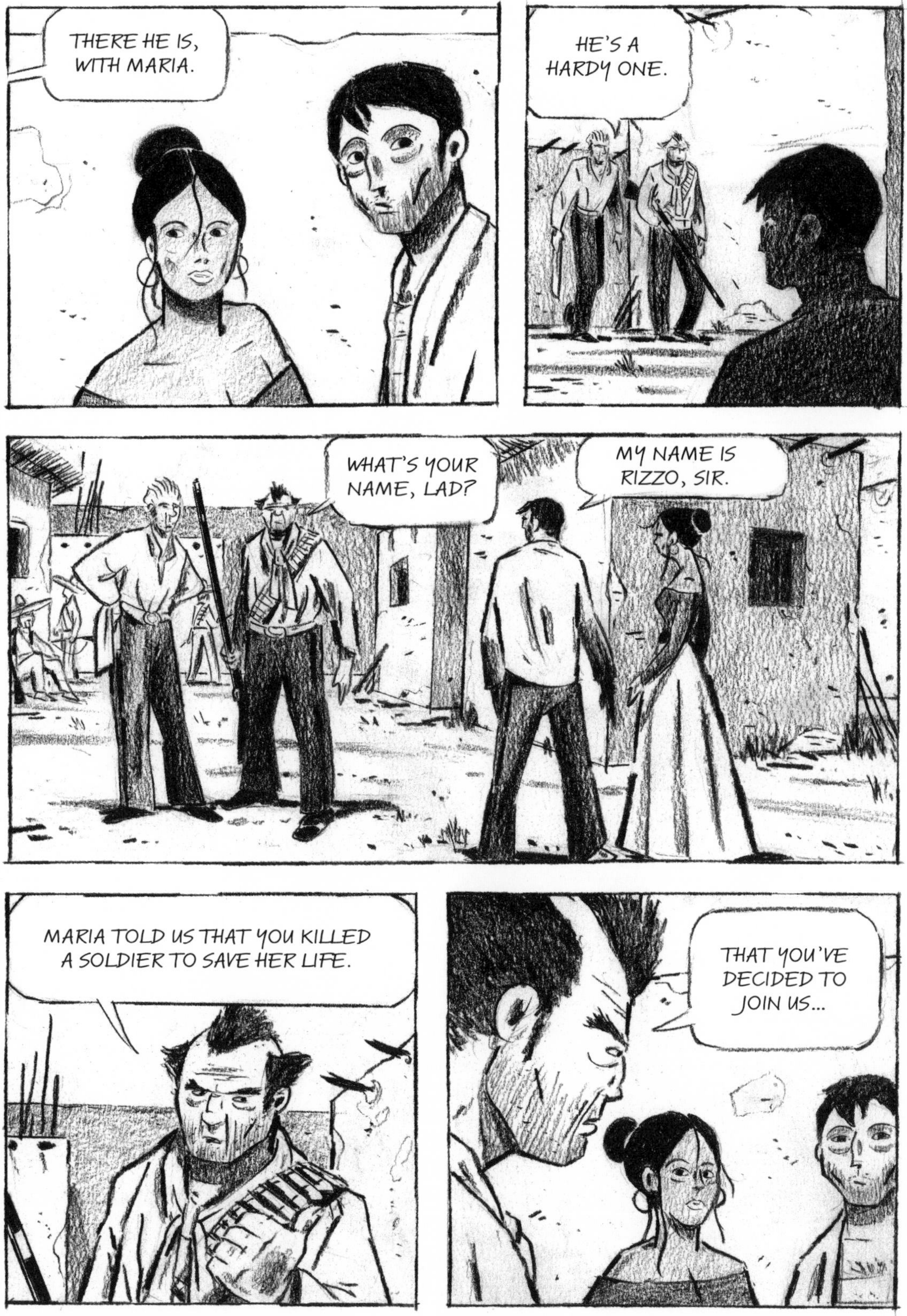
THERE HE IS, WITH MARIA.
HE'S A HARDY ONE.
WHAT'S YOUR NAME, LAD?
MY NAME IS RIZZO, SIR.
MARIA TOLD US THAT YOU KILLED A SOLDIER TO SAVE HER LIFE.
THAT YOU'VE DECIDED TO JOIN US...

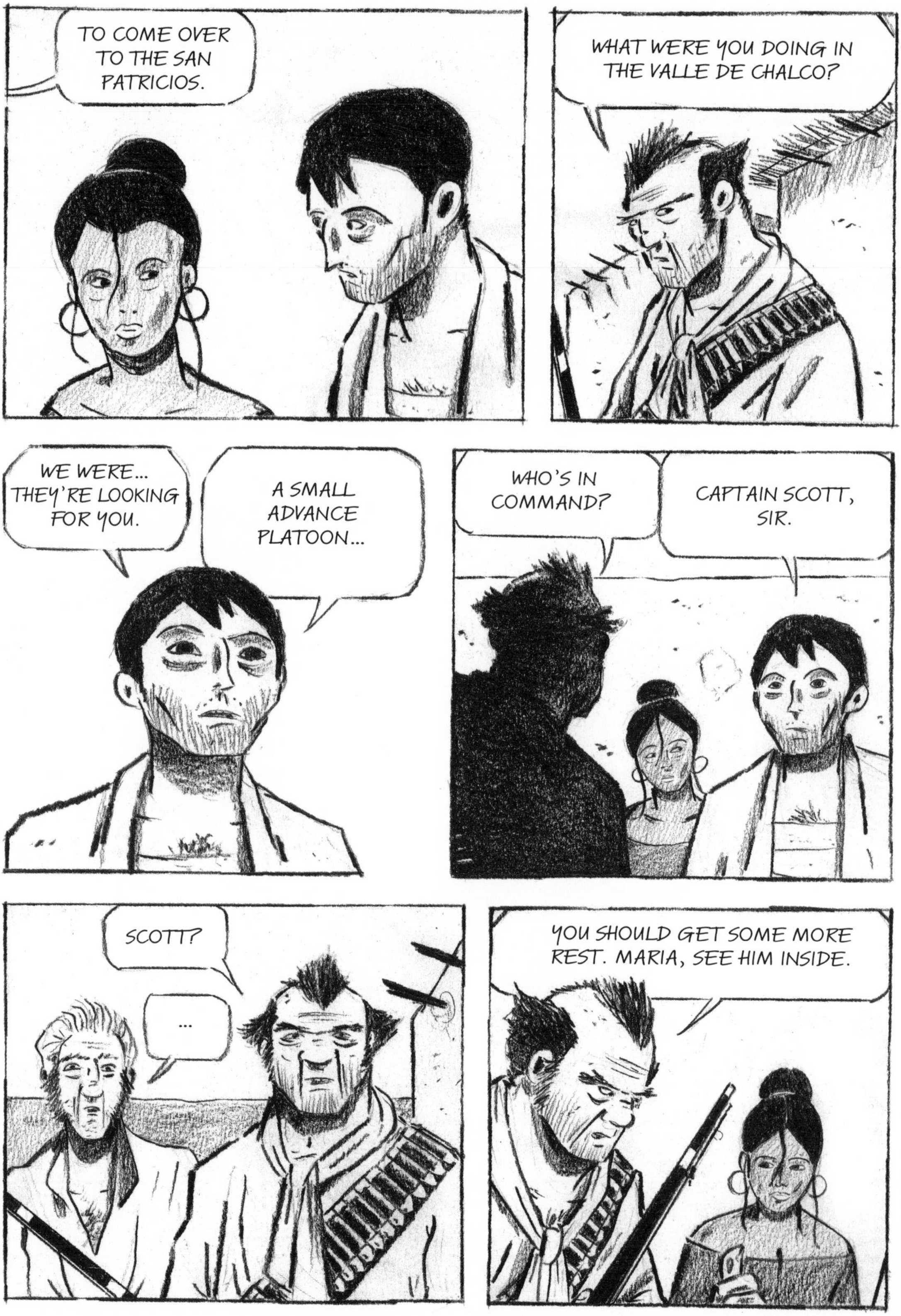
TO COME OVER TO THE SAN PATRICIOS.
WHAT WERE YOU DOING IN THE VALLE DE CHALCO?
WE WERE... THEY'RE LOOKING FOR YOU.
A SMALL ADVANCE PLATOON...
WHO'S IN COMMAND?
CAPTAIN SCOTT, SIR.
SCOTT?
...
YOU SHOULD GET SOME MORE REST. MARIA, SEE HIM INSIDE.

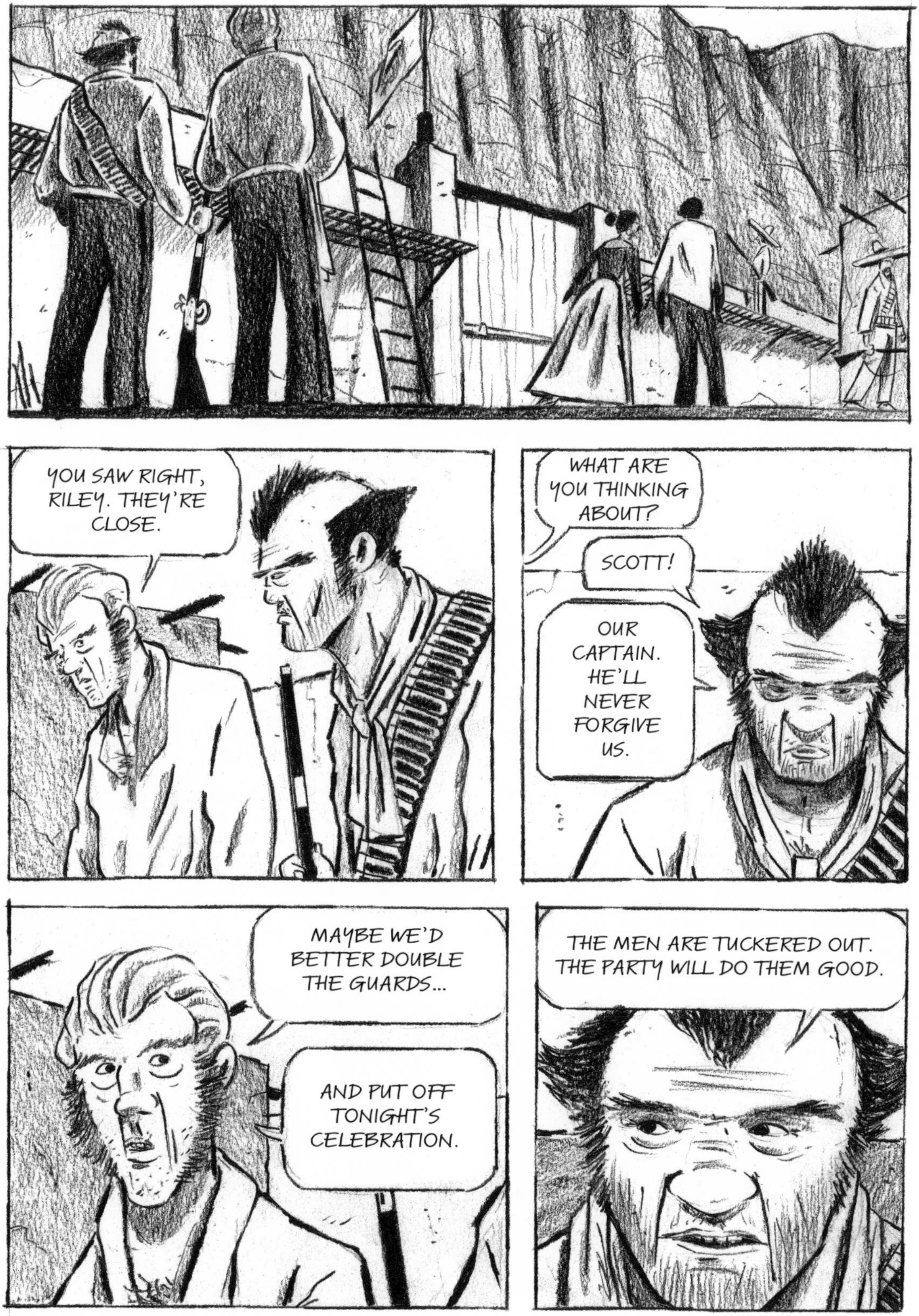
YOU SAW RIGHT, RILEY. THEY'RE CLOSE.
WHAT ARE YOU THINKING ABOUT?
SCOTT!
OUR CAPTAIN. HE'LL NEVER FORGIVE US.
MAYBE WE'D BETTER DOUBLE THE GUARDS...
AND PUT OFF TONIGHT'S CELEBRATION.
THE MEN ARE TUCKERED OUT. THE PARTY WILL DO THEM GOOD.

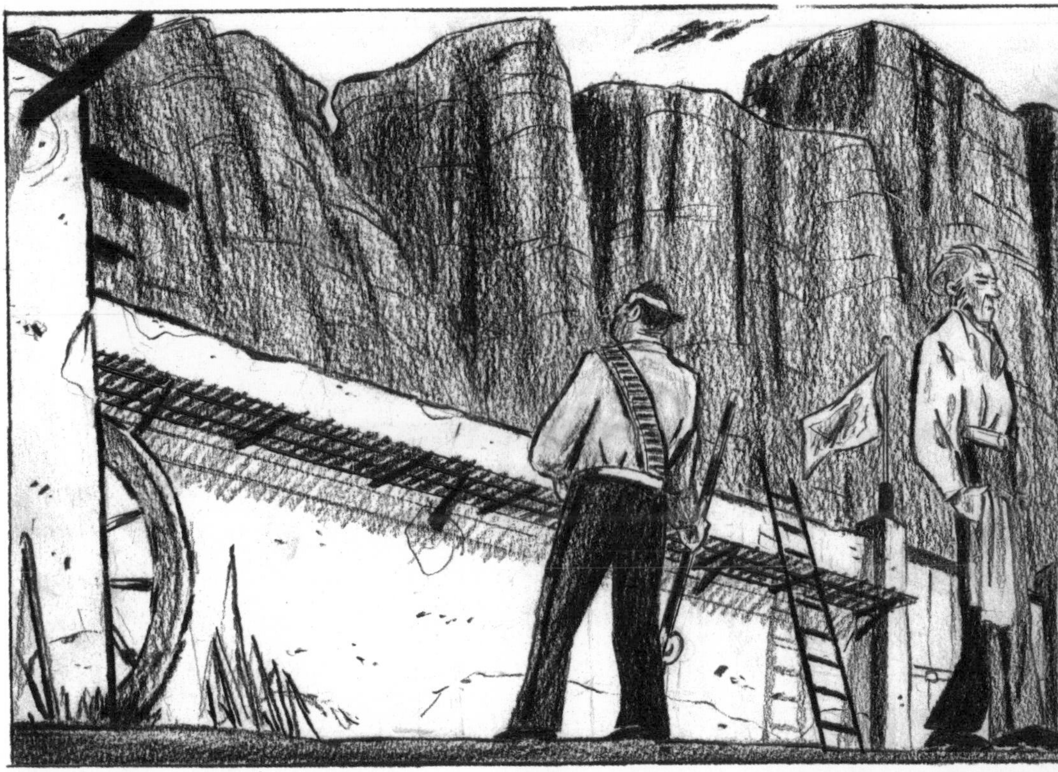

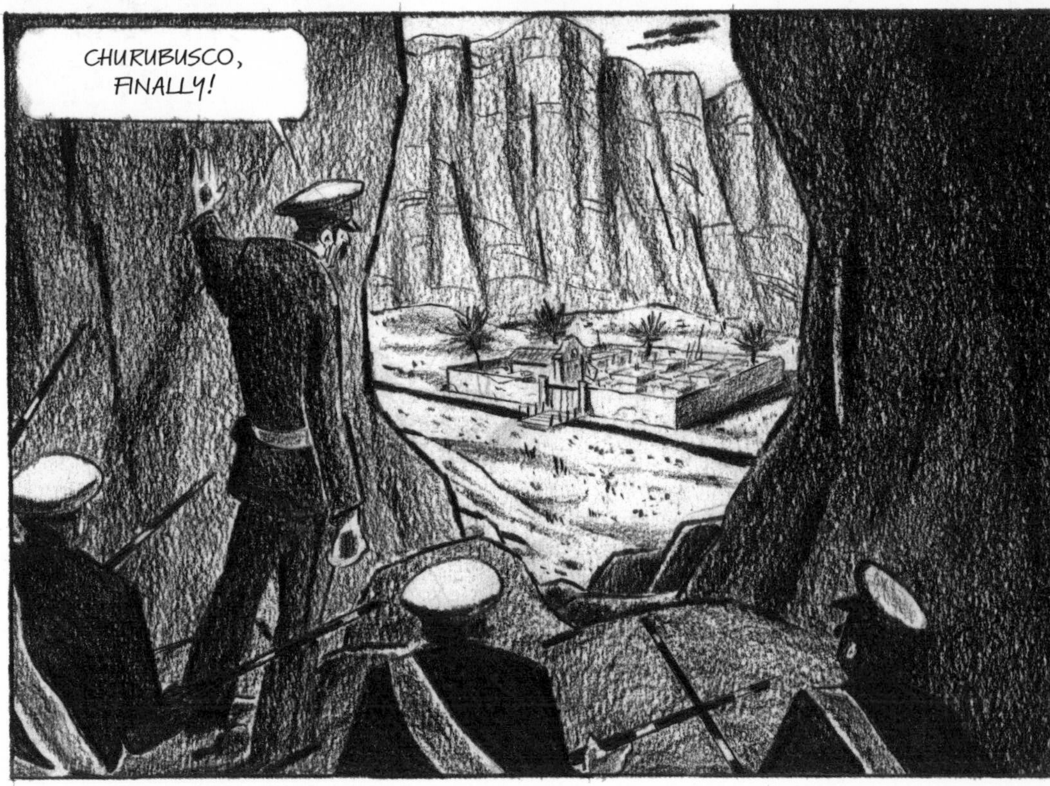
CHURUBUSCO, FINALLY!

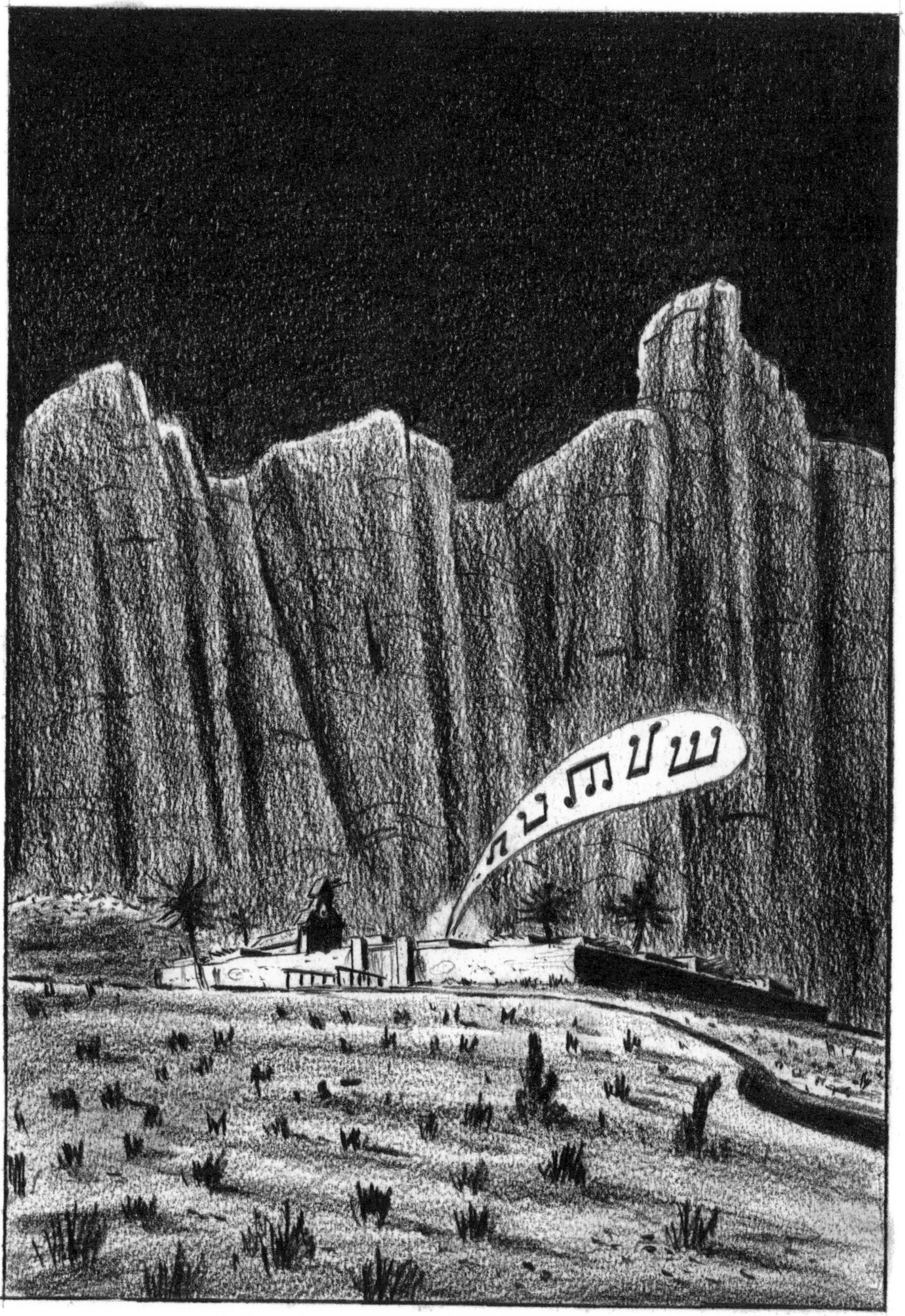

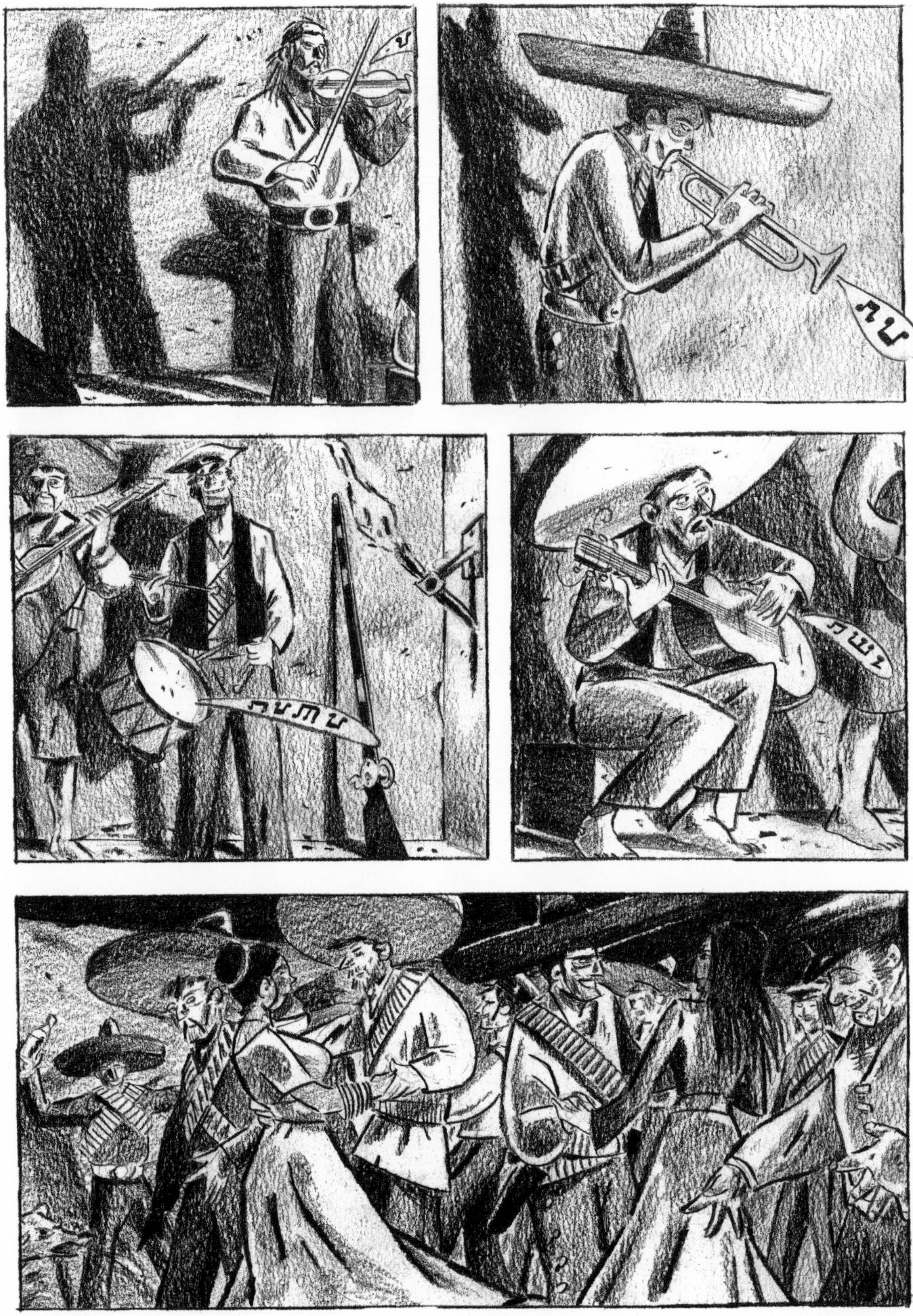

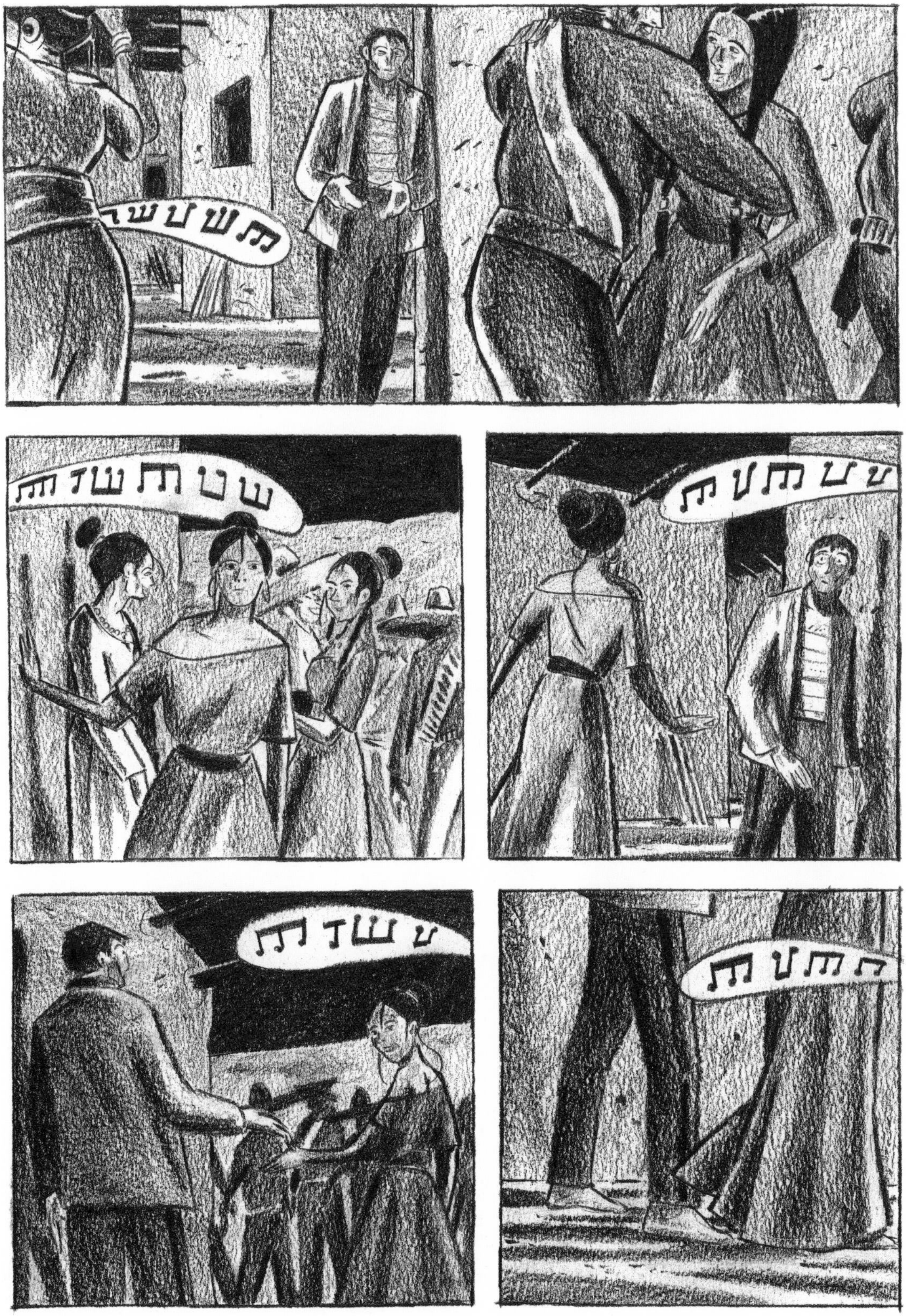

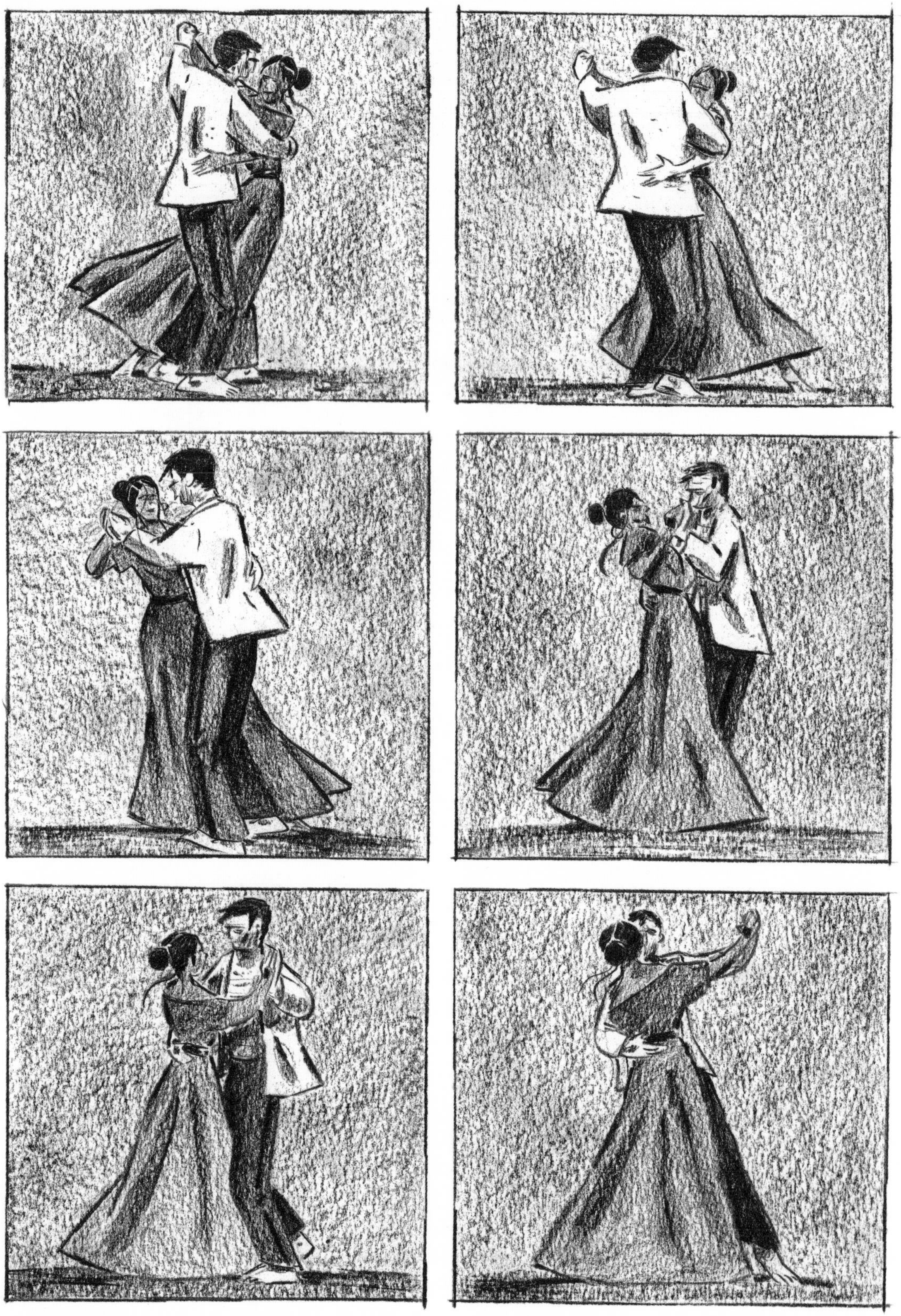

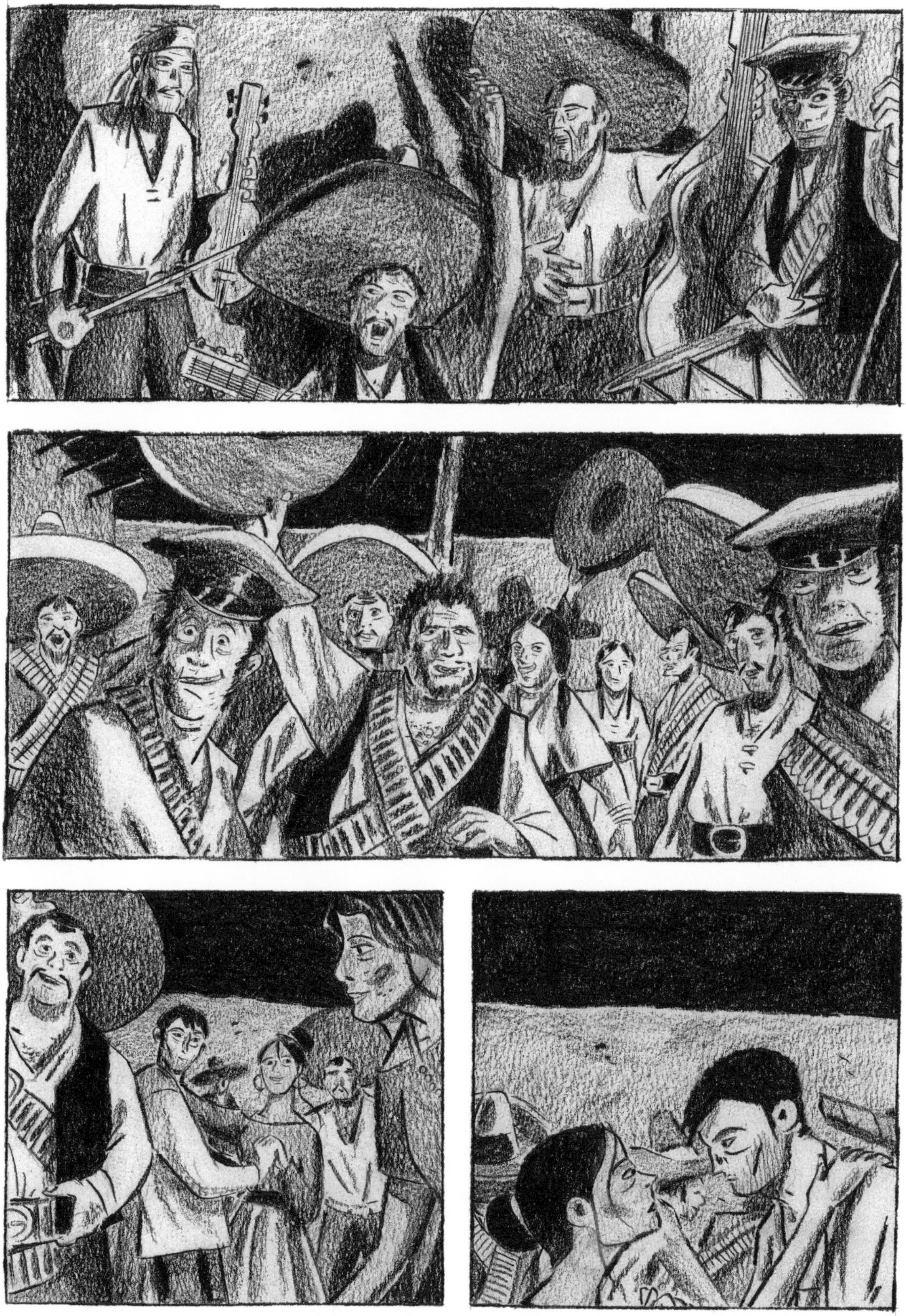

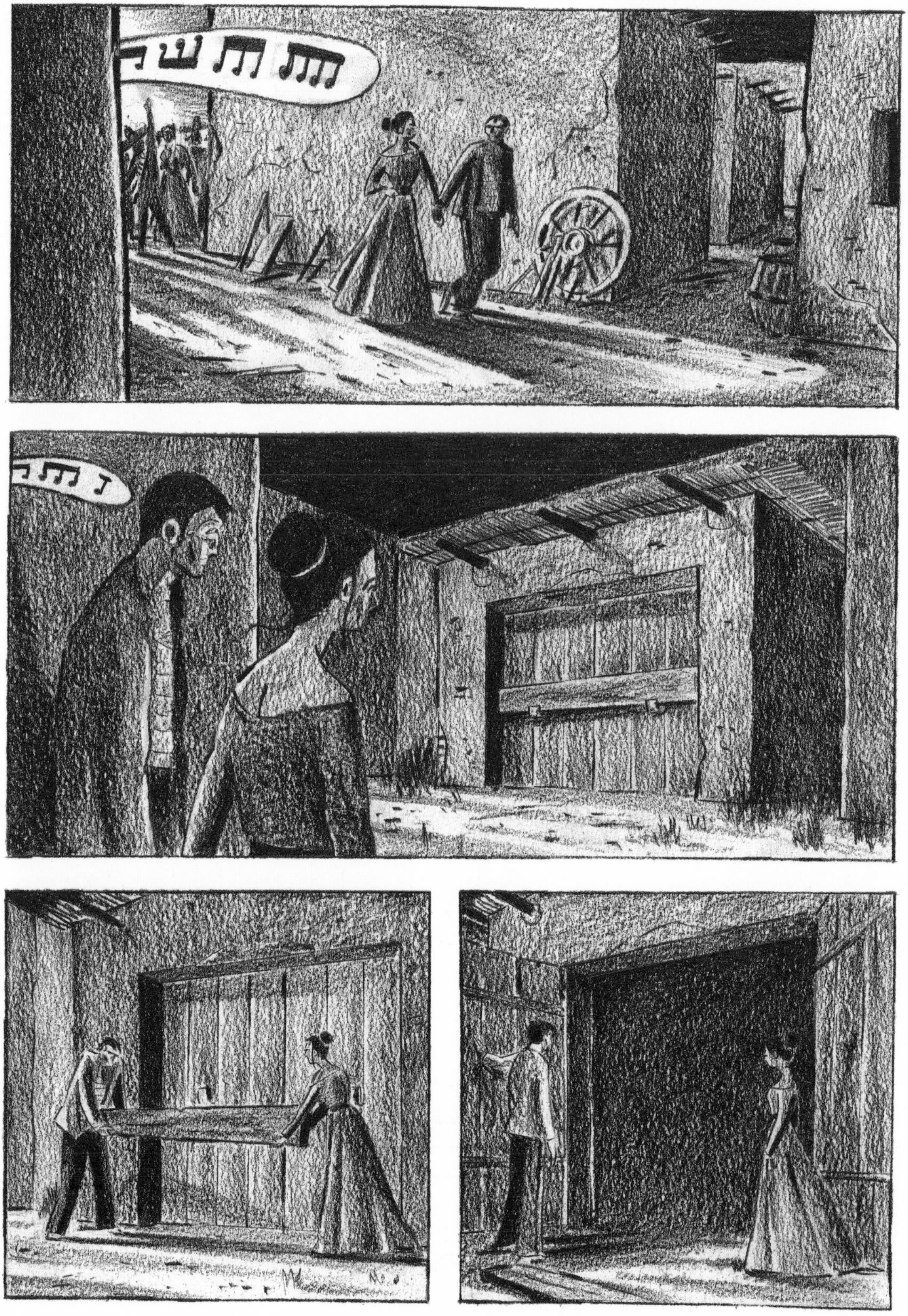

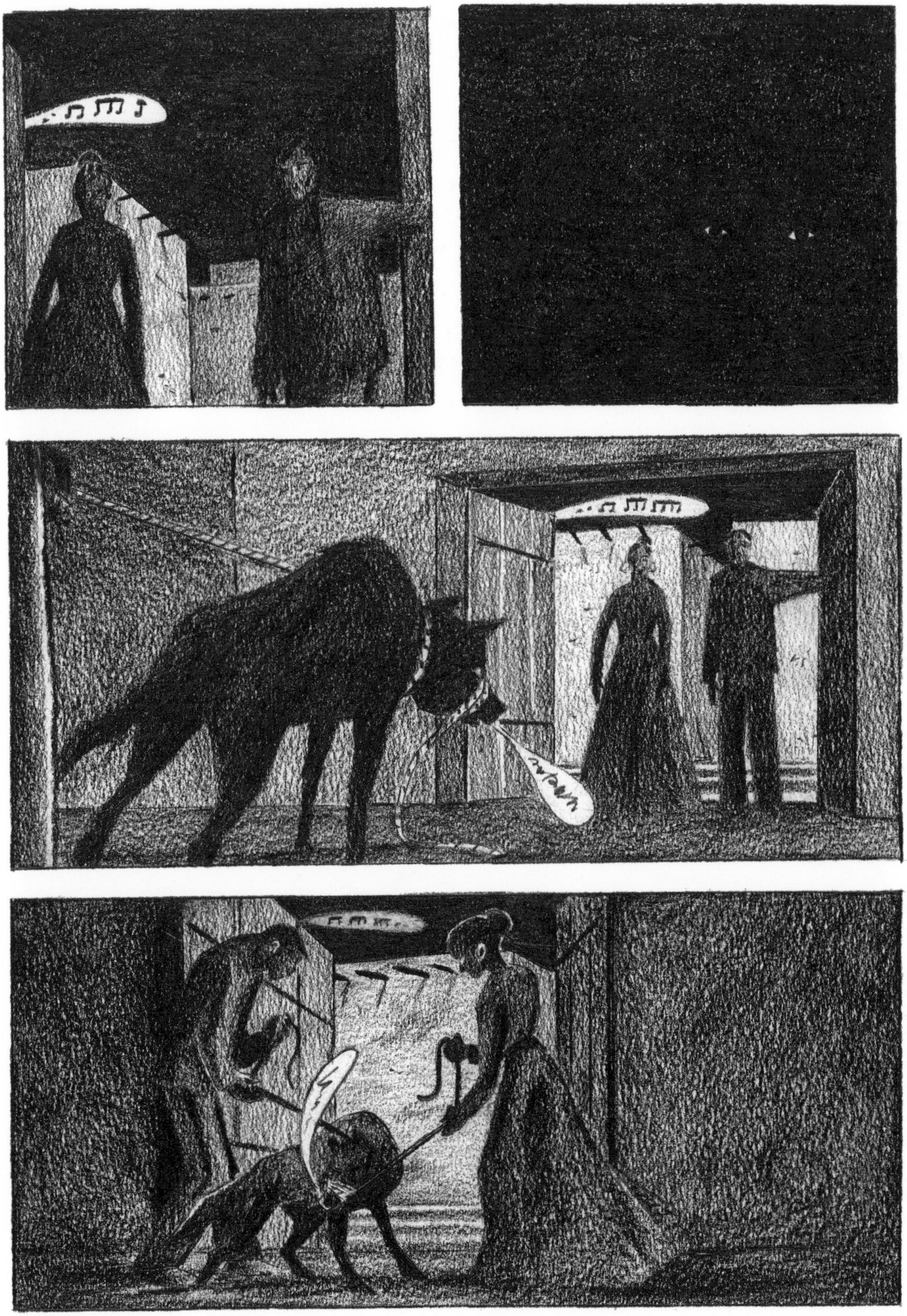

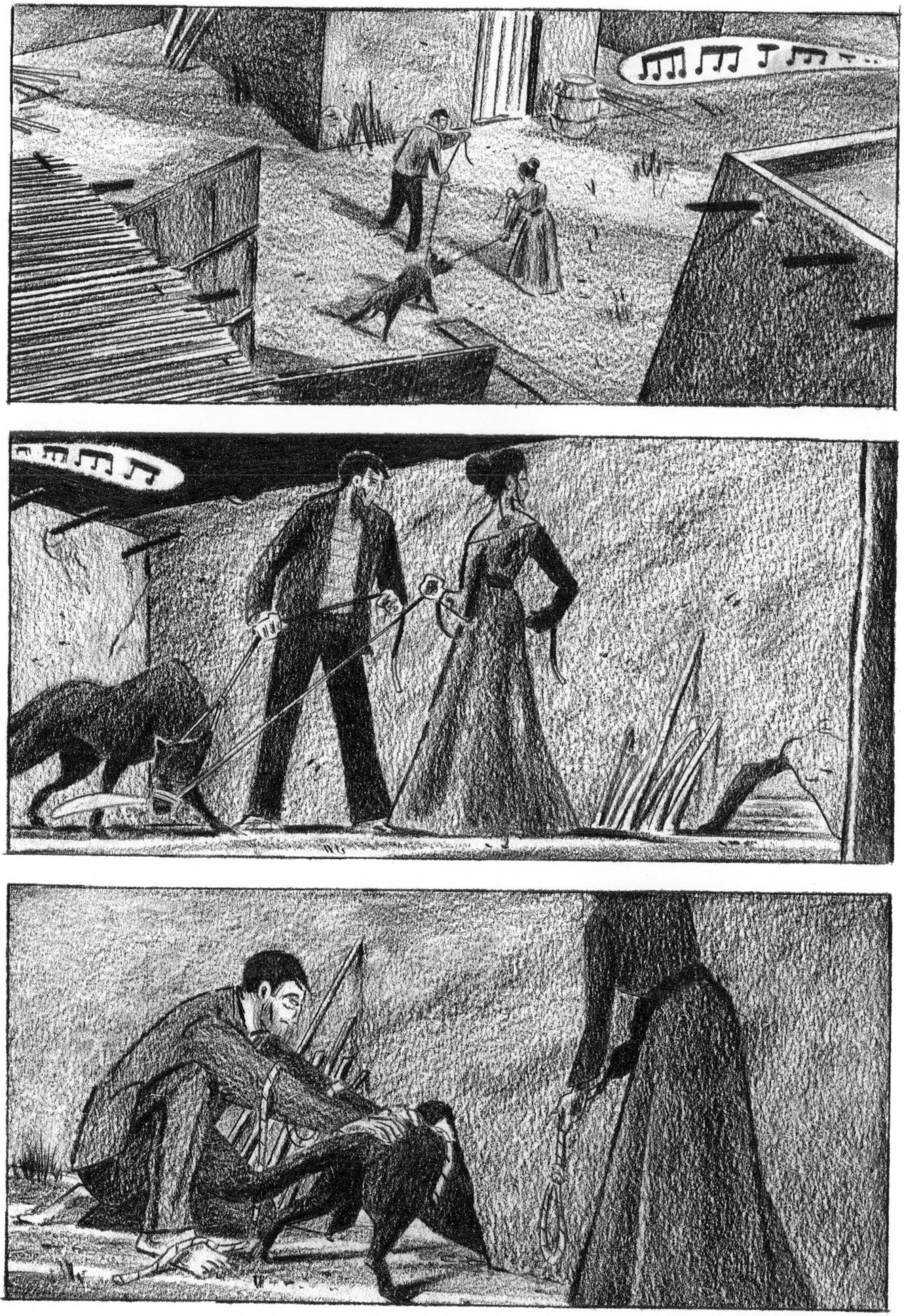

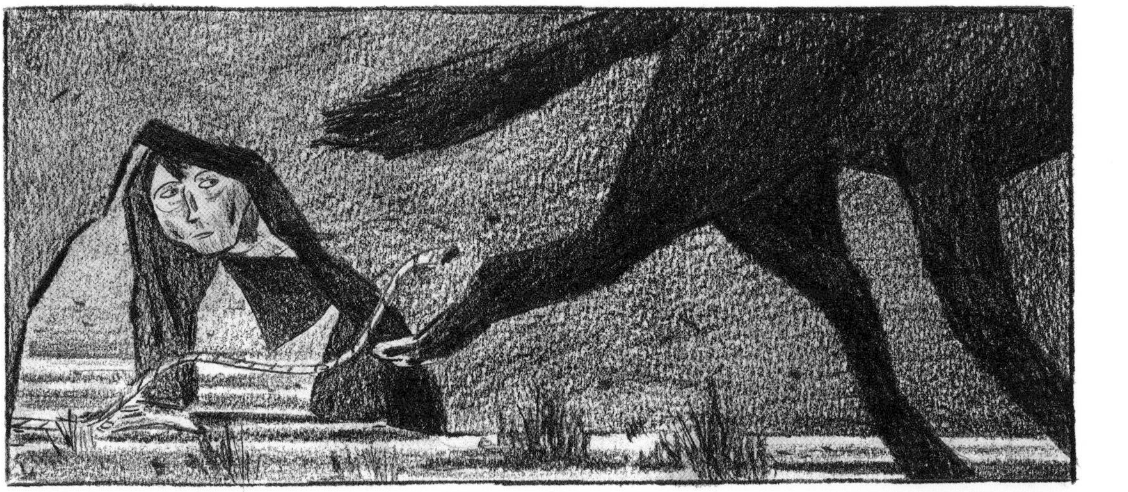

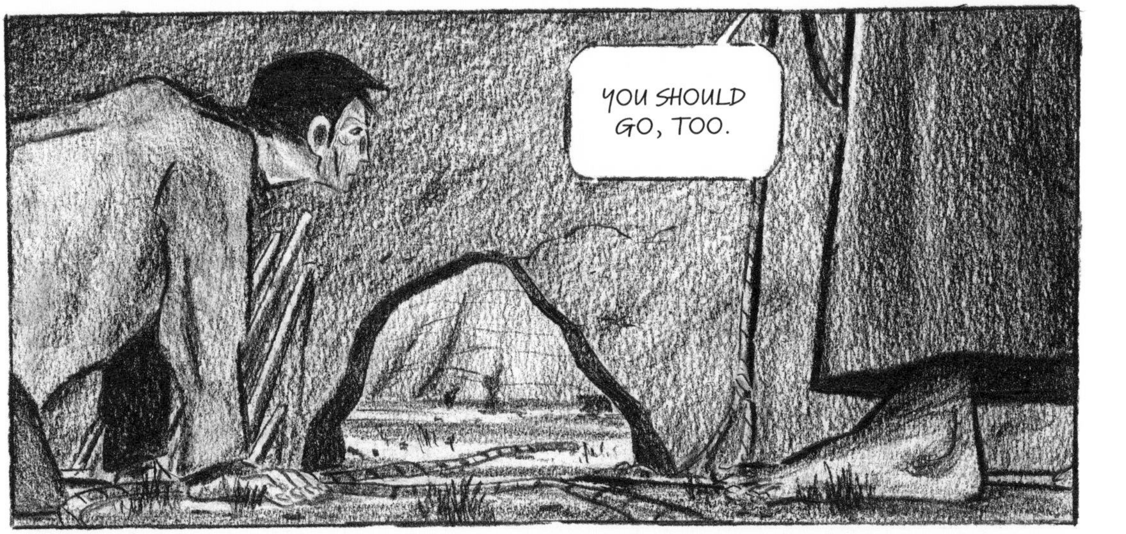
YOU SHOULD GO, TOO.

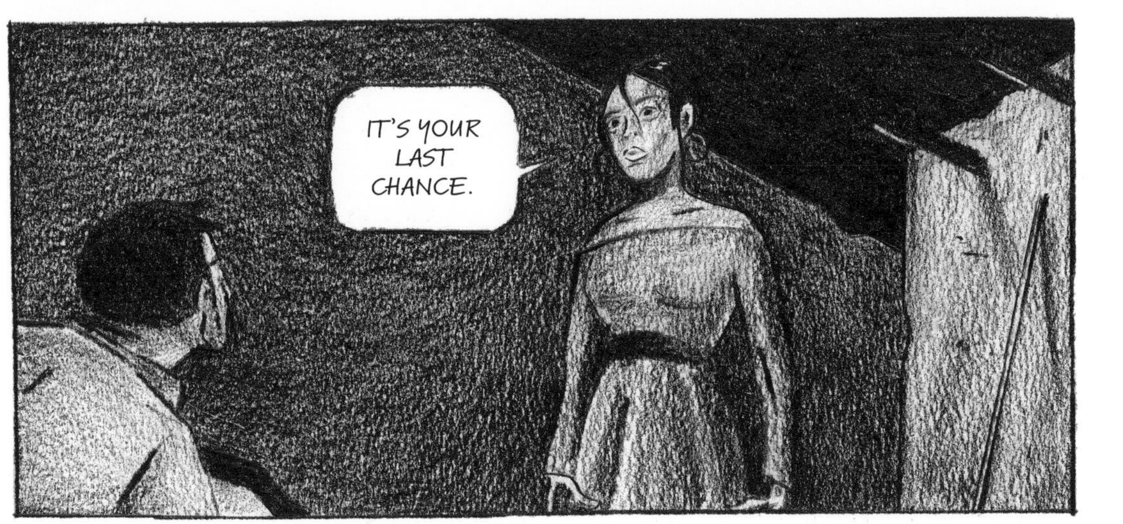
IT'S YOUR LAST CHANCE.

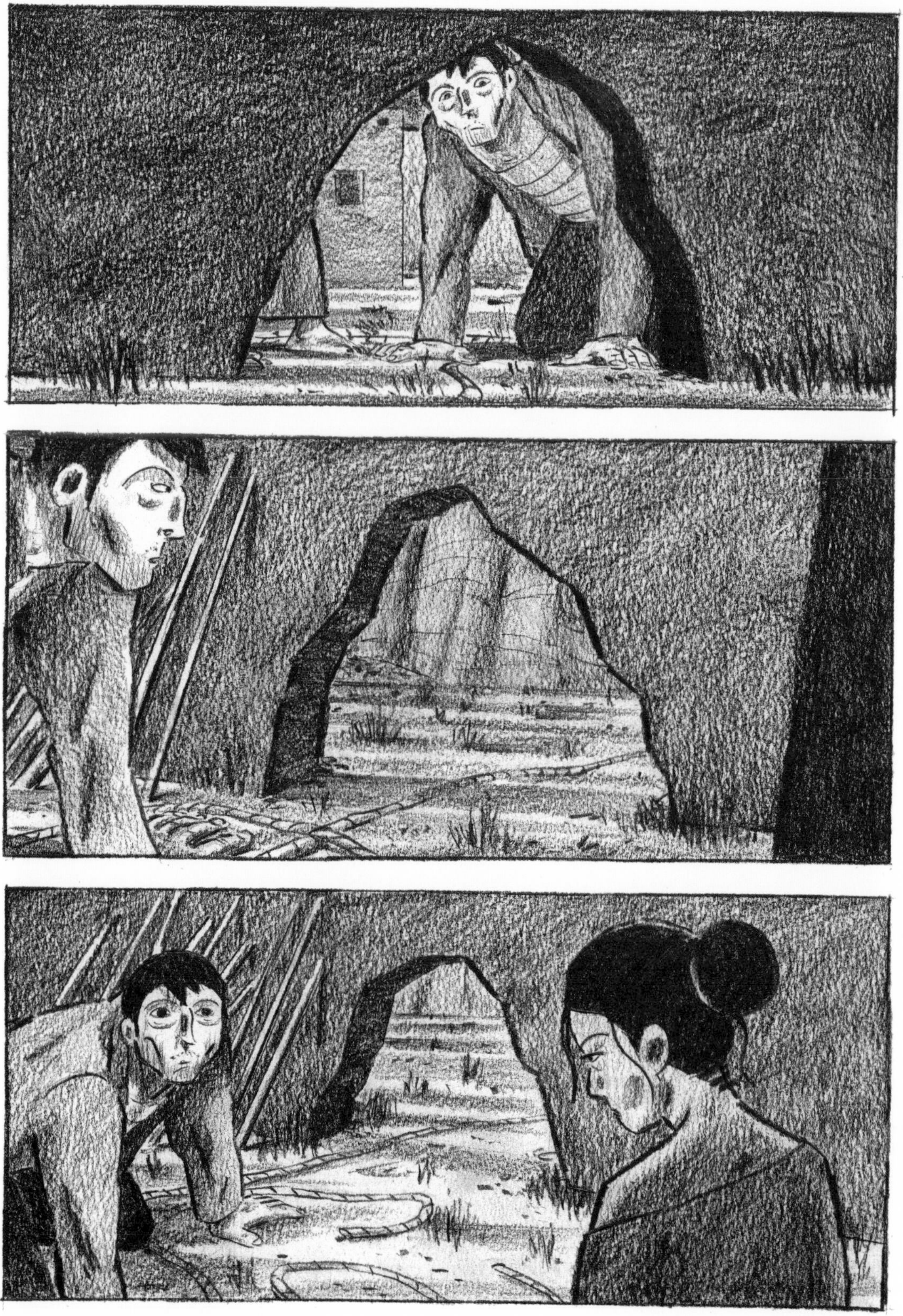

CHAPTER EIGHT

OUR LADY OF GUADALUPE

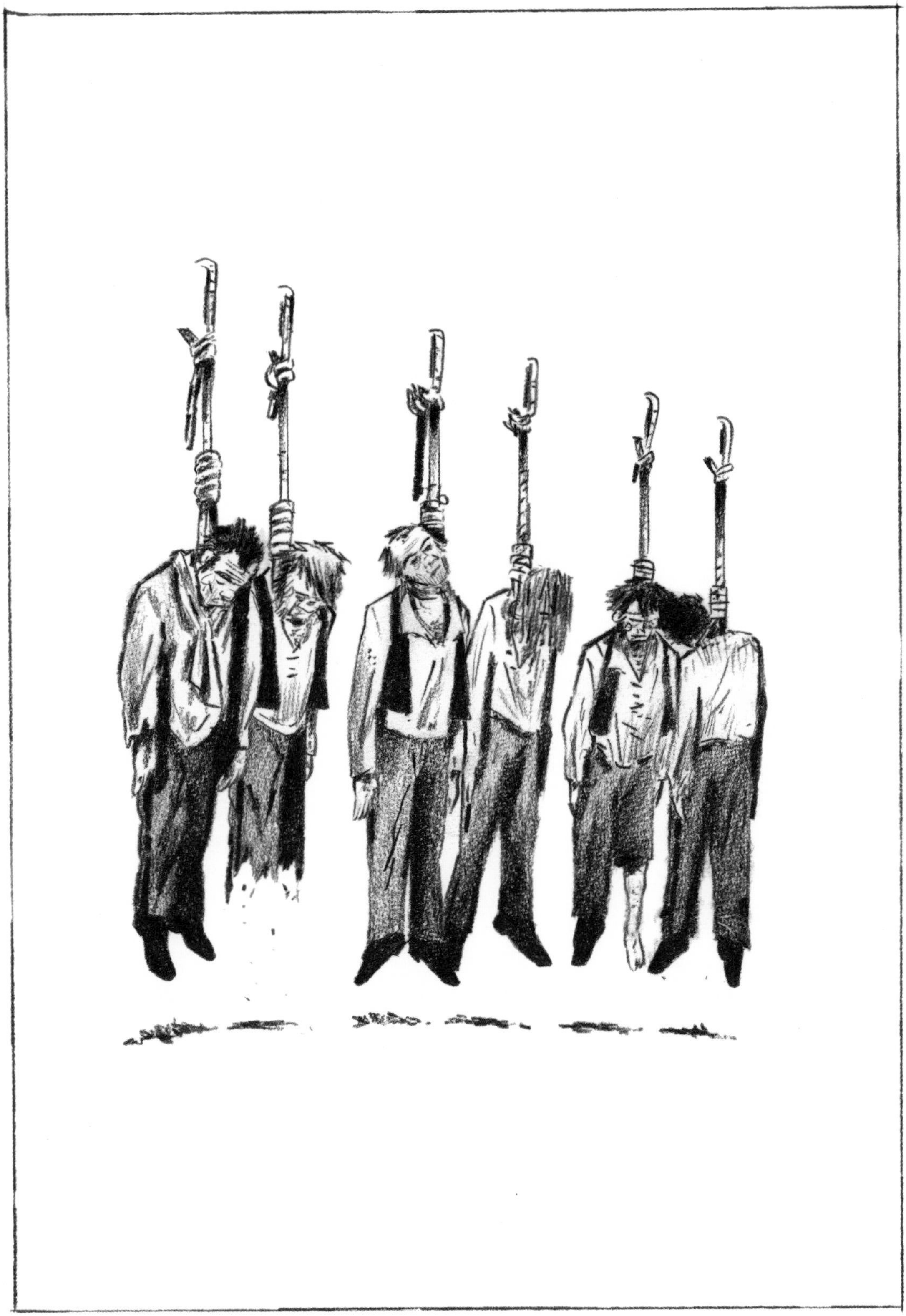

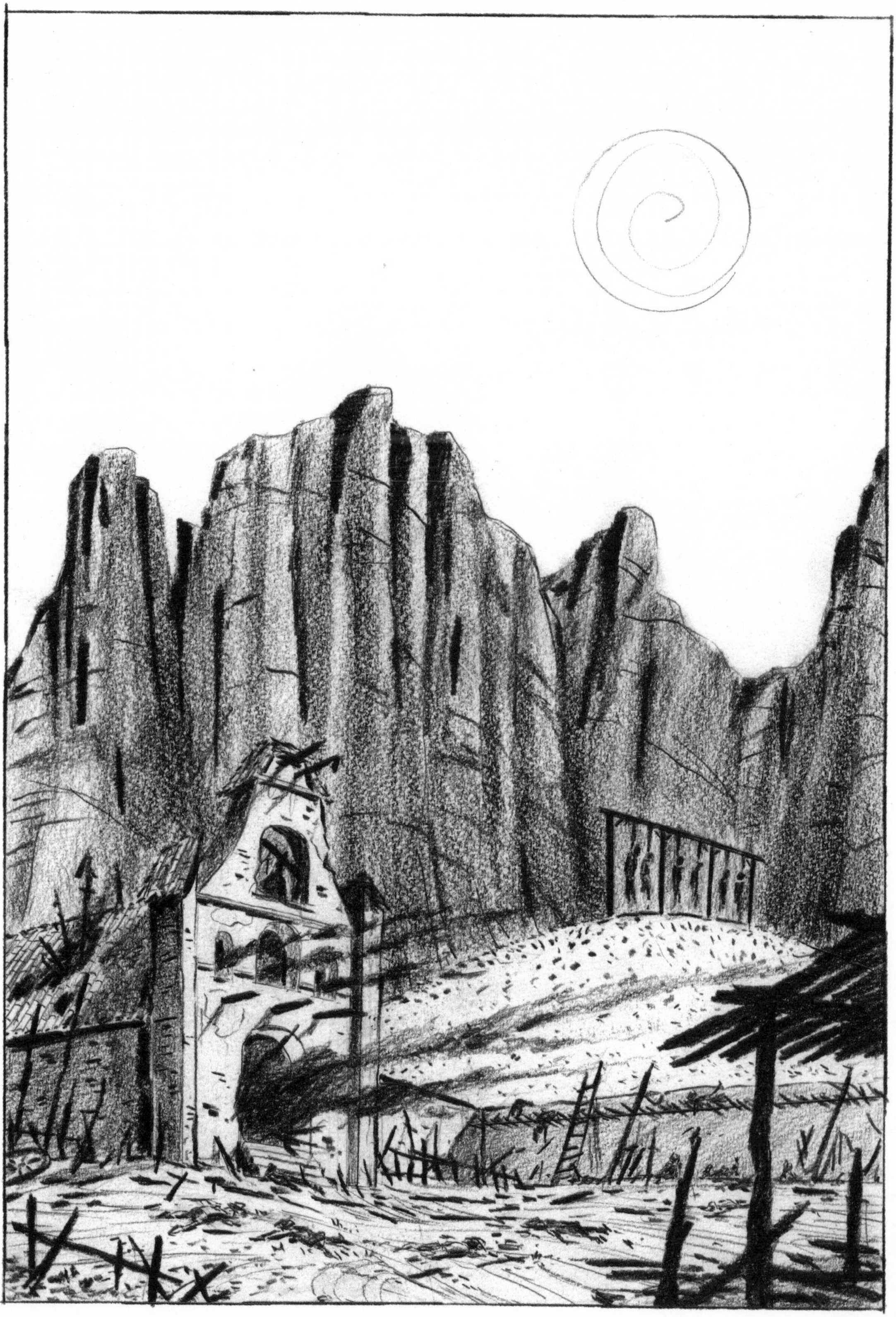

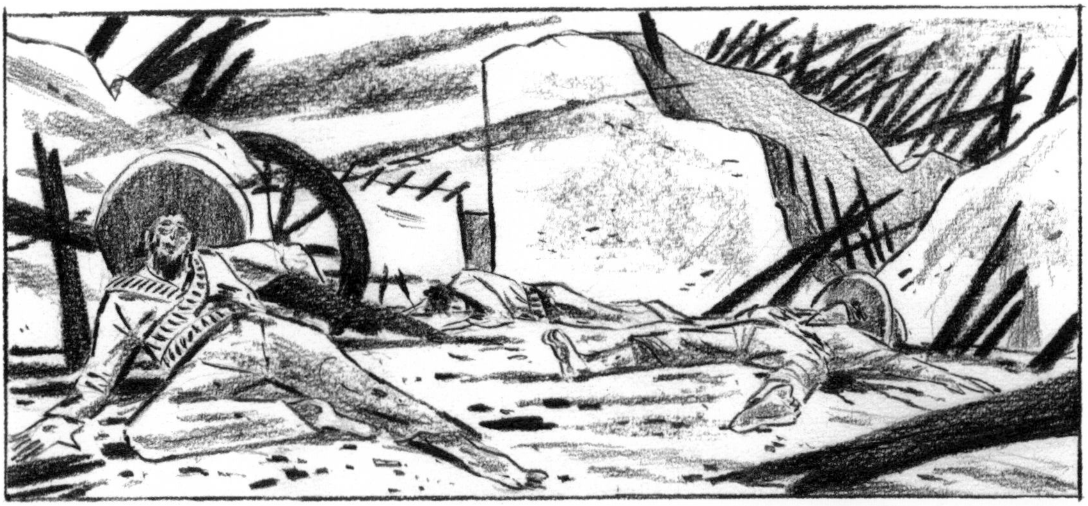

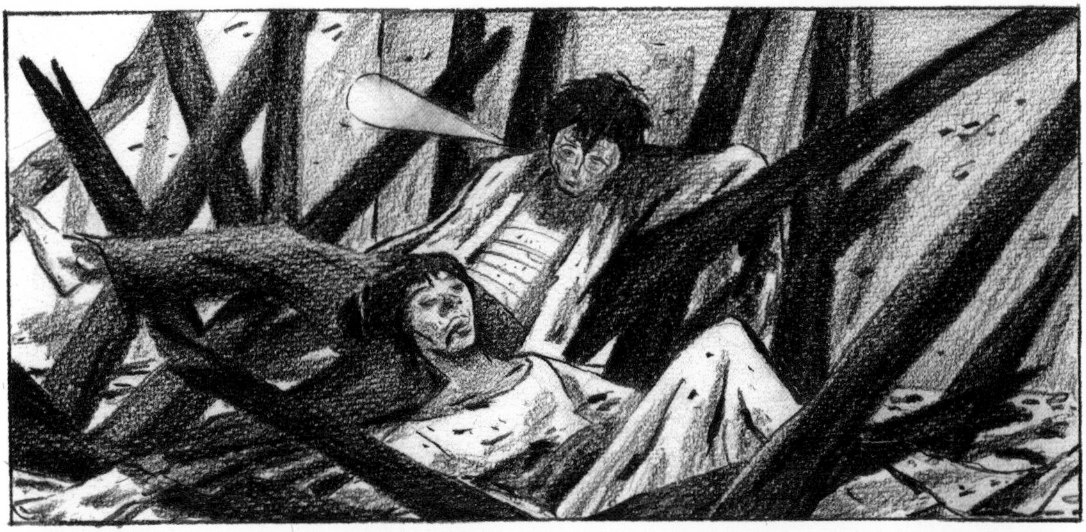

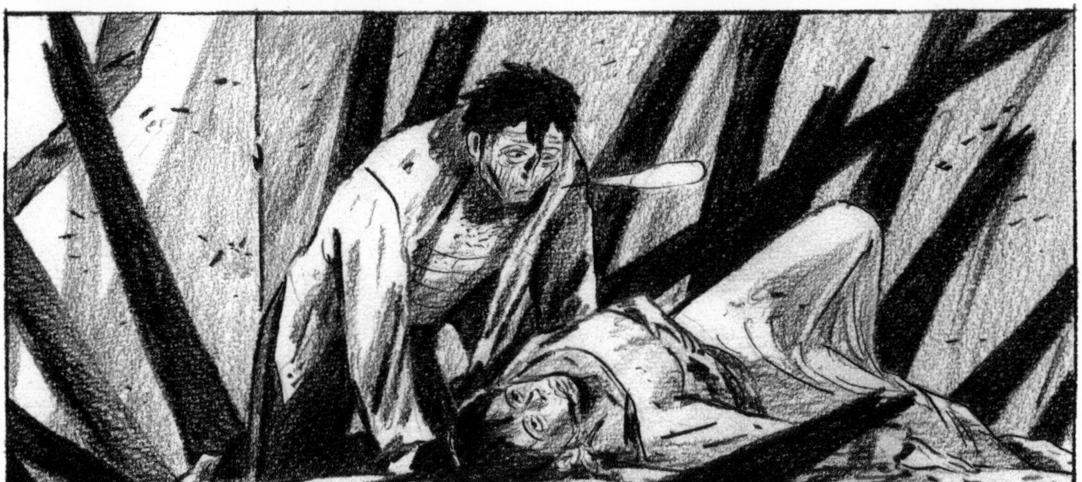

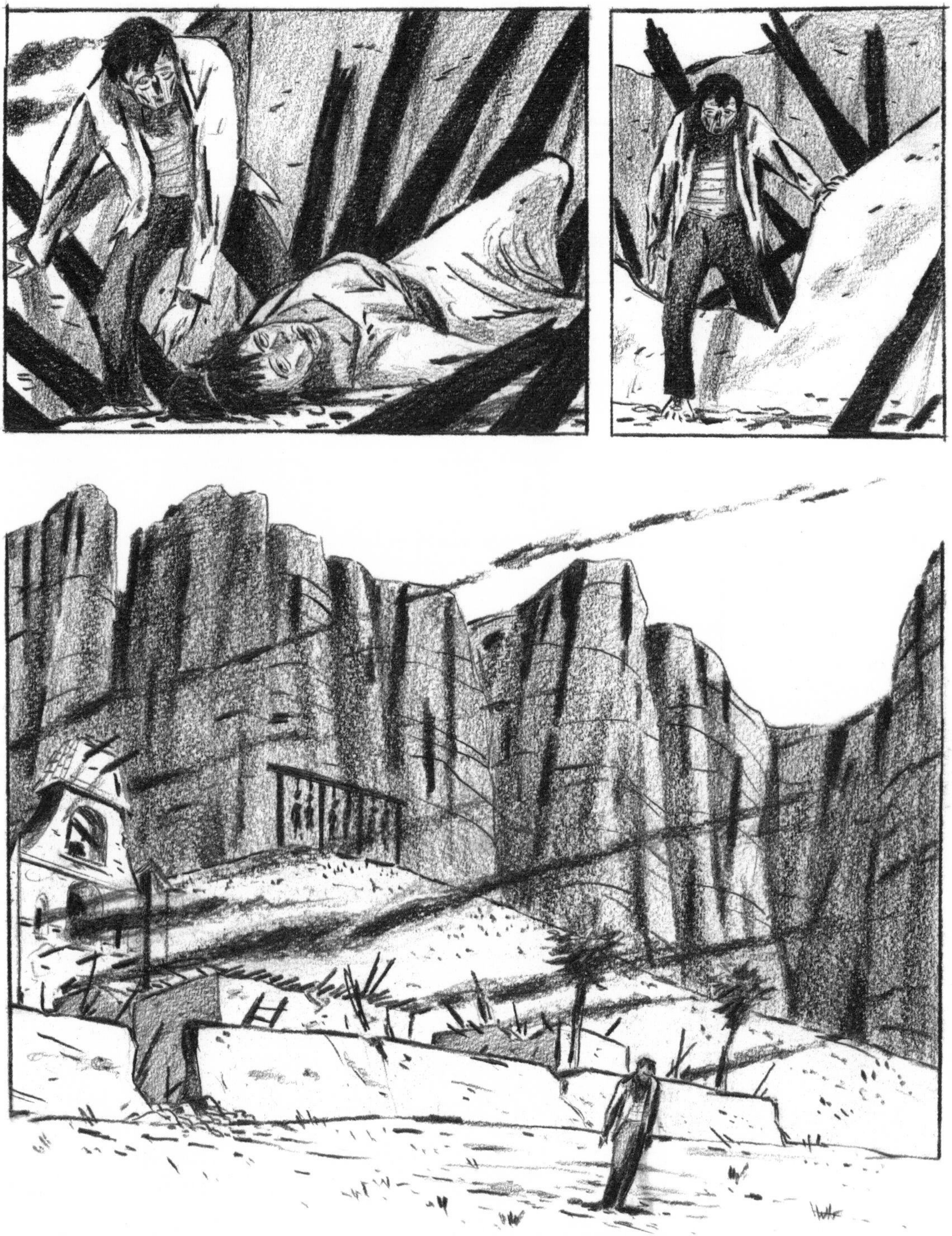

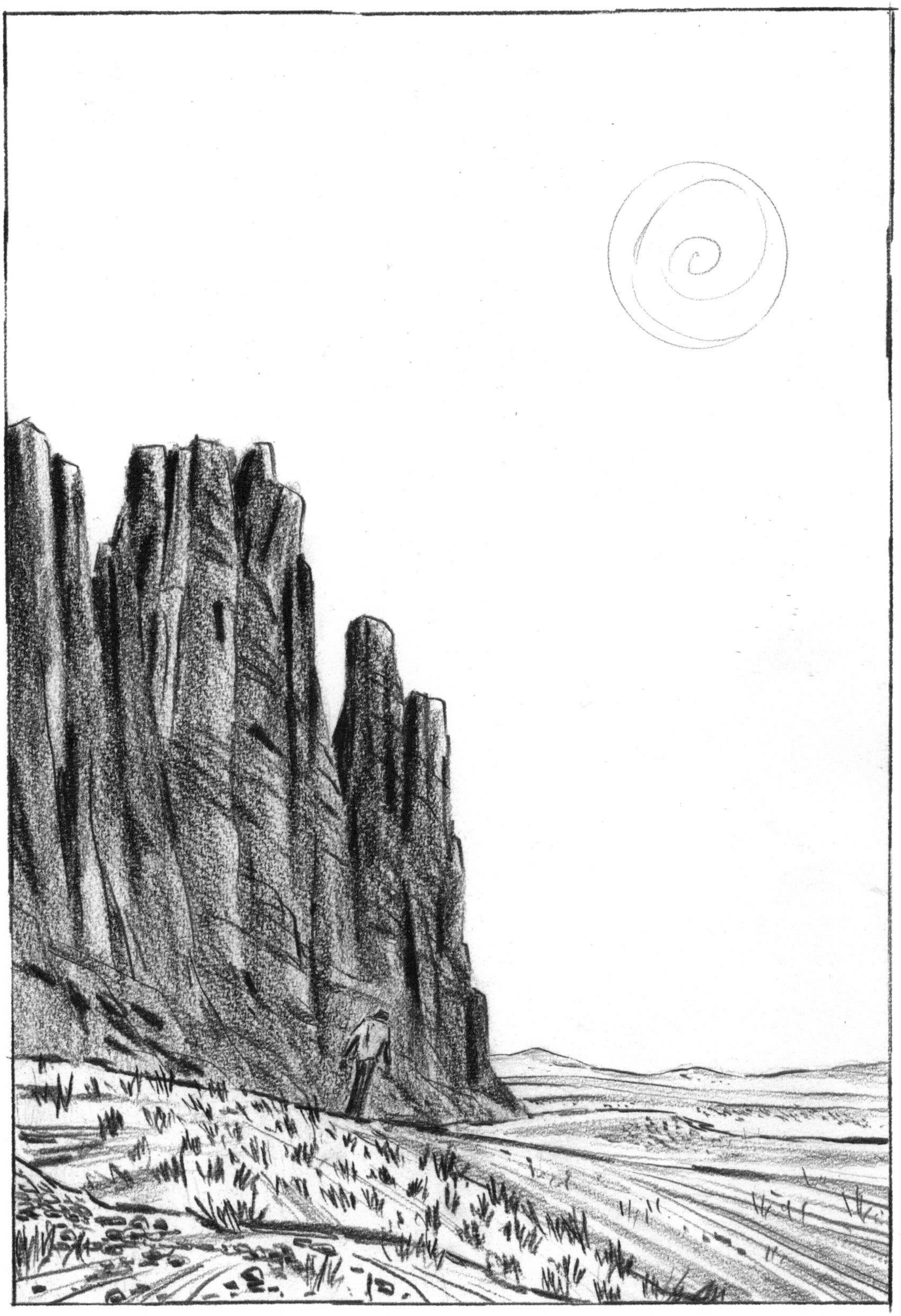

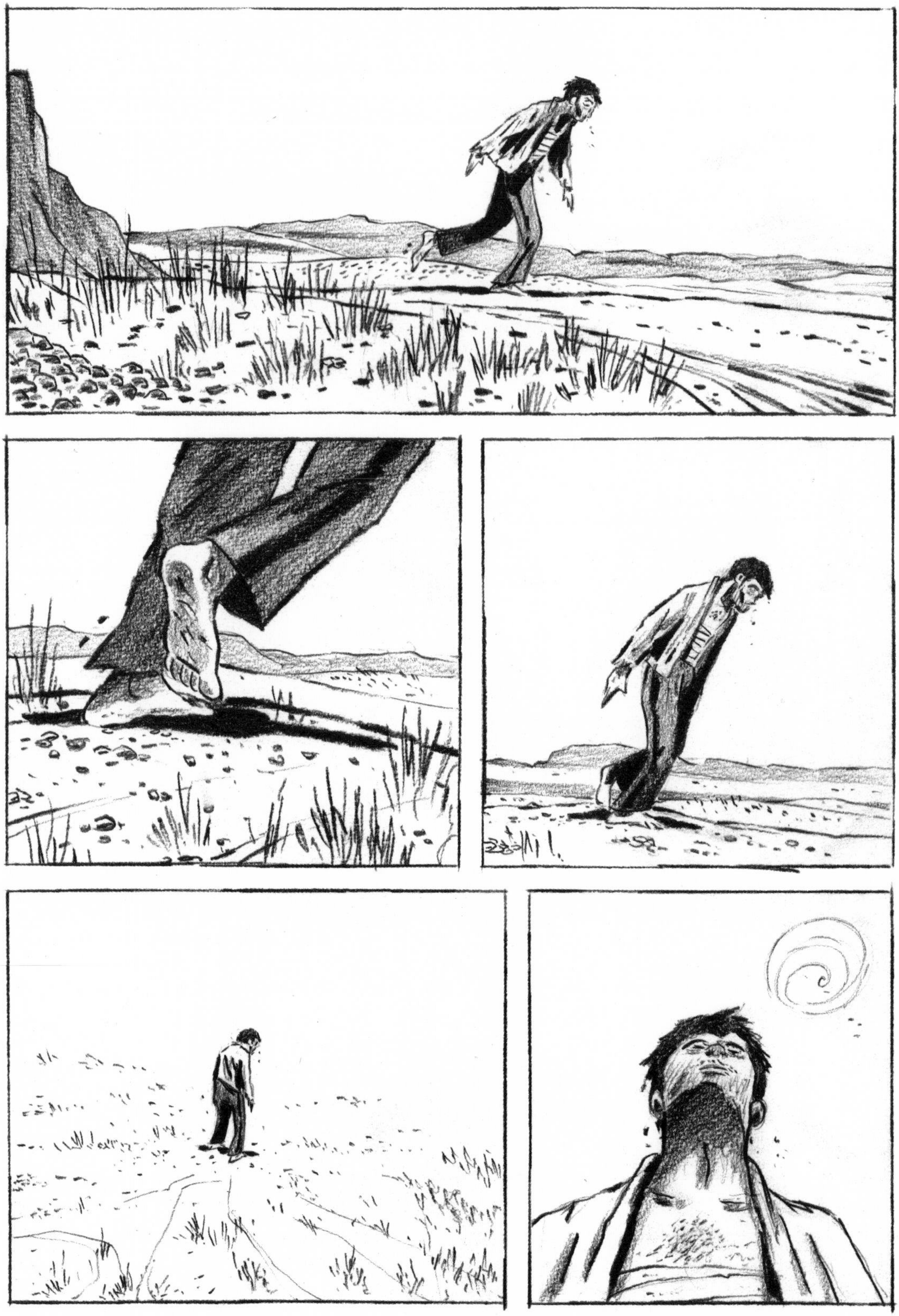

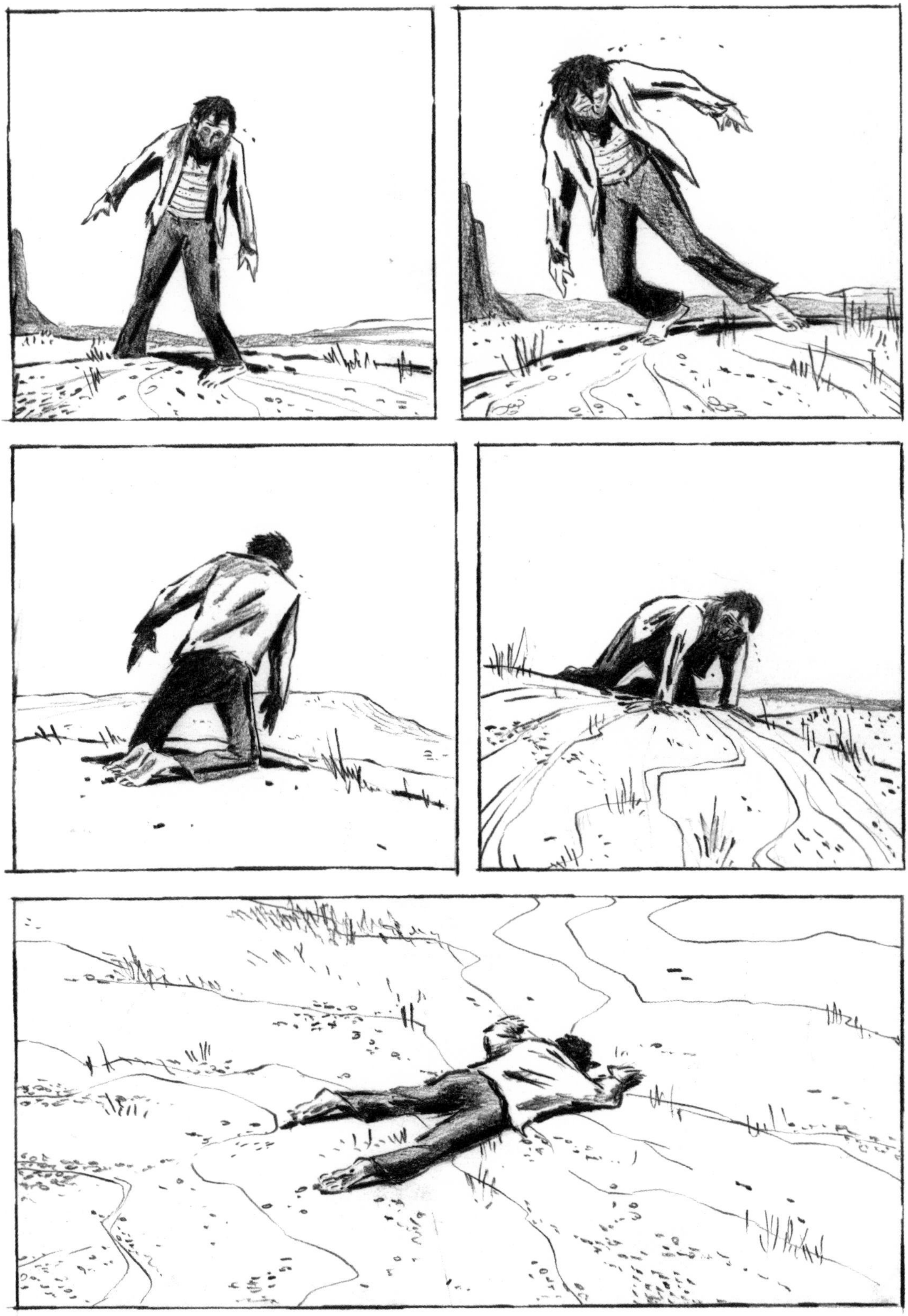

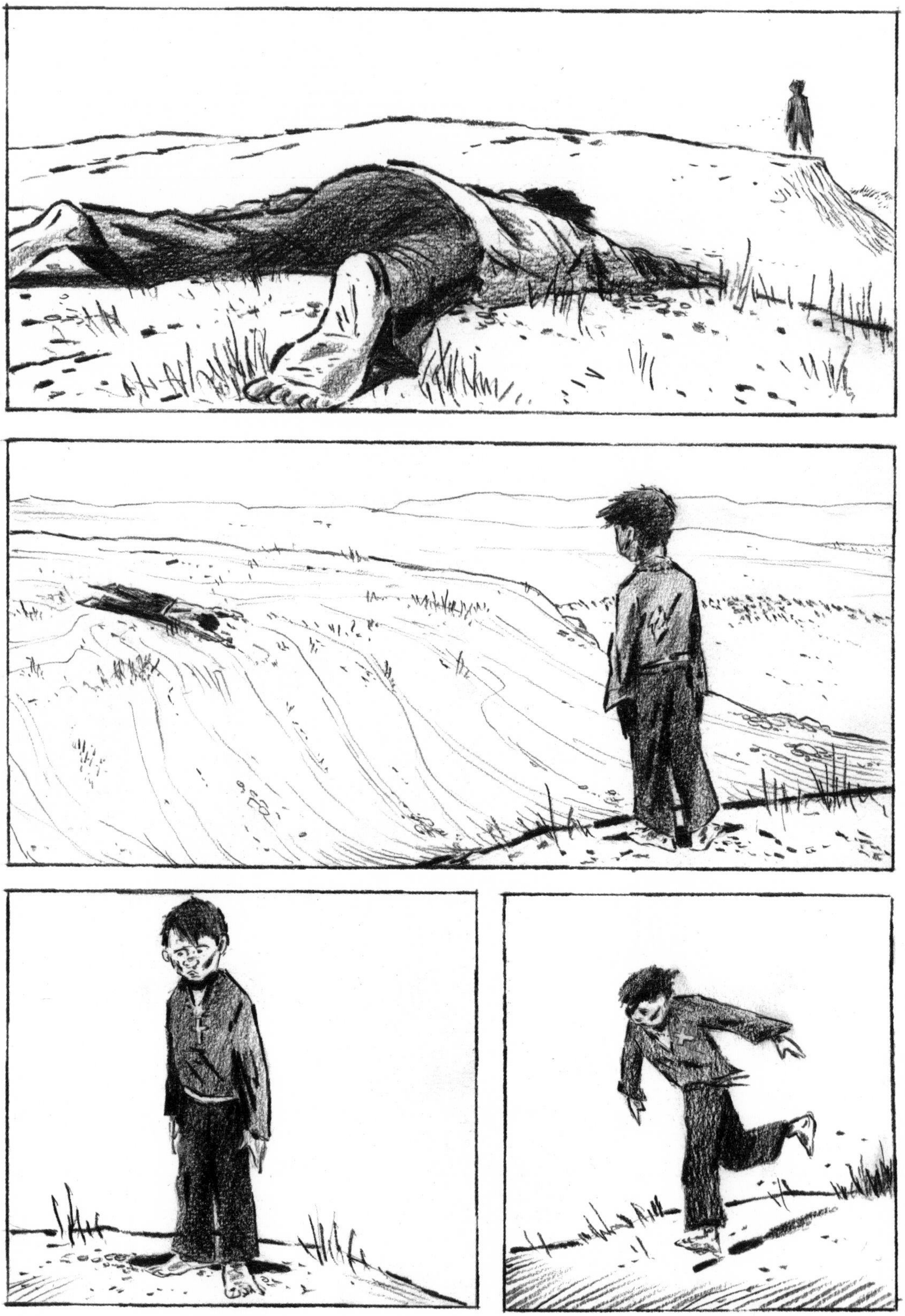

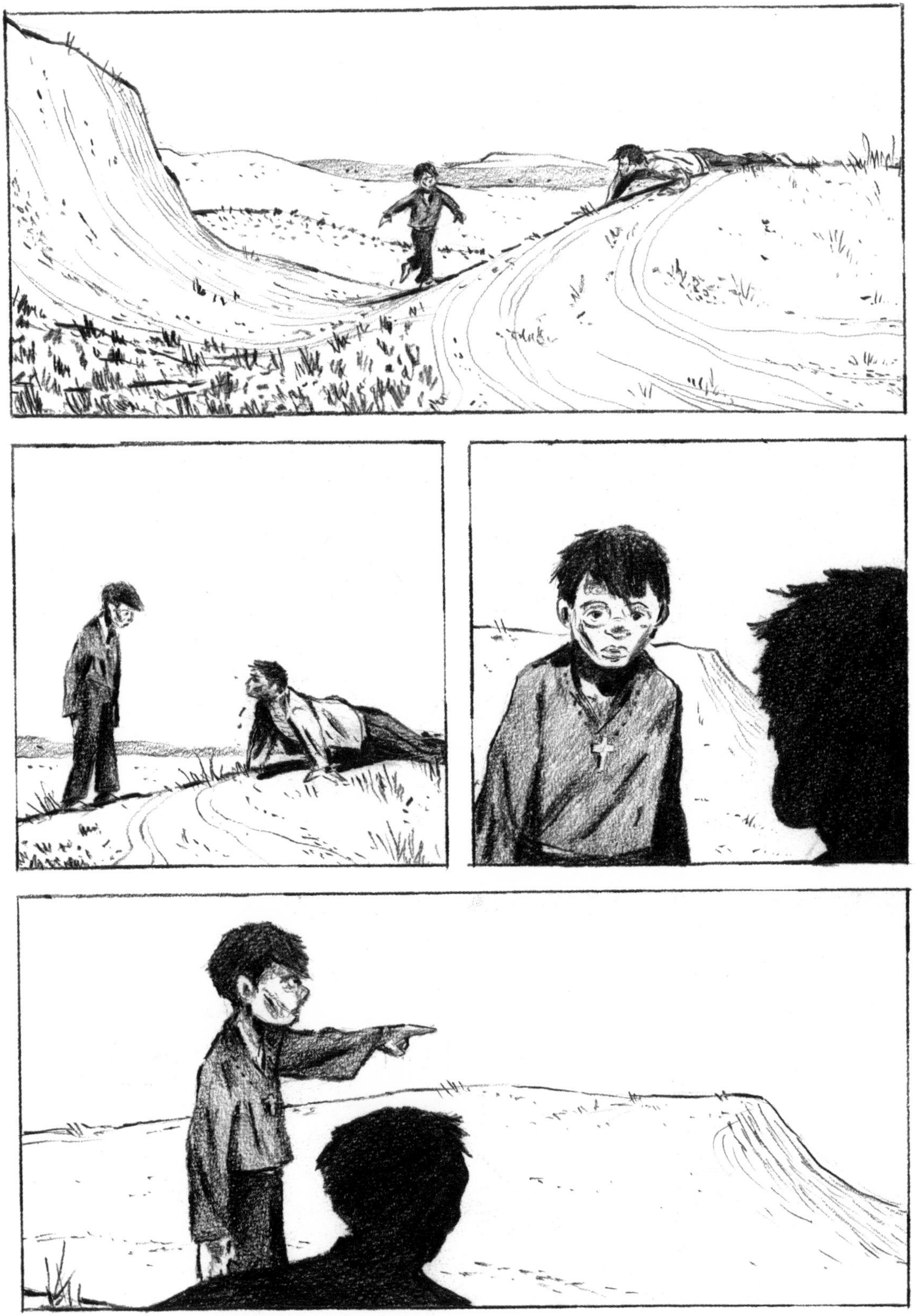

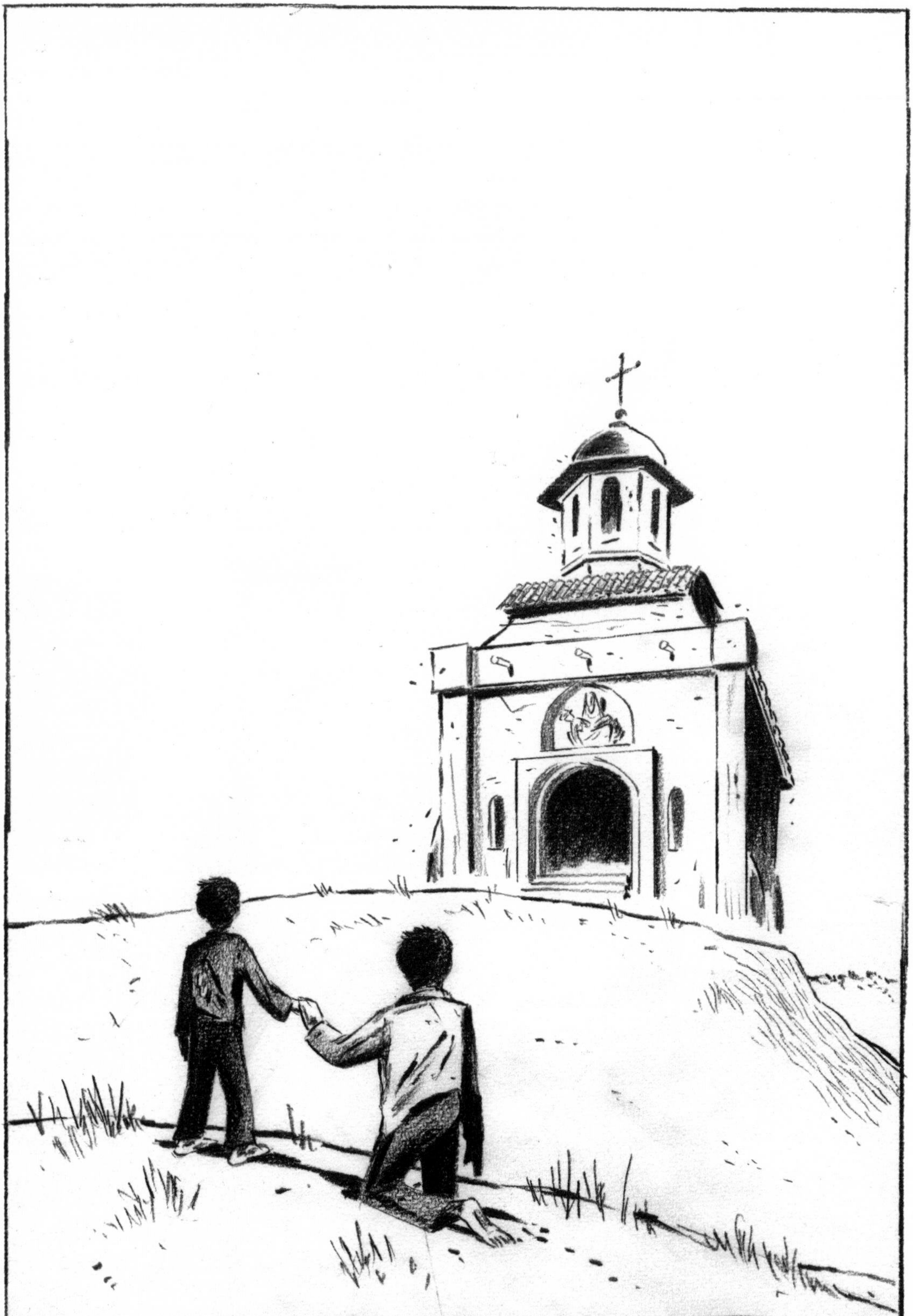

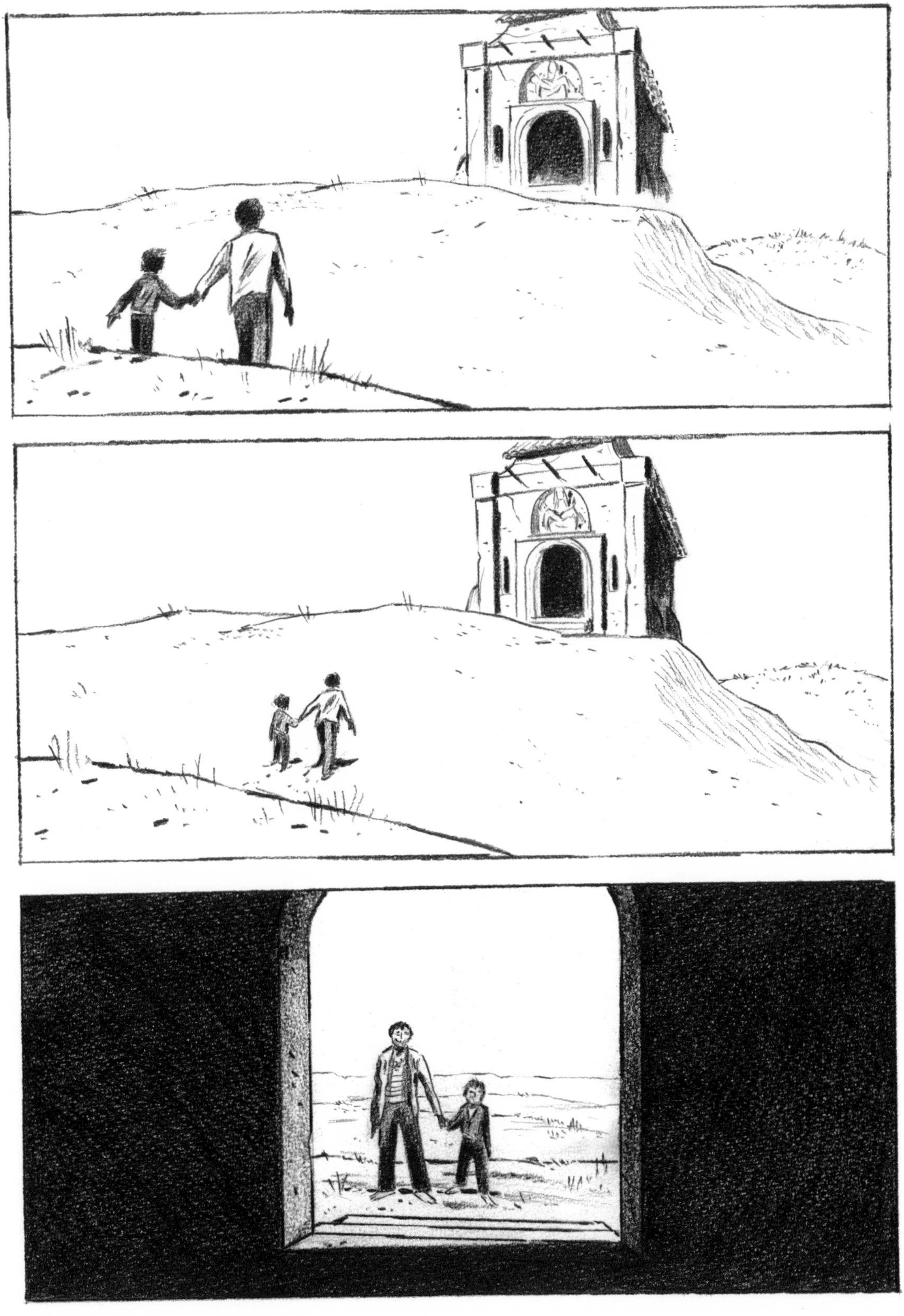

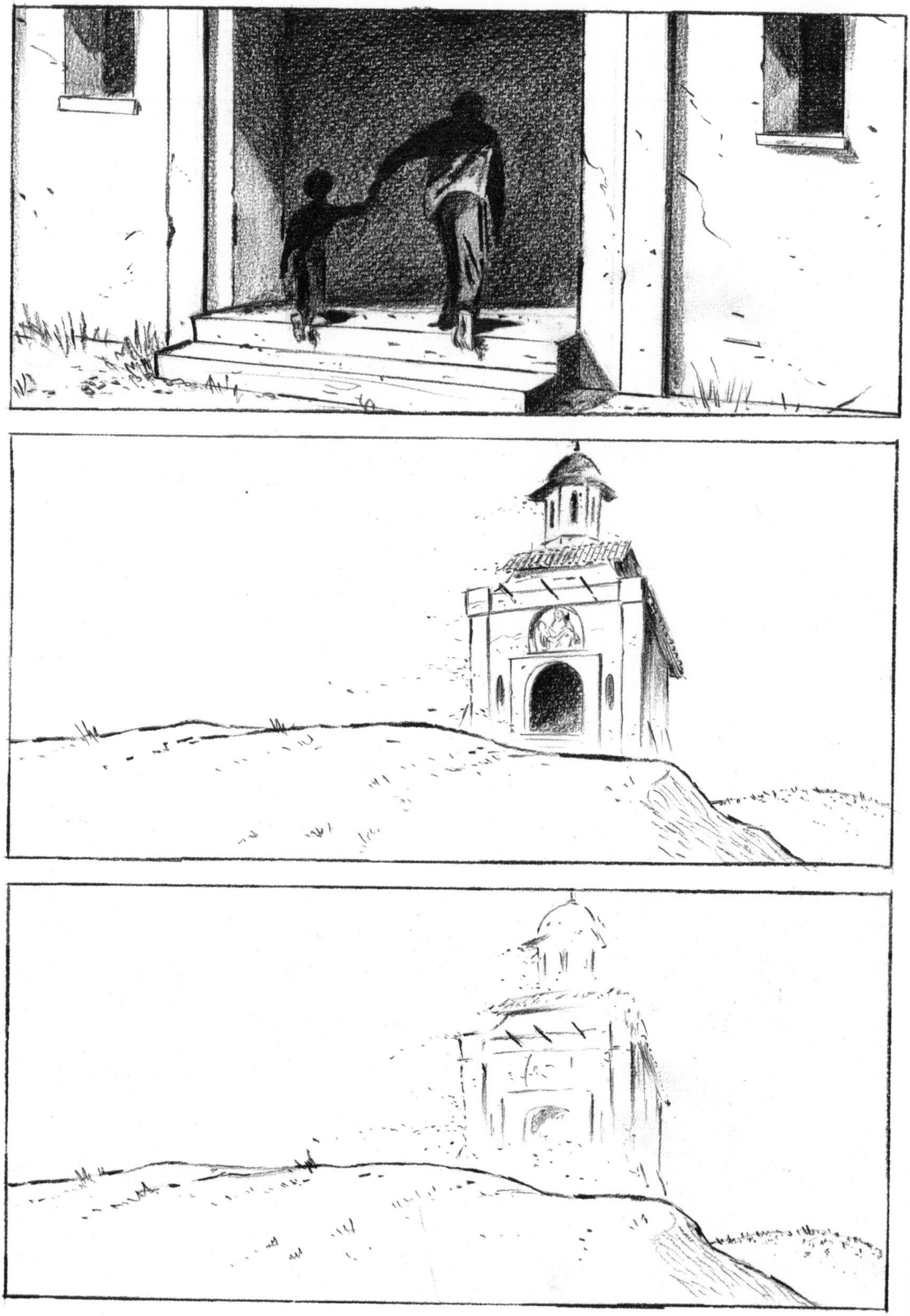

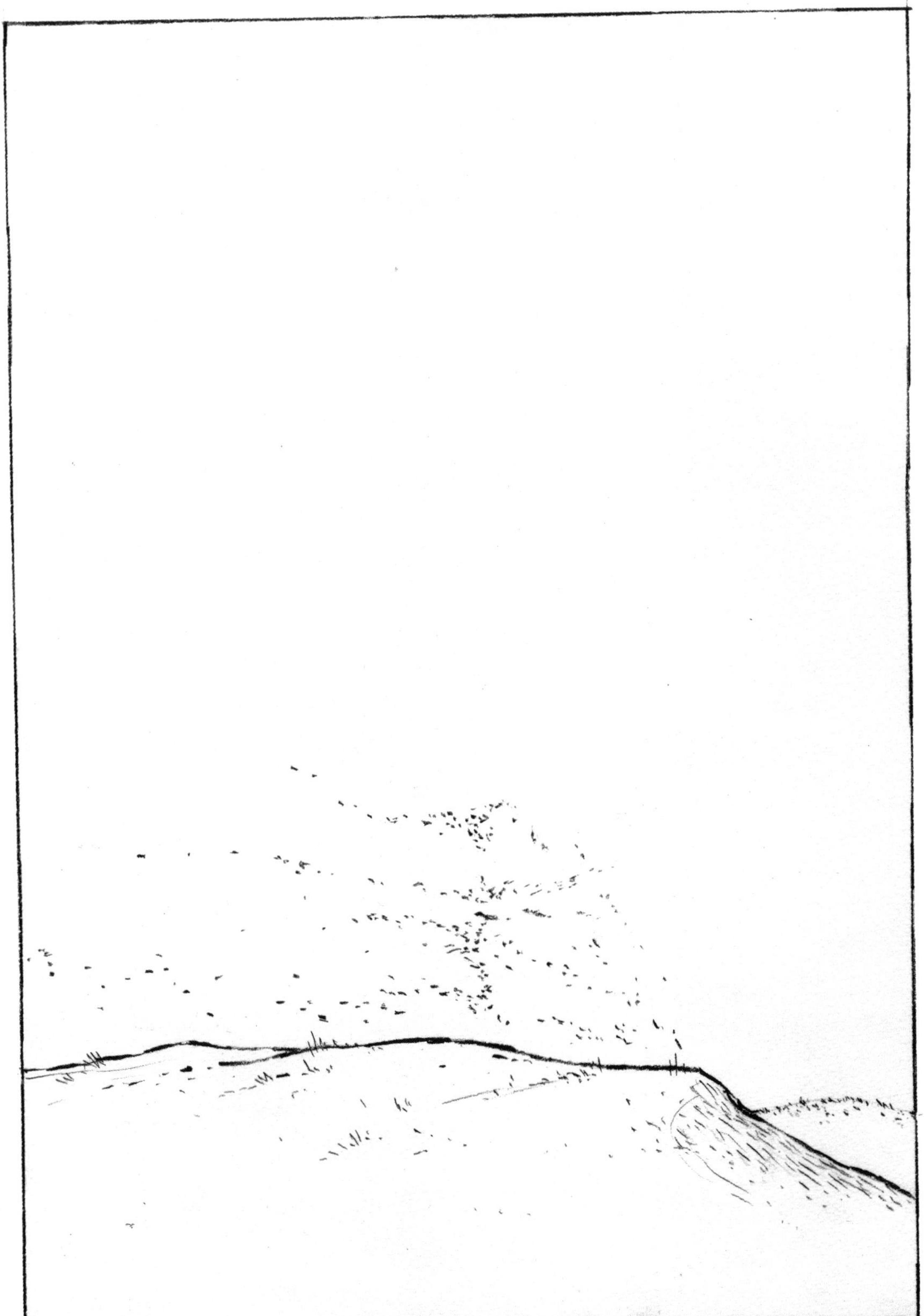

EPILOGUE

HISTORIANS GENERALLY ATTRIBUTE the desertion of the Irish and others who followed them to religious difference. They were Catholic, like the Mexicans, and were discriminated against by the American soldiers, who were mostly Protestant. My story suggests that there may have been other reasons as strong as religion that led the men to switch sides. Regardless, the Mexicans dedicated a religious symbol to the San Patricios, the Virgin of Guadalupe.

My story and its protagonist are products of invention. But reality, of course, often goes hand in hand with imagination. During my research, I found the official list of the deserters of the Saint Patrick's battalion. A hundred names or so. For each one sentenced to death, it states birthplace, age, and date of execution. Among them, I found one with an anglicized name whose origin leaves nothing to the imagination.

Garretson, Robert W./ Messina, Italy/Age 22/ 06/13/1847 hung

AFTERWORD

THE PLACES OF CHURUBUSCO

MY STORY follows but a fragment of a much larger war that ended with Mexico losing more than fifty percent of its land. Texas, California, Nevada, Utah, and parts of Colorado, Arizona, New Mexico, and Wyoming succumbed to American control. During the war, approximately 13,000 U.S. soldiers died, about 1,700 in combat—the others perishing due to scarcity and poor sanitary conditions.

The Mexican losses remain unknown, though they are estimated at around 25,000. After the conflict, the border shifted much further south, starting at Tijuana on the Pacific and ending at the opposite side of the Gulf of Mexico.

Today, there is a steel wall more than thirty kilometers long between Tijuana and San Diego, which is meant to impede the passage of immigrants from Mexico. There are other barriers at various points along the entire border.

There are underground sensors, infrared cameras, barbed wire, and watchtowers. A border in constant evolution… In the areas without any fencing, it's open desert. Migrants, accompanied by unscrupulous characters called "coyotes," often lose their lives trying to cross it.

Temperatures in the desert can reach 120+ degrees in the shade, and people have to cover over fifty miles with thick-soled shoes for protection from scorpions and snakes. The bodies of those who don't make it are left behind, never to be found again. When the barrier hits the ocean, it extends about a hundred feet into the water. On sunny days on the beach, the wall is used as a volleyball net.

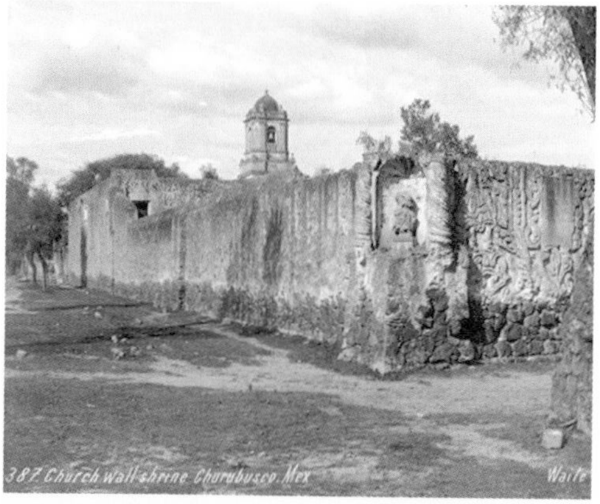
387 Church wall-shrine Churubusco, Mex
Waite

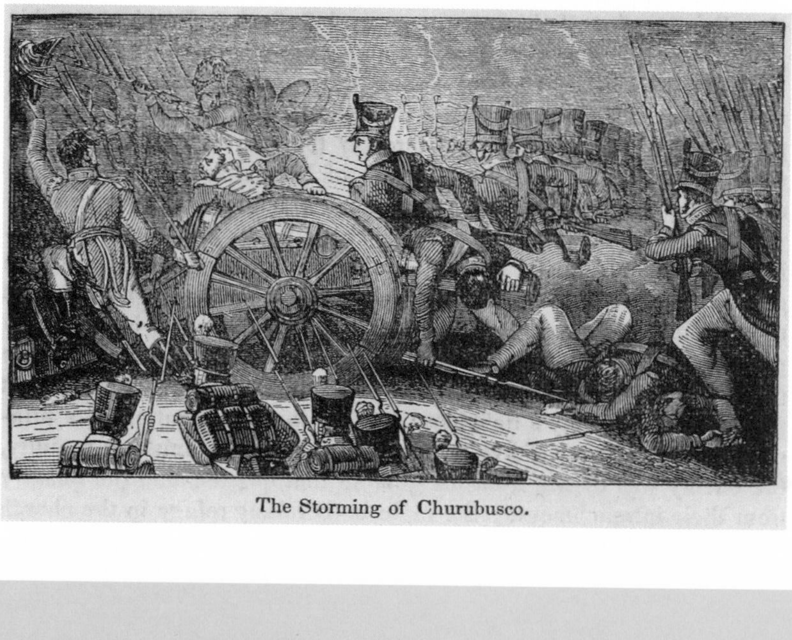

The Storming of Churubusco.

Top: The convent of Churubusco, site of the final battle of the San Patricios. The convent currently houses the military museum, the Museo Nacional de las Intervenciones.

Bottom: The Battle of Churubusco in an illustration from the period.

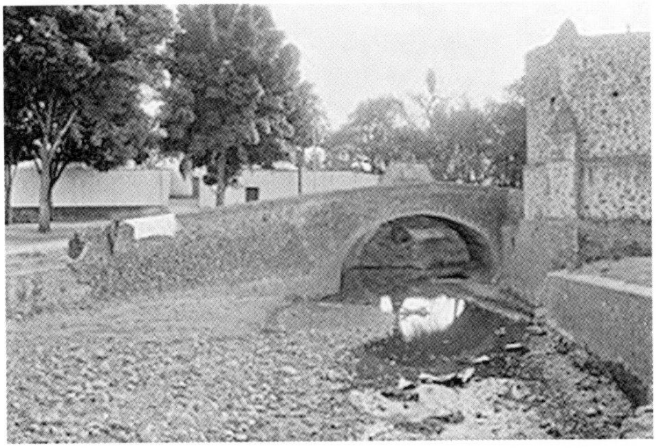

A bridge over the Rio Churubusco that runs through the neighborhood of the same name. One of the bloodiest battles of the Mexican-American War was fought on its shores, the Battle of Churubusco, which marked the end of the San Patricios.

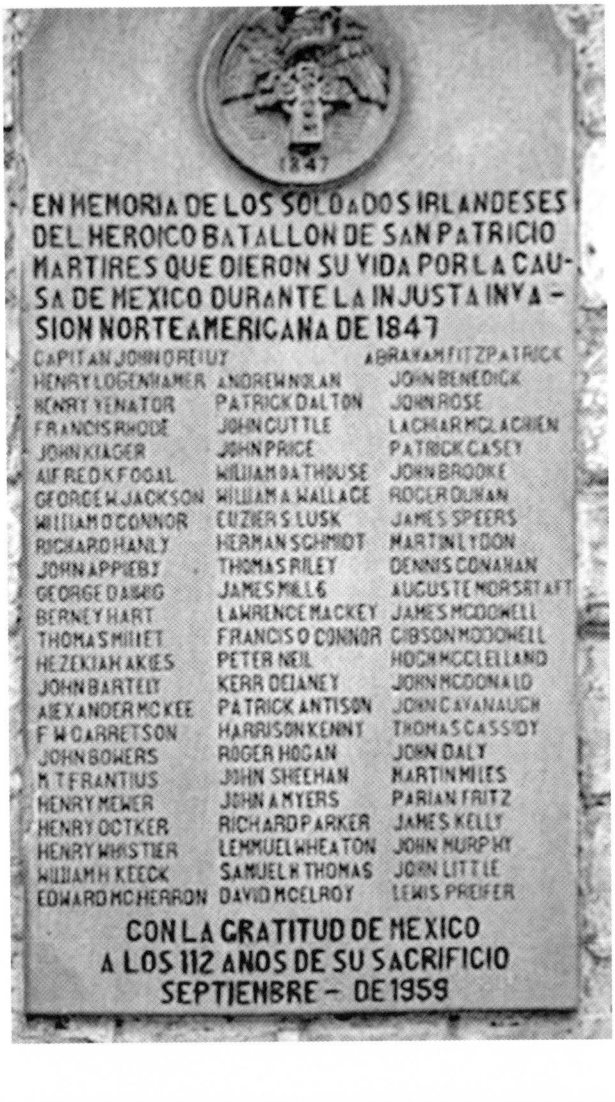
1847
EN MEMORIA DE LOS SOLDADOS IRLANDESES
DEL HEROICO BATALLON DE SAN PATRICIO
MARTIRES QUE DIERON SU VIDA POR LA CAU-
SA DE MEXICO DURANTE LA INJUSTA INVA-
SION NORTEAMERICANA DE 1847
CON LA GRATITUD DE MEXICO
A LOS 112 AÑOS DE SU SACRIFICIO
SEPTIEMBRE - DE 1959

The plate that commemorates some of the soldiers of the battalion, in the Plaza San Jacinto, San Angel, Mexico City.

ACKNOWLEDGMENTS

Thanks to:

Nicola and Donatella, who found themselves, as they say, in the right place at the right time. This story is theirs too.

Renato, for his suggestions and the enthusiasm he showed me.

The "Irish" group: Carlos, Fiona, Paddy, and the irreplaceable Manuela.

Sandri, Gianni, and Michela, who had the patience to tolerate my insecurities.

Massimo, Vanni, and Sara Valdes, for their helpfulness and kindness.

Igor, who has always supported me.

Daniela and Sarvari, who continue to follow me in my follies.